THE UPPER ROOM

Disciplines

2026

Upper Room Books®
Nashville

THE UPPER ROOM DISCIPLINES 2026

Upper Room Books® website: upperroombooks.com

Cover design: Left Coast Design, Portland, Oregon

Cover photo: Shutterstock.com

At the time of publication all websites referenced in this book were valid. However, due to the fluid nature of the internet some addresses may have changed, or the content may no longer be relevant.

Writers of various books of the Bible may be disputed in certain circles; this volume uses the names of the biblically attributed authors.

ISBN: 978-0-8358-2067-7 (print)
978-0-8358-2068-4 (enlarged-print edition)
978-0-8358-2069-1 (epub)
Printed in the United States of America

An Outline for Small-Group Use of *Disciplines*

The Upper Room Disciplines intentionally invites a diverse community of theologians and writers to meditate and offer reflections on scriptures that will nurture your soul and call you more fully to engage with the world that we are co-creating with God.

Christ is among us in fresh ways when we gather together, listening to God and to one another. We suggest gathering each week with a small group to discuss your reflections on the lectionary readings and *The Upper Room Disciplines*. Follow the simple liturgy below for a one-hour meeting. One person in the group may act as convener every week, or the role can rotate among group members.

Liturgy for Discussion

Gathering

Light a candle to signal the beginning of your time together. Enter into one minute of silence with these words:

One: Loving God, we rest, still and quiet in your embrace. With childlike trust and simple confidence, we find peace in your arms.[1]

Close the silence with a prayer or simply, "Amen."

Opening

One: God is revealed with each reading of scripture.

All: **Jesus, Immanuel, be present with us. Holy Spirit, open our ears in our conversation together and inspire us to live faithfully in the world.**

Scripture

The convener reads the scripture suggested for that day in the Disciplines.

One: The word of God for the people of God.

All: **Thanks be to God.**

Allow for a minute or two of silence.

Convener asks: What word or phrase stood out to you in the reading? What is God's invitation to you in this reading?

Group members respond in turn or as led.

Reflection

The convener reads the scripture overview for the week and then uses the following questions to guide discussion. After giving each prompt, the convener may give participants time to reflect silently or journal before inviting group members to respond aloud.

- How does the theme for the week touch your life personally? What wisdom, comfort, or challenge do you hear for the context you are living in and for the wider world?
- What relationships or situations came to mind as you read the *Disciplines* meditations this week? How were you called to act or make a response in your life this week?
- What new insight to scripture did you hear? What from the meditations has challenged your theology or discipleship this week? How might you respond to the challenge?

Praying Together

The convener invites everyone to name joys and concerns that the group can pray for now and in the coming week. The convener or another volunteer then prays for the group, closing with this prayer:

In your compassion, gracious God,
 you hear the cry of the poor, the needy, and the lonely ones.
May we also hear the cries of our brothers and sisters,
 responding in love as you have shown us in your Son,
 our Savior, Jesus Christ. Amen.[2]

Benediction

End your time with this collective benediction:

Indeed, faithful God, you have shown us the path of life
and given us a heritage of unspeakable richness.
You call us now into joyful trust of the future you bring.
We abide in you. Amen.[3]

---

[1] *Upper Room Worshipbook*, 331.
[2] *Upper Room Worshipbook*, 260.
[3] *Upper Room Worshipbook*, 236.

Contents

Foreword

The first thing that comes to mind when I think of the word *discipline* is dental floss. Hear me out—if you have been to a dentist, you have been told to floss every day. I don't know about you, but I require great discipline to make this happen consistently. Flossing is not something I look forward to, yet I know it improves my health. On late nights when I just want to fall into bed and ignore the discipline of flossing, I think of the words from one of my past dentists: "You only have to floss the teeth you want to keep." This motivating phrase inspires my discipline, particularly on the most exhausting of evenings when my pillow is calling.

An aspect of discipline occurs after one has dedicated themselves to a particular habit over a period of time: The dread, duty, or discomfort of the practice goes away. Our thoughts about the discipline move from "I really should" to "I get to." This shift often coincides with a recognition of the benefits of a particular habit or discipline. Slowly the good results outweigh the effort required, and our mind finally settles in and gives thanks. (I am still waiting for this phase in my flossing discipline, but I trust it's coming.)

Eventually, another shift happens. At some point we find that when we fail to complete the daily discipline, our bodies and our minds tell us something important is missing. I am grateful that many of my spiritual disciplines have become so integral to my well-being that when I miss them, I *miss* them. If my sabbath does not include a collective experience of worship, my day feels off. If busyness squeezes out my habit of prayer, I soon become aware that I've overlooked something vital. Whenever I miss my daily devotional time in God's word, I find that my day lacks a feeling of groundedness. Growing deeper in God's word on a daily basis and being open to the grace of God moving in our lives change us for the better. Our daily practice of reading and reflecting on scripture helps us live into Jesus' teachings from John 10:10, "I came that they may have life and have it abundantly." Time in God's word makes our lives abundant.

The Upper Room Disciplines 2026 has been carefully curated to encourage and support your discipline of time in God's word. As you strengthen this discipline, you will find your understanding of scripture deepened and your life transformed. We trust that over the course of this year, God will move in you and through you by way of the discipline of daily study. We also trust that your journey with *Disciplines* will be more enjoyable than flossing.

JEFF CAMPBELL
General Secretary/Chief Executive Officer,
Discipleship Ministries
Interim Publisher, The Upper Room

Beginnings

JANUARY 1–4, 2026 • GREG PIMLOTT

SCRIPTURE OVERVIEW: Each of this week's readings describes a beginning. Ecclesiastes describes many new beginnings as a time for one purpose to be replaced by a time for another. The psalm describes God's constant renewal of creation, in which God's relationship with creation begins anew each day. Jeremiah describes the beginning of a new season for God's people, where sorrow is replaced by joy and tears of forsakenness give way to shouts of joy. John's Prologue describes the very beginning, in which all things came into being through the Word (who "was with God and . . . was God"). Ephesians highlights the possibility of a new beginning for those of us who have been adopted into God's family through Jesus and the spiritual inheritance that is available to us through this adoption.

QUESTIONS AND SUGGESTIONS FOR REFLECTION

- Read Ecclesiastes 3:1-13. As the new year begins, how do you think God will prepare you for the various times and seasons the coming year will bring?
- Read Psalm 147:12-20. Can you recall a time of spiritual growth in which things were not going well for you and praising God was hard?
- Read John 1:1-18. Pay special attention to verse 18. How has God been made known in your life?
- Read Ephesians 1:3-14. What does it mean to you to have been adopted by God?

The Rev. Greg Pimlott is an ordained elder in the Indiana Conference of The United Methodist Church, serving Christ UMC in Indianapolis, IN. Greg is the author of *Pastoral Pause: A Practical Guide to Renewal Leave* (Upper Room Books, 2024).

New Year's Day

I was meeting with a grieving family to choose scriptures for a funeral. One of the family members knew Ecclesiastes 3 and suggested it as a possibility. The family tossed the passage around for a while, and finally someone ventured an opinion: "It's just so dark, though, isn't it?" I hadn't thought of this scripture in that way, but as my eyes skimmed over the words in response to the family member's objection, I could see their point. *A time to kill. A time to break down. A time to hate.*

As a society, we've moved away from the idea of funerals and more toward celebrations of life. Families say things like, "We want the service to be cheerful and upbeat, not somber and sad." There's hardly room for ideas like killing and hating at a celebration. Sometimes it feels like there's hardly room for death and resurrection.

These themes also make Ecclesiastes 3 an unlikely choice for New Year's Day. Some of us have just finished an all-night party, and we're looking ahead to a new year, a fresh start. Who wants to think about death and loss and breaking down at a time like this? Yet this scripture reminds us that the year ahead is as likely to bring death as it is to bring life. Some years bring peace; other years bring war. Some years we have more baptisms than burials; some years it goes the other way.

There will surely be plenty of reasons to celebrate in the year ahead. It could be, though, that our greatest moments of spiritual deepening will occur when hard times come and we turn our faces toward God, who will be with us through the good times and the hard times alike.

O God, you give us each season in turn. Guide us through everything this new year will bring, and help us ever to seek your face. Amen.

FRIDAY, JANUARY 2 ~ *Read John 1:1-9*

This passage always startles me a little when I come across it in the lectionary, shortly after the beginning of the year. We encountered it only a couple of weeks ago in a darkened sanctuary on Christmas Eve, framed by the gentle flicker of Advent candles and the quivering anticipation of children anxious to get to sleep so Christmas morning can arrive. It seems natural to find it there; these verses of John's Gospel seem custom-designed to be accompanied by earnest worshipers raising their candles and singing "Son of God, love's pure light" (UMH #239).

What, then, do these first verses of John hold for us in the cold, clear light of January? Christmas has come and gone. The candles from Christmas Eve have been packed up with the rest of the decorations and put away until next November, when worship teams and altar guilds will scour closets and church basements searching for them. Why pull John's Prologue out again so soon, as though we're resurrecting Christmas Eve before we've had the chance to tell the rest of Jesus' story?

The Prologue of John's Gospel is not just the beginning of Jesus' story; it is Jesus' story. The Word was with God. The Word was God. Without Jesus nothing that is would be, and nothing that would be would truly live.

As our Christmas Eve services come to an end, we extinguish our candles as though we've gotten our fill of light for the year and now it's time to snuff it out. Encountering these verses again so soon reminds us that nothing can extinguish the light: not the powers and principalities of this world; not the animosity or indifference of society; not even our own short attention spans. The true light, which enlightens everyone, was coming into the world. Christ has come, and he is here to stay.

Light of light, life of all, fill us with the true light which enlightens all people and can never be extinguished. Amen.

SATURDAY, JANUARY 3 ~ *Read John 1:10-18*

Verse 18 is tempting to skim over, coming as it does at the very end of this passage. Life and light catch our eye along the way. John's prophetic testimony reaches our ear long before we get there. Grace and truth grab hold of us and won't let go. Who could blame us, then, for being so emotionally and spiritually spent by the time we get to the end of the Prologue that we overlook a verse that has the power to bring us to our knees? "No one has ever seen God. It is the only Son, himself God, who is close to the Father's heart, who has made him known."

Is there even an analogy that fits? The only ones that come to mind are wildly inadequate. Ancestors I've never met, and those of my spouse, are reflected in my children's features. (Not the same). A mirror reflects an image around a corner that we otherwise wouldn't see. (Not even close).

The theological claim stands on its own, unique in its power and brashness. We can know the unknowable divine, see the unseeable God, and encounter the one who made heaven and earth in Jesus of Nazareth. John will use the rest of his Gospel to flesh out what this means as he introduces us to this man, Jesus, who is fully human and fully divine. John the Baptist proclaims him; the twelve disciples serve and celebrate and deny and betray him; Mary Magdalene is the first to preach the gospel as she announces his resurrection. We'd do well to linger for a moment before we move on to all that, though, and just sit (or kneel) with this truth: It is the Son, who is close to God's heart, who makes God known to us.

Christ our Savior, thank you for showing us the fullness of the Triune God. Amen.

SUNDAY, JANUARY 4 ~ *Read Psalm 147:12-20*

SECOND SUNDAY AFTER CHRISTMAS

The psalm begins with an affirmation: "How good it is to sing praises to our God, for he is gracious, and a song of praise is fitting." What follows is an inspiring list. God gathers outcasts and heals the brokenhearted! God sends rain to make the hills come alive with grass! God provides food for all the creatures that walk and fly and crawl across the face of the earth! God grants peace and good harvest and hope and love! When we see those things happening around us, it's not only good to sing praises to God; it's easy.

But what about other times in our lives, when things aren't going so well? When the rains don't come, and the crops don't grow, and peace and hope and love are hard commodities to come by? When we're sitting on the banks of the rivers of Babylon, trying in vain to sing the Lord's song in a strange land? When the waters have come up to our neck, and the flood sweeps over us?

Thankfully, the psalm doesn't say righteousness depends on us finding it easy to praise God, nor does it insist that praise must come easily to us if we are to be found faithful. Blowing wind and flowing waters can refresh the earth and our spirits; they can also sweep away houses and capsize boats. Falling snow can cover the landscape with a peaceful stillness; it can also make roads impassable and cause pile-ups on the highway. It is not our circumstances that determine our need to praise. Whether it is easy or hard, we are called to praise.

Whether all seems well in our lives or nothing seems well, God is constant. So too is our responsibility as God's people to "Praise the LORD!"

Help us to praise you, O God, in good times and hard times. Fill our hearts with songs of praise! Amen.

Serving God with Peace and Humility

JANUARY 5–11, 2026 • KENJI KURAMITSU

SCRIPTURE OVERVIEW: These scriptures explore the kind of world God is interested in building and the kind of holy people who will inhabit it. The grand scope of the natural world as well as the inner workings of human hearts are evoked to suggest divine mastery over these spheres. The prophet points to the day when God's servant will bring justice to all people. In the psalm, God's voice resounds on the earth with might and power. In Acts, Peter witnesses to the fulfillment of the promise in Isaiah. The Gospel tells of the arrival of the Spirit, confirmed by the heavenly voice of affirmation. Faithful people will cultivate humility and peace. In the scriptures for the week, we can notice a theme of following God's call in our lives despite human hierarchies or fear. The power of God's voice guides our work to recognize belovedness in ourselves and others, especially during difficult times.

QUESTIONS AND SUGGESTIONS FOR REFLECTION

- Read Isaiah 42:1-9. When has God helped you to act in ways that build peace and goodwill? In situations when you have not lived up to those values, what has helped you return to that center?
- Read Matthew 3:13-17. What does it mean to you to be beloved by God? Recall times in your faith walk when you have felt close to the love of God and times when you have felt far from it.
- Read Psalm 29 several times. Where have you seen God's glory and majesty in creation?
- Read Acts 10:34-43. How do you narrate the story of your faith? What about Peter's rendering stands out to you?

An ordained Episcopal minister in Chicago, IL, Rev. Kenji Kuramitsu, LCSW, is Associate Dean for Community Life at the University of Chicago, Rockefeller Memorial Chapel and an adjunct professor of Pastoral Care at McCormick Theological Seminary.

MONDAY, JANUARY 5 ~ *Read Isaiah 42:1-4*

This Servant Song lyrically depicts one who acts with tenderness, compassion, and responsibility toward others—one who cares for others, protecting those who are easily broken, marginalized, and wounded. This is a person who would cup their hands with dignity around those who have been forced to live as fragile wicks of flickering candles, nearly extinguished by life. While Christians hold that Isaiah's prophesied leader was most fully revealed in the person of Jesus Christ, our text also invites us to consider ways to cultivate these traits in our own lives and in our own unique areas of stewardship.

In the Hawaiian language, the term *kuleana* is used to describe a person's sphere of sacred responsibility. One's *kuleana* may be a plot of land, a family unit, a church, a workplace. This focus can change over the course of a person's life as roles evolve between child, student, parent, pastor, elder. In this worldview, each individual's actions are innately connected to a wider web of being and belonging.

The image of a servant who meets the people with such reciprocal tenderness stands out precisely because far too many leaders carve a swath through our world with reckless abandon. Unlike the wise counselor who pauses before speaking, who exercises compassion for the poor, and who is invited to places as far as the farthest islands, these figures reject restraint, wielding force in a way that ultimately masters and narrows them. The divine does not delight in the cheap, conquering power of such kings. In God's political economy, gentle leadership, protection of the weak, and consistent service are more highly prized than any crown. God invites each of us to more closely hew our lives to such service.

Lord, guide me in ways that align with your call for wisdom and peace. Make me an instrument in the furthering of thy justice and goodness to all the ends of the earth. Amen.

TUESDAY, JANUARY 6 ~ *Read Matthew 2:1-12*

EPIPHANY

King Herod's reputation as a man of violence must have preceded him. His stature as a ruthless leader reverberates not only throughout the biblical text, but also among his contemporary writers who documented his brutality and terror. What did these pilgrims from the east make of this tyrant who schemed to maintain his fragile power, whose warped vision finally held a glimpse of profound insight? The paranoid king perceived correctly, alongside his visitors, that the helpless babe portended a real threat to his rule, that this Christ would inaugurate a way of being that would trouble an *ancien régime* built on reprisal and domination. Anxiety from leaders ripples downwards, and the entire city trembled with Herod's contagious and brittle fear.

The faithful foreigners who made their way westward must have only clung to the dim promise of this strange light in the sky, a star of anticipation and mystery. It is not easy to travel beyond one's own cultural, religious, and geographical boundaries, hoping against hope that truth and transformation might be found at the end of the journey. Yet, like Bethlehem, these humble figures were chosen by God to play a role in birthing something new.

The magi's openness to God's dreams and stars poignantly condemns the petty power squabbles of emperors and kings. How open are we to the leading of the divine in our day? How willing are we to acknowledge the unexpected people and places that God chooses to honor?

Jesus, star of heaven, light of the world, guide us as we seek to walk according to your ways. Transform the hardness in our hearts, that we may faithfully serve you. Amen.

WEDNESDAY, JANUARY 7 ~ *Read Psalm 29:1-5*

We make the passage of our short lives as created beings in a world spoken into existence by God. The psalmist muses on this divine declaration cascading over the face of the deep, writing for ancient peoples who saw water as a symbol of chaos, instability, raw power. It is not hard to relate to this worldview when we witness a waterfall, a whirlpool, a hurricane making landfall, or the blackest depths of the sea; we increasingly register the risks associated with this element in our time of climate crisis, as creation endures anew all manner of such peril.

Watery disorder being marshaled by a steady voice calls us back to the story of creation. It is also echoed in Jesus' calming interactions with storms and choppy seas. In all of these instances, God's holy words create the conditions for the grandeur of creation and the small miracles that shape our daily lives to blossom.

Though God's voice can sometimes come to us as a quiet whisper, a tugging of the conscience, a nudge from the Holy Spirit, this passage reminds us that it can just as readily land in our lives with a blistering force that can splinter cedars. Such awe should be inseparable from our worship and praise. A voice that shakes the earth can also fasten us securely upon this fragile planet. As we strive to steward well the land which feeds us, God's voice calls to us with clarity and steadiness, laying bare the reality of our utter dependence upon the earth and all those heavenly beings who shape our inner and outer worlds.

God, call out to us in the fierceness and fray of our lives. We thank you for the miracle of life, for mice and mountains. Grant that the feebleness of our hearts be perfected in the fullness of your mercies. Amen.

THURSDAY, JANUARY 8 ~ *Read Acts 10:34-43*

We human beings are spectacularly skilled at placing ourselves into distinct groups and hierarchies. Sometimes these sortings are relatively innocuous. Yet a brief survey of the troubled history of our species testifies to the ways that marking ourselves by apparent differences can distort the divine dream for our world. Against a culture that too readily slipped into a place of suspicion, fear, and privileging of certain groups over others, Peter preached of a God who cannot help but show impartiality toward all. Unlike us, God cannot be bought or bribed, seduced or swayed toward granting unjust favor. Participation in God's waking dream is universally available without distinction, offered freely to all who seek justice and peace.

In certain business settings, entrepreneurs are asked to develop a thirty-second "elevator pitch," imagining what they would say given the opportunity to make a case for themselves. Stand-up comedians often polish the best few minutes of their material into a "tight five"—the best jokes trimmed of any fat—in case they are ever called up on stage last-minute and need to demonstrate their chops. Likewise, as Christians we never know when we will be called upon to give a testimony about the hope that dwells within us. The writer of Luke–Acts provides one such vivid example of the distilled essence of the gospel: Jesus was baptized, healed others, worked against evil, and was killed by being hanged on a tree. Deuteronomy considered those who suffered such a death to be cursed by God, yet after such an ignominious end, Peter preaches, and God's favor fell upon the Lord's servant. Jesus' rising back to life and sharing food and drink are potent reminders of the divine invitation to all of creation to join God's continued breaking into our world.

Redeemer God, tear down all human divisions, for we each belong to you. Instill your gospel in our lives with the healing and justice that you alone can perfect. Amen.

FRIDAY, JANUARY 9 ~ *Read Matthew 3:13-17*

From the chaos of creation and the psalmist's mystical visions to Christ quelling storms on the Sea of Galilee, the scriptures are replete with God's voice echoing across waters. Matthew's scene of Jesus' baptism by John is another such holy moment, when the heavens themselves open up and a voice publicly claims Jesus as God's Son. This is a declaration of approval as well as delight, witnessed by a crowd who oversees a divine blessing on the beginning of Jesus' public ministry.

Christ models the modesty of a true leader, approaching a figure as imperfect as John to be baptized, and declaring his allegiance to God's righteousness. Jesus' descent into the roiling waters of the River Jordan is also his ineluctable joining in solidarity with the suffering of humanity, just as he would descend after his crucifixion to preach liberation to the captives of death. Jesus' "immediate" rise from these waters speaks to God's commitment to raising up all those in whom God takes pleasure.

It must have been jarring to go from the mountaintop experience of being claimed by God to the desert-valley experience of being tempted in the desert. At our baptism, God does not promise an easy road ahead but does promise to be with us, always, through whatever experiences we traverse next. Like Jesus experienced an evolution in the roles of his life as marked by his baptism, so too do our own ministries and responsibilities shift over time as God beckons us upon new waters. While it is sometimes scary to take that next, most faithful step, we can remember that just as God takes pride in God's beloved, so too can we find home within God.

Jesus Christ, humble us and draw us closer to your freely given love and mercy. Wash us clean of our sins, that we may delight in your righteousness and grace. Amen.

SATURDAY, JANUARY 10 ~ *Read Isaiah 42:5-9*

We draw breath more than twenty thousand times per day, an act often done unconsciously. Yet our breath can also serve as a powerful anchor for our attention whenever we turn our awareness to those steady, fragile waves lapping at our inner shores. Many world traditions invite focus upon the breath as a meditative practice. The writers of the Hebrew scriptures distinctively understood this sacred, ordinary, rhythmic act to be a gift granted by the same God who created the heavens and the earth.

Our God does not only sweep tectonic plates with grandeur, but also tenderly grips an elder or infant by the hand. God works in large and small ways to guide us. As the magi were drawn toward God's bright star, so too are all who are enclosed in darknesses, wrought by physical and metaphorical confinement, drawn toward freedom. God's servant does not stand in the way, but instead urges us to widen the lens of empathy to fully appraise and welcome those outside our immediate field of vision.

The same God who gives us breath knows how many more breaths are measured for us to draw before we return to the earth. No matter how much we might long to know what is to come—how an election, a relationship, or a new venture will come to pass—God has access to insight across time in a way that defies mortal understanding. While it can at times be excruciating to live with this uncertainty, we can take courage in God's invitation to join an unfolding plan of healing and justice, in God's use of our faithfulness as an instrument to bless the entire world.

Holy Spirit, transform us. Open our eyes to the invisible connections that shape our world. Once again, tear down the walls that cleave us from one another, that all penned in by wire and shame may behold your piercing light. Amen.

SUNDAY, JANUARY 11 ~ *Read Psalm 29:6-11*

Baptism of the Lord

Even after floodwaters recede, it is immediately evident exactly how high the water rose. Watermarks etch the walls of the houses at ankle, knee, abdomen, eye-level—leaving a lasting imprint of the damage done.

Our lives are also often marked in relation to events which leave us reeling in their wake: the loss of a loved one, the ending of a significant relationship, a betrayal or hurt from a community we love, a health crisis. At times these events have the effect of stripping our mental forests bare, contorting our self-understanding, leaving us with a feeling of being utterly exposed to the elements. In such seasons, it is essential to remember our ultimate belonging in the God who never leaves us abandoned. Radically, today's reading describes God's enthronement as established not in creation, but in God's triumph over the floodwaters—suggesting that we too can relate to ourselves in light of what catastrophes we have overcome.

The late Rev. Dr. David D. Daniels III was fond of speaking of baptism as leaving a "watermark" in our lives, stamping us as Christ's own forever. Divine favor and belovedness fall upon us like so much rain in our baptisms. When life aches, we might also give God thanks for those events we count as blessings: the birth of a child or a grandchild, pilgrimage or travel to a place that transforms our relationship with the world, the triumph of a marriage after a period of intense struggle.

All the thunders of human artillery, of fighter jets breaking the sound barrier, of our harsh inner voice of self-recrimination—none can match the power of God's voice, calling us to make peace within ourselves and this world.

Creator God, draw us closer to your vision for our lives. May we live according to your holy purposes. Amen.

The Voice of Faith

JANUARY 12–18, 2026 • JAN TURRENTINE

SCRIPTURE OVERVIEW: Scripture consistently portrays faith as an identity-forming spiritual quality that acts and speaks. Isaiah demonstrates unwavering confidence in God, regardless of circumstances, and a mission to be light in the world. The psalmist's faith produces hope in God's deliverance and "a new song" that proclaims God's salvation to others. Paul's portrait of faith includes an identity and giftedness that enable believers to fulfill God's purposes. The Gospel of John reminds us of the power of testimony in pointing others to Christ.

QUESTIONS AND SUGGESTIONS FOR REFLECTION

- Read Isaiah 49:1-7. How does your faith give you confidence?
- Read Psalm 40:1-11. What does your "new song" of faith say?
- Read 1 Corinthians 1:1-9. How does your faith keep you from harmful distractions?
- Read John 1:29-42. How do you point others to Jesus?

Jan Turrentine has worked in Christian publishing as an editor and writer for over 35 years. She lives in Nashville, TN, and is a member of West End United Methodist Church.

MONDAY, JANUARY 12 ~ *Read Isaiah 49:1-4*

Nevertheless. How do you hear that word? Is it a long sigh of resignation, of giving up? Or do you hear in that word a song of faith, trust, confidence, and determination?

When Hurricane Helene made landfall in Florida in late September 2024 and continued its inland march across several other states, two friends of mine in Western North Carolina watched helplessly as rushing water flooded their property. Within minutes, one of their cars and some business equipment were gone, and two rental units were destroyed. Yet the social media updates of these friends rang with gratitude and hope. They didn't sugarcoat the tragedy, but neither did they resign themselves to that present reality. *Nevertheless,* the post said. *Regardless of this, God has been good to us. God is faithful, and we will move forward.*

For God's servant Israel, "nevertheless" (CEB) was the sure resolve that, despite how things looked, God had a plan. Even in the face of God's rebuke and judgment for the people's unfaithfulness—and notwithstanding Jerusalem's destruction—God's plan was not only for God's people but specifically for this servant. God knew him, called him by name, held him in the divine grasp, protected him, and wanted to work through him. He was tired and weary, his strength depleted. "Nevertheless," God's servant proclaimed, his future, his purpose, his success, his well-being depended not on his own strength but on the strength of his God.

With each challenge we face, each problem, adversity, or pitfall, we get to choose the nature of our "nevertheless." We can drop our heads and sigh with defeat, or we can remember the One who knows us, calls us, equips us, and holds us. We can declare with confidence like Israel: "Yet surely my cause is with the LORD and my reward with my God."

Gracious God, teach me to have a "nevertheless" kind of faith in you regardless of my circumstances. Amen.

The opening verses of Isaiah 49 record a turning point in the life of Israel, God's servant. After objecting to God's call to the point of weariness, he acknowledges the insufficiency of his own strength and embraces the strength of God. He accepts the honor of being the one who will "restore Jacob to God" (CEB). Yet that, says God, is not enough. God's vision is much broader and extends beyond Israel's people "to the end of the earth" (CEB).

It's interesting that God reveals that larger vision of salvation after Israel accepts this call. Surely the mission of restoring God's people to God and returning them to their land seemed overwhelming. How could Israel do more?

You will do it, God says, because "I will also appoint you as light to the nations" (CEB). God's servant can complete the task because God calls him, equips him, appoints him, strengthens him, and fills him with the light of salvation. Israel's identity as light is also his mission and his message.

The intensity or brightness of light depends on its source. Not only did Jesus say, "I am the light of the world" (John 8:12), he told his disciples, "You are the light of the world" (Matt. 5:14). Like God's servant Israel, divine light forms our identity, our mission, and our message. Everywhere we go, we carry the light of Christ.

In many churches, worship services begin with an acolyte entering the sanctuary carrying a torch then lighting the candles on the altar, representing Christ, the light of the world. At the conclusion of the service, the acolyte extinguishes the altar candles, save one. Relighting the torch before the last candle is extinguished, he or she then carries the symbolic light of Christ out of the sanctuary, inviting worshipers to take this light with them into the world.

Light of the world, shine through me. Amen.

WEDNESDAY, JANUARY 14 ~ *Read Psalm 40:1-4*

Occasionally in church services of my childhood, someone would "give their testimony," dramatically recalling how God rescued them and gave them new life. The "pit of death" and the "mud and filth" of the psalmist's story was their story too (CEB). Their passion and conviction powerfully moved others to renewed trust and faith in God.

Each of us knows the desperation of feeling somehow trapped in a relationship, a job, or some other circumstance. We know the helplessness of feeling the metaphorical ground beneath us shifting, knocking us flat. We know the anguish of crying out to God for help, hoping God will hear and respond. Even if we cry out for a very long time, even if we must wait for God to act, we—like the psalmist—wait with hope. God's past faithfulness assures us that God will lean down, lift us up, and place us once again on solid ground.

But that's not all God does. God gives us "a new song," "a song of praise." It's a song meant not only for us but also for those who find themselves mired in hopeless situations, some floundering and fearful, others haughty and defiant. Our stories of God's faithfulness can spark hope both for those who know they need God and for those who proudly cling to their self-sufficiency. Our songs bear witness to the amazing love and grace of the God who saves.

The individual stories behind our songs vary; they may be dramatic or rather ordinary. Either way, they are the backstory. The real story others need to hear comes in the song we sing through our lives of service and praise of the God who leans down, listens, lifts us up, and sets us on solid ground.

Faithful God, remind me of the powerful song you have placed within me, and give me the courage to sing it. Amen.

THURSDAY, JANUARY 15 ~ *Read Psalm 40:5-11*

A couple of years ago, I met a woman who was looking for work—odd jobs of any kind, really. She had numerous skills: housekeeping, painting, construction, electrical work, lawn maintenance, garage organization. Impressed, I hired her for a specific job at my house. At one point, she took a break and came to where I was working at my kitchen table, several Bible translations and commentaries spread before me. She was curious, and when I told her what I was doing, she began to speak freely about her faith.

Her life experiences had been very different from mine. Her past was filled with abuse and pain. She had at one point been trafficked by her then-husband and had suffered through some unspeakable situations. Yet she was positive, hopeful, and determined that her life moving forward would be a good one. She was enrolled in college and working toward a specific career. Like the writer of Psalm 40, God delivered her and gave her "a new song" (v. 3).

It's unclear the specifics of the psalmist's earlier situation, but we know it was dire. What is clear is the gratitude. Beginning with verse 5, the psalmist turns from speaking about their deliverance to speaking directly to God, praising and thanking God for the wonderful things God has done. God had been so good, so faithful, that it was impossible for the psalmist to enumerate everything God had done. What could express sufficient gratitude to this One like no other? God, the psalmist knew, didn't want sacrifices and offerings. What could they do?

God's will was for the psalmist to share God's faithfulness, salvation, loyal love, and trustworthiness with others. Rather than keeping God's goodness quiet, the psalmist "didn't hold anything back" (CEB). Neither should we.

God, help me to speak about you with a boldness that holds nothing back. Amen.

FRIDAY, JANUARY 16 ~ *Read 1 Corinthians 1:1-9*

Paul's first letter to the Corinthian church opens with words of encouragement, gratitude, and affirmation. He reminds them of their identity as God's people, their connection to Christ's followers everywhere, and the riches and spiritual gifts they have received through Christ. He also affirms God's faithfulness to them and their partnership with Jesus Christ.

This context is significant because much of the rest of this letter consists of Paul sternly admonishing them over attitudes and behaviors inconsistent with the faith they profess. They are divided and quarreling, engaged in sexual immorality, involved in lawsuits with fellow believers, inappropriately partaking of the Lord's Supper, misusing spiritual gifts, and even denying Christ's resurrection. Their problems are so pervasive that they are distracted from their purpose and have lost sight of the people God called them to be. With their focus averted from Jesus, their testimony is threatened.

We're not so different. Distractions surround us. The problems the Corinthian Christians faced could easily take hold in our lives and in our churches, compromising our testimony about Christ and distracting those who need to hear the gospel message.

But they don't have to. The gifts and graces the Corinthian Christians received are ours too. Like them, we "have been made holy to God in Christ Jesus"; we are "God's people" (CEB). And we are not alone. We join with "all those who call upon the name of our Lord Jesus Christ in every place" (CEB). We are in partnership with one another, with Christians everywhere, and with Christ. We have everything we need—the limitless grace of God, spiritual gifts, and "every kind of knowledge" (CEB)—to live into our calling to bear witness to God's love and salvation. We can't afford to get distracted. Our message is too important.

Loving, saving God, keep my focus on you and your call. Amen.

SATURDAY, JANUARY 17 ~ *Read John 1:29-34*

The "A" on my 11th-grade English paper brought a smile, but the note my teacher added beneath it made me think. "Use your voice to create change!" she said, encouraging a reserved teenager with deep feelings and big opinions to use a gift she saw in me.

One of the most interesting voices in the New Testament is John the Baptist. His public ministry was relatively short: Some scholars estimate it lasted only about six months. Yet it was so important that he spent much of his life in the wilderness preparing for it. John's unique mission was to prepare people for the coming of the long-anticipated Messiah.

Living into his calling involved not only knowing who he was but also who he was not. He was not the Messiah, Elijah, or a prophet. He made that clear to Jewish religious leaders who questioned him. "I am the voice," he told them (John 1:23). His witness, his testimony, came from his identity as the voice God used to point people to the Messiah.

The people needed this voice because the Messiah God sent was not at all what they were expecting. Even John, with his clear grasp of his own identity and purpose, did not recognize Jesus at first. He anticipated the Messiah; he expected the Messiah. But even he did not recognize Jesus until he "saw the Spirit coming down from heaven like a dove, and [resting] on him" (CEB). Once he saw, he called out to others to "Look!" and see "the Lamb of God who takes away the sin of the world" (CEB).

Our world is filled with voices proclaiming all kinds of messages, but none is more important than those voices that point to Jesus. Our voices, in the form of both our words and our actions, are the vehicles God uses to carry the message of Jesus.

God, make my voice strong and my message clear. Amen.

SUNDAY, JANUARY 18 ~ *Read John 1:35-42*

New Testament readers notice almost immediately that John's Gospel is different from Matthew, Mark, and Luke. Its uniqueness provides a biblical portrait of Jesus we would not otherwise have. John's distinct features include careful use of different writing styles like poetry, narrative, and dialogue; brilliant imagery illustrating theological truths; and specific details of interactions and conversations. Significant dialogue comes in Chapter 1, setting in motion Jesus' ministry that forever changed the world. Following beautifully crafted poetry about the Word—Jesus—and John's testimony that paved the way for Jesus to enter the scene, people began to follow him.

On two consecutive days, John encounters Jesus and boldly declares him as "the Lamb of God who takes away the sin of the world!" (v. 29, CEB). Just as boldly, he announces, "I have seen and testified that this one is God's Son" (v. 34, CEB). That's all it took. Immediately, "two disciples heard what he said, and they followed Jesus," (CEB) spending the remainder of the day with him. Such a simple introduction, yet profoundly life-altering.

It's no small thing to point someone to Jesus. It is, in fact, the most important thing we can do. We can do it with words, but we also do it with the way we live our lives. As people whose identity is "Christian," our words, attitudes, actions, priorities—everything about us—should point to Jesus Christ. That's the thing about faith in Christ. It permeates every area of our lives, changing us from the inside out. It remakes, renames, redefines, and redirects us. It gives us a message, a mission, and a voice that points to Jesus.

Sometimes the voice of faith gently whispers. Sometimes it joyfully sings. Sometimes it shines a light into darkness. Sometimes it offers hands to serve. But always, it points to the One who saves.

Lord, use me to point others to you. Amen.

Texts of Trauma and Hope

JANUARY 19–25, 2026 • PATRICK B. REYES

SCRIPTURE OVERVIEW: Certainly, these texts have been placed together in the lectionary to point to Jesus as the central figure in our tradition and text. With the exception of the psalm, the other three texts are typically seen to build on one another. Matthew refers to the Isaiah text. The Isaiah text refers to a future Prince of Peace. Paul's letter places Jesus above all religious leaders. Together, they point to Jesus as the Messiah. But the texts have more to say to us than merely reflecting on Jesus' centrality in our tradition. The texts offer another way to think about how to recognize and respond to trauma and suffering. We can see the pain that inspired the writing of each of these texts and resist the urge to solve each instance with the arrival of a savior. We can dwell in the suffering, come to know it, and see what might emerge on our own journey toward healing.

QUESTIONS AND SUGGESTIONS FOR REFLECTION

- Read Isaiah 9:1-4. How has God's love freed you to find your calling?
- Read Psalm 27:1, 4-9. When have you called out to God? How has God helped you turn your cries to praise?
- Read 1 Corinthians 1:10-18. How does your community of faith regard its leaders? How does your community's regard of its leaders shape the body of believers?
- Read Matthew 4:12-23. How have significant changes in your life (like a loved one's death or a career change) allowed your ministry to grow?

A Chicano writer, theologian, and executive leader, Rev. Patrick B. Reyes, PhD, is the Dean of Auburn Theological Seminary and the bestselling and award-winning author of *The Purpose Gap* (Westminster John Knox, 2021) and *Nobody Cries When We Die* (Chalice, 2016). He is a board director for the American Academy of Religion and is the Co-Dean of the Freedom Seminary for the Children's Defense Fund.

MONDAY, JANUARY 19 ~ *Read 1 Corinthians 1:10-18*

In his letter to the Corinthians, Paul lists all the leaders the people in Corinth are following and calls them out for dividing themselves amongst these teachers. We might say we follow any of a number of famous preachers and religious leaders today. Paul challenges his readers, saying those distinctions do not matter.

This week we celebrate the Rev. Dr. Martin Luther King Jr., one of many faith leaders from the civil rights era. Preachers and teachers often return to his words and teachings. Even as a bald, desert-based Chicano pastor and theologian committed to nonviolence, I chose to study in at Boston University because of King's legacy, having been told by a pastor that, as a student of social movements and a nonviolent organizer, I should consider the school of the prophets.

It would be tempting to say that I follow Rev. Dr. Martin Luther King Jr. Certainly I learn from him and others who have come after him. Yet is Christ divided? We are in an age when society, and certainly Christianity, feels more divided than ever. Rather than choose sides, perhaps Paul is reminding us to stay in the tough conversations with all Christians, to bridge divides among the church, and to work to heal communal and denominational wounds.

I wonder how we might live into the unity part of the dream that Rev. Dr. Martin Luther King Jr. cast from the steps of the Lincoln Memorial. How might we not just quote the prophet but actually live into his dream by honoring Paul's request to close the gaps in the community? In many ways, I think King was hoping we would catch this dream, a dream of a playground where all children could play, or as Paul says, one body. Could we realize the dream?

God above all leaders, remind us of the dream, a dream to be one body, a community baptized in your name. Amen.

TUESDAY, JANUARY 20 ~ *Read Matthew 4:12-23*

Years back, I was talking with a close friend about the abuse she and her children were experiencing. As a pastor and a scholar who is also a survivor of childhood abuse, I listened, cried, and drove for what seemed like hours as we talked on the phone, only to find myself parked in front of my childhood home—the very place where I had experienced the worst parts of my life. Confused, I sat there staring at my house of horrors, reminding myself that no person desires nor deserves to suffer.

In Matthew, Jesus returns from the desert after resisting temptation, only to hear that his cousin John has been arrested. He immediately flees to the Land of Zebulun and Naphtali. These spaces were conquered and violated time and time again; their inhabitants "lost." It is curious that Jesus would go to these places where violence and trauma had marked the land for generations. We could do a simple reading of the text and point to Jesus fulfilling the text in Isaiah (9:1-4). But again, we have to wonder, why these places?

Where do you turn to when life seems hopeless? When you are overwhelmed and the trauma feels too much, where are you drawn to return? Think about those places, whether that be your inward landscape, technologies, or places of significance for you. When we return to these sites of trauma, we learn from our past experiences and are able to seek insight and healing. Like memorials, these sites of past violence become the sites of survival, learning, and hope. Perhaps we return to these places to remind ourselves *never again*. Perhaps we go to these places to remember how far we've come. Whatever the reason, we return as Jesus did and find the redemption that is offered by our great God.

Creator who knows our loneliness, be with us in our time of need. Journey with us to those places in need of healing. And be with others who struggle alone this day. Amen.

WEDNESDAY, JANUARY 21 ~ *Read Psalm 27:1, 4-9*

We have been here for a long time, *mijo.*" I was young when I learned that my people have been on this land for generations. When I was older, I learned about the ways the land and people were colonized and about the attempted genocide of my relatives and other Indigenous people. I live on land that should feel familiar, and yet I am surrounded by the descendants of those who sought to harm my ancestors.

The psalms are songs to the divine, cries that reflect hope as much as despair. They remind us of the power of songs, dances, and cultural traditions. I know David's pain. I hear it in our drumming and our sacred songs, calling out to the Creator to show us their divine face.

I often wonder how others feel in moments of desperation. I wonder what songs they sing, what cries they give, what hymns they choose to reflect their pain. When enemies surround us, do we still look for the beauty of the Lord?

For those of us from cultures and traditions where singing, dancing, and speaking our language has been outlawed, this psalm reflects this pain. And yet it is not just my pain alone. Because I share the psalms with so many different people and different cultures, I know that you have also experienced the isolation expressed in the text. It is in this shared experience, even if only through this one piece of scripture, that you and I both know the pain of being surrounded by our enemies. My grandma is not just talking to me. She is talking to you as well. She is reminding you that you have been here too.

How will we share this deep divide?

To the God of those who dance and sing our songs, of storytellers and keepers of our cultures, remember us, as we remember your people, and honor them with this land that belongs to all God's creation. Amen.

THURSDAY, JANUARY 22 ~ *Read Matthew 4:12-23*

The US surgeon general recently issued an advisory on the loneliness epidemic. Loneliness, he writes, is killing us. "It is associated with a greater risk of cardiovascular disease, dementia, stroke, depression, anxiety, and premature death. The mortality impact of being socially disconnected is similar to that caused by smoking up to 15 cigarettes a day, and even greater than that associated with obesity and physical inactivity." He adds that half of all US adults report feeling lonely.*

Jesus surely experienced one form of loneliness in the desert; learning that his cousin—the person who leapt for him in the womb—has been taken by the state is a completely different form of isolation. But Jesus does something remarkable. Instead of sinking deeper into isolation, he reaches out. Jesus ends this passage by calling his disciples.

Those of us in the church understand the ways the church mirrors society, and it is no different for the loneliness epidemic. We are facing great shifts in our religious institutions. As Christians facing our own loneliness and isolation, Jesus' action can show us the way forward. In these tough times, we can call on the community. When we at our lowest, Jesus reminds us that this is precisely the time to start our ministry and call the people together. This is true for leaders and participants. When people gather, healing happens. Jesus is modeling what Shawn Ginwright and Rev. Dr. Emma Jordan-Simpson have both called "healing-centered leadership." We can cultivate ministry practices that push us to turn outward and invite other disciples to journey with us. It is this outward turn that allows our inner wounds to heal.

---

*https://www.hhs.gov/surgeongeneral/priorities/connection/index.html

God of the healers, watch over us as we call on all disciples to heal in your name. Amen.

FRIDAY, JANUARY 23 ~ *Read Isaiah 9:1-4*

Isaiah was written largely during the exile. It was written during great pain and suffering and is a cry for another way. It is a futurist text—imagining, hoping, exploring what it might feel like to be free.

I connect deeply with part of verse 3: "They rejoice before you as with joy at the harvest." Every year, my community celebrates the harvest before the long winter. This practice has occurred for generations. Corn, beans, and squash (the three sisters) are the centerpiece of our meals. From tamales to tortillas—and what we put inside each—the harvest represents new life. I know what the harvest smells, looks, tastes, and sounds like. I feel the corn husks under my hand, the rough edges that will soon be smooth from cooking. I smell roasting corn, cooked squash, beans, and the steam that rises to my nose when unrolling the tamale. The spices from the mole sauce—chocolate, nuts, seeds, and dried chilies ground to a paste and cooked down—offer tastes of something ancient and exciting. I know the sounds of family gathering, laughing, and celebrating our time together during harvest. What a gift!

At the same time, I am not sure what to do with the tension of the spoils language that immediately follows this verse. As quickly as I relate to the first metaphor of the harvest, I recoil from the second, imagining—instead of exultation—the death and destruction that accompanies victory and plunder.

This is the tension of our scriptures. Even as we recall the joy of hearing these verses, perhaps as recently as this past Advent season promising the arrival of the Christ child, we cannot ignore the full reality of our stories of faith. There are no easy answers. And by not accepting easy answers, we sit with the struggle and look to the hopeful future of true freedom in God.

To the God of our past and future, accompany us as we celebrate the harvest by honoring your name. Amen.

SATURDAY, JANUARY 24 ~ *Read Psalm 27:1, 4-9*

Why is this the world I was born into?

I often find myself confronted by pain and trauma, asking *how could this happen?* Cancer. Death of children. Violence against loved ones. Global environmental destruction. Societal and political divides appear to have no end. Wars occur across the globe and generational suffering needs healing—and even if the wars have ceased, the memory and trauma remain. For some of us, we are displaced people trying to make a home in a land that is hostile to us. For others, we are on ancestral lands that have been occupied and taken from under our very feet.

As we move to the end of this week, our texts remind us that this violence is not new. Being surrounded and overwhelmed by those who do not have our health and happiness in mind is not new. This world is marked by violence. That does not mean the violence and suffering are necessary, but rather, the texts offer us some guideposts for how our ancestors met and dealt with the trauma of their lives.

For Matthew's Jesus, returning to the scriptures and sacred places identified in his tradition, as well as gathering support from others, encouraged him. For David and Isaiah, their futurist vision of a healed world that draws on the history and traditions of the community inspired them to continue.

What historic pains and traumas do our communities face? For what do we need a futurist vision? Sit with these texts for what they are—cries of pain, songs of trauma and hope, and reminders that we have been here before. Know the ancestors of our tradition are walking with us on this day and every day.

God of our ancestors, provide a futurist vision for us as we become good ancestors in your name. Amen.

SUNDAY, JANUARY 25 ~ *Read Isaiah 9:1-4*

We each have a choice to make. We can be a good ancestor, a keeper of a sacred fire that burns for generations, tended to and nurtured. Or, we can fade away like a candle that served its time and is extinguished.

We've spent seven days together journeying through sacred lands, telling stories. Who did we honor and name? How many people like the Gospel writer, Isaiah, David, Chloe, Paul, or Jesus can we name as good ancestors?

David wrote songs for a particular historical moment and for a specific group of people. Paul's letter was tailored to a particular group of people who were focused on the leaders of their time. A good ancestor is not one who comes up with the universal truth that everyone should know—pastors and religious leaders fall into this ego trap all too easily.

Instead, a good ancestor lives a life that makes space for future generations to thrive. They focus on loving the community before them, writing them songs and letters, addressing their particular fears and hopes. A good ancestor explores the depths of the moment while placing it in the context of previous generations. A good ancestor reminds their people that God's people have been here before.

Reflect on your ancestry. How are you faithful to your Christian and familial roots? Cast your vision seven generations from now. What will the community you now serve need? Who are they? What challenges are they facing? What songs, prayers, letters, and expressions of faithfulness are you offering now that might guide them in times of change? What story will you leave them so that when they look to the past, they can see a healed future?

God, we pray for the fire-keepers. In a world that tries to put their light out, we ask that you sustain their spirit so that their ministry and light may shine for all to see. Amen.

Unshaken

JANUARY 26–FEBRUARY 1, 2026 • OLENA TOVIANSKA

SCRIPTURE OVERVIEW: The prophet Micah calls us to take the way of justice, mercy, and humility. The psalmist shows that the mountain of God's truth is available for the blameless. Both are not only judgments but also provide prophetic hope. In Paul's first letter to the Corinthians, he shows that righteousness, holiness, and redemption are given in Christ on the Cross. The mountain of blessedness in the Gospel of Matthew seems desperately impossible to hike, but Christ shows us that it is he who is our way to live a truthful life right where we are.

QUESTIONS AND SUGGESTIONS FOR REFLECTION

- Read Micah 6:1-8. What does it mean "to act justly and to love mercy and to walk humbly" in your everyday life?
- Read Psalm 15. The psalmist claims that the requirements for dwelling with God relate to how we treat others. How does this affect the ways you seek to be in God's presence?
- Read 1 Corinthians 1:18-31. How is the Cross foolishness for the people of our time? What is the power of the Cross for you today?
- Read Matthew 5:1-12. What compels you to want to be blessed, knowing Jesus' definition? What concerns you about being blessed according to this definition? How are the beatitudes gifts?

Olena Tovianska lives in Irpin, Ukraine, where she works as a translator with English and Chinese languages. In her ministry, she explores how performing arts can be used in communal worship to heal traumatized communities.

MONDAY, JANUARY 26 ~ *Read 1 Corinthians 1:18-31*

Paul says "Jews ask for signs"—they want to make sure that God is in control. Israel has survived big, godless empires throughout its entire history; to accept that God has become an object of a shameful punishment by a pagan invader is scandalous. The One who is understood as having full control over the course of the history doesn't seem to have any control on the Cross. Jesus' crucifixion reminded Jews that they didn't have control over their lives as long as there was an invader speaking the language of torture and death. Those who brought Jesus to crucifixion had found illusory stability by cooperation with the imperial power. From their perspective, Jesus not only failed to find a proper coping strategy with the reality of occupation, but he also jeopardized their own coping strategy. Jews saw the Cross from one side—as a total loss of control.

In the same sentence, Paul says "Greeks desire wisdom." The Cross is foolish to those who seek to use wisdom to understand the experience. Both Jews and Gentiles see the Cross as the point of zero power and control. But they don't see the other side of the Cross—love. The only thing that could make God end up on the Cross is love: Love without a milligram of coercion; love that doesn't conquer or convince. When we question what sign the Cross shows us or what wisdom could be gained from such a violent act, the answer to both is love.

Sometimes things happen that make it seem like God has lost control. For me, it was a full-scale invasion of my country. How can there be another big war in Europe after the Holocaust? How can such things happen if God has not lost control? In such moments, I pray to always see another side of the Cross—the depth of God's love.

Lord, when I look at the Cross, help me not to lose sight of your love, as it is the only power to live a faithful life. Amen.

I am living in the midst of genocidal war. Three years in, *injustice* is another word for *reality*. Yet I see that acts of justice provide hope—and hope for a more just world can be enough on which to survive in the face of unspeakable despair and violence.

The prophet Micah says God's people are to "do justice." The very first act of justice for Christians is the prayer Jesus taught us: "May your [just] will be done on earth as it is in heaven" (Matt. 6:10). The prayer resounds in our upper room of hope, but that room can easily turn into an ivory tower unless we take our work for justice into the public square. We can bring justice into the world by way of the second requirement of Micah: Loving "kindness" or "mercy" (NIV) by offering it to the suffering ones.

As for the third, is there a litmus test for walking humbly? It might be a refusal to believe that others' children are less important. How can children be killed by bombs and missiles, kidnapped or sent away from their parents? How can they live without food, water, medical care, and safe schools if we don't accept that they are less important?

Each of these three requirements seems so simple until we stop spiritualizing them and put them into the realm of our everyday interactions. Then they seem to be hardly possible. But the trial Micah describes is not only a judgment—it is also a hope. God's faithfulness, which was fully expressed on the Cross, is the embodiment of justice, mercy, and humility. The beauty of God's love looks straight into the ugly face of our depravity. Justice doesn't skip the difficult parts but meets us where we are by the mercy of Jesus. His resurrection is the invitation to share in his courage and to hike the mountains of the Lord, the mountains of justice, mercy, and humility. Christ will hike with us.

May the mountains of the Lord become witnesses to the just and merciful acts of your church. Amen.

WEDNESDAY, JANUARY 28 ~ *Read Psalm 15*

Who can be in God's sanctuary? The author of this psalm describes a person whose acts, words, and values are all aligned. This alignment is called *integrity*.

Is integrity even possible today? Some scholars have described our current reality as "post-truth." This designation indicates a time when emotional appeal is more influential than fact, challenging the notion of what truly is important. I ask myself how we can dwell in God's sanctuary of truth when everything and nothing matters at the same time. In the midst of such chaos, how can we make the right decisions?

A "post-truth" reality challenges the idea of wholeness. The more fragmented our lives are, the more vulnerable we become. Into this setting comes a pack of perpetrators sensing our open wounds. Some translations of verse 5 use the word *usury,* which is the practice of lending money with unreasonably high interest, exploiting the vulnerable circumstances of another. Exploitation, though, is broader than a financial matter. Propaganda does exactly this, exploiting deep human fears and anxieties.

None of us can attain a perfect level of wholeness, as the natural state of being human is all about contradiction. But God is continually creating new and wondrous opportunities: In Jesus we are called to be his sanctuaries. He has made his dwelling within us and empowered us to be people of integrity as a prophetic sign in the fragmented world.

Our stance in the public space will not be shaken if we choose integrity. Being unshaken doesn't mean that others will not try to shake us off, but their shaking will not knock us off balance. The gift of the indwelling of the Lord is perseverance, both of individuals and of the church, the body that proclaims the power to uplift by hope and truth amid cynicism and despair.

Holy God, help us to be your sanctuary of truth, a prophetic sign of wholeness in a broken world. Amen.

THURSDAY, JANUARY 29 ~ *Read Micah 6:1-8*

A court hearing is not always an exciting event to attend. Of course, it does depend on our reason for being there. If we are seeking justice, we would look forward to the trial; if we are to be judged, we would likely hope it never comes. Before God, we are both the plaintiff and the defendant at the same time, seeking justice but also having much to be judged for.

For the case, God calls the people to remember what God has done, all the way from their deliverance from slavery to their entry into the Promised Land. It was a chain of ups and downs in their faithfulness, but God didn't act toward them out of the scarcity of their trust; God acted out of the abundance of God's mercy. God's actions do not reflect the ugliness of our state, but the beauty of God's love.

Though the practice of sacrifice was a part of the God-given law, the prophet uses irony to show how miserable our attempts at covering our transgressions are. No offering is sufficient. We could not give "thousands of rams" or fill ten thousand rivers with oil. Nor does God desire the more intimate sacrifice of family. No, the Lord has made clear the requirements. "To do justice and to love kindness and to walk humbly with your God" are not abstract ideas the prophet makes up, but the things God has shown him. Through these actions we glimpse God's character. Through these actions we offer to God the right sacrifices that adequately respond to God's saving grace and allow God to work through us in the world.

Lord, may mercy be my eyes, seeing how you cover my wounds with your love. May humility be my ears, hearing that I am as important to you as the one who is next to me and the one who is far from me. May justice be my guide as I seek to follow your will in this world. Amen.

FRIDAY, JANUARY 30 ~ *Read 1 Corinthians 1:18-31*

The very same passage from First Corinthians can be perceived in a radically different way than how we considered it earlier this week. It depends on the status of the one who is in contact with the message: "perishing" or "being saved."

All the sin and evil of humanity find their full expression on the Cross. Isn't this life scary if people can crucify God? The Cross says: "Yes, it is scary, but that's not the whole story." The Cross doesn't show us only the reality we see, and it doesn't fix it instantly either. Instead it shows us the One who creates the ultimate reality and invites us in. God doesn't let torture and death have the final word; God comes with resurrection and hope.

In a world structured around the prevailing wisdom of "power," the Cross is an invitation to define reality by the love of God. The love of God is the only power that gives us courage for living our lives faithfully right where we are. No matter how little control I feel like God has over my life or in this world which seems to be falling apart, God's love is enough for me to take a risk of living by God's righteousness, holiness, and redemption.

"Perishing" is not taking God's love seriously, not giving it a chance. "Being saved" is letting God's love define my reality. This love seems as foolish now as back then. It is much easier to see myself as an insignificant dot in the cosmos than as the apple in the eye of God's love. But this love is still as powerful as it has always been. "Love is strong as death," says the Song of Solomon (8:6), and here comes Love, which is stronger than death, bringing the hope of resurrection.

Lord, give me courage to let your love define my life. Amen.

SATURDAY, JANUARY 31 ~ *Read Matthew 5:1-12*

I joined the church back in the 1990s during a wave of revival in Ukraine. We used to say, "May God bless you!" to the people sitting beside us after worship as another way to say "goodbye." We still say it now, though much less, and I often wonder if we would still say "May God bless you!" if both the speaker and the hearer had the same idea of blessedness as Jesus.

Lest popularity distract him from the true picture of the world, Jesus leaves his followers and takes a hike up the mountain instead. His disciples come to him. The verbs of action are only used for Jesus and the disciples. Have the crowds joined them on the mountainside? We can't tell for sure from the text. Being a disciple is different from being one of the crowd. This uncertainty of the text leaves us with the choice of which group we want to join. We traditionally interpret the beatitudes as gifts, but what if they are not? What if they are an invitation, an open invitation for a hike to the mountain of God?

Who are these people Jesus calls blessed? Those who don't live by the illusions of this world: They are poor, and they hunger and thirst as nothing of the world can fulfill them. They don't succumb to illusions. They mourn, as mourning makes us fully present to reality. They have seen the kingdom with their heart, and they live by its values in a world where the kingdom is not obviously visible: amongst the meek, merciful, pure in heart, and peacemakers. They realize what usually happens on the way: insulting, false accusations, and persecution. But they have the courage to carry on.

Lord, give us courage to follow you up the mountain. Amen.

SUNDAY, FEBRUARY 1 ~ *Read Matthew 5:1-12*

Who does Jesus call blessed? The big dreamers—those who refuse to agree with things as they are—are blessed. Those who claim nothing as their own, who don't cling to the things given but instead hold the hand of a Giver, are blessed. The mourners who don't avoid injustice and evil, those who don't see righteousness as something optional but as the only way to live, those who refuse coercion and tend the wounds of human fragility—Jesus calls them blessed.

Verse 9 speaks to me in this moment. Who are the peace-makers in times of haunting wars? God calls them God's children. If wars like the one I live in construct the reality of millions of others on this planet, does God have so few children? Where are those who are ready to face the ugliness of war, who don't dismiss the wounds and tragedies but plant seeds of courage to stand up for the victim and confront the aggressor?

If these beatitudes are invitations, who would dare to accept such an invitation? Who would have enough courage to be called blessed? It is much easier to read this text as a piece of poetry—an intensely metaphorical excerpt, left by an ancient teacher. But Jesus is not giving us his teaching, he is giving us himself as "the way and the truth and the life" (John 14:6).

Maybe it's not that Jesus calls it a blessing to be persecuted, to mourn, or to feel extreme hunger or thirst, but that this very life of God is able to make us genuinely blessed even when we do mourn, hunger, and struggle for justice, peace, and righteousness. Jesus has become our peace in times of war and our righteousness in the realm of sin.

God, help me to remember that you are what encourages me to accept the invitation and to partake in the life you design in the face of whatever may come. Amen.

Lighting God's Way

FEBRUARY 2–8, 2026 • JOEL T. P. FITZGERALD

SCRIPTURE OVERVIEW: This week's scriptures juxtapose the light of God's alternative kingdom with the hurtful way humans tend to operate. Isaiah asks if our worship helps the downtrodden or if our internal schisms distract us from mission. The psalmist notes that the blessings of the righteous flow to those who shine their light by helping the poor and oppressed. In First Corinthians, Paul makes explicit the way of God as an alternative path from the ways of this world, suggesting that God's wisdom is something this world cannot begin to comprehend. In the Gospel, Jesus invites us to be salt and light through obedience to the full calling of God; a calling made clear in the Law and the Prophets.

QUESTIONS AND SUGGESTIONS FOR REFLECTION

- Read Isaiah 58:1-12. When have you chosen the fast of form over substance, fasting only to show off or to battle with others? When have you chosen the fast of breaking the bonds of injustice?
- Read Psalm 112:1-10. When have you felt fulfilled in helping others? Who did you help and why?
- Read 1 Corinthians 2:1-16. How have you felt the Spirit moving in your life? Where has the Spirit led you into ministry?
- Read Matthew 5:13-20. How have you been salt and light in the world? How could you let your light shine?

Rev. Joel T. P. Fitzgerald is a United Methodist pastor serving The United Methodist Foundation of Michigan. He is the husband of Rev. Erin Fitzgerald and the father of two boys.

MONDAY, FEBRUARY 2 ~ *Read Isaiah 58:1-9a*

In today's reading, Isaiah starts off nice and easy. "Shout out; do not hold back! Lift your voice like a trumpet!" But then the record scratch comes. We're not shouting praises; we are shouting remonstrances. God wants to get our attention to ask us some hard questions. Are we seeking God's favor even as we fight and quarrel with one another? Do we go off to church assured of our righteousness even as we oppress those who work for us? Ouch.

As a pastor, this calling out stings. I've run around trying to get ready for worship on a Sunday morning while folks in my town go homeless. I've spent hours upon hours in navel-gazing church meetings while kids in my son's school didn't have winter coats. I've offered God the fast of following rules while overlooking the deeper purpose for which those rules were made.

Yet Isaiah doesn't say we should throw out worship or rules or even committee meetings. What Isaiah *is* asking, though, is whether all these things serve the ultimate purpose of God's kingdom. It's not a question of whether to fast or to help the poor, whether to worship or to lift up the oppressed. The question is, rather, how does our fasting equip us to help the poor? How does our worship lead us to lift up the oppressed?

Like any good preacher, Isaiah doesn't leave us with reproach. Instead, he tells us what happens when we offer our bread to the hungry: Our light will break forth, our healing will spring up, and we will be in community with God.

God, help my worship and my fasting align with your kingdom. Help the work that we do always lead to your beloved community. Amen.

TUESDAY, FEBRUARY 3 ~ *Read Isaiah 58:9b-12*

What do we do when we've experienced loss? How do we move forward? Isaiah seems to know human psychology, suggesting one common response to loss is lashing out at others. Instead of looking at root causes, or being self-reflective, we want to blame others, to externalize our grief and fear onto some scapegoat. This can make us feel good in the moment. It can alleviate our immediate distress. But it does not actually fix anything. It doesn't rebuild that which we've lost.

A little more gently than yesterday's reading, Isaiah suggests how to rebuild that which we've lost. Isaiah counsels us to stop bickering and blaming one another. Instead, Isaiah wants us to focus on the afflicted and hungry, to put our efforts toward helping those in need. This work, not mere religious obligation, is what will bring God's favor. This work, not infighting and contention, is what will help restore that which has been lost.

Isaiah ends with a lovely image of a restored world, where the walls have been rebuilt and the streets restored. Tellingly, such a world comes not through force or coercion. It comes not through winning any type of fight. Rather this new world comes through doing the small, hard work of restoration. In our world of constant change and seemingly ever-present conflict, it can feel like this small work carries no weight. Given all the loss of this world, how can volunteering at our local food pantry, or sitting with a grieving widow, or standing against injustice make any difference? Isaiah's answer is that it makes *all* the difference; indeed, that it is the *only* way by which the walls will be rebuilt.

Gracious God, may I live my life in line with your path, that I may be called "repairer of the breach." Amen.

WEDNESDAY, FEBRUARY 4 ~ *Read Psalm 112:1-10*

The psalmist continues Isaiah's theme of righteousness as a beacon of God's way. Rather than lay into us for failing to be righteous, though, the psalmist connects God's goodness with the actions of the righteous and their just rewards. The psalmist offers a positive case for one who follows God's path; namely, they will receive riches and blessings, happiness and delight.

In our society, we often assign righteousness to those who are successful. Did you succeed in politics, commerce, or culture? God must be smiling on you. Are you important, followed by millions on social media, have a popular podcast? Surely you must have done something right.

Yet such success is not a sign of moral righteousness. Rather, the psalm suggests that righteousness is not based on our outcomes but is an outgrowth of our behavior. The psalmist goes through what the righteous do. They act with grace and mercy; they give to the poor and are steady in the face of turmoil; they act with justice and are not afraid when evil comes. In contrast, the wicked are made angry by this behavior, grinding their teeth at how the righteous behave.

We see in the psalm a glimpse of God's alternative way. The way of God is the way of self-giving love, of solidarity with the poor and oppressed. It is the way of justice and constancy, a way that remains even when the winds of this world seem to be blowing in the other direction.

God, help us take the path of righteousness, even when it is hard, even when the world wants us to go the other way. Help us act righteously on behalf of those who go without. Amen.

THURSDAY, FEBRUARY 5 ~ *Read 1 Corinthians 2:1-16*

In this passage from the first letter to the Corinthians, Paul waxes a bit ironically about his inability to communicate well. He downplays his eloquence and knowledge. He talks of the fear with which he came to the people, relying merely on the wisdom that comes from God. This God-borne wisdom stands in contrast to the folly of worldly thinkers.

When I was in seminary, I worked at a church whose primary mission was to serve unhoused and marginalized people. Our church would meet on Saturday night for a meal and Bible study, followed by a worship service. My senior pastor insisted that everyone had something useful to contribute, so right after the sermon we had a "talk-back" time where anyone could share what they got out of the sermon.

Monday through Friday I would be immersed in high scholarship, learning big words like *hermeneutic* and *exegesis*. Then, on Saturday, I would go to church and try to relate what I was learning to people who might not have a place to sleep, or who might be barely holding on to recovery, or whose many jobs couldn't pay all the bills. I felt the dichotomous nature of my two "worlds" keenly. I also learned important lessons about understanding your audience and relating the message of scripture in words and spirit and examples that mean something to them.

That's not to say that scholarship is not of God or that the ideas my parishioners espoused lacked eloquence or depth. Rather, as Paul relays, the wisdom of God can come from anywhere, the academy or the street. The source is less important than if the content points toward God's alternative path of love and justice. That's a kind of wisdom that can be found anywhere followers are willing to look.

Gracious God, help us hear your voice, even in unlikely places. Help us heed the wisdom that points toward your reign. Amen.

FRIDAY, FEBRUARY 6 ~ *Read 1 Corinthians 2:1-16*

My wife and I have a running joke. If there is a breakdown in communication, one of us will say to the other, "This would be a lot easier if you could just read my mind." The joke gets at the reality that it is hard, even in the closest relationships, to really know what someone else is thinking. Many communication issues, whether in personal relationships, work settings, or even church, often boil down to our inability to fully communicate what's in our own heads or to fully perceive what is on someone else's mind.

Paul suggests that we can know the mind of God because we have God's Spirit residing in us. But how do we really know if we have the mind of Christ? How do we know we are acting as Christ and not being misled by our human bent toward self-aggrandizement?

I think knowing the mind of Christ is less about what we know or think or feel; rather, I think knowing the mind of Christ is about what we do. In this week's scriptures, we see again and again how showing the light of God's path is the most important work. We can study and pray, taking in God's "mind" through scripture and by understanding on a logical level what it means to follow Christ. But our thoughts and prayers can only go so far. It's our actions that truly show the result of God's work in our lives.

Showing the light of God's path is done through how we treat the most marginalized among us. How do we know we have the mind of Christ? It's less about thinking the right thoughts or feeling the right feelings. It's about doing the work of God amongst those who are oppressed and dispossessed.

Dear God, help us know your mind. Help us discern your Spirit. Help us bear the fruit of your presence in our lives. Amen.

SATURDAY, FEBRUARY 7 ~ *Read Matthew 5:13-16*

By this point in the Gospel of Matthew, Jesus is well into the Sermon on the Mount. He gives the well-known instruction to be salt and light. A master of metaphors, Jesus gives instructions here to encourage those listening to consider the results of their work, not as an effort to manage the outcomes but to remember the purpose. Salt is there for taste. If salt loses its taste, what is its purpose? Light is there to show others the way. If we have a light and hide it, what's even the point of having a light? Why build a city on a hill if you don't want others to see it? Jesus asks his disciples to be salt and light through their actions—to act in such a way that others see and taste the beloved community Jesus is instituting.

Jesus' call in this passage raises the tension of *being* versus *doing*. Jesus says we are salt and light, but then says that being salt and light means showing it to others. So, is our saltiness something internal to us once we are in relationship with God—something we *are*? Or is our saltiness something we exhibit in the world—something we *do*?

In Jesus' telling, being and doing are interrelated. A light has the quality of being a light, and because of that quality it helps people see. Salt has the quality of saltiness, and by its very nature salt makes food taste better. Following Christ is both about our inner being—about conforming ourselves to the mind of Christ—and about how we exhibit that inner nature out in the world. One leads to the other. In following Jesus, we are light and salt, and our inner being manifests itself in the work we do for God's kingdom.

Dear God, let me live my life so that in my work, others may see the light of your grace. Amen.

SUNDAY, FEBRUARY 8 ~ *Read Matthew 5:13-20*

After talking about salt and light, Jesus returns us to righteousness. Is righteousness just a state of being? Or is righteousness about what we do in the world? This passage seems to complicate a simplistic division between grace and law. Here Jesus says that we must be the light of the world, and we must fulfill all righteousness.

But what is the righteousness that Jesus asks us to fulfill? Returning to the Hebrew Bible readings, we see righteousness exhibited through solidarity with the poor, giving ourselves to others, and refusing to participate in the dominating systems of this world. For us, this may mean following the disciplines that help us connect with God, engaging in worship that reminds us of God's grace, or reaching out to the lost and hurting of this world.

As the son of two United Methodist pastors, I grew up in the church. My earliest memories are of church events and meetings, of the rhythms and seasons of the church year. I feel at home in these traditions and ways of doing church. Yet I must recognize that there is a difference between doing church the way I know and love and the righteousness of God. Too often, though, we in the church confuse the two. We think following a certain tradition or a certain rule is what it means to be righteous. If this week's scriptures teach us anything, it is that the righteousness of God is often in the alternative, marginalized places.

And that is truly good news, that even in a world of hurt and chaos, God's light still shines on our path. That we, even in our frailty and brokenness, can be beacons of the light of God's grace.

God, continue to shine your light on my path. In this tumultuous world, help me reflect that light on others. Amen.

Glorious Transformation

FEBRUARY 9–15, 2026 • BETHANY BARNETT

SCRIPTURE OVERVIEW: A cloud, not dark, but burning like fire settles atop Mount Sinai: This is the Word of the Lord. In the unmediated presence of God, we cannot help but be utterly transformed by the experience. Jesus, even the one who is himself divine, begins to glow when God shows up in person. The author of 2 Peter recalls this mountaintop experience, and the psalm praises the tradition of anointed ones. We must also be transformed by the bright, life-changing appearance of God. When we see the light of God shining in a dark place, some of us run in fear, others tremble unable to move, still others stand in awe of God's glory. The same God who transformed Jesus Christ is at work in us. We will never be the same.

QUESTIONS AND SUGGESTIONS FOR REFLECTION

- Read Exodus 24:12-18. Read slowly, paying attention to all five senses. What do you think Moses saw, touched, smelled, and tasted?
- Read Psalm 2. When have you seen people in power do something antithetical to the will or character of God? What is this psalm's response to that action?
- Read Matthew 17:1-9. What would it be like to stand in the full presence of God? What would God tell you?
- Read 2 Peter 1:16-21. What is God doing in your life to transform your heart? What can you do to accept God's work in your life?

Bethany Barnett is chief editor and owner of Theology Edits LLC, where she edits Christian material for writers, publishers, and organizations. She is currently pursuing a Master of Theological Studies at Perkins School of Theology.

MONDAY, FEBRUARY 9 ~ *Read Exodus 24:12-18*

Reality is elusive in Exodus 24. The thick descriptions of God are paradoxical. At first, God's presence is described as a cloud covering the mountain, but the very next verse references "the glory of the LORD," which suggests a degree of brilliance and brightness. Finally God is described no longer as a cloud but as a "devouring fire" reminding readers of the bush where Moses first met God: The bush that was on fire but never burned up (see Exod. 3:2).

How can God be a dense cloud and blindingly bright all at once? This is not the only way Exodus 24 seems to slip out of reality and take on an otherworldly quality. Beginning in verse 9, the passage describes Moses at the base of the mountain with the Hebrew people and then once, twice, and a third time he walks up Mount Sinai to be with God. Every time you think he's in the presence of God he slips back down into the presence of the people.

Some scholars suggest these paradoxical descriptions of God and the trifold ascent up the mountain happen because the editor of Exodus combined three competing oral stories and simply kept all of them instead of choosing one coherent narrative. But the repetition allows new bits of information to be unveiled in a circular way, each time exploring the same subject in a new light. It's like turning a jewel in the sunlight or watching an instant replay from a different angle at a ball game. Each of the three tellings has the opportunity to reveal deeper truths about God. How does each change the way we understand God and God's commandments?

God, open my eyes. Help me to see you and your work in the world in fresh ways. Amen.

TUESDAY, FEBRUARY 10 ~ *Read Matthew 17:1-6*

God has a way of bringing the most unlikely people together throughout scripture, but this one really takes the cake. God joins Moses, the leader of the ancient Hebrews; Elijah, a quirky Israelite prophet; and Jesus, the Son of God. What are we to make of this trio?

In Jesus' day, there was somewhat of a religious debate between those who believed the Jewish law was most important to follow and those who believed the teachings of the prophets were more important. But God doesn't want any divisions. God created both the law and the prophets so we would learn how to love.

Much like Exodus 19 tells of God giving the Ten Commandments to Moses on Sinai, the book of Matthew tells of God revealing the greatest commandments through Jesus. The first comes in Matthew 7:12: "So in everything, do to others what you would have them do to you, for this sums up the law and the prophets" (NIV). The second comes in Matthew 22:37-40, where Jesus tells the people that the law and prophets both hang on loving God with all your heart, soul, and mind and loving your neighbor as yourself. Moses, the one who brought the law to the people, and Elijah, the first of the major prophets, appearing together with Jesus, the Son of God, shows how the law and prophets ultimately work in service of God's love.

God brings these people together to settle the question of which code of ideals to follow. By uniting Moses, Elijah, and Jesus together on a mountaintop, we get to understand, and be transformed by, one rule: the law and prophecy of love.

God, you are love. Show me how to find unity in things that seem opposed to one another. And in everything, let me show your love. Amen.

WEDNESDAY, FEBRUARY 11 ~ *Read 2 Peter 1:16-21*

A lighthouse is a powerful lamp that guides people safely to shore. Most people experience it from a far distance, spotting it many nautical miles away from the rocks. When sailors see a lighthouse, they are alerted to the dangers of a rocky shoreline. Sometimes, though, the sight is a hopeful reminder that land is close.

Although many sailors use the light of a lighthouse to safely navigate around the shoreline, few people actually climb the steep stairway that leads to the light itself. The bulb of the lighthouse is blinding at such a close distance. It would be very difficult to approach and impossible to look at directly. The intensity of this powerful, lifesaving light is what God is like. Although many people are guided by God's overpowering light from a distance, prophets are the few who approach this light head-on.

Prophets are the ones who climb the steep sides of a mountain to reach the bright place where God dwells. They see God face-to-face and are utterly transformed in the presence of the Holy One. From God, they receive an important piece of wisdom that they take back to the people: important instructions that tell everyone about the path they are following, both the dangers of the path they are walking down and the hope of safe passage for those who follow God's guidance.

Peter stood on the mountain when Jesus was transfigured. He witnessed the overpowering glory of God. Now the wisdom of that moment is transferred to us through this writing. How does the wisdom of Peter's instructions act like a lighthouse in your life?

God, you are the light shining in the dark. Light up my life and reveal the best path forward. Help me stay near to your word and to those who have seen you face-to-face so that I might be led to life. Amen.

THURSDAY, FEBRUARY 12 ~ *Read Psalm 2*

Many psalms are attributed to David, and even more reflect the experience of a king anointed by God. Psalm 1 sets up the "wheat and chaff" metaphor. Psalm 2 continues the separating of the "good" from the "bad" by contrasting other world leaders with the king of Israel. It accuses the kings of other nations of wickedness, whereas it lifts Israel's king up as the anointed one, the begotten son of God.

We're used to labels like "anointed," "begotten," and "Son of God" referencing Jesus. But there is a whole library of literature in the Hebrew Scriptures that made these terms mean something significant to Israel long before Jesus took to the scene. These terms were coined for David—to talk about the difference between him and other kings. While these phrases may have been popularized to describe David's intimate relationship with God, over time they became warped. Instead of indicating relationship, these titles were used as a taunt, demanding other kings "kiss the ring" or be destroyed.

Although the same words are later used to describe Jesus, he flips the script. Rather than coming as a king, Christ comes as a poor day-laborer. Instead of coming to conquer other nations, Jesus comes to be destroyed by the principalities and powers. David claims power; Jesus, the Son of God, gives it up willingly.

David and Jesus each display an intimacy with God. Although David uses his relationship with God to leverage power, Jesus uses his relationship with God to care for humanity. What does this say about the character of God? Name specific kinds of power you have been entrusted with. How will your relationship with God influence the way you will choose to wield this power?

Jesus, Son of God, help me be like you. I need your grace so I can follow in your footsteps. Amen.

FRIDAY, FEBRUARY 13 ~ *Read 2 Peter 1:16-21*

The phrase "cleverly devised myths" in verse 16 is provocative. It suggests that Peter is arguing that he didn't just make up a story about the Transfiguration. But the phrase *sophizō mythos* has a wide range of meanings. A different translation could easily read, "We did not follow wisdom sayings when we made known to you the power and coming of our Lord Jesus Christ." This translation emphasizes the fact that Peter didn't just read about this event. Peter, unlike other religious teachers, tells stories he saw with his own eyes.

When I was young, my elderly Sunday school teacher told us about the time she was rescued in a snowstorm. She was driving home late at night during a blizzard. Just when she started to panic about being unable to see the road ahead, a truck materialized in front of her. It made every turn she needed to make to get home up to and including parking in front of her house. She pulled safely into her driveway, but when she turned to thank the truck driver, the truck had vanished and the tire tracks ended right where she had seen it park. She believed it had been an angel who had guided her home.

Although my teacher's retelling of Bible stories up until that point had been somewhat dry, she lit up when she told about her own brush with the Divine. Her encounter with an angel must have occurred fifty or sixty years before, but, despite the decades, I could see she was still affected by the memory.

Peter's encounter with God is much the same. He tells his stories about God in a different way than other religious teachers because he doesn't tell stories that happened centuries ago to other people. He's passionate about the stories he tells because they happened to him.

God who sees me face-to-face, reveal yourself in undeniable ways. Let me see you in ways I have only read about. Amen.

SATURDAY, FEBRUARY 14 ~ *Read Exodus 24:12-18*

One of the Hebrew words for *sin* is sometimes translated as "to miss the mark." The word in Exodus 24:12 translated in the NRSVUE as *instruction* can also be a verb translated as *to shoot*. These translations call to mind the sport of archery, where an archer attempts to hit a mark with an arrow. They make us think of the "law" of God as a way of shooting our arrow at the target, like a skilled archer teaching us how to hit the bullseye.

As many archery athletes know, you have to practice a lot to hit the target. It takes a good coach to instruct you. You have to listen to that coach and follow their instructions. But that doesn't replace the many hours you'll put into trying and failing to hit the target. I used to think that sinning was always terrible, even when I messed up in small ways. But I've come to learn that reflecting on how I've failed and confessing it is an opportunity to learn. I have the freedom to practice hitting the target again and again until I can consistently get it right.

I think that's part of the challenge of religious practice today. Religion is rarely seen as a life-long art to be learned. It often becomes just a list of rules to follow, which causes harm to people instead of helping them. Jesus exposed the failure of that mentality and reminded us that the root of the Torah is loving God and people. We are going to miss the mark—it is part of the process of learning. The point isn't to get it right every time, but to keep trying. We can practice turning our eyes toward God's love for all people. We can try over and over again to love others better, using God's law and the teachings of Jesus as a guide.

God who teaches us to aim true, thank you for your instructions. We could not learn without them. Thank you for your example of love that guides our lives. Amen.

SUNDAY, FEBRUARY 15 ~ *Read Matthew 17:1-9*

TRANSFIGURATION SUNDAY

This is my Son, the Beloved, with whom I am well pleased." These are the words God says to confirm Jesus' identity at his baptism in Matthew 3:17. After Jesus is baptized, Matthew says that he is driven into the wilderness to fast and overcome temptation. When he returns, Jesus calls his disciples, gives his famous Sermon on the Mount, begins healing people, and teaches in parables. By the time he is transfigured, he is a well-established teacher. God repeats the words from his baptism, but this time, adds "Listen to him!" Everything that Jesus says should be taken as seriously as if God said it.

Rereading Matthew in this light, I'm struck by Jesus' interpretation of the law. Jesus has a high opinion of God's law, but his understanding seems to be foreign to the people, even though they too have studied Torah. Jesus scolds leaders for elevating human tradition above God's commandments (see Matt. 15:1-9) and he restores the spirit of God's law by retelling the law in a new way. In the Beatitudes (see Matt. 5:8-10), Jesus blesses people whom God's law protects but human tradition has overlooked. He shows people how to fast and pray for the sake of growing with God instead of as an ego boost, and he teaches them to use the law to straighten out their own behavior instead of using it to judge others.

Many times I have had to take a hard look at Jesus' teachings and admit that I have been following society's trends and traditions instead of following God's rule of love. But it is in following God's law of love that we are transformed.

God, you are my teacher. Help me listen to you so that I can be transformed in your love. Thank you for the instruction you have given me through Jesus, the Word made flesh. Amen.

Lead Us Not Into Temptation

FEBRUARY 16–22, 2026 • KAROLINE LEWIS

SCRIPTURE OVERVIEW Anticipating the season of Lent, the testing of Jesus in the wilderness takes center stage. The story of Jesus' temptation and the accompanying texts often set the tone for this season in which we reflect on areas of our lives where we are tempted to place our desires over God's. We are invited to imagine what difference it makes that Jesus himself was tempted and consider how our own times of testing manifest in our lives of faith. The Genesis texts, frequently referred to as "The Fall" or "The First Sin," point to the beginning of sin entering the human story. In the passage from Romans, Paul tackles the relationship between our sin and Jesus' death and resurrection. The psalmist speaks to the importance of the confession of sins. Jesus' model of prayer to not be led into temptation (Matt. 6:13) becomes a daily discipline for our journey through Lent.

QUESTIONS AND SUGGESTIONS FOR REFLECTION

- Read Genesis 2:15-17; 3:1-7. Which commands of God do you find particularly difficult to follow? Why do you think Adam and Eve succumbed to the temptation to disobey God?
- Read Psalm 32. Remember a time when you were forgiven, or forgave someone, for a transgression. What did that forgiveness feel like?
- Read Romans 5:12-19. How do you understand the differences Paul draws between Adam and Christ? How do those differences relate to your own experiences of having your sins forgiven?
- Read Matthew 4:1-11. How does Jesus' experience of temptation help you take comfort or make you question your ability to resist temptation?

Rev. Karoline M. Lewis, Ph.D. is Marbury E. Anderson Chair in Biblical Preaching at Luther Seminary in St. Paul, MN.

MONDAY, FEBRUARY 16 ~ *Read Matthew 4:1-11*

When reading of the temptation of Jesus in the wilderness, whether in Matthew or in the Gospel of Luke, it's easy to conclude that since even Jesus was tempted, temptation must just be a part of following Jesus. While it's true that temptation is a part of life, Jesus' temptation is unique. In our English translations, it sounds like the devil wonders if Jesus is the Son of God. The Greek text (the original language of the New Testament) does not imply this. Rather, the devil's inquiry includes affirmation on the part of the devil of Jesus' identity: "If you are the Son of God (and you are)." The devil knows perfectly well who Jesus is. The question is, does Jesus?

Jesus' wilderness testing comes on the heels of his baptism, where he has heard God's affirmation from the heavens, "This is my Son, the Beloved, with whom I am well pleased" (3:17). What gets put before Jesus are not your garden-variety temptations, but a testing of Jesus' very identity and his obedience to God. Yes, Jesus passes the test, but only because he knows who he is.

Our experiences of temptation are often less about falling into some unforgivable sin and more about forgetting who God has claimed us to be—God's very own children. In moments of trial it is all too easy to forget the promise from the heavens that is ours as well. We listen to the voices of powers bent on manipulation rather than to God's voice that lifts up the meek.

The devil in the wilderness exposes the kinds of tests Jesus will face over the course of his ministry. We too stare down temptations in our lives, temptations that take advantage of us, prey on us in moments of weakness, and try to get us to question who we are as God's beloved. But we know who we are.

Dear God, lead me not into those temptations that try to pull me away from what I know to be true—that I am your beloved child. Amen.

TUESDAY, FEBRUARY 17 ~ *Read Romans 5:12-19*

Paul's understanding of sin equates it with death. He makes a direct comparison between the sin of Adam that separates and the obedience of Christ which reunites. Just as Adam's sin became an inherited trait that leads to death for all humanity, Christ's obedience becomes an overpowering inherited trait that leads to life.

I am not sure that we typically connect sin with death in our understanding today. Instead, we have a smaller, action-oriented view of sin, categorizing our sins as all the immoral acts we wish we didn't do. Our sins cause us regret, remorse, even fear that somewhere they are being counted against us. And we tend to be quite accomplished in pointing out the sins of others. But Paul sees sin a little bit differently here. For Paul, sin has a singular nature. It is all that works against God. Sin is an entity that pulls us away from God. Our sinful actions are the result of a broken relationship with God and of being separated from God. When we are not in a right relationship with God, it is no wonder we do not make the best choices, and those choices can lead to death. Death is not just the literal loss of persons to mortality. Death happens, says Paul, when we find ourselves so apart from God that it feels like the abyss has swallowed us whole. Death means such a separation from God that we can't see the resurrected life made possible through Jesus and cannot live, therefore, in life-giving ways.

We believe that we have already been made right with God, already been reunited through Jesus. In Jesus, not even death can separate us from the love of God. God's grace is given for all through the life, death, and resurrection of Jesus. This is our Lenten promise.

God of grace, when we feel apart from you, remind us once again that nothing in the whole world can separate us from your love. Amen.

WEDNESDAY, FEBRUARY 18 ~ *Read Matthew 6:1-6, 16-21*

Ash Wednesday

In Mark, Jesus' first act is an exorcism. In Luke, it's a sermon back in his hometown of Nazareth. In John, it's the miraculous and abundant sign of turning water into wine. But for Matthew, the inaugural act of Jesus' public ministry is the Sermon on the Mount, narrated in chapters 5–7. Jesus sits his followers down and teaches them what it means to be a disciple.

You may have noticed that following Jesus is not for the faint of heart. So Matthew has Jesus begin his ministry with lengthy instruction on what it means to commit to discipleship. The Ash Wednesday reading falls in the middle of this pedagogical lesson and warns against religious practices done for the sake of attention and admiration. This is a worthwhile teaching at the beginning of Lent as millions of Christians choose to adopt a practice to mark the season, whether abstention from certain foods and drinks or adopting a habit that might bring one closer to God. No matter the choice, it is tempting for us to think that everyone wants to know about it, to do it to impress people, or to engage in the practice for the sake of the practice itself. Jesus calls our motivations to task.

Jesus reminds his disciples past and present that our religious practices, our behaviors of faith, are done to increase our trust in who God has claimed us to be. As we are reminded on this Ash Wednesday that we are dust and will one day fade away, we are also reminded that our "treasure" is protected from the decay of this world. How we act in the world reveals whether our practices are truly for the glory of God.

God, you call us to be a light to the world that shines your love and glory. During this season of Lent, accept my offerings and sanctify me. May my heart and my treasure both be with you. Amen.

THURSDAY, FEBRUARY 19 ~ *Read Genesis 2:15-17; 3:1-7*

God's warning to Adam reminds me of all the times I would give my two sons a similar admonition. And as soon as I uttered, "Don't do (fill in the blank)," of course, they did it. It never failed.

This story in Genesis states a truth about our human condition we would rather avoid—that time and time again we gravitate toward the forbidden or what we know could be bad for us. Even though God offers us abundance—Adam can eat from every other tree in the garden—we zero in on the one thing we aren't supposed to do. And thus ensues an endless series of questions. "Really? What would actually happen if I did it? Is it really that big of a deal? You probably just said that to scare me." These questions take hold, convince us that they are reasonable questions, and all of a sudden, we have sidelined the promises placed before us.

Perhaps we ask these questions because the abundance all around us is too hard to believe. Perhaps it is because trusting God—if we are honest—is just really hard. Trust means letting go of control; it means giving ourselves over to God when we're not sure how it will all work out. And few of us enjoy being in such positions.

During the season of Lent and getting closer to the Cross, it becomes even harder to believe in God's promises. How can life come out of death? How can Jesus' empty tomb mean resurrection for me? Maybe one of the gifts of these forty days is to give us time to ask these questions of ourselves and with one another. Maybe Lent is our season to learn to trust once again.

God of abundance, when we see only what's not possible, come near and remind us of all that you have in store for us: more grace than we can ever imagine. Amen.

FRIDAY, FEBRUARY 20 ~ *Read Psalm 32*

In a study Bible I have on my desk, the title for this psalm is "The Joy of Forgiveness." This title equates happiness and joy as the outcome of forgiveness, as the psalm begins, "Happy are those whose transgression is forgiven." But forgiveness is complicated, and the joy or happiness that comes from forgiveness often seems a long time coming.

We want to forgive, but so many things hold us back. We want to be forgiven, and yet deep down we believe we are not worthy of forgiveness. And too often forgiveness is simplified as the other side of the apology equation. We have this sense, as the title suggests, that forgiveness should be an easy act and an immediate balm. But the fact that there is this psalm dedicated to forgiveness may suggest otherwise. As God's people, we are called to forgive those who trespass against us. But forgiveness is a process. It takes intentional work—the bigger the trespass, the more time and work necessary. Jesus instructed us to pray that we can give and receive forgiveness. And he instructed us to pray a lot, because forgiveness is hard work.

Psalm 32 is an appropriate pairing with texts that speak about sin and temptation, especially as we transition into the season of Lent. Psalm 32 invites us to consider the role of forgiveness in our lives of faith. When have we held forgiveness back? When have we offered it too freely? But Psalm 32 also brings us into the joy of forgiveness known fully in God. We are truly blessed, another possible translation for "happy," because we can be fully honest with God who promises to hear us and meet us with steadfast love. It's not easy, but on the other side is gladness in the Lord, rejoicing, and shouting for joy.

Forgiving God, in your love we have our joy. Like the psalmist, in your endless mercy, may our voices praise you. Amen.

SATURDAY, FEBRUARY 21 ~ *Read Psalm 32:3-5*

According to the psalmist, one critical factor when it comes to forgiveness is confession. Confession is incredibly difficult because it means acknowledging accountability. Confession gives witness to responsibility. Confession means fessing up to what we have done and what we have left undone, being exposed for the hurt we have caused.

A confession is not the same as an apology. We hope that apologies come with adequate contrition. But often the apology does not name the actual wrong committed. "I'm sorry" often assumes that the harm does not need acknowledgment but rather, we can simply move on with our lives as if nothing happened. But confession is a critical component of forgiveness, whether that forgiveness is given or received. And when we don't confess our sins, says the psalmist, we can actually feel it in our bodies. Holding our confession has a negative somatic result. When we hold on to the wrongs we have done, our strength to go on will be overshadowed by guilt. Guilt is like the tormenting heat of summer, beating down on us mercilessly. But in confession, there is release. As The Message translates Psalm 32:5, "Then I let it all out; I said, 'I'll come clean about my failures to God.' Suddenly the pressure is gone—my guilt is dissolved, my sin has disappeared."

Confession is not a solution, but a step toward letting go of guilt's grip. And confession to God is a way to keep and even strengthen our relationship with God. God listens, always, not to say "I told you so" or "I knew it" but to affirm the never-ending presence of God's love. We can be completely honest and open with God, and it is in that knowledge that rejoicing is possible.

God of mercy, because you forgive us endlessly, we are free to forgive others. Help us to live in the joy that comes from honesty, trust, and forgiveness. Amen.

SUNDAY, FEBRUARY 22 ~ *Read Matthew 4:11*

First Sunday in Lent

It would be easy to interpret this concluding verse of Jesus' temptation in the wilderness as a reward for withstanding the devil's wiles. Jesus made it! All forty days! And so the angels show up to wait upon him, a sign of God's approval: "Good job, son!" Yet it's important to note that the word *diabolos* which is typically translated as "devil" can also mean "enemy" or "adversary." And enemies and adversaries are never going to go away, not for Jesus and not for us. The resistance to Jesus' hoped-for kingdom of God will lead to Jesus' arrest, trial, and death. Jesus' temptation in the wilderness was not a one-time exam to see if he could pass. Instead, his trial during those forty days foreshadows the opposition that will be constant for him and for all who follow him.

The sudden appearance of the angels is better translated as, "angels began to serve him." The presence of angels represents the presence of God. This speaks so much truth into our lives of faith. As we begin our own forty-day journey toward honoring Jesus' death and resurrection, the angels' presence with Jesus reminds us that God is present with us.

Opposition to the kingdom of God is constant. We are not promised relief from temptation but endurance. The promise of Matthew 4:11 looks forward to Jesus' words that end Matthew's Gospel, that Jesus will be with us always (28:20). It also looks back to the beginning of the Gospel, reminding us of Jesus' true identity and purpose—as Immanuel, God with us (1:23). We are never alone.

God, Immanuel, help us to remember that no matter what we experience in our wilderness, you are always with us. We know the wilderness and its challenges will always be there; help us to trust in your presence. Amen.

Stepping Out in Faith

FEBRUARY 23–MARCH 1, 2026 • MARK FELDMEIR

SCRIPTURE OVERVIEW: Scripture tells story after story of persons who step out in faith into the unknown. Having received a divine call to leave his country and kindred, Abram journeys to an unfamiliar land, following God's promise that he will beget a nation and by him all the families of the earth will be blessed. While on pilgrimage to Jerusalem, the psalmist looks toward the hills and asks the timeless question, "Where does my help come from?" The apostle Paul argues that it was through Abraham's faith, not through his obedience to the law, that the divine promise was realized. Under the cover of darkness, Nicodemus, a religious expert, seeks answers from Jesus about the mysteries of God.

QUESTIONS AND SUGGESTIONS FOR REFLECTION

- Read Genesis 12:1-4a. When have you sensed God calling you to new places or possibilities?
- Read Psalm 121. Where do you turn for strength and solace in times of trouble? How have your most challenging experiences pointed you to God's presence?
- Read Romans 4:1-5, 13-17. When do you worry that your faith doesn't measure up to that of others? Why does God "gift" us with "grace" instead of "pay" us with "wages" like workers?
- Read John 3:1-17. Why does Nicodemus visit Jesus at night? When have you had to start something all over again?

Rev. Mark Feldmeir is Sr. Pastor at St. Andrew United Methodist Church in Highlands Ranch, CO, and the author of five books, including his latest, *Life After God* (Westminster John Knox, 2023).

MONDAY, FEBRUARY 23 ~ *Read Genesis 12:1-4a*

Abram, who later becomes Abraham, receives an improbable divine call to leave his homeland and journey to an unfamiliar land that God will reveal to him. God promises Abram that he will be the father of a great nation, but Abram's calling appears fraught with challenge.

First, Canaan, the land God promises to give Abram, is already occupied by Canaanites. And it would seem unlikely that those Canaanites, upon Abram's arrival, would greet him with a welcome party and say, "If you'll just give us a moment, Abram, we'll start packing up." Second, at seventy-five-years old, fathering a nation from scratch would seem a bit ambitious for Abram, if not entirely absurd, especially considering he has no children. Finally, as far as we can tell, Abram has no religious credentials to speak of, no diplomatic experience in nation-building, and no family to accompany him on his journey save his wife Sarai and his nephew Lot.

But Abram still answers God's call, choosing to believe what he cannot see, leaving behind the familiar for the unknown, and making the perilous journey that will expose him to uncertainty. Abram is a model of faithfulness not so much because of *what* he believes, but *how* he believes. He relinquishes the security of the present and accepts the vulnerability that comes whenever we pursue God's new possibilities for the future.

Every day, moment by moment, God calls us into new places where possibilities for new life abound. Whether it's a call to move across the country for a new job or a call to walk across the street to reconcile with a neighbor, every divine call involves risk, demands vulnerability, and requires us to leave the familiar, comfortable places we've always known—stepping out in faith, believing what we cannot yet see.

Loving God, embolden me to embrace the unknown in pursuit of your good possibilities for my life today. Amen.

TUESDAY, FEBRUARY 24 ~ *Read Genesis 12:2-3*

What gets you out of bed every morning? Abram has a reason for living that gets him out of bed every morning. When Abram receives the promise that God will make of him a great nation, God informs him that "in you all the families of the earth shall be blessed." But this translation from the NRSVUE fails to capture the magnitude of Abram's God-given mission. Some scholars believe it should read, "*by* you all the families of the earth shall be blessed," suggesting that Abram is not some passive religious figurehead, but has an active, urgent role in the world. The so-called "families of the earth" are not expected to come to him seeking his blessing. Abram's mission is to actively go and bless them.

The beginning of Abram's story in chapter 12 marks a shift in Genesis. For eleven chapters, Genesis tells in broad strokes the story of God creating the world and engaging with all of humanity—from Adam and his descendants through Noah and his descendants, until we land on Abram. Chapter 12 zooms in on the origin of what will become the chosen people of Israel. Yet from the very beginning, God is clear that Abram will bless not just the families of his own nation, but all the families of the earth. What God is to do through Abram is for the entire world.

Imagine that God might be calling you, like Abram, to actively bless others. The notion that we can bless others is mostly foreign in the modern world. But as descendants of Abram, we too are called to bless all the families of the earth. To bless someone is simply to call forth or invoke grace, wholeness, or what Hebrew scripture calls "shalom" upon them. We bless others by sharing God's love and grace in every encounter.

God of Grace, let me be put to work for you today, that all the families of the earth may be blessed by you. Amen.

WEDNESDAY, FEBRUARY 25 ~ *Read Psalm 121*

Psalm 121 is one of fifteen "Psalms of Ascent" the people of Israel sang or recited on their way to Jerusalem for Israel's holy festivals. It speaks of the dangers pilgrims might encounter on their journey: heatstroke, foot injuries, being 'stricken by the moon' (a mental condition in the ancient world from which we get the word *lunacy*), and evil. The psalmist, looking toward the hills, wonders, "From where will my help come?" It's an ageless question. To whom will we turn for strength and solace in times of trouble? To what will we look to satisfy our deepest needs? Through these dangers, says the psalmist, we have only one true source of help in life: the God "who keeps Israel."

But do we have any gods other than the one who keeps Israel? Some scholars believe the psalmist, when looking toward the hills, sees the high places in Canaan where the altars to Baal and the fertility poles to Asherah had been erected. Israel had been commanded to dismantle the Canaanite shrines, but not all had been destroyed. Remnants of Canaanite religion remained in the Promised Land and forms of idolatry persisted. Perhaps the psalmist, in looking toward the hills, glimpsed the allure of the false "help" up there and needed reassurance that "My help comes from the LORD, who made heaven and earth."

We too can lift our eyes to the hills around us and see today's most alluring sources of "help" in life. Our cultural idols are many: religious certitude; workaholism; hubris; political loyalties; our obsession with appearance, achievement, and money; to name a few. Yet the psalmist trusts that beyond the hills—beyond even this present journey—it is only the God who keeps Israel who "will keep your going out and your coming in from this time on and forevermore."

You are my true source of help in life, O God. When I am surrounded by so many false gods, keep my going out and my coming in, today and forevermore. Amen.

THURSDAY, FEBRUARY 26 ~ *Read Romans 4:1-5*

It's easy to think of Abraham and Sarah as incomparable, even perfect, models of faith. After all, they left everything behind at God's sudden call to birth a new nation in a foreign land against seemingly impossible odds and with such unquestioning obedience. Yet we know their faith was riddled with uncertainty and even fits of disobedience.

On one occasion, Abraham, aware of Sarah's alluring physical beauty, is so worried people might kill him to get to her that he claims she's his sister so he can dangle her in front of mighty Pharaoh (see Gen. 12:10-20). When it becomes apparent that Sarah is unable to conceive a child of her own, she gives her maid, Hagar, to Abraham, hoping to at least start a family this way (see Gen. 16). Only later, she becomes so jealous of Hagar that she demands that Abraham throw both Hagar and her son into the desert to die (see Gen. 21:8-21).

If you've ever worried that your faith doesn't measure up to that of Abraham and Sarah, Paul's message is good news. He reminds us that if God viewed Abraham and Sarah as "workers," God would have been obligated to pay them wages. But God didn't see them as workers, nor did they see God as an employer. Instead of wages, God gave Abraham and Sarah a gift called grace. God didn't accept them because they were perfect people but accepted these naturally flawed people for God's own sake. That emboldened Abraham and Sarah, flaws and all, to trust God completely as they fulfilled their unique calling.

As children of Abraham and Sarah, we never have to work to earn God's acceptance. Because we are not God's "workers" who are due wages, we are never justified by any good work. We are justified only because of God's gift of grace given to us.

God, accept me and use me just as I am today. Help me to rest in your grace as I seek to do your will. Amen.

FRIDAY, FEBRUARY 27 ~ *Read Romans 4:13-17*

In our human relationships, promises are much easier to make than to keep. We know both the regret of having made promises that we've broken and the betrayal when others have failed to uphold the promises they've made to us. Broken promises are especially painful when we've put our trust in those we know and love most deeply—those whom we assume will fulfill their commitments, act in good faith, and have our best interests in mind. Trust can take years to build, but only moments to break.

One way to safeguard that trust, or to avoid having to trust another altogether, is to enter a contract. Whereas a promise is a commitment made by one person to another, a contract is a mutually binding agreement between the two. Contracts eliminate the need for trusting others—even in relationships we might consider loving. Contracts not only mitigate risk and protect us from the possibility of getting hurt, but they also ensure that there are no surprises. Usually not fulfilling the terms of the agreement has consequences. If both parties fulfill their end of the deal, everyone knows what to expect.

But the apostle Paul reminds us that in matters of faith there is no contract. Our relationship with God is held together by a holy promise that rests solely on grace. Trying to earn what God desires to give us by doing everything we are told to do, or by perfectly following the law, would be like trying to fill out all the right forms and signing our name on the dotted line of a contract we could never actually fulfill. It would eliminate personal trust in God completely and turn this holy promise into something like a business deal. Faith has no terms and conditions or fine print. While faith always has risk, we can rest assured: faith also has a promise grounded in grace—a promise God will never break.

God, give me the courage to trust you and the strength to follow you wherever the road may lead today. Amen.

SATURDAY, FEBRUARY 28 ~ *Read John 3:1-3*

By all appearances, Nicodemus lacks nothing in life. As a Pharisee, he is set apart from other Jews. As a member of the Sanhedrin, he serves on Judaism's version of the Supreme Court. With his enviable resume of degrees, he is one of Jerusalem's most recognizable influencers. Nicodemus is an icon of Jewish faith and practice. Everything in his life is in its proper place.

Yet he comes to Jesus at night, under the cover of darkness, ostensibly because something is still missing in his life—something about which no one must know. Maybe after all these years of climbing the ladder of religious certainty and celebrity, Nicodemus is like the old greyhound on the racetrack that has finally caught the coveted rabbit—only to discover that the rabbit he's been chasing isn't actually real. Nicodemus has likely been pursuing a faith that is all about ascertaining unquestionable truths about God and scripture, observing certain religious laws and traditions, and maintaining his public image as a scripture-answer man. It's a kind of faith he can control and manage, a check-the-box kind of faith focused on the externals—but one that seems to have left him lacking, still searching for something real.

Maybe what brings him to Jesus under the cover of darkness is the inner conflict he feels—that we all feel—whenever religious certainty becomes a substitute for a deeper, ever-evolving communion with God. Just when we assume we have a handle on God, by God's grace—like Nicodemus—we feel an impulse to keep searching and growing. We sense that maybe we do not have all the answers, or that our answers no longer lead us to what is real or life-giving, or that our answers are preventing us from asking some potentially life-changing questions, like the one Nicodemus asks Jesus that night: "How can anyone be born after having grown old?"

Loving God, draw me to the light of your grace today, and reveal to me what is real and life-giving. Amen.

SUNDAY, MARCH 1 ~ *Read John 3:3-17*

Second Sunday in Lent

When Jesus says no one can see the kingdom of God without being "born from above," it's an invitation to unlearn old answers, to relinquish all that we assume makes us acceptable in this world, and to surrender our need to be in the driver's seat.

Nicodemus scoffs at the proposition. "How can anyone be born after having grown old?" he asks. I don't think Nicodemus is being a literalist. I think he understands what Jesus means. What he's telling Jesus is, "I've worked so hard to get where I am, to believe what I believe, and I'm just too old now to turn around and start all over again." That's when Jesus utters the most oft-quoted verse in all of scripture: "For God so loved the world that he gave his only Son, so that everyone who believes in him may not perish but may have eternal life."

Perhaps you've been taught that "perish" refers to hell, "eternal life" refers to heaven, and "believing" in Jesus will determine whether you will perish in hell or receive eternal life in heaven. But it's more likely that Jesus, as he looks at Nicodemus standing before him in the darkness, sees someone who is already perishing and desperately longing for life—right now.

When we are working so hard to have all the answers and keep up appearances and play the part, it can be exhausting to the point of perishing. What is vital and eternal inside us begins to die. Jesus offers us an alternative to "perishing." He calls it being "born from above." It's akin, he says, to becoming like a toddler all over again and being led by the hand by a God who moves freely through this world like the wind blowing through the trees. It is eternal life that we can access right here, right now.

God of Life, I surrender to you whatever within me is perishing and longing to be reborn. By your grace, may I experience eternal life today. Amen.

Trusting in God

MARCH 2–8, 2026 • DONG HYEON JEONG

SCRIPTURE OVERVIEW: The overarching theme of this week's lectionary reflection is trusting in God. The passages from Exodus and Psalms narrate the troubles of the Israelites in the desert, inviting us to reflect upon the realities of trusting in God in the midst of life's difficulties. The reading in Romans continues the theme of trust whereby we are invited to trust or boast only in what God has done for us on the Cross. Finally, the reading in John depicts the Samaritan woman as an exemplary figure of faith who believed in Jesus as the Messiah. She didn't require miracles to have faith; she found the miracle and her faith in her encounter with Jesus.

QUESTIONS AND SUGGESTIONS FOR REFLECTION

- Read Exodus 17:1-7. When has God's provision sustained you through tough stages of your spiritual journey?
- Read Psalm 95. What object, image, or memory serves for you as a symbol of God's faithfulness?
- Read Romans 5:1-11. How have you discovered God's grace in your life when life's troubles seem to overwhelm you?
- Read John 4:5-42. When has letting go of your expectations or rules allowed God to work freely in your life or in the lives of others around you?

Dong Hyeon Jeong is an associate professor of New Testament Interpretation at Garrett-Evangelical Theological Seminary. He is the author of *Embracing the Nonhuman in the Gospel of Mark* (SBL Press, 2023).

MONDAY, MARCH 2 ~ *Read Exodus 17:1-4*

I cannot blame the Israelites for complaining. Even if they were liberated from slavery and witnessed the parting of the sea—or perhaps because of these experiences—I understand why they cried out to God for help. Food and water are matters of life and death. As the father of two young children, I demand food and water for my children for their survival. I am struck more by Moses' response than the Israelites' complaining. What were they supposed to do in their dire situation? Should they have just suffered quietly as they were forced to do so under the Egyptian empire?

I wonder about the appropriateness of identifying the Israelites' behavior with the Yiddish expression, *kvetch,* which in English has come to mean *complain. Kvetch* can be understood as constantly nagging or complaining, perhaps over trivial matters. And trivial matters do happen. However, I understand that the spirit of *kvetching* stems from the desire not just to complain but also to hold on to the promise of survival and protection. How can the Israelites live out the promises of God if they suffer and die in the desert? How are they to praise God and share God's *hesed* (grace) when they themselves do not know what that means anymore?

As a parent, I get exhausted when my kids complain incessantly. And yet I also know they do so because they trust that I am the person to ask for help, because I am their parent. And so we can see the complaints of the Israelites as a sign of their trust. They are asking God for help, not turning to other gods and goddesses out there. Their hope is only with God.

God of hope, we seek you in our difficult hours. We believe that you are with us and will never leave us hungry or thirsty. Even if the world says otherwise, our hope remains in you. Amen.

TUESDAY, MARCH 3 ~ *Read Exodus 17:1-7*

The miracle of water coming out of a rock is not the only miracle in this passage. In verse 6 God tells Moses that God will be standing in front of him on the rock of Horeb when Moses strikes the rock, in front of everyone to see. With the focus on the miraculous water, it's easy to miss the visible presence of God. To see the staff that performed the ten miracles not that long ago bring water from a rock would already be enough for me to believe. But to see God standing in front of Moses would be too much.

In this season of Lent, Exodus 17:1-7 invites us to remember and acknowledge those moments when God is present in our lives. God is not only present in moments when our prayers are answered. God's presence is not contained within the changing or betterment of our conditions. Rather, God is present in each moment of our lives. The challenge is acknowledging that presence. Lent then becomes an opportunity for us to practice witnessing God's presence by lessening our egos, giving up our insatiable drive to make the world go around us, and releasing our incessant demands that we expect God to meet.

Exodus 17 invites us to remember God's goodness in our lives. We remember the staff that turned the Nile into dry ground (Exod. 14:15-25). We remember how God turned the bitter water of Marah into sweet and drinkable water (15:22-25). We remember the manna in the mornings (16:1-36). I do hope that our prayers are answered by God. Yet even if it feels like God is nowhere to be found, I believe that God is with us. All I have to do, particularly during this season of Lent, is remember how overwhelmingly good God has already been to me.

God of wonders, we thank you for the miracles of life and the blessings you have bestowed upon us. Forgive us for forgetting how you always watch over and love us in so many different ways. In your loving name we pray. Amen.

WEDNESDAY, MARCH 4 ~ *Read Psalm 95:1-7*

I love reading biblical passages that speak about how God is directly involved in the creation of our beautiful world. Inasmuch as that sounds simplistic, to speak of God's direct involvement theologically implies that we see God's presence, imprints, and other expressions of divine manifestation in nature. Since the trees are created by God, then we can learn about the divine through the trees. Theologians call this kind of imprinting *panentheism* or the understanding that God is revealed in every part of creation, not only in humans.

As I write, I continue to hear reports of the aftermath of hurricanes Helene and Milton, two back-to-back storms that devastated parts of the southeastern United States in the fall of 2024. It is one thing to say that I experience God in a majestic tree; it is another to speak of God's presence in nature after the devastating blow of a hurricane. More than a hundred people died, thousands lost so much, many lost everything. Throughout the world, we are witnessing how climate change continues to devastate so many lives. In the midst of all of these calamities, how do we see God our Lord as maker and shepherd when we have lost so much as a result of the very creation that God has created?

I am confused, terrified, and broken by the loss around me. And yet the psalmist invites me to declare that God is the rock of my salvation. Declaring my faith in God is not just a task for good times; faith must be deeply manifested in troubling times. I don't have easy answers for destruction and loss, particularly that which comes as a result of natural events. One day, I hope that I will see as God sees. Until then, I will rest in God's goodness that I know is present with me even in the midst of the storm.

Merciful God, we seek you, our Lord and Shepherd. We pray for all of our brothers and sisters who are struggling right now. May your loving arms protect and guide them. Amen.

THURSDAY, MARCH 5 ~ *Read Psalm 95:8-11*

Psalm 95 says that God loathed the Israelites for forty years. But did God actually do so? I struggle to reconcile the image of God as loving and forbearing with the loathing, swearing, and vengeful images of the divine I read in this passage.

Before jumping to conclusions, I researched other possible interpretations of this passage. I have found out that Hebrews 3:7-11 echoes Psalm 95:8-11, not verbatim but close enough. Exodus 17:1-7, Psalm 95:8-11, and Hebrews 3:7-11 were written at distant times and locations; however, through these disparate passages one can trace a collective memory shared by the authors of what happened at Meribah. Perhaps, then, Psalm 95:8-11 is not a verbatim transcript of the divine's action, but a collective memory of what the people have felt in response to their testing God. Instead of a factual account of what happened, maybe this is the author's interpretation of the consequences for not trusting God in the midst of their struggles.

The Bible speaks about God hardening people's hearts to force them to choose the wrong action. Many other passages just make God look bad, as well. Every time we encounter these texts, we should take a pause and reflect on what these passages actually tell us about one another and ourselves. Perhaps we can see in them not a vengeful God but representation of how the authors of these texts felt about their own actions. The authors are warning us not to repeat their mistakes. It's not that these passages are not truth, but the truth in them may not be the immediate message we first see.

Loving God, we seek to understand your ways as we hope to build the beloved community you have created us to be. Forgive us for failing to seek the goodness in one another and in all of your creation. Amen.

FRIDAY, MARCH 6 ~ *Read Romans 5:1-5*

With so many atrocities happening in our world right now, praying for peace is not just a perfunctory action anymore. We desperately want peace in our divided, contentious world. Romans 5:1-5 is a great passage to reflect upon when it comes to hoping for peace in this world. Paul declares that we have peace with God through our Lord Jesus Christ.

Paul expresses his sentiments for peace not as a perfunctory salutation or empty declaration. Rather, this peace that Paul declares is laden with liberating and subversive implications. Paul writes from within the enslaving systems of the Roman Empire, in which everyone is forced to live according to the *Pax Romana* (Roman Peace). This so-called Roman "peace" was more a threat to fall in line or else be met with a sword. For Paul, Christ provides the pathway to God's peace.

Paul's subversive understanding of peace does not avoid conflict; rather, this peace seeks liberation from oppression, even if affliction ensues. Paul knew about the afflictions that followers of Christ would have to endure simply by declaring that Jesus Christ is the Lord and the bringer of peace. And yet Paul shares his experience of faith that the Holy Spirit will pour God's love into his readers so that they will survive and even thrive in and beyond the oppressive systems of their world.

To believe in Jesus Christ is to believe in God's love as we endure the afflictions of our lives too. Our hope for peace is not in some future return of Christ; it is for peace to become a present reality. It is not about buying insurance for the afterlife or a talisman for protection. Christ's peace empowers us to endure the afflictions of the world and to change them for ourselves and for others, right here, right now.

God of hope, we thank you for empowering us to face the tribulations of our lives. Inspire us to be agents of your peace, bringing liberation in your name. Amen.

SATURDAY, MARCH 7 ~ *Read Romans 5:6-11*

Hubris is the type of pride that leads to failure. It is a dangerous path. We start to think so much of ourselves that we make mistakes and act immorally, thinking that we are above others, exempted from the law and any form of responsibility. Hubris allows us to believe that we do not need the love and care of others. The pinnacle of hubris is when we intentionally choose to boast of our sins.

Paul could have described himself and the church with power-driven words, colonial expressions, and hyper-masculine innuendos. Instead, Paul chose to describe himself and the church as weak and ungodly, as sinners and enemies, as people in need of justification. He did so not to glorify shame or to silence the church but to uplift and center the salvific works of Jesus Christ. Sometimes Paul's words are misconstrued to indicate that all humans are worthless, yet I don't think that's what Paul was trying to say. Paul is reminding us that we do not save ourselves. God is the first mover, the first reconciler, who graciously saves us through Jesus Christ. We are justified by God while we are sinners, before we even chose to believe.

This is why I believe in Jesus Christ. In my weak and ungodly moments, God invites me back into the fold of divine grace, imploring me to repent of my sins and live once again a sanctified life. There is no greater gift than for God to love us, not just unconditionally, but even before we ask to be loved. That is why Paul invites us to only boast of what Christ has done for us on the cross. Such an invitation does not negate our good works or the importance of uplifting individual voices. Rather, humility keeps us guided by the reconciling love of God.

God of reconciliation, we thank you for the grace you have shown us through the cross. We boast of your enduring love for all. Amen.

SUNDAY, MARCH 8 ~ *Read John 4:5-42*

Third Sunday in Lent

The point of the conversation Jesus has with the woman at the well is never about her having five husbands, yet readers of this text gravitate toward that point. We do not even know why she had five husbands. Was it because she was forced into levirate marriage, the practice of marrying your deceased/incapacitated husband's brother(s) so that the first husband's lineage will continue? Were her husbands, one after another, conscripted by the Roman army to fight and killed in battle? Whatever the reason, the fact that she has had five husbands is not the point. The point is Jesus knows who she is. Jesus truly sees her and loves her.

While the twelve apostles of Jesus have a hard time believing in Jesus as the Messiah, the Samaritan woman trusts in Jesus because of their one conversation. She does not require a supernatural event to believe; all she needs to hear is that Jesus knows her and is willing to speak to her, to be in relationship with her.

Living in the twenty-first century implies that we might not see miracles as they were reported to have happened during the time of Jesus. And yet we do still hope for and witness miracles in our lives. We witness God's miracle when we are empowered to love one another and to fight for justice. The Word of God is most compelling when it is manifested through visible signs of love. We share God's love when we pay attention to the people around us—when we seek to know them as full people, to know their story and to understand their perspective. Others come to believe in the Messiah, the Christ, because the miracle that truly speaks to us all is love.

God of wonder, we thank you for your presence in our lives. Empower us to care for one another. Be with us as we witness to your love in this world. Amen.

Journeying to Discernment

MARCH 9–15, 2026 • DONNA K. WHITNEY

SCRIPTURE OVERVIEW: All four scriptures for this week explore the importance of discernment. The Gospel reading uses images of vision and blindness to engage deeper reflection about ethical and spiritual awareness and the ways in which we are to respond to what we discern. The reading from 1 Samuel illustrates Samuel's journey into discernment and invites us to consider the degree to which we see ourselves and others as God sees. The Twenty-third Psalm suggests that in our deepest darkness, there remains the possibility of an encounter with God. In Ephesians, the writer uses images of sleep and death as foils for the truth of Christ. Embedded in the epistle is an apparent contradiction that invites discernment regarding silence and speech.

QUESTIONS AND SUGGESTIONS FOR REFLECTION

- Read John 9:1-41. How do you understand healing as distinct from curing? What practices does your spiritual tradition offer for engaging your own inner capacity for healing and wholeness?
- Read 1 Samuel 16:1-13. Who do we as individuals and communities fail to see as God sees them, maybe even failing to see them at all?
- Read Psalm 23. Recall a difficult time in which you encountered God in a particularly deep way. How do your inevitable experiences with suffering and evil challenge and/or strengthen your faith?
- Read Ephesians 5:8-14. What do you as an individual want to wake up from? What do you want to wake up for?

The Rev. Dr. Donna K. Whitney is an ordained minister serving Metropolitan Interdenominational Church in Nashville, TN. She is a retired physician and a poet. She provides trauma-informed care at Healing Minds and Souls, a faith-based community organization that provides education, resources, and support for fostering wholeness.

MONDAY, MARCH 9 ~ *Read John 9:1-41*

Who sinned? From ancient times to now, illness and disability have often been attributed to sin—usually the sin of an individual. Science and medicine offer alternative explanations, and so does Jesus. But the question still stands. In shamanic traditions, illness was considered evidence of disordered relations in a community, whether the community was aware of it or not. Healing meant more than curing an individual body in the modern Western biomedical sense. Healing in shamanic traditions and in the culture of first-century Palestine meant reaching wholeness whether or not a cure was achieved. Healing meant restoration to a sense of belonging in one's own skin and in community. Healing reached beyond individuals and individual bodies.

Who sinned? The question still stands today. When Black people in America are disproportionately affected by diabetes and hypertension, who sinned? When whole neighborhoods are without a grocery store, who sinned? When millions lack access to health care they can afford, who sinned? When residents of Louisiana's "cancer alley," home to the most toxic air and water in America, watch their environment and their bodies decay, who sinned?

Certain Pharisees thought that Jesus had sinned, having violated the sabbath on a technicality. When they ask Jesus, "Surely we are not blind?" Jesus confirms that they are not. They aren't blind because they have seen what is possible. They have seen healing that goes beyond the simple cure. They have seen healing that means wholeness for individuals and communities. They have caught a glimpse of the kingdom of God, and yet they try to hold it back. Like Jesus, Reverend James M. Lawson Jr. often said, "We don't have to live like this." And we don't.

Thank you, God, for healing that goes beyond a cure. Thank you for sight to see beyond what is and to behold what is possible. Amen.

TUESDAY, MARCH 10 ~ *Read John 9:1-41*

When we read about the miracles performed by Jesus, and when we pray for miracles, we should take care that we're not asking for magic. There were plenty of self-proclaimed magicians running around in first-century Palestine, but Jesus wasn't one of them. Magicians use deception and sleight of hand to get us to give our power to them. Jesus uses love and truth to let us access our own power. Jesus heals not by magic but by engaging a person's own innate capacity for healing. Look closely at the way the blind man was healed. Jesus spits on the ground and spreads the mud on the man's eyes. But it is not until the man participates in his own healing by entering the pool that his sight is restored. The healing that Jesus offers taps into the intrinsic wholeness of a person. The healing that Jesus offers doesn't take away anyone's power. It activates a person's own power, the person's own innate capacity for healing and wholeness.

Maybe this is why certain Pharisees were displeased by the healing recounted in this passage. Some of these Pharisees were used to having a particular type of power: a "power over," a power that disempowers others. But Jesus doesn't trade in "power over." Jesus invites us into our own wholeness, into our own authentic selves. And when we are healed into wholeness, we no longer accept external "power over" from anyone who cultivates power for power's sake.

While the beginning of the passage deals with physiologic sight, by the end, the conversation shifts to spiritual and ethical sight. If, like the Pharisees in the text, we now see the possibility of wholeness, then like them we have the responsibility not to stand in the way of the healing that brings that kingdom into being.

Merciful God, help us to accept your invitation into healing and wholeness for ourselves and for the world. Amen.

WEDNESDAY, MARCH 11 ~ *Read 1 Samuel 16:1-13*

Notice the development in Samuel's capacity for discernment. The first son of Jesse that he sees seems like a perfectly good candidate to be king. But the Lord tells Samuel that Eliab is not the one, and he gives Samuel some guidance as to the matter of discernment: "Do not look on his appearance or on the height of his stature . . . for the LORD does not see as mortals see; they look on the outward appearance, but the LORD looks on the heart."

Samuel seems to learn quickly, because as the next six sons of Jesse pass before him, it is Samuel and not the Lord who is able to say confidently that none of the six is the chosen one. When David finally presents himself to Samuel, it is again the Lord who speaks: "Rise and anoint him, for this is the one." But it was Samuel who had the discernment to ask about an eighth son and Samuel who insisted on seeing the young man before even sitting down to eat. By this point, the Lord is no longer correcting Samuel, but confirming Samuel's discernment.

Samuel learns how to look into the heart rather than being distracted by appearances. Whom do we dismiss or fail to even see based on superficial appearances?

Samuel asks if there is another son. Someone was being overlooked, maybe because he was the youngest, maybe because he was regarded as just a simple shepherd. But Samuel wanted to know who was missing. We would also do well to inquire who is missing. Who is missing from the pews in our sanctuaries? Who is missing from our consideration as we select leaders? Who is missing even from the narratives in our scriptures?

All-seeing God, we pray for the gift of discernment. We pray for open, wise, and compassionate hearts and minds, so that we might see ourselves and see one another as you see us. Amen.

THURSDAY, MARCH 12 ~ *Read Psalm 23*

This very familiar and beloved psalm is often read in moments that call for comfort—when facing tragedy, illness, or death. A close read reveals that the psalm offers comfort, not because it dismisses or denies suffering, but because it acknowledges life's harsh realities. The NRSVUE translates verse 3 as, "he restores my soul." Other translations use *strength* (GNT) or *life* (CEV)to identify that which God renews or revives. All translations suggest a near-death experience either of the body or the soul—perhaps both. The rod and the staff that comfort and console offer such comfort and consolation precisely because suffering is woven into the very fabric of human life.

The poet who wrote these lines didn't write them because there is no dark valley, nor out of wishful thinking that God would remove the valleys. We all go through dark valleys. Everyone has been there. The psalmist didn't write these lines to deny the dark valleys. The psalmist wrote these lines because no matter what the valley, no matter where, no matter when, no matter how deep, no matter even if the valley is of our own making—in every valley, God is there. God is there because God is everywhere. God is with and within every one of us.

Psalm 23 is very much a here-and-now psalm, evoking images of lush vegetation and quiet waters, anointing oil and abundant nourishment. The final verse is often taken to suggest eternal life, but the Judaic context and the original Hebrew do not support that interpretation. The familiar King James translation says, "I shall dwell in the house of the LORD forever," but other versions indicate this dwelling will continue until the end of this life. God is not waiting to dwell with us after we die; God is present in this very life, in this very moment.

With Psalm 23 as a focal point, offer a prayer of thanksgiving to God.

FRIDAY, MARCH 13 ~ *Read Ephesians 5:8-14*

In this letter, the writer invokes themes of light and sight, contrasting light not only with darkness but also with sleep and even with death. In the midst of this exhortation to live "as children of light," the writer seems to make a contradiction. First, the writer says, "Take no part in the unfruitful works of darkness; rather, expose them." Then, in an apparent contradiction, the writer says, "For it is shameful even to mention what such people do secretly." So which way is it? Expose wrong-doing or don't even say out loud what evil deeds are being done?

The light we need here is the light of discernment. We should consider when it is best to expose wrong-doing, and when it is best to keep quiet. If we are to expose wrong-doing, when, where, and in the presence of whom is it best to do so? Discernment means examining our motives: Do we expose wrong-doing as gossip or in an effort to provide a path to correction? We can examine the difference between calling out—publicly naming a wrong in a way that produces shame—and calling in—naming a wrong with the intent of inviting another into deeper understanding and the possibility of reconciliation. If, instead, we believe it is right to stay silent, do we know when our silence is a product of our own shame or a reflection of cowardice? Do we know when our silence is a gesture of wisdom and mercy?

The writer's apparent contradiction invites us into reflection, allowing us to acknowledge opportunities to practice discernment. When we seek wisdom around our decisions of when, where, how, why, and in front of whom to speak and to keep silent, we make stronger decisions that better reflect God's goodness into the world.

God of wisdom, help us to know when to speak and when to keep silent. Help us to know the difference between silence born of courage and silence born of fear. Help us to use our speech only for those things that are pleasing to you. Amen.

SATURDAY, MARCH 14 ~ *Read Psalm 23*

Everyone's life moves through "the darkest valley" in one season or another. There is no walking around the valleys, no flying over them, no tunneling under them, no standing to one side and refusing to go through. What many of us fear even more than moving through the valley is getting stuck there. The valley can feel like a hopeless place, a place from which there is no exit. The valley can be a painfully lonely place. The valley can be a place saturated with evil. The psalmist doesn't deny the existence or the pervasiveness of evil. But no matter how desperately lonely we may feel, the psalmist insists, "I fear no evil, for you are with me."

Sometimes in the midst of trouble, we ask how God can allow us to suffer. We may ask, "Where is God, anyway?" We may wonder if God is anywhere at all, if God is even real. Yet the valley is often where we finally turn to God, finally experience the presence of God.

That direct experience with God can only be described indirectly, poetically, and the psalmist gives us poetry to convey what flows from that experience. The psalmist says, "Surely goodness and mercy shall follow me all the days of my life." The psalmist comes into an awareness of the goodness and mercy of God that follow us all, just because God is God. And because of the psalmist's transformative encounter with God, they leave their own trail of goodness and mercy in the world. Our encounters with God's goodness and mercy can inspire us to do the same.

Good and merciful God, may my deeds of goodness and mercy live in the world as your goodness and mercy follow me. Amen.

SUNDAY, MARCH 15 ~ *Read Ephesians 5:8-14*

FOURTH SUNDAY IN LENT

In the ancient world, sleep and death were seen as closely related phenomena, understandably. To the outside viewer, someone sleeping and someone who has died appear similar. Through medical technology, we now know much more about how the brain functions during sleep. We instead are baffled by the waking sleep in which our brain waves show the activity of alertness, yet our minds are numb to the reality of what's going on around us, numb sometimes even to what's going on inside us. This is the waking sleep that suggests a death of the soul. And powerful currents in our culture today—as there were in the ancient world—prevent us from being fully awake to the reality we live in. They prevent us from acknowledging the powers that defend and sustain the status quo; the powers that create poverty, homelessness, and hunger; the powers that perpetuate racism, sexism, homophobia, ageism, transphobia, xenophobia, and the other evils that we sometimes accept as simply "the way things are."

The whole trajectory of the scriptures says that no matter what the status quo looks like, no matter who and what might sustain it, no matter how many cultural and spiritual sedatives might be offered to us (think technology, social media, advertising), we can wake up. We can wake up to the myths, lies, distortions, and misrepresentations that saturate our communal life. Just like the sun can wake us up in the morning, the writer of this letter insists that the light of Christ can awaken us too, even in the challenges of the times we live in.

God of love and light, may we have discernment to know light from dark. Give us the ability to discern what is pleasing to you, the strength to live into the ways that please you, and the grace to let your light shine in and through us. Amen.

Faithfully Waiting on Resurrection

MARCH 16–22, 2026 • ELIZABETH W. CORRIE

SCRIPTURE OVERVIEW: God is the source of life and therefore triumphs over death. This does not mean, however, that our lives will be without hardship or death. The psalmist cries out impatiently. The exiles in Babylon remain in captivity. Mary and Martha mourn Lazarus. Even Jesus himself cries for his friends. But as we await the resurrection of the dead on the Day of Judgment, we also have a taste of resurrection now. This is what it means to set our minds and attitudes on Christ, experiencing the power of the Holy Spirit as we journey in trust and hope together with our fellow sojourners in Christ's church.

QUESTIONS AND SUGGESTIONS FOR REFLECTION

- Read Psalm 130. When have you longed impatiently for God? How can you lean on these ancient words for comfort during these times?
- Read Ezekiel 37:1-14. What do you believe will happen after you die? How does Ezekiel's vision relate to this? Does it change how you think about resurrection?
- Read John 11:1-45. What do you believe Jesus means when he proclaims that he is the resurrection and the life? How does this relate to your own understanding of death and resurrection?
- Read Romans 8:6-11. How can you cultivate a mind that is set on Christ? How would this change some of the ways you currently act or think?

Elizabeth W. Corrie, PhD, is Professor in the Practice of Youth Education and Peacebuilding at Candler School of Theology, Emory University in Atlanta, GA. She serves on the General Board of Global Ministries and is a lay member of the North Georgia Annual Conference of The United Methodist Church. She attends Neighborhood Church UMC in Atlanta.

MONDAY, MARCH 16 ~ *Read Psalm 130*

The psalms are the songs of the Israelites, and this psalm, part of the Songs of Ascent (Pss. 120-134) most likely functioned as a pilgrimage song for people journeying toward Jerusalem to the Temple for religious festivals. It is striking, then, to imagine the psalmist crying out from the depths—while crying out from emotional depths, the author is also crying out from geographical depths along the journey up to Mount Zion. Asking the Lord to listen and give mercy, the psalmist waits in hope to be forgiven and made ready to worship at the Temple.

Notably, this psalm stays in the moment of waiting—we do not arrive at the destination nor receive an answer to the prayer. We move in and through the depths while continuing to look upward, trusting that God's great redemption will come in God's time. But trust and hope does not necessarily make it easier to wait on God. The psalmist's longing is so passionate it must be said twice: "More than those who watch for the morning, more than those who watch for the morning." Who has not had a terrible night, perhaps while ill or while sitting at the bedside of someone who is dying, and faced that terrible hour before dawn, when we feel most separated from the sleeping world around us? Who has not cried out from the depths of a seemingly endless season of grief, contrition, or distress, asking God to listen and give mercy? God's promise will be fulfilled, but waiting on it may be painful, even lonely.

What can we learn during this Lenten season from our psalmist's cries? We can lean on the psalmist's faithfulness and find solace in the shared longing. We can seek assurance in knowing we stand in a tradition that shows us how to cry out—even impatiently—to God.

Pray this psalm repeatedly, and join your cries and your hope to these ancient words.

TUESDAY, MARCH 17 ~ *Read John 11:1-35*

The story of the raising of Lazarus continues beyond these verses, but it is worth dwelling on these scenes before the event. Jesus and the disciples are staying on the other side of the Jordan. They have left Jerusalem because the religious leaders who opposed him threatened to stone and arrest Jesus. They are hiding out, or at least re-grouping. While there, Martha and Mary, the sisters of Lazarus, send word to Jesus that Lazarus is ill.

Jesus loves this family, and they love him. According to John's Gospel, Jesus has stayed with them in Bethany before. It's clear they support Jesus' work. Later in the Gospel, Jesus will visit them again, and Mary will engage in an extraordinary expression of love by anointing Jesus' feet. And yet, as close as they are, he decides not to go to them immediately upon hearing of Lazarus' illness. When he finally arrives, both Martha and Mary confront him, separately using the same words: "Lord, if you had been here, my brother would not have died." They sent word, and his response was delayed. They cried out from their depths, and, like the psalmist, they waited with their whole being at Lazarus' bedside, praying for mercy.

When Jesus is confronted by this crying out of the depths, he cries too. Why? Perhaps it too much to see his beloved friends suffering under the power of death. Perhaps even his knowledge that not only Lazarus but all these fragile people before him will one day be resurrected doesn't assuage the grief of the moment. Perhaps he too feels the pain of losing Lazarus, even knowing it is happening for the glory of God and will soon be over. In this scene we see Jesus at his most human, and in this moment, he suffers with us, even as he knows that the suffering will pass.

Jesus, beloved friend, thank you for crying with us. Dry our tears with hope and trust, as we know that what you ask of God, God will give. Amen.

WEDNESDAY, MARCH 18 ~ *Read Ezekiel 37:1-14*

Even the best action movies cannot compete with the awe-inspiring vision of Ezekiel. A valley filled with bones like the wasteland of a battlefield, the noise and quaking as the bones come together and become enfleshed, the four winds rising to enter these thousands of bodies to stand them up, a restored people like an army ready to march.

Imagine hearing about this vision as an exile in Babylon, desperate and longing for God and for your homeland. Imagine what it would mean to feel utterly cut off and forgotten by the people you have left behind, to have no hope of return in your lifetime. Your bones are "very dry"—long dead with nothing left to revive. And yet through Ezekiel's prophecy you receive word that your bones, and all the bones of your people, will live again.

This vision is not only the hope of exiles. It is also the hope of all of us who face mortality. This vision is among the scriptural sources for Jewish and Christian understanding of resurrection. We don't believe resurrection to be merely a survival of a disembodied soul, but a full restoration of our entire beings, our entire selves—including our bodies. This full-bodied resurrection takes seriously all of what it means to be human. Our physical bodies are an integral part of our being, connected to our soul and mind and spirit. Ezekiel's vision assures us that all of who we are will be resurrected and united with God.

Ezekiel's prophesy reminds us that wherever we are, we will return home, and when we come home, our whole being will be restored and embraced.

God of the exiles, heal and embrace my full being, and make these bones live! Amen.

THURSDAY, MARCH 19 ~ *Read Ezekiel 37:1-14*

God commands Ezekiel to prophesy over the dry bones, and he does. But at the end of the great noise and quaking, when sinews join bones, flesh is added, and skin covers these bodies, there is not yet breath. These reconstituted bodies are still dead. So God commands Ezekiel to prophesy to the breath. The Hebrew word used is *ruach,* which can be translated not only as *breath,* but also as *wind* and *spirit.* The breath comes from the four winds, from all of God's creation. Indeed, this moment in which the winds enter the dead bodies and make them live again reminds us of God's original creative act in Genesis 2:7, when God breathed life into the creatures God made from the earth.

God is showing Ezekiel and the ancient Israelites—and us—that God, and only God, is the source of life. The very dry bones, bones so completely dead that no hope of resuscitation could be imagined, have indeed come to life again, and it is by this sign that we know that God is the Lord.

How often do we forget that we are not the source of our own breath? In our busy lives, we exercise our agency and make many decisions that shape the paths our lives take. We work hard, and we support ourselves by this work. We earn things and we buy things with those earnings. It is no surprise that we tend to live as though we are self-made. But we began Lent with ashes—from dust we came, and to dust we will return—and it is fitting that we dwell not only on our "dust," but also on the miraculous breath that enlivens us every moment. That is how we know that God is Lord.

Breathe deeply, using your belly. As you breathe, give thanks to the Lord God who draws on all creation to place this breath in you, this moment, and every moment.

FRIDAY, MARCH 20 ~ *Read John 11:17-45*

When Jesus arrives in Bethany, Martha comes to meet him. Though she confronts him by saying that Lazarus would not have died had he been there, she affirms her faith that Jesus can ask anything of God and God will give it. Does she believe Jesus can raise her brother from the dead?

It doesn't seem like it. When Jesus goes to the tomb and asks the stone to be removed, she objects, worried about the smell. Lazarus has been dead for four days—in Jewish tradition, this is beyond the point when resuscitation is possible. But Martha does believe in resurrection, the understanding of bodily resurrection on the last day informed by Ezekiel's prophecy. She also believes that Jesus is the Christ coming into the world. As readers, we bear witness to Martha's understanding of death, life, and resurrection transforming in real time. Yes, Lazarus will rise again on the last day. This was already part of her theology. Yes, Jesus is the Christ, the Messiah promised to redeem Israel. This was already part of her theology. What was not part of her theology, until that moment, was that Jesus the Christ is *currently* the resurrection and the life. Her beloved friend—the man standing before her who has stayed in her house—has taken resurrection into himself and transformed what resurrection means. We live eternally in Christ, both now and in the last day.

This is too mind-blowing to grasp immediately, but it is through the raising of Lazarus that Jesus demonstrates that God is the source of resurrection and the source of all life, and therefore the one who overcomes all death. Just as God commands breath into the dry bones in Ezekiel's vision, God, through Jesus, commands Lazarus out of the grave—so that we know that Christ is Lord.

Lord Jesus, you are my resurrection and life. Help me to know eternal life in you today, as well as on the last day. Amen.

SATURDAY, MARCH 21 ~ *Read Romans 8:6-11*

Paul contrasts two ways of living: a life based on selfishness and a life based on the Spirit. Paul is talking about mindset, how we focus or govern our minds. The Common English Bible translates it as "attitude." Having an attitude of selfishness makes us hostile to God and leads to death. Having an attitude that comes from the Spirit leads to peace and life. And Paul reminds us that our enslavement to sin and death is overcome by resurrection—the same God that breathed life into dry bones and called Lazarus out of the tomb is in the Son who triumphed over death on Easter and who sent the Spirit to live in us even now.

We can cultivate an attitude rooted in the Spirit when we remember that we are not the authors of our own lives, but that only God can make dry bones live. We can cultivate an attitude rooted in the Spirit when we remember that Jesus is our hope for eternal life. We know intellectually this is true—we have the theology—but when we smell death, as Martha did with her brother, it is hard to know this in our bones.

What practices help you cultivate an attitude rooted in the Spirit? Lenten practices such as prayer, fasting, or acts of service help us cultivate such an attitude. As we draw close to the end of Lent, we must consider how we will carry that attitude throughout the rest of the year. In Galatians, Paul writes of the fruit of the Spirit, evidence of a life lived in the Spirit: love, joy, peace, patience, kindness, generosity, faithfulness, gentleness, and self-control (5:22-23). What practices help you remember resurrection, even in moments when you wait, desperately, in the midst of death? How can you draw on these practices in your Lenten journey and beyond?

Creator God, you are the only source of life. Redeemer God, you call me out of the grave. Sustainer God, you set my mind on you and bring me peace. Amen.

Fifth Sunday in Lent

As we come full circle to our pilgrimage psalm, it is worth rereading, and even memorizing, as it shows us how to wait actively, how to journey toward God in and through the depths with trust and hope. The psalmist cries, just as Mary cries in her suffering, and we know that Jesus cries with us.

But something else happens as well. The psalmist cries out to God and then turns to address the other travelers. Remember, they are pilgrims headed to Jerusalem, heading to the Temple for worship. While still in the moment of waiting, perhaps impatiently, the psalmist is confident that the Lord is faithful and loving and will provide redemption to all the people. The psalmist does not travel or wait alone.

Neither do we. The God who brings dry bones to life and promises exiles a return home, healed and restored in their full selves, the God whose Son transforms our understanding of resurrection and invites us to eternal life, the God who sends the Spirit to free us from selfishness and resets our minds on life and peace—this God is the God we go to worship, together. On this day, we head to worship, surrounded by communities of support. As you journey to join your people in worship, know that while the waiting can be difficult, it does not have to be lonely. Allow your whole being to hope in God's promise, and join your people on this Lenten journey toward Easter.

Gracious God, as I prepare this day to worship you, I give you thanks for fellow pilgrims. Be with us as we continue our Lenten journey together toward Easter. Dry our tears and revive our dry bones as we set our minds on you. Give us trust, hope, peace, and life today, and every day. Amen.

The Risk of Obedience

MARCH 23–29, 2026 • JUAN GATTINONI

SCRIPTURE OVERVIEW: The readings this week have a common theme of the risk in obeying and following our Lord. We move toward Palm Sunday when we will once again journey with Jesus through his Passion. The decision to give his life for the salvation of the world was not easy; Jesus needed the certainty that this was the will of God. Isaiah and the psalmist describe being treated with contempt, beaten, and rejected. In reciting the earliest known Christian hymn, Paul in Philippians emphasizes how Christ surrenders his glory and is subjected to humiliation and death. Even when the reasons and teachings of our Lord are logical or valid, they require a leap of faith and personal acceptance, not without risk. If Jesus trusted and gave himself, we can do so too.

QUESTIONS AND SUGGESTIONS FOR REFLECTION

- Read Psalm 31:9-16. It is said that fear warns of possible dangers. When have you experienced fear? What was the result of your experience?
- Read Isaiah 50:4-9a. What specific, special tasks (small or large) do you feel that the Lord has given you?
- Read Philippians 2:5-11. Jesus invites us to adopt an attitude of humility. When have you accepted this invitation? When have you failed to be humble?
- Read Matthew 21:1-11. Where are you in the Palm Sunday story? How do you respond to Jesus as he enters?

Rev. Juan A. Gattinoni was born in Buenos Aires, Argentina. He is a retired pastor of The Methodist Church, professor of theology at the University of the Latin American Educational Center of Rosario, Argentina, and a musician and composer of religious songs.

MONDAY, MARCH 23 ~ *Read Psalm 31:9-16*

We begin our journey to Palm Sunday with Psalm 31, a psalm attributed to David. Surely the fear that King David felt in the moments he stood before the giant Goliath was different from the concern expressed in Psalm 31. David could see Goliath in front of him; he could measure his size and the size of the danger. Those who attack in the psalm avoid direct confrontation, leaving the psalmist to fade away into obscurity.

The writer of this psalm speaks of the anguish and sadness of a life that is wasting away in pain and exhaustion. The cry is in terminal anguish: *If you do not help me, I am dead.* Although this situation is different from the famous fight with Goliath, in some way the response of the one suffering is essentially the same: In both situations, the one attacked looks to God for help. That famous fight came at the time when the people had asked Samuel to establish a king for them "like other nations" (1 Sam. 8:5), that is, a king who would govern according to his own will and not God's. What they got as a result was Saul. But David, no matter how many mistakes he made, always wanted to be guided by God's will.

Today the psalm asks "Let your face shine upon your servant; save me with your steadfast love." This prayer comes to us from the Aaronic blessing. It is a way of asking God to guide the way through what will come. The servant recognizes that they cannot do it on their own and needs to know what God's will is. In the dramatic situation of the psalm, and in those moments where we see no way out, where we see no light, we can pray "Let your face shine upon your servant." Like David—and, as we will see, Jesus—we can trust God to guide our way.

Dear Lord, I am in distress. Let your face shine upon me. Guide me daily because I want to follow in your footsteps. Amen.

TUESDAY, MARCH 24 ~ *Read Isaiah 50:4-9a*

The point of persevering against an adversary is not to support our opinion of what is best, at least if we want to follow Isaiah's thought. It is about conveying the Lord's will or wisdom. There is a difference, isn't there? We encounter ideas to protest against or fight for all the time. Our anger may flare up quickly in these situations, especially when we face injustice. But Isaiah's words are a reminder to be rational and create strategies that allow us to overcome situations of injustice. Yes, the text encourages us to have words for the tired, for the needy, for those who are oppressed in times of darkness. But these words are based on the word that the Lord gives, a word we hear when our ears are open to God's wisdom. Before we can act, we must discern what comes from God. We tune our ears to listen to God, and God gives us the wisdom to draw up the strategy of what to do and how to raise the hope of those who are suffering.

Even after all that discernment, and with an open ear to what God commands, the struggle may still continue. Our path forward may not be easy; we may still face problems, rejection, aggression, and more. The prophetic word is often rejected, as it was so many times in the days of the prophets. But we take a total risk for God: We commit ourselves, not because of our interests and our decisions, but because our guidance is from God who gives us strength. We affirm with the prophet "The Sovereign LORD himself defends me—who, then, can prove me guilty?" (GNT). It is not always easy to commit to the work God calls us to. But we can remember that if the Lord sends us, the Lord will not abandon us.

Thank you, Lord, for the challenges that you put in our hands. Give us assurance that we are directed by your Holy Spirit to face them. Amen.

WEDNESDAY, MARCH 25 ~ *Read Philippians 2:5-11*

Because of their lyrical construction and the fact that they are often set as poetry, these verses are generally considered to be a hymn, likely a hymn written before Paul composed this letter to the Philippians. Perhaps it was a hymn known to his audience, and Paul used the words to reinforce something familiar. Or perhaps Paul was introducing this language to the readers of his letter, sharing something already known in other circles to teach them the way to live the faith. The tradition of using music to instruct in the faith lasts through the centuries. In Martin Luther's time, popular music was incorporated to sing the faith. Charles Wesley wrote thousands of hymns to express his understanding of faith. Today we know that singing in church is a fundamental way of shaping and sharing what we believe. It is not only what is preached or prayed that touches the human experience: Hymns and songs mark and transform lives.

This hymn in Philippians speaks of Jesus and his humility. Jesus released any right he might have had to exalt himself. He did not act on any pride, power, glory, or sense of self-esteem that would have raised him above others. He became humble without limits, without negotiation or speculation. He was first in line and went to the last place. Incredible, isn't it?

Paul likely added the phrase before the hymn when writing to the Philippians, which says: "The attitude you should have is the one that Christ Jesus had" (GNT). Paul invites us to have this attitude and asks us to stop being "first in line," to be among the humble who serve, love, forgive, and have no pride to boast. And we are invited to this attitude not only within the four walls of the church, but in all of life itself. Let us have the attitude of Christ in every encounter—humility!

Thank you, Lord, for your Son, Jesus Christ, who loves us even when we always want to be "first in line." Make me humble like Christ. Amen.

THURSDAY, MARCH 26 ~ *Read Matthew 26:6-13*

We do not know exactly why this woman appeared with her alabaster jar of very expensive perfume and anointed Jesus with it. Here in Matthew, as in Mark and John's Gospels, those gathered complain that the perfume could have been sold for money—to help the poor, they protest, though the narrator of John notes that these motives might not have been so pure (12:6). Jesus, however, sees the value of the gift as it is given. There will always be people who are poor, Jesus points out, and we have to wonder if those complaining had any particular need in mind. Did they know the name of the "poor" they wished to serve? Jesus reminds them that he is right in front of them, and that he will only be with them a short time.

We are accustomed to thinking that everything is governed by economics, politics, social classes, and how much money we have. Yet Jesus was not going to become richer and more powerful because he was anointed with expensive oil, nor would the problem of poverty be solved by selling the expensive perfume. Our world doesn't work like that. This act is an act for God's kingdom.

So what does it say about how God's kingdom works? In the economy of Jesus, the gesture of love that the woman makes is more valuable than what the precious perfume might have bought. Gestures of love, however small or insignificant they may seem, transcend the moment. Even Jesus says "wherever this gospel is preached all over the world, what she has done will be told in memory of her" (GNT). We have been led to believe that a bank account is what ensures life. But it is love that engenders and sustains life. It is the love of God in Christ that makes our life eternal, now and forever.

Dear God, we do not worship you and praise you so that you fill us with gold. Fill us with your spirit of love. Amen.

FRIDAY, MARCH 27 ~ *Read Matthew 26:30-35, 69-75*

Certainly Peter has the best of intentions when he says, "I will never fall away." Peter is sure that he will not abandon Jesus. His love for Jesus is not in doubt. Perhaps Peter thinks that his declaration of faithfulness puts him on a level of superiority above the others. His statement carries an air of bravado. Or perhaps Peter truly believes he has it in him to follow Jesus to the very end. Either way, his actions will not correspond to his words.

Jesus acknowledges this instantly. And it is only a few moments that Peter's courage lasts. Peter undoubtedly had the best of intentions; he had all the love and respect for the master too. But he is the same as everyone else, like all the humble people who accompanied Jesus into Jerusalem only to abandon him. Peter doesn't even recognize his failure. It's not until the rooster crows that he is almost pulled from a dream—or, better yet, a nightmare—and realizes that what Jesus spoke has come true, that he is just as fallible and mistaken as all the others.

What are we to take from Peter's denial? This story is a clear indication that any of us can follow in Peter's footsteps and deny Christ. And it would be easy to summarize that this story teaches us that no one can be truly faithful. But more significant than Peter's failure is Peter believing himself to be a better disciple than the others, that he could be a leader because of his merits, or that he was a better person than his companions. Peter cannot earn his place as the "rock" on which Jesus will build his church (Matt. 16:18). The lesson in that respect mirrors the lessons we learn from the other passages of scripture this week—the importance of humility as a virtue of the kingdom.

God, inspire in me the humility of Christ, that which advances the coming of your kingdom on earth. Amen.

SATURDAY, MARCH 28 ~ *Read Psalm 118:1-2,19-29*

In our verses from Psalm 118, we read of the psalmist's praise and thanksgiving for God. The full psalm oscillates between thanksgiving and petition. The psalmist praises God's goodness while also asking God for deliverance from distress. We see some of that petition in verse 25, but mostly praise—praise in the familiar language that we who gather in worship tomorrow will echo as we remember Jesus' triumphant entry into Jerusalem: "Blessed is the one who comes in the name of the LORD!" The writers of the Gospels saw this psalm as pointing toward Jesus as the Messiah, seeing in its praise and thanksgiving to God the indicators of salvation that God was providing through Jesus.

While this psalm extols God for God's saving works, the distress the psalmist feels seeps through. This praise is in the face of challenge and struggle. And as we begin the final week of the Lenten journey, traveling with Jesus from the celebratory procession into Jerusalem straight to the Cross, we hear in this psalm our own cries of need. This psalm, written by a person of faith, tries to affirm that whatever challenge we face, God is the answer. God is our salvation. God will deliver us.

A song that we sing in my church asks God for guidance, indicating that we are tired of our ways that have failed, and we don't want to fail anymore. It is the words of a constant prayer affirming the certainty of a life on God's path. God has prepared a way for us. The way is narrow, hard, opposed to everything the world teaches us. In following God, we risk losing everything of earthly value. But we gain the glory of the Lord. Therefore, as Jesus said: "Thy will be done."

Lord, there is nothing more important to me than the life you gave me. Just a few drops of your great love and my life is reborn. Amen.

SUNDAY, MARCH 29 ~ *Read Matthew 21:1-11*

Palm/Passion Sunday

The entrance to Jerusalem followed a prophecy that had been announced long ago by Zechariah (9:9). The people would immediately realize what was happening. They would also recognize that this king was not like those of the neighboring or dominant countries. Christ's work was not about subduing subjects but about transforming lives, changing the world with people who understood that the kingdom of God was coming and that this kingdom was unlike any other earthly kingdom. When Jesus argues with Pilate and says to him, "My kingdom does not belong to this world" (John 18:36), he isn't only speaking of the origins of his kingdom but also talking about his strategy for bringing that kingdom to earth. The kingdom of God, the kingdom whose essence is love, was already present; it was already showing itself, but it was not yet complete, not full. Christ's kingdom wouldn't come with overwhelming force that establishes rule through control. Christ's kingdom comes as an invitation to a different way of living.

Jesus enters Jerusalem to affirm that his kingdom of love, justice, and peace is possible. Jesus enters our hearts as well to tell us that his kingdom is possible in our lives and in our world. He enters simply and humbly because his kingdom is not built on violence, hatred, opposition, or the domination of the strongest. His kingdom becomes a reality wherever love rules. His strategy was to give his life, so that love would triumph—and he succeeded! Christ lives and reigns among us!

Dear God, I do not always understand that love is the way to live in your kingdom. Thank you for the master who continues to invite me to love one another. Amen.

The Emotions of Holy Week

MARCH 30–APRIL 5, 2026 • DAVID WILSON

SCRIPTURE OVERVIEW: Although we anticipate the celebration of Easter, this week's readings remind us to slow down and walk through Holy Week. The passage from Hebrews recalls the suffering of Jesus on the Cross, and Psalm 36 provides poetic imagery of the suffering servant. Both lead us to keep our focus on Jesus. The readings from John and Matthew guide us through the emotions of Jesus' journey to the Cross—betrayal, conflict, denial, and hope. These themes guide us along the journey of Holy Week and empower our Easter response: to share the story of resurrection and to live out the command to love one another.

QUESTIONS AND SUGGESTIONS FOR REFLECTION

- Read Isaiah 42:1-9. How have you responded to God's call on your life? How often has that call changed?
- Read Psalm 36:5-11. What would your poem to God look like this week?
- Read Hebrews 12:1-3. How do you stay focused on Jesus? What imagery in this passage do you think relates to staying focused?
- Read Matthew 28:1-10. Think about a time that you had good news to share and could not keep it to yourself.

Bishop Rev. Dr. David Wilson, first Native American Bishop elected in The United Methodist Church, currently serves the Great Plains Episcopal Area of Kansas and Nebraska.

MONDAY, MARCH 30 ~ *Read Isaiah 42:1-9*

I recall my Hebrew Bible course in seminary well. It was a fascinating class, probing deeply into the stories that I had only read individually or in worship. Our study of Isaiah was one that I recall vividly. We looked at the three sections of this book, and the professor talked about the authorship. As a young seminary student, I thought that the authorship of Isaiah was a given—the author was Isaiah. Imagine my surprise at learning the three sections of this book were likely written centuries apart. We discussed whether the writer of Isaiah was referencing Jesus, the Messiah. When one reads today's passage and other verses from Isaiah carefully, it's easy to see why many believe these verses are about Jesus. He is prophesied to come and deliver the people, to bring justice and hope.

Others say these verses are about the prophet Isaiah, or the nation of Israel, which did not live up to God's expectations. In essence, both failed. The people were disobedient and did not listen, and they looked to the arrival of this Messiah to make all things right.

We are told in this passage of a God who created a covenant with the people who will be a light to the Gentiles. Christ is the "model" of the covenant that we are given for our lives.

That covenant with us today is as valid as it was for the people who first experienced this passage. God continues to be faithful to all whether we are successful in responding to God's call on our lives or not. And God calls us to do the same with one another. Christ lived the model of calling us out of darkness into the light that he created by his presence in the world. We are called to do the same—to help others see light when it doesn't seem possible. We are called to promote and to live out justice in all the places we are sent.

Creator God, help me to be your presence of light to a hurting world this week. Amen.

TUESDAY, MARCH 31 ~ *Read Psalm 36:5-11*

I taught an Introduction to the Bible course for many years at Oklahoma City University. I tried to think of new ways to teach the Bible to help students understand its formation and purpose. As I taught Psalms, I talked about how the psalmists were persons who would pour out their hearts to God through this religious poetry. It could be through their joy, turmoil, praise, lament, or any variety of emotions. I explained that the psalmists were among the first to be so open and direct with God. Most others were too afraid to question God.

I invited my students to write modern-day psalms that described their feelings on situations they experienced. Most did a great job of expressing frustration, joy, lament, and more. I told them there was no way I could grade their writings, as their honest words of how they were feeling toward a situation or toward God were not mine to judge.

The psalmist models this act of expressing emotions, describing God's faithfulness and righteousness, and using beautiful imagery to try to understand the awesomeness and unfailing love of God. I love verses 8-9: "You give them drink from the river of your delights. For with you is the fountain of life; in your light we see light." The psalmist is using what they have seen and experienced to try to describe who God is and the love that God has for the world.

This passage connects with our experiences this Holy Week as we not only journey toward the Cross but also consider the love God has for the world. I invite you to do what I asked my students to do: Take time to write a psalm of how you are feeling about God's love for you today.

Gracious God, enable me to share your love as I sense people and places that yearn for light. Amen.

WEDNESDAY, APRIL 1 ~ *Read Hebrews 12:1-3*

I have run the Oklahoma City Half Marathon many years. This marathon was established to honor the victims of the 1995 Oklahoma City bombing, a terrorist attack that claimed 168 lives.

I train a lot for the 13-mile race. It takes much time and energy to stick with the plan in order to be healthy and able to complete the race each year. I know I can finish the race, but I always have in mind a time frame within which I want to finish. Running the race itself is an exhilarating experience for me as thousands cheer for runners throughout the route. At times I have started the race only to want to quit part of the way through. When that happens, I think about the hours and hours of practice I have put in, and I push on. I fight through the pain, discomfort, elements of weather, and other challenges to get to the finish line. I keep my focus on finishing the race.

This passage from Hebrews is a great parallel to my running. Much of running is mental, and it takes a lot of focus to get across that line. The author of Hebrews writes of that which slows us down on our spiritual journey, the sin that just won't let go. We cannot handle it by ourselves, but we can keep our eyes focused on Jesus as we stay determined and focused on the presence of Christ all around us. What wonderful imagery for us when we face challenges in our lives.

Hebrews tells us that Jesus endured the Cross and ignored the shame for the sake of joy. We share that joy on Easter Sunday as we think about Jesus staying focused on his journey to the Cross for all of humanity.

Creator God, help me to keep focused on you this week as I experience joy all around me. Amen.

THURSDAY, APRIL 2 ~ *Read John 13:1-17*

Maundy Thursday

Many of us will participate in special services throughout Holy Week. One of the most humbling and uncomfortable services for many is the washing of one another's feet. I recall a meeting that I attended years ago of people from all over the country. One attending pastor had been assigned to do the devotion. He surprised all of us by incorporating a foot washing. We had no notice and were not prepared for the humbling experience.

As I participated in the service, I thought about the disciples who were gathered with Jesus that day. They probably had a long day of travel, and, unlike my group, they had walked wherever they went. Their feet were dusty and dirty, and they were not prepared either. Peter was the one who had the nerve to stand up and say, "You are not washing my feet!" Peter's opposition was because Jesus was their leader, and in the eyes of Peter, this task was not something for a person in authority to do.

But Jesus illustrated what it means to be a servant leader. Leaders are not greater than those who follow them, Jesus was saying. Jesus set an example to all who were there of what he expected of them as they continued their work as a disciples.

Jesus is our example too. This act is a command from Jesus to love one another, just as he loves us. The rituals of Holy Week help to bring home the love that Christ has for the world. We can't just talk about love; we must illustrate that love through our daily acts. We are called to do no less.

Giving God, may my rituals of serving you and others be fitting for you and your kingdom. Amen.

FRIDAY, APRIL 3 ~ *Read John 18:1-19*

Good Friday

Betrayal is one of the most difficult emotions to experience. Betrayal comes in many forms, some of which come from those closest to us. Betrayal is hard to overcome. It takes time, prayer, and patience to forgive those who betray us. Often the closer we are to a person who has betrayed us, the more difficult the recovery.

Reading of Judas' betrayal of Jesus has always been a challenge for me. What catches my attention is that Jesus knew it was coming. He had already called it. It is part of a necessary plan, as Jesus knows his fate is the Cross.

However, Judas' betrayal isn't the only one Jesus faces. Peter denies knowing Jesus, a betrayal in itself. Peter was one of the most faithful disciples; many believe he was Jesus' favorite. Yet after Jesus is taken away, Peter denies knowing Jesus not just once, but three times. By this time, Peter has chosen violence in attempting to prevent Jesus' arrest by cutting off the ear of the high priest's servant, and, as we saw yesterday, Peter didn't want Jesus to wash his feet. Throughout the last days of Jesus' earthly life, Peter fails him in so many ways.

Peter and Judas both regret their betrayal of Jesus. But Peter goes on to continue as a faithful follower, introducing Christ to many throughout the rest of his life. His words of love and service to Christ continue to this day. The role of Peter shows us that the love of Christ overcomes any of our faults and failures. At times we will get it right, and at other times we will fail. In every moment, we rely only on the grace of God.

Loving God, assist me always as I work to get it right as I serve you and your kingdom. Amen.

SATURDAY, APRIL 4 ~ *Read Matthew 27:57-66*

HOLY SATURDAY

I think of the types of loss that we face in our lives. Some losses are expected after long illnesses, and some losses are sudden. In whatever way death comes, we are never fully prepared for it. We face the various forms of grief that are natural to all of us.

As a pastor, I have helped many with this grieving process. Right after a loss, we quickly go through the motions of preparing for the service and burial, often without being able to fully take in what has happened.

Joseph, Mary Magdalene, and the other Mary are doing just that. Joseph is very generous to offer his own tomb for the burial. The two Marys are there to mourn the loss of Jesus, doing all that was expected and staying with the body until the end. Many Native American services do not conclude until the relatives and friends have made sure the casket is completely covered with dirt. I think of this ritual as I read of Mary Magdalene and the other Mary sitting in front of the tomb. They loved Jesus so much that they did not have the capacity to worry about the authorities, who would know they were followers of Christ by their presence at the tomb and could have arrested them as well. The same was true for Joseph who risked his own arrest and death when he asked for the body of Jesus.

This story is like a scene in a good movie that points to the rest of the story that is to come. The sorrow of those at the tomb combined with the authorities' suspicion that followers of Jesus will come and take his body give hints of how this story will end. We as followers of Christ know the rest of this story and look forward with hope and joy.

Creator God, give me words of hope to speak to those who are grieving this day. Amen.

SUNDAY, APRIL 5 ~ *Read Matthew 28:1-10*

EASTER

Several Muscogee-Creek tribal churches in the Oklahoma Indian Missionary Conference have a special ritual for their services of Holy Communion. The women bake the leavened bread and prepare the elements for the service. Whenever they are ready, they stand at the door of the church and process in with the elements. It doesn't matter at what point of the service they are ready, if the pastor is preaching or others are singing. They come in when they are moved to bring in the elements.

Only the women prepare the elements, the table, and more. They sing a Muscogee hymn as they process in. This tradition honors the women who first saw the risen Christ. The women are called to care for the elements as a way of remembering the role of the women in the Easter story. Through this act, they continue to tell the story.

The women who encountered the risen Christ were frightened yet full of joy. Jesus empowered them to go and tell the others, which they did. Now we are to do the same. We are called to tell the story of the love of Christ for the world. May we see the magnificence of God as the psalmist shared through our reading this week. May we serve one another through servant leadership. May we work through grief in our lives, knowing the One who brings comfort to all. And may we be about the work of justice for the sake of the world.

O Risen Lord, I begin this day with the joy that I serve a risen savior! Amen.

Believing and Testifying for Jesus

APRIL 6–12, 2026 • MIGHTY RASING

SCRIPTURE OVERVIEW: As humans, we rely so much on our senses that it is sometimes difficult to believe something we have not directly experienced. We may not have seen Jesus, but through the words and actions of his followers, we experience his love and grace. In Acts, Peter quotes the psalm, boldly sharing about God's presence in human life and the powerful expression of that presence in Jesus. The verses in First Peter point to the inheritance that God has in store for us. God's grace sustains us when we face trials. Lastly, the passage from John shows Jesus meeting Thomas where he was while stressing the importance of believing even without seeing him.

QUESTIONS AND SUGGESTIONS FOR REFLECTION

- Read Acts 2:14a, 22-32. Whose faith story has influenced you in your faith journey? Who can benefit from listening to your faith story?
- Read Psalm 16. Reflect on a time when you encountered a disaster. What prayers did you utter? How did God answer your prayers? How can you be an answer to the prayers of others experiencing a similar situation?
- Read 1 Peter 1:3-9. What trials have you faced that eventually strengthened your faith?
- Read John 20:19-31. When have you wrestled with doubt? How did other Christ followers help you deal with deep faith questions?

Mighty Rasing is a published author, blogger, and lifelong United Methodist. Born and raised in the Philippines, he moved to the USA in 2015 to serve with Discipleship Ministries. He also writes poetry and fiction in his native tongue, Ilokano. He lives in New Braunfels, TX, with his wife and their three boys.

MONDAY, APRIL 6 ~ *Read Acts 2:14a, 22-32*

I loved listening to my grandmother's stories. I marveled at how she and my grandfather crossed the Cordillera Mountain Range in the Philippines to move from the western side to the eastern side of Luzon Island before the building of wide and paved highways. I've only read about World War II, but she told me how her family experienced and endured the Japanese occupation in the 1940s and how the American armed forces eventually helped the Philippines win the war.

My grandmother's experiences took place several decades before I was born, and it was fascinating to connect her stories to my own journey and to the history and developing story of the Philippines.

In today's reading, Peter stands up and preaches to the crowd. That was not an easy thing to do given his humble background. But he encountered something special and life-changing when Jesus called him to follow. He experienced, first hand, the life and ministry of Jesus. He saw Jesus preach, heal the sick, confront hypocrisy, and show compassion to so many. Peter even walked on water with Jesus. He also connected the story of Jesus to the bigger story of God's people, and he saw God's promise fulfilled in the resurrection of Jesus.

As an eyewitness to the life of Jesus, the words of Peter carried weight. The Holy Spirit was working in him, giving him strength and courage to proclaim what he had seen and heard. The Holy Spirit was also at work in the hearts of the people listening to him. In the same way, when we tell our story as Christians who follow Jesus, the Holy Spirit works in us, as well as in the hearts of those who listen.

Dear God, thank you for the courage and strength of your followers who testify and live out their faith publicly. Help me to do the same. Amen.

I grew up in the northeastern part of the Philippines, which is visited by about twenty typhoons annually. When we heard the forecast on the radio, we would hunker down for a day or two and wait for the typhoon to arrive. The sky would go dark as heavy clouds rolled into our town. Strong winds would buffet the trees and batter the roofs of houses. Then the heavy rains would fall, marching incessantly along roofs, roads, fields, and rivers. While strong typhoons were passing through, I remember my father and mother—both United Methodist pastors—praying for God's protection over us, our church, and the community we lived in.

When the sky cleared and the typhoon left, we would discover a trail of destruction. One time, a tree in our yard was uprooted. At another house we lived in, one edge of a piece of galvanized iron roof was rolled up. Still at another time, flood waters came into a room in our house. Elsewhere in the community, it was often worse: Rice fields ready for harvest were flooded; livestock was washed away; and in some cases, lives were lost.

Every year, stronger storms bring devastation to thousands of people around the world. We cannot avoid the destruction brought about by these natural disasters, and often all we can do is pray and flee to a safer place. We can cry out to God for refuge just like the psalmist. While dealing with the aftermath of such disasters, God can show us the way of life through the support of friends, family, and even strangers. I'm always amazed at how people work together cleaning up debris, making repairs, and encouraging one another. After all, God often answers prayers through the people around us.

Lord, provide succor and protection for those who suffer from the effects of natural and human-made disasters. Amen.

WEDNESDAY, APRIL 8 ~ *Read John 20:24-31*

Do you remember the early days of social media? If you had a baby or got a pet, went to Disney, a beach in Thailand, or climbed the Eiffel Tower in Paris, you *had* to post it on social media. I posted about the food I ate, the places I visited, and any new experience I had. My friends and I often joked that if we had an experience—good or bad—and we didn't post about it on social media, had it even happened?

In the first century, Thomas was not present when the other disciples encountered the resurrected Christ. In the absence of smartphones, cameras, and social media, people relied on good, old fashioned stories passed by word of mouth. But Thomas wanted more than that: He wanted to see and feel the wounds of Jesus. Thankfully, Jesus met him where he was and showed him his wounds. Thomas believed and exclaimed, "My Lord and my God!"

Just like Thomas, we often want proof before believing, before committing. I sometimes wish to have a supernatural experience like seeing a burning bush, hearing an audible word from God, or experiencing some kind of miracle. Those experiences are few and far between, though. I am reminded of Jesus' words to Thomas: "Blessed are those who believe without seeing me."

The people around us may not see the actual, physical Jesus. But they can see him through stories from the Bible, through our words of encouragement, through the stories of how God has been working in our lives, and through our acts of kindness. We can follow the example of Jesus when he healed the sick, fed the hungry, set the captives free, and showed compassion to all kinds of people. The world may not see the physical form of Jesus, but they can see the resurrected Christ in each of us who follow him.

Pray for those who struggle with doubt and with deep spiritual questions.

THURSDAY, APRIL 9 ~ *Read 1 Peter 1:3-9*

When I was a child, my parents would often encourage me to study well because education, they said, was the only inheritance they could give my siblings and me. While public school is almost free in the Philippines until high school, it can be expensive to support a child through college. Even then, the support of the parents might not be enough.

I have had my fair share of challenges and difficulties in pursuing this inheritance. My monthly allowance from my parents would sometimes be delayed. In my third year of college, I wanted to shift to another degree program, but I could not. It would have meant staying in college an extra year, and we could not afford that. Some of my peers sometimes skipped meals to make ends meet while others unenrolled for a year or longer to earn funds for their education.

It took me four years of hard work to graduate from college, fighting off distractions and persevering through challenges. I knew that once I graduated, I could build a career that would support me and my sense of mission in this world. Thankfully, with support from my parents, extended family and friends, and working part-time as a freelancer, I was able to afford and finish college. My parents were proud, and I knew that I had done my part in working for this inheritance of education.

Today's passage speaks of a priceless inheritance, one that we can not yet see but that God has in store for us. This inheritance does not mean an easy, carefree life here on earth. We must endure trials, trials that will challenge our faith but will lead to wonderful joy. We may not be able to see the fruit of this inheritance right away, but we can trust Jesus who is faithful and who walks with us.

Lord, help me keep my eyes on you and on the inheritance you have for me when the trials come. Amen.

FRIDAY, APRIL 10 ~ *Read Acts 2:32*

In 2006, I was elected as the national president of the United Methodist Youth Fellowship in the Philippines (UMYFP). I headed a small team of young people who were in charge of producing resources for youth work in the Philippines, running meetings and leadership conferences, and implementing projects. It required a lot of hours. I also had a full-time corporate job, which I felt was a good career track for me. However, the workload became more and more challenging and I came to the point where I needed to choose between these two commitments.

I weighed my options. I prayed. Then I talked to friends and other youth leaders who had held the position before me. Many of them shared stories of God's faithfulness and provision as they served as full-time volunteers in the UMYFP.

We are surrounded by stories. We accept some stories more readily than others because of our relationship with those who tell the stories. The more we trust the storyteller, the more we accept the truth of the stories we hear. In Acts 2, Peter preached to his fellow Jews and residents of Jerusalem, sharing the story of Jesus: his life, suffering, death, and resurrection. He bolstered his testimony by saying that he and the other disciples were "all witnesses to this." Some people doubted and claimed they were drunk. But also about 3,000 people were added to their number that day. I imagine that these 3,000 trusted and accepted the story and testimony of Peter and the disciples.

I ended up resigning from my corporate job. I trusted the stories of other youth leaders and friends that I talked to. But more than that, I trusted God and ended up experiencing firsthand the goodness and provision of God after saying "yes" to serving.

What stories from others have supported you in your journey of faith?

SATURDAY, APRIL 11 ~ *Read 1 Peter 1:6-7*

One afternoon in my second year of college, I had a deep conversation with a friend about college, life, and faith. Before we parted, he asked me a difficult a question: "If you lost everything, would you still follow God?" It was a pretty serious question for my 19-year-old self. I wasn't ready to delve into it.

On my way back to my dorm room, my phone kept buzzing with text messages. A fire was raging near where I lived. I was getting worried. And when I arrived, I saw the charred remains of my home: only the facade remained. My jaw dropped and my knees buckled. Everything I owned at that time was burned—my books, a small TV, all my clothes, cassette tapes, my old journals, term papers I was working on—all of it had been lost to the fire. The only thing I had left was the guitar I had borrowed from a friend and the clothes I wore that day.

Today's reading talks about our faith being tested "as fire tests and purifies gold." Let me tell you, it's not easy to go through the testing of fire. But when we endure trials, our faith remains strong, and when we cling to the grace and promise of God, we emerge victorious, joyful, and wiser.

After the fire, friends from my campus ministry helped me get back on my feet. My father came from the province to Manila and treated me to a shopping spree. I got new clothes and everything else I needed. I was thankful for this cloud of witnesses who served as God's hands and feet to me when I was going through the fire. But more importantly, I knew and felt that God was there walking with me as well.

What fires have you gone through in your life? How did God walk with you through those fires?

SUNDAY, APRIL 12 ~ *Read John 20:19-29*

Have you ever had an experience so incredible that when you shared it with friends, they did not believe you? Imagine being one of the disciples who discovered the empty tomb on Easter morning. Imagine seeing Jesus appear several times in different places. But when you share with the other disciples—particularly Thomas—that Jesus is risen, they don't believe it. I can almost see the reaction of Peter with his usual impulsiveness and brashness. I can imagine the reaction of brothers James and John who, at one time, fought about who would get to sit beside Jesus. When your sharing is met with skepticism rather than excitement, it can dampen the excitement you feel.

When we share stories and testimonies about our faith and experiences with God, not everyone will believe. Some will echo Thomas and say, "unless I see it or experience it, I will not believe!" Anticipating this reaction could sometimes be enough to keep us silent about wonderful things God has done in our lives.

The disciples were sure of what they saw and experienced: They were witnesses to the wonderful things that Jesus did during his life and ministry, as well as the things that happened after his suffering, death, and resurrection. They talked about it and shared it with their family, friends, and even with strangers.

Sometimes sharing our story and experience of faith is enough. We can trust that Jesus works in the hearts and minds of people around us. This is what John Wesley, the founder of Methodism, called prevenient grace: the kind of grace that draws people to God even before they commit to following God. Some people will doubt, some people will question, but we share our stories of faith anyway with confidence, love, and compassion.

Lord Jesus, help me share my story and journey of faith with the people around me. May they see and feel your love through me. Amen.

God's Promises

APRIL 13–19, 2026 • MEG LYBECK-SMOAK

SCRIPTURE OVERVIEW: The scriptures this week are rooted in the promises of God for the people of God. In Acts and Luke, the promises of God's love evident in the sacraments of baptism and Communion are uplifted. The psalm speaks of God's promise to be with us, even—and especially—during times of suffering when we call out to God in prayer. First Peter claims God's promise to be faithful to us, as we humans are in turn called to be faithful to God and to live out our faith in communities of God's beloved.

QUESTIONS AND SUGGESTIONS FOR REFLECTION

- Read Acts 2:14a, 36-41. As you think about your baptism, how have the vows you made (or that others made on your behalf) brought you closer to God and to claiming God's promise of love in your life?
- Read Psalm 116:1-4, 12-19. When have you cried out to God in prayer during a time of suffering in your life and experienced God's promise to hear your petitions?
- Read 1 Peter 1:17-23. How do you witness God's promise of faithfulness to you when you respond by living your faith in community?
- Read Luke 24:13-35. When has the celebration of Holy Communion opened the eyes of your heart anew to God's promise of salvation for you?

Rev. Meg Lybeck-Smoak serves as the Pastoral Care Director and an ACPE Certified Educator for a long-term care community in Milwaukee, WI. She enjoys spending time outdoors, traveling, reading, and being with her spouse, two daughters, and other family and friends. Meg is an ordained Elder in the Wisconsin Conference of The United Methodist Church.

MONDAY, APRIL 13 ~ *Read Acts 2:38-39*

I was raised in a family active in The United Methodist Church. Though infant baptism is common in the denomination, my family decided not to have me baptized until I was older. When my friends from eighth grade youth group began confirmation classes in the fall season, I did too. I learned about the history and traditions of our denomination within Christianity. I wrote a faith statement, which helped me discern and claim my own beliefs within the church.

That spring my friends decided to confirm for themselves the vows taken for them at their baptisms. I chose to be baptized in the church at the confirmation service. My baptism was more than thirty-five years ago, and I still remember the sacred moment when my pastor made the sign of the cross on my forehead with the baptismal waters.

In today's scripture, Peter tells the people, "Repent and be baptized every one of you in the name of Jesus Christ so that your sins may be forgiven, and you will receive the gift of the Holy Spirit." Baptism for Christians is a sacrament of initiation into new life with membership into the community of faith in Jesus. Peter's call to repentance also speaks to a radical change of mind and spirit for those who choose to follow this call. When we repent and choose to come back to God from the sins that separate us from God and others, we are restored to right relationship in the family of God. Our repentance means that God's promised blessings may be realized in our lives. This promise is for all who believe.

Gracious God, we give you thanks for your promise to always be with us, through the gift of the Holy Spirit, given to us through baptism. Amen.

TUESDAY, APRIL 14 ~ *Read Acts 2:14a, 36-41*

Peter's sermon in today's scripture passage occurs on Pentecost, and he appeals to the crowd with passion and conviction by saying, "Therefore let the entire house of Israel know with certainty that God has made him both Lord and Messiah, this Jesus whom you crucified." The scriptural narrator tells us those present are "cut to the heart," and they ask, "What should we do?"

When we separate ourselves from God and others, we want to know how we can make things right. On a recent rainy Monday morning, I was feeling cranky and entirely out of sorts. Our family had accidentally overslept that day, and in our rush to get out of the house on time, I had spoken harsh words to my spouse and teenage daughters. I had also missed my quiet devotional time with God because of our shortened morning routine. I felt very disconnected.

At the retirement community where I serve as a chaplain, we have a beautiful ecumenical chapel. Between services that day I found the chapel empty, and I decided to go and sit for a few moments. While I sat there, breathing deeply, I listened. It took a few moments to quiet my thoughts, but once I did, I heard the lovely "shuush" of the raindrops falling on the chapel roof. The sounds of the rainwater reminded me of God's promises through the baptismal waters. I asked God to forgive me for my distance from God and my impatience with my family. Immediately I could breathe more deeply and felt at peace. I later texted my loved ones and apologized for my bad mood. The rest of the day I felt more connected to God and to my community.

Forgiving God, thank you for calling us to repentance and offering us your forgiveness through Jesus, in whose name we pray. Amen.

WEDNESDAY, APRIL 15 ~ *Read Psalm 116:1-4*

The subtitle of Psalm 116 is "Thanksgiving for Recovery from Illness." The psalmist begins with words of devotion for God, "I love the LORD because he has heard my voice and my supplications." I am struck by the power of this proclamation, because only in three other places do the psalms specifically speak of love for God: Psalm 5:11, 31:23, and 40:16. As Psalm 116 continues, we understand that love for God grows out of God's fulfilled promise to save the psalmist's life.

I once suffered with a bad case of stomach flu. Neither food nor fluids would stay down for four days. I felt terrible: weak, nauseous, dizzy, sharp stomach pains, and a pounding headache. I cried out to God in prayer multiple times, asking to be delivered from my suffering. I prayed as the psalmist did, "O LORD, I pray, save my life!"

On the fifth day of my illness, I awoke and felt better. I tried a tiny sip of water, and amazingly it stayed down. As the day continued, I regained my strength and was able to feel well. Knowing that God had been with me throughout that difficult time and had heard my prayers gave me hope that when I call on God, I will be heard.

In verse 2 of Psalm 116, the psalmist affirms that because God has listened, a life-long commitment has been established. We pray to God always, in good times and in bad. That is true in our human relationships, as well. When we love someone, we are in constant conversation with them. We speak and are listened to, and they speak, and we listen to them. So it is with God.

Healing God, thank you for the promise that you always hear us when we pray. We love you, God, and trust in your promise to turn our suffering into abundant life. Amen.

THURSDAY, APRIL 16 ~ *Read Psalm 116:12-19*

Psalm 116 focuses on thanksgiving to God for the blessings God has given us. The psalmist wonders how to fully express the deep gratitude felt when God's promises to us are fulfilled. In verse 13 lifting the "cup of salvation" references the Jewish tradition of blessing four cups during the Passover meal in celebration of the Exodus. In the Christian sacrament of Communion, we too lift the cup of salvation as we remember Jesus' sacrifice for us to fulfill God's promise of forgiveness of sins and eternal life.

In both verse 14 and verse 18 of Psalm 116 the word "vow" is used, in which the psalmist vows, or promises, to give thanks and praise to God for all that God has done for us. Verse 17 of the psalm says, "I will offer you a thanksgiving sacrifice and call on the name of the LORD." At the time I am writing this meditation we are preparing to celebrate the Thanksgiving holiday in the United States. Thanksgiving is a time in which many people set time apart from the everyday to gather with loved ones and intentionally give thanks to God for life itself and for all of God's blessings. As a result of this gratitude for God's blessings, we may also feel called to respond by sharing our time and gifts through acts of service to others.

This psalm is traditionally read on Holy Thursday, because of its connections to Jewish Passover and Christian Communion. Psalm 116 reminds us of God's promise to give us life and life abundant. Because of God's gracious promise to us, people of faith vow to give thanks and praise to God in return, and we vow to serve others as visible signs of our faith.

God of promise, we are grateful for all that you have done and continue to do for us. Help us to respond with gratitude to you by serving others in Jesus' name. Amen.

FRIDAY, APRIL 17 ~ *Read 1 Peter 1:17-23*

It is easy for us to focus on the material things of this world. Every day we go to work, drive the kids to school, cook meals, prepare for the next day, and try to get enough sleep. Then we get up the next day and do it all over again. These things are important, and we need to pay attention to them. But when our focus on the physical is so narrow that we fail to see the wider spiritual realm, we separate ourselves from God.

Today's scripture from 1 Peter is a reminder that our holy God calls us to be holy people. This letter of encouragement to faith communities claims our call: From the foundation of the world God has destined us to be God's people. As members of God's family, God has destined Jesus to redeem us. God's amazing work in Jesus as Savior of the world is mirrored through God's works in us as those who live out faith and hope in our lives. We are called not to be consumed by the "perishable" things of this world (silver or gold, in verse 18) but to live new lives which are "imperishable," embodying the "living and enduring word of God."

First Peter calls us to respond to God's promise of faithfulness by being faithful to others. We are to live with "genuine mutual affection" and to "love one another deeply from the heart." Loving others deeply, genuinely, and with mutual affection is not easy to do. We live in a polarizing time, politically and religiously. And yet our call as people of faith is not to focus on that which is perishable but to broaden our perspectives to the imperishable.

God of hope, help us to focus our whole being on your living and enduring word. We seek to live out our faith by loving one another as you love us. Amen.

SATURDAY, APRIL 18 ~ *Read Luke 24:13-29*

Luke's Gospel account of the walk to Emmaus in chapter 24 is a powerful example of God's promise to be with us always. Nothing in this life, including death, can separate us from God's love. Yet at times we struggle to recognize God's presence in our midst.

In today's scripture two of the disciples are walking along the road and talking about the recent events of Jesus' trial, crucifixion, and his body's disappearance from the tomb. As they go along someone comes to join them. The Gospel narrator tells us this third person is Jesus himself, "but their eyes were kept from recognizing him."

The colloquial thinking is that seeing is believing. But sometimes we see God and still do not believe. God is in the beauty of the sunrise, in the smile of a loved one, in the laughter of children, and in the kindness of strangers. Yet how often do we bear witness to such occurrences? How often do we fail to see God's presence with us through these events?

As the disciples and their traveling companion come to the end of their journey, it is close to evening. The man with them walks ahead as if to continue on alone. This action reminds us that Jesus does not force himself upon others. It connotes that faith is a voluntary response to God's grace. The disciples invite him to remain with them—"Stay with us, because it is almost evening and the day is now nearly over"—and he accepts their hospitality. God is with us, always, even when we fail to recognize God's presence.

Immanuel, God with us, thank you for the reminder that nothing can separate us from your love. Help us to recognize you in all the people and events we encounter each day. We pray this in Jesus' name. Amen.

SUNDAY, APRIL 19 ~ *Read Luke 24:30-35*

At the beginning of today's scripture passage, Jesus reveals himself to the disciples through Communion. "When [Jesus] was at the table with them, he took bread, blessed and broke it, and gave it to them. Then their eyes were opened, and they recognized him."

When we gather with our faith community around the Communion Table, our invitation is the same as that given to the Emmaus disciples: to recognize God's promises to us. As we take the bread and cup, remembering that Jesus gave himself for all of us, we may see God in a new way. We see not only with our eyes but also with the eyes of our hearts. When God opens the eyes of our hearts, we may accept the promise of forgiveness of sins and life eternal with God, through Jesus.

The disciples present at the meal excitedly ask one another, "Were not our hearts burning within us while he was opening the scriptures to us?" With renewed insight into God's promise of redemption through scripture and Jesus' actions through celebrating Communion, the disciples spread the good news of Jesus' resurrection: "The Lord has risen indeed."

Our call as modern-day disciples of Jesus is the same now. We gather and feast on God's good gifts of salvation with the sacrament of Communion. Then we take that good news out into the world and share it through our words and actions. "Then they told what had happened on the road and how he had been made known to them in the breaking of the bread."

Saving God, we are grateful for your promises of forgiveness of sins and life eternal with you. Help us to see and accept these promises anew each time we gather for Communion. May we share this good news of your promises in all that we say and do, always. Amen.

The Abundant Life

APRIL 20–26, 2026 • MAGREY R. DEVEGA

SCRIPTURE OVERVIEW: Each of the passages this week describe different and complementary aspects of the life of faith. In Acts, we see Christian community in its infancy, when the first Christians gathered to share in the power and wonder of God. In the iconic Psalm 23, we see ourselves as sheep in the fold of God's provision, receiving care and courage to endure the valleys of life. In 1 Peter, we remember the sacrifice of Jesus, whose woundedness guarantees our healing. And in John's Gospel, we hear of Jesus as the gate through which we can be in a full and life-giving relationship with God. Taken together, these passages remind us of essential qualities—wonder, care, courage, healing, and salvation—that comprise the abundant life.

QUESTIONS AND SUGGESTIONS FOR REFLECTION

- Read Acts 2:42-47. Imagine what it was like to be in the first Christian community. What aspects of their activities do you see evident today? How can you recapture a sense of awe and wonder for God?
- Read Psalm 23. What memories do you have of reading and hearing this psalm throughout your faith journey? When has it brought you comfort? In what ways do you identify with the various scenes of this psalm now?
- Read 1 Peter 2:19-25. What does the cross mean to you? What difference does it make for you to acknowledge and embrace the sacrifice that Jesus made for you?
- Read John 10:1-10. How has Jesus been a good shepherd to you? How has he been the door through which you have experienced abundant life?

Rev. Magrey R. deVega is Senior Pastor of Hyde Park United Methodist Church in Tampa, FL. He is the author of thirteen books, including *Questions Jesus Asked: A Six-Week Study of the Gospels* (Abingdon Press, 2023).

MONDAY, APRIL 20 ~ *Read Acts 2:42-47*

In the wake of Pentecost, we find the early Christians conducting activities familiar to faith communities today: fellowshiping, breaking bread, singing songs, learning and growing, serving others. But before they undertook any of these programmatic aspects of Christian community, they experienced awe and wonder.

Unlike the corporate actions of fellowship, discipleship, and service, which they could initiate and create together, the sense of awe and wonder had to "come upon them" from God. It came from a source external to them. They could not manufacture it; they had to be open to receiving and experiencing it.

This invites a question for individuals and churches: When is the last time you have felt awe and wonder in regard to God and your faith? In fact, how often do you sense awe and wonder in any aspect of your life?

When we began to emerge from the COVID-19 pandemic, we longed for wonder and became more attuned to it. We traveled to national parks like never before. We relished the joy of being together like never before. We learned to appreciate the simplest things in life with greater attentiveness than ever.

This scripture passage invites us to be more intentional about sensing the awe and wonder that is all around us, in every moment. We can make it a goal every day to pay attention to the wondrous moments—from the breathtaking to the subtle—which we attribute to God, offering these blessings upon us. It may require disengagement from the stressors of life, temporarily unplugging your conscious attention to these challenges and inviting moments of exercise, rest, or creativity. This will allow the genius and imagination of our subconscious to awaken us to the surprises and serendipities that are all around us. Pay attention to the awe and wonder of God all around you.

God, open our eyes to your awe-inspiring presence and power all around us. Amen.

TUESDAY, APRIL 21 ~ *Read Acts 2:42-47*

The first time Christians gathered in community—before there were impressive sanctuaries, paid professional staff, and denominational structures—they focused on four essential communal practices. They worshiped together. They grew in their faith by learning together. They cared for one another in fellowship. They engaged in service to others. These comprise the four core practices of Christian community: worship, grow, care, and serve. They are rooted in four of the most important Greek words in the New Testament that describe the activities of the early Christians: *Kerygma,* meaning "proclamation." Christians gather to proclaim the good news of Jesus Christ, often in the context of worship. *Didache,* meaning "teaching." Christians gather to deepen their discipleship through study, learning, and training. *Koinonia,* meaning "fellowship." Christians gather to care for one another and strengthen bonds of love and prayer. *Diakonia,* meaning "service." Christians extend the reach of God's love to those in need in their communities and around the world.

For any church to be healthy and balanced, all four of these activities should be conducted with equal vitality. A church without inspiring and God-honoring worship becomes too much like an exclusive social club. A church without effective disciple-making processes becomes too shallow in its commitments and convictions. A church without fellowship becomes too prone to divisive infighting. And a church without effective missions and outreach becomes too focused on its own needs. If any one of these four pillars is missing or out of balance, it is like a table with a short leg or a car with a flat tire.

How would you characterize your church's effectiveness in each of these areas? And how can you help improve them?

God, thank you for the gift of community. Guide us in becoming the church you have called us to be. Amen.

WEDNESDAY, APRIL 22 ~ *Read Psalm 23*

Tucked amid the tranquil images of Psalm 23, between green pastures, still waters, and an eternal dwelling place, there is this inescapable reality of life: the valley of the shadow of death. We cannot skip past it, because it is in the middle of the psalm. Literally and literarily, it is right in the middle.

My friend and terrific preacher James Howell notes a very important shift in this psalm in the way the psalmist refers to God. In the beginning of Psalm 23, the psalmist refers to God in the third person, as if talking about God. "The LORD is my shepherd." "He makes me lie down." "He leads me." "He restores my soul."

But somewhere along these six verses, the psalmist shifts the reference to God from the third person "he" to the more intimate, more direct second person "you." It is as if the psalmist has made a conscious decision at some point to not just talk *about* God but to talk directly *to* God, in a deeper, more personal connection with God. "Your rod and staff . . . comfort me." "You prepare a table." "You anoint my head."

That is a remarkable shift. And where does that happen in this psalm? Yes, right in the middle, right in the valley. This points to one of the central truths in this psalm. It is in the valley that we can experience God most closely and most personally. As painful and as inescapable as the valleys of our lives are, they can be and often are the most transformative moments in our lives, for that is where we discover a relationship with God who is with us. "Yea, though I walk through the valley of the shadow of death, I will fear no evil: for thou art with me" (KJV).

God, thank you for journeying with me through life's highs and lows. Even when I am in my darkest valleys, thank you for being with me. Amen.

THURSDAY, APRIL 23 ~ *Read Psalm 23*

In modern day Israel/Palestine, just east of Jerusalem, there is a wilderness called the Wadi Qelt. It is a deep valley, surrounded by steep, imposing cliffs dotted with caves and crevices. One can easily imagine how threatening the Wadi Qelt was thousands of years ago. It was a dangerous place to walk, especially alone, with the constant threat of wild animals and thieves lurking behind every corner.

According to Jewish tradition, this is the place where the psalmist was inspired to write the Twenty-Third Psalm. Not overlooking some green pasture or tranquil water. Not in a place of serenity, but of danger and fear. This was the place where the psalmist realized that his entire view of God shifted. God was not distant or absent, largely disconnected from his suffering, but was close by, whose rod was there to ward off bandits and wolves, whose staff was there to rescue him when he was in danger.

Biblical scholar James Limburg offers a fascinating bit of insight into Psalm 23. In the King James Version of this passage, the phrase "Thou art with me" is exactly in the center point of this psalm. Twenty-six words precede this phrase, and twenty-six words follow it.

This psalm is, in itself, a literary valley in which all the tranquil moments of our past (pastures and waters at the beginning of the psalm) and all the hopeful dreams of our future ("the house of the LORD" at the end of the psalm) converge in the center of the psalm, in the crucible of our darkest valleys. The psalmist would remind us that only when we go through those painful moments can we experience the one truth that will enable us to experience both tranquility and hope: "Thou art with me."

God, thank you for being with me amid the hardest moments of my life. Thank you for your rod and staff, which comfort me. Amen.

FRIDAY, APRIL 24 ~ *Read 1 Peter 2:19-25*

Go to any local bookstore and you will likely find a section titled "Self-Help," entirely devoted to ways to improve a person's life. Book after book guides us toward maximizing our mental, physical, emotional, and relational strength. Publishers crave the opportunity to sell the next bestseller teaching the masses how to help themselves. It works in selling books, and there is something to be said for wanting to improve yourself. But in matters of sin and salvation, here's the bottom line: Self-help does not save.

Passages like today's remind us that Jesus did for us what we could not do for ourselves.

In one of Rembrandt's most famous works titled *The Three Crosses*, we see a glorious depiction of Jesus on the cross with the two thieves at his side. It is rendered in stark grays and blacks, except for the inbreaking light from the heavens, signifying God's holiness cast into a world of sin.

Off in the shadows of the image is a figure. You can barely see the person, except for his hands, burying his face. He appears grieving, overcome with emotion.

Many art critics have concluded that this person is none other than Rembrandt himself. He included himself in this scene as a way of acknowledging that he deserved the fate of the cross; he was responsible for sins that put Jesus there. The figure is therefore not just expressing grief or guilt but also gratitude to God. Rembrandt recognized that Jesus took his place and did for him what he could not do for himself.

In matters of sin and salvation, self-help does not save. God has given to us an amazing gift: salvation through Jesus Christ.

Gracious God, thank you for Jesus, and for what he did for us on the cross. May we live our lives in grateful response and commitment to you. Amen.

SATURDAY, APRIL 25 ~ *Read John 10:1-10*

In Jesus' day, shepherds lived on the fringes of society. So, for Jesus to name himself as the Good Shepherd in this text may have been a shock to the original hearers of John's Gospel. He was, in effect, saying that he would become the object of ridicule and scorn in much the same way that common shepherds were. These words would have upended the expectations of John's audience.

But here is the more surprising reversal by Jesus. The conventional wisdom was that the shepherd would often surrender his sheep for the slaughter, both for food and to be sacrificed in the Temple, so that people could restore their relationship with God. But in John's Gospel, Jesus flipped that conventional understanding upside down. He declared himself as the one who would "lay down my life for the sheep . . . I lay it down of my own accord" (10:15; 18)

This Good Shepherd was not going to lead his sheep to slaughter but would allow himself to be the sacrifice, to die in their place.

No wonder his critics did not understand him. How could the sacrificer become the sacrificed? It just seemed so hard to believe. But in the grand scope of the gospel message, it makes perfect sense. For Jesus not only gave himself up for us; he then empowers and calls us to give of ourselves for others. Through Jesus' act of self-giving, he shows us how to take up our cross daily and follow him. For "No one has greater love than this," Jesus said, "to lay down one's life for one's friends" (John 15:13).

So, what things in your life need to die in order for others to really live? What call to sacrifice is Christ giving to you?

God, thank you for sending Jesus, who gave himself up for us. Strengthen me to do likewise, offering myself in service to you and those around me. Amen.

SUNDAY, APRIL 26 ~ *Read John 10:1-10*

Jesus set up a dichotomy between two different kinds of influences on our lives. One leads to life and the other to destruction. Which influence will we allow into our lives? Which "door" will we choose?

I remember the game show *Let's Make a Deal*. The host, Monty Hall, would offer contestants a chance at taking home whatever was behind the doors they chose. Depending on their selection, they received either a fabulous prize or a comical dud. Wouldn't that show have been a whole lot easier if contestants could have received a sneak-peak behind those doors? That's not the way the game worked, and that's not how life generally works. But Jesus gives us an advantage. He said, "I am the door" (NKJV). Behind this door is life—abundant, hopeful, and healthy life, the kind that God intends for us. That's the kind of life Jesus came to give us.

Behind Door #2, though, is the thief. In broad terms, the "thief" is anything that would distract us from receiving the abundant life that Jesus can give us. It is anything that prevents us from experiencing the forgiveness, freedom, and joy of God's image alive within us. What are the thieves in your life that threaten to "sneak in, steal, and destroy" you? Maybe it is a brokenness in your relationship with others, or a failure both to forgive and to be forgiven. Maybe it is a constant worry about your future, or a nagging addiction that is damaging you or others. Or maybe it is a confrontation with your own mortality.

Here's the good news. You don't have to choose those doors sight unseen. You know what's behind them already. So, choose Door #1. Choose Jesus, who is the door that leads to abundant life.

God, enable me to choose the abundant life you have for me. And strengthen me to turn away from all that prohibits me from choosing you. Amen.

God Is a Trustworthy Refuge

APRIL 27–MAY 3, 2026 • PUMLA NZIMANDE

SCRIPTURE OVERVIEW: The readings for this week have the common thread of dependence upon God. In each reading, someone is facing hostility or suffering. In Acts, Stephen is stoned to death for his belief in Christ. In John's Gospel, the disciples struggle with Jesus' prediction of his death. Peter tells the scattered believers not to fear despite the hatred in society, and the psalmist cries to the Lord for rescue from his persecutors. Yet in each text is also a turning point toward God for the solution to the suffering. God is a trustworthy refuge who will sustain all people through the difficulties of life. Turning to God shapes our response to suffering.

QUESTIONS AND SUGGESTIONS FOR REFLECTION

- Read Acts 7:55-60. Think of a time when you were victimized and hurt by people. How did this make you feel? What is the likelihood of you pronouncing Stephen's words, "Lord, do not hold this sin against them"?
- Read Psalm 31:1-5, 15-16. When have you experienced God as a refuge and rock in your life?
- Read 1 Peter 2:2-10. Think of a baby drinking milk from a mother. Draw parallels between God as mother and yourself as the baby. What images and thoughts come to mind as you focus on this idea?
- Read John 14:1-14. In what ways are you troubled? Take time to be still and to bring the matters that trouble you before God in prayer.

Rev. Pumla Nzimande is the Presiding Bishop of the Methodist Church of Southern Africa. She is a liberation theologian and an advocate for justice, practical ecclesiology, and transformation. She is known for developing, mentoring, and equipping leaders.

MONDAY, APRIL 27 ~ *Read Acts 7:55-60*

Stephen was a faithful follower of Christ and a church leader who performed great miracles and wonders through the Holy Spirit. These great acts and miracles posed a threat to the order of the day, and he was accused of blasphemy. He was brought before the Sanhedrin, the council of the nation, to plead his case or face death. Even with this threat hanging over him, he continued to preach what was deemed to be offensive to the Jewish interpretation of scripture.

The anger of the Sanhedrin reached its climax when he claimed to see the heavens open and the Son of Man standing at the right hand of God. This was enough to infuriate the Sanhedrin to the point of wanting him killed. Believing that their interpretation of scripture was supreme, the accusers turned to Leviticus 24:13-16, which prescribed stoning as the appropriate form of punishment for blasphemers. Stephen was dragged out of the city and stoned to death.

Stephen suffered through one of the most painful methods of punishment, but he did not fight back or seek to escape. Instead, he submitted his spirit to the faithful hands of God. He believed the glory that awaited him after death far surpassed his present suffering.

Mob violence is real and continues to happen in our world today. An increasingly common form of mob violence is found in digital spaces where people are bullied and shamed. While digital spaces preclude the physical results of violence, the emotional trauma can be as damaging. When violence—emotional or physical—is inflicted on us, we are invited to find shelter in God. It is from God that we gain the strength to press on. Stephen prays and petitions for his offenders. He dies the death of a faithful servant who trusts in the faithful God who is our refuge.

Lord, help me to face suffering and pain in the confidence that in you I have a refuge and helper. Amen.

TUESDAY, APRIL 28 ~ *Read Psalm 31:1-5*

From the outset the psalmist declares their full trust and dependence in God. The psalmist further pleads with God for deliverance from being put to shame.

I recall the fear that I experienced as a young girl when approaching an adult for help. I was taught that children must be seen and not heard. To me this meant that I should hold back any requests for help. One day during the cold months of the year, I lost my school jersey. For days I suffered and went to school without a jersey because I was too afraid to approach my parents and own up to having lost it. I thought that I needed to suffer in silence rather than risk making my needs known. Eventually, I plucked up enough courage to speak to my parents and state my case. To my surprise, they were already aware of my need and had a new jersey for me in the cupboard. All that I had needed to do was speak to my parents and confess. I could not believe that I had suffered so much when my parents had already provided for my needs!

God is a good parent who provides for our every need. It is not always easy to approach God with our needs, but we are encouraged to come before God and to make our needs known through prayer. We become more confident in approaching God when we regularly spend time with God and develop faith and trust in God's supremacy. God provides for our every need. God comes to our rescue. Approach God with confidence knowing that God is your provider and refuge.

Lord, "great is thy faithfulness! Morning by morning new mercies I see, and all I have needed thy hand has provided. Great is thy faithfulness, Lord, unto me" (UMH 140). Amen.

WEDNESDAY, APRIL 29 ~ *Read 1 Peter 2:2-3*

The author of First Peter draws parallels between children of God and newborn babies. Similar to babies who need milk for their sustenance and well-being, Christians need the spiritual milk that will nurture us and help us grow in our salvation.

Christians understand Christ's salvation as deliverance from sin and its consequences. Such deliverance is brought about by faith in Christ. When we experience salvation, we become like newborn babies in the gospel, alive in Christ and yet needing to grow day by day into his likeness. Without spiritual milk, we will never mature into Christians who can resist temptation and sin and live out our calling in the church and the world.

The writer encourages believers to hunger after the things of God and not the things of the world, which are fleeting and offer no contribution to spiritual growth. What is our spiritual milk? These are the things that facilitate our spiritual growth, also known as spiritual disciplines: prayer, meditation, solitude, fasting, Bible study, journaling, service. The more we practice these disciplines, the more they nourish our souls and strengthen our walk with Christ. God our refuge has provided all that we need in order to grow in discipleship. As a mother holds and feeds her newborn, God holds us and wants to see us mature in our faith. All that God asks of us is that we latch onto those edifying things that help us grow in faith.

Thank you, Lord, for your salvation plan. I commit myself to feeding on your word and to the practice of spiritual disciplines so that I may grow in my walk with you. Amen.

THURSDAY, APRIL 30 ~ *Read 1 Peter 2:4-10*

The imagery of a building being erected calls to mind the process by which stones are chosen. Stone workers choose from the available stones, finding those that fit together well and provide strong support from the foundation up. Not all stones fit the builders' needs. A cornerstone is particularly integral to the strength of a building. These special stones are chosen carefully to ensure the success of the project. Here the writer of First Peter gives specific attention to a stone that has been rejected by the builders, and yet this stone becomes the cornerstone for the building. In the same way, Christ is the cornerstone for our salvation.

The writer says that we too are being built into a spiritual house so that we may become a holy priesthood. Through this text we are reminded that we are a spiritual lighthouse, a beacon of hope to our broken world so that people may find refuge in us. It does not end there: Resounding throughout the text is our call to be a royal priesthood; a people consecrated into the service of God; a people called to sing praises to God in thought, word, and action; a people called to holy living. The privilege of this calling does not happen through our own strength and knowledge but through Christ who has reconciled us to God so that we may be called children of the light.

Christ the chief cornerstone is still rejected by many today as people live their lives without a personal relationship with him. It becomes our duty to call people out of darkness into his wonderful light so that their lives too may be built upon the solid rock.

God, my Refuge and Strength, help me in my living and dying to reflect your grace and call all into the joy that I have found in you. Amen.

FRIDAY, MAY 1 ~ *Read Psalm 31:15-16*

The Greeks understanding of time is twofold. *Chronos* refers to quantitative time that is measured by clocks, and *kairos* is time that cannot be quantified but is measured by its quality. *Kairos* refers to an opportune time, a moment, a God-appointed time and season. When the psalmist says "my times are in [God's] hand," the psalmist speaks of both *chronos* and *kairos*. *Chronos* measures the days allotted to us by God, and *kairos* speaks of the schedule on which God releases God's plans for us at God's appointed time.

When we live a life of submission to God, we surrender to God's will and direction for our lives, and that includes the way we use our time. It seems that twenty-four hours in a day is no longer sufficient. People are always in a hurry to get from one place to the next, to beat the red traffic light, to save a few minutes here or there. Instead of causing us to slow down, the COVID-19 pandemic thrust us deeper into the Fourth Industrial Revolution, a period marked by the ever-increasing merger of our physical and digital lives. Now many of us work from home, blurring the lines of our lives even further.

God is drawing us into moments of order, discipline, and stillness so that we can make the best of each moment while-looking after our spiritual, mental, and physical health. We may work harder and harder each day, but if we do not commit our time to God, we will chase after the clock and miss those *kairos* moments of being pleasantly surprised by God. Look and wait in anticipation for those *kairos* moments, and do not allow the race of life to deprive you of them.

Help me day by day to live in the awareness that you are at work in my life. Quiet the noise in my heart so that I can see you more clearly. Amen.

SATURDAY, MAY 2 ~ *Read John 14:1-7*

The disciples had journeyed with Jesus for three years throughout his earthly ministry. They had heard him speak on many occasions of his death and resurrection. All this talk of separation from their leader caused the disciples great discomfort and distress. As Jesus prepares to leave them, he reassures them that such separation is temporal and that reunion will come. It is encouraging to know that at the end of our life's journey, we have a home. We have a place that has been prepared for us.

The disciples were worried about what had not yet transpired. Just the thought of separation was enough to cause them concern. Sometimes we worry about the future: We fixate on what could go wrong, and we want to control the outcome. Jesus consoles his disciples and assures them that the separation is not eternal. This is a text of comfort and also a text of trust. We are called to trust that all things will work out for good in the end. We are called to trust that Christ, our friend and Lord, will never abandon us but will always provide a way for us to be reunited with him and reconciled to God. There is always a way home to God.

While this text speaks of a way to God beyond the grave, there is a way to God even in this life, through Jesus Christ who is the way, the truth, and the life. We are called into fellowship with God through him. We do not have to wait until after death in order to enjoy this relationship with God.

Dear God, help me find the way back to you so that I may enjoy the warmth and acceptance that is found only in you. Amen.

SUNDAY, MAY 3 ~ *Read John 14:8-14*

Christ made many references to God the Father while with his disciples. It is only natural that the disciples would want tangible, visible proof of God's existence. In the verses prior to these, Christ has comforted the disciples and stated that he is the revelation of God. This, however, did not stop Phillip from requesting to see God.

The desire to engage our human senses in experiencing God is natural. How I wish we could touch and see God; how I wish we could actually hear an audible voice. Unfortunately, our human senses are limited. Our physical experiences are not the ultimate expression of certain realities, in particular the spiritual ones. It takes faith and spiritual discernment to believe and trust in the unseen and yet existing things of God contained in scripture and confirmed by the witness of the Holy Spirit in our hearts.

Christ came as God incarnate so that in his living and dying, rising, and reigning we may get glimpses of the nature of God. The witness to the personhood of Christ, both human and divine, is a revelation of the nature of God. In the Gospels we learn that Christ accepted the poor and marginalized; exemplified love, joy, and humility; and modeled self-control, wisdom, and compassion.

All these reveal the nature of God to us, for Christ reveals God. We don't get a simplified image of God in scripture, yet through Christ we know even more fully the love and grace of God.

Jesus, help me to encounter you through scripture, nature, and my fellow siblings in creation. Through a life of witness, help me to reveal you to those who have not encountered your all-embracing love. Amen.

God's Great Gifts

MAY 4–10, 2026 • MARTIN WILES

SCRIPTURE OVERVIEW: Three of our passages this week touch on what God has done for us. Paul, in the Acts passage, confronts people who made space to worship an unknown God, apparently in an effort to cover all of their bases. He tells them who this unknown God is. First Peter relates the work of Christ on the cross and beyond, culminating in his resurrection. These two passages focus on God's work through Christ, and the psalmist, writing before the coming of the Messiah, praises God for all God has done. Finally, Jesus, in the John passage, reminds us of an added gift believers now have: the Holy Spirit. The Easter season gives us an opportunity to reflect on God's great gifts to us.

QUESTIONS AND SUGGESTIONS FOR REFLECTION

- Read Acts 17:22-31. What would you tell someone about God if they knew little or nothing?
- Read Psalm 66:8-20. What are some things for which you praise God?
- Read 1 Peter 3:13-22. How have you suffered for taking a stand for Christ?
- Read John 14:15-21. How do you experience God's continual presence with you through the Holy Spirit?

Rev. Martin Wiles is a teacher, pastor, author, and freelance editor who is the husband of one, the father of two, and the grandfather of seven. He pastors Buffalo Baptist Church in McCormick, SC.

MONDAY, MAY 4 ~ *Read Acts 17:22-31*

At this point in Acts, Paul is on his second missionary journey and has visited Thessalonica and Berea. Some welcome his message; others reject it. Yet Paul has viewed nothing that compares to Athens. Pagan idols and altars abound—even one to an unknown God. Paul begins to preach about Jesus and his resurrection. It seems some are willing to listen, but when Paul begins to speak of Christ's resurrection, this is too much for others and they walk away (v. 32). For Paul, Jesus' resurrection is the most important part of the story.

We put a lot of focus on Easter Sunday. When I was growing up, attending the sunrise service at my father's church was a typical part of my family's Easter celebration. I remember new clothes, putting extra effort into our appearance, and arriving at church much earlier than usual. We often saw folks we seldom saw throughout the rest of the year. Weather permitting, we might even celebrate outside where we could see the sunrise. We always made Easter into a special day.

But Easter is not just one day. This week marks the sixth week of the season of Easter, which lasts until Pentecost. And truly, our Easter celebrations should last throughout the whole year. God provides opportunities for us to explain to others why we celebrate God's greatest gift. We often speak of Jesus' life and death, but his resurrection is an essential piece of the puzzle. In fact, in another of his epistles, Paul discusses how important Christ's resurrection is for our Christian journey. He claims if it did not happen, our faith would be in vain, our forgiveness would be null and void, and our eternity would be jeopardized (1 Cor. 15:14). As we near the close of the Easter season, let's remember to celebrate Christ's resurrection and our gift of telling the world about it year-round.

God, thank you for resurrecting your son to life and empowering us to tell others about your amazing gift. Amen.

TUESDAY, MAY 5 ~ *Read Psalm 66:8-17*

I should have observed white blazes on trees everywhere I looked, both behind and ahead, but I didn't. One of the hallmarks of the Foothills Trail, which runs along the border of South and North Carolina, and of the Appalachian Trail, which extends from Georgia to Maine, is the white blazes. These small rectangles of white paint on trees or rocks mark the path. But on one section of the Foothills Trail that my daughter and I hiked, we had traveled miles without seeing a blaze. We had our guidebook, which indicated we were traveling in the right direction, but we could not be sure without the blazes. We both breathed a sigh of relief when we finally saw one. The marking helped us know we were not lost.

Throughout the Hebrew Bible and in this psalm, God reminds people of crucial markings which should elicit praise for God's great gift of deliverance.

One marking came when God delivered the Hebrews from four hundred years of Egyptian slavery. In Egypt they languished under harsh rule and ravenous persecution. But their blaze came in a man named Moses. No sooner had they escaped Egypt than they faced the Red Sea. Again, they saw a blaze when God parted the sea so that they could cross over on dry land. The psalmist recalls these stories from the Israelites' past and considers them and other markings as reasons to praise God. These signs throughout their collective history remind them of God's presence and confirm their journey as the one God has designated.

God gives many great gifts, all of which deserve our praise. God is the author of all good gifts, from creating us to guiding us by the Spirit to providing wisdom and strength. God physically delivered the Israelites but spiritually delivers us today through forgiveness. Make a list of gifts for which you can praise God.

God, your gifts are too numerous to count, and I praise you for every one. Amen.

WEDNESDAY, MAY 6 ~ *Read Psalm 66:18-20*

Once upon a time, before the internet and satellites, AM/FM radio provided needed entertainment on long car trips. I remember listening to the radio on vacations with my family. My dad would set the radio station to the one we typically listened to around town. But when we got fifty or sixty miles down the road, the station began to sound different. The signal wasn't as strong. Eventually, I could not even hear the station, or if I could, it wasn't the same station I had initially listened to. It might even be playing a different genre of music. And if we went under a bridge or passed through a tunnel, the music would disappear completely. Distance and other things interfered with us picking up the signal from the station's tower. The only cure was to move back toward the station or find another one we could tolerate.

The psalmist claimed that God would not hear him if he held sin in his heart. The psalms fluctuate between fact and feeling, sometimes making them appear confusing or contradictory. Of course, God cannot not hear as humans do. Instead, the psalmist describes his interpretation of how God feels when the psalmist refuses to repent.

God loves us unconditionally and always provides forgiveness when we ask. But when we turn from God and get too far away, it is like trying to hear a distant radio station. We can no longer hear God's Spirit speak to us clearly because we have created distance or barriers in our lives.

The cure comes through prayer. Make a daily practice of spending time with God, speaking honestly and listening carefully. Keep the airways clear.

God, I thank you for your promise to forgive me when I ask. Help me turn to you consistently. Amen.

Once a member and leader of the Communist Party in India, my friend now ministers to women and orphans. We have corresponded through social media outlets for years. Meeting Jesus transformed his life, but his decision did not come without a price. He regularly updates me on what God is doing in his area of the country. Progress, however, comes with a cost.

I will never forget one short video he sent to me. It showed a group of missionaries on their way to deliver a trunk load of Bibles when some members of the Hindu nationalist party stopped them. The extremists assembled the Bibles in a pile on the ground and set them ablaze. Then they assaulted the missionaries. Although my friend regularly shares stories of how God brings many to faith in Christ in the area where he works, the success stories are often interrupted with horrifying stories of suffering.

Throughout the Bible and the annals of Christian history we read stories of Christians who have suffered and even died for their faith. Jesus is our supreme example. As wholly innocent, Christ did not respond to his oppressors with violence, even healing when violence was committed in the midst of his arrest (see Luke 22:50-51). The example Jesus set in his suffering was to not return violence for violence. Here in 1 Peter, the writer indicates that those who abuse Christ's followers will answer for their actions and reminds us that it's better to suffer for doing good than for committing evil.

Suffering is not inevitable. But should we face suffering, at least we can face it knowing we are blameless. We are not called to be silent in our suffering, but to proclaim our faith in Christ and follow Christ's path of peace, even in the face of violence.

Jesus, help me to follow in your footsteps of peace, even when I face suffering for your cause. Amen.

FRIDAY, MAY 8 ~ *Read 1 Peter 3:18-22*

As I neared retirement age, I began passing on some of my treasured family heirlooms. I wanted to determine who received what, and I made those decisions based on their personalities and interests.

Giving away my things wasn't easy. I had to adopt a mindset of mortality. I had more years behind me than before me. At some point, I would die. But these treasures contained a type of DNA for me. My grandparents, aunts, uncles, and father had touched them. If analyzed, I might see their fingerprints. Some of the items my relatives had built. A part of them inhabited each knickknack or piece of furniture.

I explained the history of each gift to my children and grandchildren, telling them who it belonged to and how the person was related to them. For some of the items, I had to explain the purpose. I wanted them to treasure my treasures as I did and, hopefully one day, pass them along to their children.

The writer of 1 Peter tells how, through the gift of the incarnation, God bent down to humanity, giving Jesus in order that we may inherit salvation. Through Christ's legacy, we are brought to God.

Like my desire that my relatives would pass on my treasures, God desires that we do the same with the benefits of the Incarnation. We accept the forgiveness and pass on God's "bending down" to others. We put our fingerprints on the prize but realize we do not really own it. It belongs to all people. Don't forget to pass along what God has given you in Christ.

God, I am forever grateful for the gift of Christ. Empower me to share that gift with others, telling of your love and mercy that is available to each and every person. Amen.

SATURDAY, MAY 9 ~ *Read John 14:15-21*

I can only imagine the look on one of my children's or grandchildren's faces were I to give them a present with nothing inside. Initially, they would show excitement, especially if they were young—a present from Mom, Dad, Meme, or Pop. They might pause long enough to see who it was from, but then they would tear into the package, wondering whether it contained something from their birthday or Christmas wish list.

But suppose I had put nothing in the box—just wrapped an empty container. The glow on their faces would soon vanish. The grandchild probably would think my mind was slipping or I'd just forgotten because of my age. My children might assume I was playing a cruel joke on them.

Jesus promised a gift that his followers could not see. It might have seemed like an empty box to them at times, but the present would be far from a disappointment.

Jesus often hinted at what lay ahead for him and other believers, but most who heard him were slow learners. Many imagined a conquering king, not a suffering servant. Finally most understood, but disappointment set in. Their container felt empty. Jesus, however, soothed their fear and sorrow, promising that he would send a Comforter, the Holy Spirit, to abide with them after his return to heaven. They would not be able to see the Spirit, but they would feel its presence in their lives and realize the fruit of God abiding through their actions and ministry.

God's gift of the Spirit enables us to do God's work. The Spirit produces love, joy, peace, patience, goodness, faithfulness, kindness, and self-control, combined with unique spiritual gifts given to each person. Together, we possess a powerful gift from God that gives us comfort in turmoil and courage to do God's work. Let God's great gift move you into God's plan for you.

God, help me depend on your Spirit to do your work. Amen.

SUNDAY, MAY 10 ~ *Read Acts 17:22-31*

Full-service filling stations were not only places where everyone went to fill their vehicles with fuel. When a customer pulled up to the pump, an attendant appeared, asked how much fuel the person wanted, and then filled the tank. The attendant also checked the oil level, cleaned the front windshield, and checked the tire pressure while the tank filled.

Later, convenience stores with gas pumps became popular, but these weren't full-service stations. Customers pumped their own gas, which made prices cheaper. But we lost the one-on-one interaction with the attendants and drove around in vehicles with dirty windshields, low oil, and low tire pressure. Full-service stations became more and more rare.

As Paul walked the streets of philosophical Athens, he noticed a plethora of gods. One statue was even entitled "To the unknown God," maybe just in case they missed one. Paul, however, told them about a "full-service" God. This God was the one for whom they had no name.

Self-service is the name of the game these days, and there's certainly nothing wrong with doing something ourselves if we can. Google and YouTube are excellent instructors. Some things, however, require full service. Our spiritual life is one of these—we need the full-service God Paul preached about. And full service is one of God's great gifts to us, providing us salvation, grace, forgiveness, guidance, and accountability.

In response to God's gift, we are called to be in full service for others. As God fully serves us, God also wants us to turn and serve others. Doing so entails serving with the right motives, coming from a place of sharing the gift we have received.

Holy God, may I always depend on you for guidance and support as I share your gift with others. Amen.

Chaos Versus Control

MAY 11–17, 2026 • ABBY K. NORMAN

SCRIPTURE OVERVIEW: Despite the fact that this week comes between Easter and Pentecost, two celebratory feasts, the passages this week do not feel very celebratory. In fact, they all point to a liminal space in which the speaker proclaims that God is in control, while also admitting that things feel very chaotic. In Acts, Jesus ascends, once again defying the hopes of his followers for an earthly kingdom. This scene recalls Psalm 68, where the Lord rides on clouds. In the Gospel, Jesus anticipates his departure and prays for his followers. Peter talks about a trial testing Christians. It is easy to gloss over suffering and confusion as we move between two seasons that highlight the power of God. This week allows us to acknowledge we are not the first people to sit in the discomfort of this liminal space. It is not impossible to hold both of these truths at the same time.

QUESTIONS AND SUGGESTIONS FOR REFLECTION

- Read Acts 1:6-14. When have you experienced the power of community?
- Read Psalm 68:1-10, 32-35. Recall a time when you recognized God's power. How might that have been a foretaste of God's kingdom? What hopes are expressed in this passage?
- Read 1 Peter 4:12-14; 5:6-11. What hardships are described that feel similar to your experiences today?
- Read John 17:1-11. What does it mean for you and your congregation that Jesus prayed for unity among his followers?

Abby K. Norman lives in Atlanta, GA, with her college sweetheart turned husband and their two hilarious teens. She spends her working hours teaching at a micro-school for neuro-diverse kids and being the head wrangler of the youth and children at her beloved church, Eastside. She believes that if we are going to have a world that loves one another, we have to raise kids who know they are beloved. When not working, she runs her mouth on the internet under the handle @abbynormansays on all platforms.

MONDAY, MAY 11 ~ *Read Acts 1:6-14*

The disciples got surprised again. After the shock of the Crucifixion and the delight of the Resurrection, Jesus literally floats off into the sky. I know it is easy to think of the disciples as dolts that never could figure out what was happening, but in their defense they were pretty consistently living in unprecedented times. Their savior and friend died, was buried, and rose again.

Even with his multiple warnings, why wouldn't the disciples continue to think that Jesus was going to be with them forever? And then one day, poof, he is in the sky and gone. They are aghast, agog. What in the world do they do now? Literally what in this world are they supposed to do when Jesus isn't here anymore? The angels couldn't be more clear: Friends, he will come back how he left. So in the meantime, it is time to get back to work.

Recently America experienced yet another unprecedented election season. On voting day my friend and I distracted ourselves from fretting about the election results by getting our sanctuary ready for the next season. At the end of the day, we were still proud of the work we had done. The next day as I went to work as a middle school teacher of neurodiverse kids, I was glad that was the work I was doing. It turns out that the times are often unprecedented, but the work to which we are called remains the same. When Jesus comes back, or our political will is fulfilled, or the normal we wish for is returned to us, I hope that time finds us doing the work God is calling us to do.

God, we don't always know what to do. We feel shocked and surprised; we freeze like deer in headlights. Show us our one next step. Be with us as we get back to work. Amen.

TUESDAY, MAY 12 ~ *Read Psalm 68:1-10; 32-35*

Psalm 68 provides a beautiful description of God's restorative work. God is described "as a father to the fatherless, a defender of widows" (v. 5). These verses share a beautiful redemption story, where people are restored relationally—the lonely being restored into families—and also systemically—the prisoners set free with song. It describes God going out before God's people, rain in the desert, an abundance of showers and a bounty that is designed for the poor. This sounds pretty great, right?

As a literature teacher I teach that in certain texts the start of the passage happens before the first written words. The events implied before the beginning of this passage is really where this psalm begins, which leads to some questions. Why is the psalmist asking God to arise, to show up? Where has God been? And when God shows up, why is this writer asking God to scatter their enemies? What are the enemies doing?

The psalmist envisions enemies well-organized and in formation close by—a terrifying prospect. What must the psalmist be feeling when they ask for their enemies to be scattered? I empathize with this writer. I often don't see any good news. In my darkest moments it does feel like the enemy of everything I have ever wanted for this world is well-formed and closing in.

When the forces of darkness feel like they are winning, I can spiral very fast. Yet this is not the direction the psalmist takes. Instead, the psalm imagines a God who makes a way for a more beautiful and just world. The doom and gloom fall away, and the hope of what could be and how God will make it so becomes the focus.

Lord, help me to see the ways you want to break through, even—especially—when it feels like my enemies are closing in. Amen.

WEDNESDAY, MAY 13 ~ *Read 1 Peter 4:12-14*

Peter is writing to first century Christians who live in a very precarious situation. They experience persecution, from verbal slights by neighbors all the way to difficulty getting jobs or selling goods at market. It's unclear what the "fiery ordeal" Peter speaks of in verse 12 actually references, but suffice it to say they do not have it easy.

Peter acknowledges these hardships. He is in no way spiritually gaslighting his readers, telling them that God is in control so they should be happy or that everything is actually fine. Peter reminds them that their suffering has purpose. They suffer alongside Christ, who experienced the ultimate suffering. Peter reminds his readers not to be surprised when a world that has always been radically hostile to Jesus and his message continues to be so. The persecution of God's people is not new.

Christianity today has come a long way from the humble roots nurtured by Peter and his fellow disciples, but those of us who follow Christ today may still face challenges to the choices we make—sometimes even by other Christians. Acknowledging this provides me comfort in my own unprecedented time that actually is more precedented than I want to admit. I can remember that I am not the first person to feel like everything around me is unsure. I can rejoice in the fact that while the world is the same, I have been changed, so maybe the world has changed because I am in it. Isn't that the way Jesus works?

God, help me to remember when times are especially hard, that this is not the first time you are experiencing this unrest. You have always been faithful to your people. Amen.

Ascension of the Lord

Who do we think we are? No, really. Who do we believe ourselves to be? I grew up the third sister in a trio of girls who happened to be good at mostly the same things. We were all in honors classes, preferred English classes to math classes, sang in the choir, marched in the band, and tried out for the musicals. By the time I got into high school some of my teachers didn't bother to learn my first name, simply calling me Ms. France. At times this was frustrating, but mostly I liked it. The assumptions the teachers were making were true. I did like words and music and being in the plays. By thinking I was good at these things and having the adults in my life reinforce that belief, I grew into more of who I wanted to be. I became the story we were all telling about me.

As Christians, who do we think we can become? That question can only be answered in the context of who we think God is and what we think God can do. Remember, this letter was written only one generation after Jesus was resurrected. Perhaps no one receiving this letter saw the Resurrection in real time, but likely they met someone who did. Though Paul, the author, did not see the Resurrection, he had a powerful interaction with Jesus that changed him forever. The people that Paul is writing to need to remember who God is and what God does. The Ascension is another glorious event in which God showed us who God is. When we remember who God is, we remember what it means to be made in the image of God.

God, may we ground ourselves in you. We know who we already are thanks to your great power. Remind us who we are becoming. Amen.

FRIDAY, MAY 15 ~ *Read 1 Peter 5:6-11*

I had two babies very close together. Sixteen months is not enough time to forget any of the details of the first time I birthed a baby. Instead of this making me dread the second time around, it made me more excited. I knew what I was getting into this time, and that gave me great comfort. I did it before. I could do it again. Was it going to be hard? Yes. Was it going to be painful? Yes. Did I know for sure that I was capable of withstanding labor and coming out on the other side clutching a baby to my chest? Also yes. The first time around I had reminded myself of my mother and sister and cousins, all the women in my life who also had experienced childbirth and come out victorious. The second time, I reminded myself of my own experience.

Knowing that there would be pain involved helped prepare me for childbirth. No one goes into a birthing class and hears, "Oh! I don't know why you are here! This isn't a big deal at all!" Part of the preparation is facing the fact that it is going to hurt so you can figure out a way through that pain.

Peter here is reminding us that there are evil forces in this world, and they want us to fail. These forces prefer the unjust chaos they benefit from over the peace of Jesus. Peter is not suggesting we just ignore these troubles. Rather he suggests we face them head on, remind ourselves that we are not the first ones facing hardship, and recognize that believers all over the world are also with us in the hardships. We can take refuge in the truth that we can get through trials just as our siblings in Christ have done. God sustained them and will also sustain us.

Lord, when we are in the middle of the hard stuff, feeling like the enemy is on the prowl, remind us who you are and whose we are. May we be comforted and bolstered by what you have done before. Amen.

SATURDAY, MAY 16 ~ *Read John 17:1-5*

I am a Christmas person. I just love it. Some of the first religious writings I tried out were for the season of Advent. Mary, the mother of God, is my favorite character in the Bible. Everything about her and her life engages my curiosity. With this deep love for Advent and Christmas, I spend a lot of time thinking about Jesus as a baby in a manger, which is why I think this particular passage is a little jarring to me. Even though I know that Jesus is and was and always will be, I need the reminder that it has always been true that Jesus was there when the world began, that Jesus has already taken redemption to completion, that Jesus exists outside of time's constant move in one direction.

This passage speaks to the authority that Jesus Christ has and also what Jesus has already done with that authority. Jesus has saved us. Jesus has claimed us as children of God. Jesus has finished the job, and it ends in glory! This is also an interesting passage because while it highlights the eternal nature of Jesus, it also shows Jesus bound by the time we live in.

Belief in things like the virgin birth, the Resurrection, and the Ascension exist in tension with the daily reality we see with our eyes. This passage reminds me that both can be true—that both have always been true.

God, keep us grounded in space and time, and remind us that you have already won; your kingdom reign already is. Amen.

SUNDAY, MAY 17 ~ *Read John 17:6-11*

Jesus prays for me.

Since I was a little girl, I have sung that Jesus loves me, and I do believe this to be true. But all too often I think we imagine Jesus' love as something that happened a long time ago that we still talk about because it was so powerful. This passage challenges that belief. This passage shows Jesus actively praying, not just for the disciples but for all who believe in him throughout time. Jesus has a prayer list and it turns out I am on it.

Jesus also calls me his, claims all of us who choose to follow him. For the Gospel writer, this is the way our inheritance is passed down: from God to Jesus to the apostles to all who follow who make up the church. Jesus' words encourage his followers not to see his death and later ascension as abandonment, but as fulfillment of his task on earth. Leaving, Jesus passes on the authority to his followers so that the work will continue.

Jesus prays for our unity in that work. This doesn't mean that we are totally symbiotic and operate in full agreement as one mind all of the time. Jesus is praying this pretty immediately preceding the Crucifixion and Resurrection. What we now call Holy Week is littered with moments of Jesus not understanding what God is doing, not wanting to continue, feeling like God has abandoned him. The work that God and Jesus do through the actions of Jesus was not clear and lined out and easy. It was tumultuous and confusing for Jesus at times. So what does that mean for us? It means even when it is hard, one of the tools Jesus gave us to overcome those challenges is one another. We don't always have to agree or even understand fully, as long as we commit to walk with one another until the end.

God, as we look toward the next thing that feels surprising or scary, may we remember that you have gone before us and even pray for us by name. Amen.

In the Power of the Spirit

MAY 18–24, 2026 • DENISE KOHLMEYER

SCRIPTURE OVERVIEW: Many contemporary Christians wrestle with the theology of the Holy Spirit, as there are innumerable facets to the Holy Spirit. As such, the Spirit often remains the most mysterious person of the Trinity. The Spirit is powerful and active, and we understand the role of the Spirit within larger truths about God and God's activities in the world. God empowers the disciples on Pentecost by the Spirit, and the psalmist emphasizes the role of the Spirit in creation. Paul tells the Corinthians that the Spirit enables us to recognize Jesus as Lord and serve one another. John tells of Jesus' promise of "rivers of living water," indicating the coming Spirit. We have much to be grateful for in the presence and power of the Holy Spirit as it empowers us to serve and reach others.

QUESTIONS AND SUGGESTIONS FOR REFLECTION

- Read Psalm 104:24-34, 35b. As a wonderfully made, Spirit-filled member of creation, how do you see yourself fitting into the work of God?
- Read Acts 2:1-21. How are you fulfilling your calling as an ambassador for Christ?
- Read 1 Corinthians 12:3b-13. How does your faith guide you to a tension between sameness and difference that might help you create a diverse unity among your family or faith community?
- Read John 7:37-39. The Spirit pours through us so that we bless others. How will you yield to the Spirit today to bless someone?

Denise Kohlmeyer is a freelance writer and administrative assistant at the non-profit Phil's Friends. She lives with her husband in the Chicagoland area and is a member of Chapelstreet Church in Geneva, IL.

MONDAY, MAY 18 ~ *Read Acts 2:1-12*

Now that Jesus had ascended into heaven, we see that God is doing something different. That something new was the inauguration of the church, of which Peter was to be the rock. But to launch the church, the disciples first must be given power and authority, which were imparted to them on the Day of Pentecost. As they were gathered in a house, a sudden rushing wind filled it—and the disciples as well—so much so that these Aramaic-speaking men began communicating in several foreign languages. Devout Jews who had traveled to Jerusalem from other nations to celebrate Pentecost miraculously heard the gospel being proclaimed in their respective tongues. Utterly amazed and bewildered, they asked one another, "What does this mean?"

What it meant was that these listeners were hearing the wonders of God through Jesus being declared for the first time. And in hearing this good news, they had the opportunity to call on the name of the Lord and be saved (v. 21).

For the disciples, it meant that they were graduated to apostleship ("sent ones") and were now qualified to speak authoritatively on behalf of Jesus Christ. To fulfill this new ministry, they were given the Spirit, who empowered them with the courage to speak God's truths.

What does it mean for us today? As ambassadors of Jesus Christ (2 Cor. 5:20), we too are empowered to share about God's great grace. Through the infilling of the Spirit, we can boldly proclaim the good news. To do so, however, requires daily connection and humility with God. We must pay attention to God's work in our lives and trust the guidance of the Holy Spirit in order to be powerful, effective witnesses for our great God.

God, fill me with your Spirit so that I may unashamedly and boldly declare the wonders of your grace and kindness that lead to salvation. Amen.

TUESDAY, MAY 19 ~ *Read Acts 2:13-21*

While the majority of those who heard the apostles' miraculous proclamations at Pentecost were amazed, some were skeptical and mocked the apostles. "They have had too much wine," they claimed dismissively.

Peter, now filled with the Spirit, was quick to correct these naysayers and pointed them to the prophet Joel—with whom they would have been familiar. Joel had once declared that God did this very thing in days past with the prophets. God had infused them with the Spirit to enable them to prophesy, an act for which many of them suffered grievously.

Now God was doing it again, and Peter was proof. In fact, so profound was Peter's first evangelistic sermon and the outpouring of the Spirit in the hearts of the hearers that three thousand people were baptized (v. 41).

Sadly, skepticism and mockery are still some people's go-to responses upon hearing the gospel. Yet Peter tells us how to respond to hostile detractors. We are not to shy away from engaging with them; nor are we to become argumentative, as we may be tempted. Rather, we are to "always [be] ready to make a defense to everyone who asks you to give an account for the hope that is in you, yet with gentleness and reverence" (1 Pet. 3:15, NASB). The story of Pentecost inspires us to know that the Holy Spirit is God working through us, enabling us to communicate God's grace, love, mercy, and compassion with a self-controlled tongue and gracious speech.

Gracious God, use me mightily to proclaim your good news and your grace that saves through faith. Empower me, by the work of your Holy Spirit, to share this good news with gentleness and reverence, so that others may see your love through me. Amen.

WEDNESDAY, MAY 20 ~ *Read Psalm 104:24-34*

I can get lost in the poetic rhythm of this psalm. The psalmist is extolling God's creation with beautiful word pictures. I can readily imagine the mythical beast Leviathan—elsewhere in scripture painted as a creature of chaos and evil—frolicking like a puppy within the great sea.

Imagery of this kind helps us to understand the creative mastery of God. Creation was not random or disorderly but came about through strategic order and purpose. God created with skill, beauty, and even humor (consider the blobfish or fried egg jellyfish). God also created with the assistance of the Holy Spirit, who was present at the beginning, hovering over the waters before they parted to fashion dry land habitable for both humans and creatures (Gen. 1:2).

The psalmist reminds us too that not only did God create every living creature, but God also sustains them. Everything on earth is dependent on God for breath and bread to survive and thrive. This dependence is beautifully phrased in verse 27, which says all parts of creation "look to you," painting an emotive picture of a child who looks to their parent for safety and sustenance. This beautiful image inspires us to seek a closeness with God, such as we would with a gracious parent who lovingly cares for our every need.

Finally, the psalmist bursts into spontaneous and exuberant worship, singing the praises of the Almighty Creator. "May the glory of the LORD endure forever." As believers we understand, like the psalmist, that this is the right and reverent response to our Creator for the magnificent and mysterious world which is gifted to us.

God, your creation is marvelous and wonderful. I love to delight in it—in the animals, the sunsets, and fellow humans—and in you, most especially, my God and my Creator. Amen.

THURSDAY, MAY 21 ~ *Read Psalm 104:35*

Yesterday's reading demonstrated a believer's response to contemplating and delighting in God's creation. Yet the psalmist acknowledges those who scorn God and refuse to acknowledge God as Creator. They refuse to give God the credit and the glory. Instead, they scoff and spurn God.

Having seen the glory of God's creation, the psalmist is unable to believe that others could continue to not see. Evidence of God is all around: "Ever since the creation of the world God's eternal power and divine nature, invisible though they are, have been seen and understood through the things God has made" (Rom. 1:20). Creation testifies to God's sovereignty and power. God has made God's attributes as plain as the clouds in the sky and the grass on the ground. God is everywhere. One cannot walk outside, even on a stormy day, without observing God's handiwork. Yet some people ignore the obvious. And in doing so, they miss the truth.

We are not exempt from missing the truth of God's creation. Even those of us who proclaim to follow God can miss the mark and refuse to give God credit for all of creation. We miss this mark through both big and small actions, from simply not taking time to notice the gift of God's creation to abusing the earth and devaluing the gift we have received.

Yet our gracious God is always longing for us to recognize the gift and to sing praise. When we pay attention, evaluate our choices and actions, and work to care for God's creation, we, like the psalmist, can exclaim, "Bless the LORD, O my soul. Praise the LORD!"

Oh Lord, how great and countless are your works. In wisdom you made them all. To you alone belongs all glory and power and honor. Amen.

FRIDAY, MAY 22 ~ *Read 1 Corinthians 12:3-6*

I work for a nonprofit and most of the time we work well together when setting goals. But on occasion each of us has a different vision for or opinion about our work. In those instances, unity is lacking. Planning can stall and nothing gets done.

Yet regarding spiritual gifts, God equips us all differently in pursuit of a uniform goal of service. We understand God to be revealed in three ways, as Father, Son, and Holy Spirit. Some identify these three personas as Creator, Sustainer, and Redeemer. Each of these revelations of God complements the others, working beautifully in diversified unity. We understand the Spirit as the distributor of spiritual gifts, the person of the Trinity who empowers individuals with gifts to work for God's purposes in the world. Jesus put into practice those gifts and thus acts as our model of faithful living. He showed mercy to those he encountered; he taught people in parables that pointed to God's kingdom; and he served by healing, feeding, and much more. Now it is through us, his disciples, that these works continue here on earth, through the employment of our spiritual gifts. It is God, then, who controls the divine outworking of our gifts, for "his good pleasure" (Phil. 2:13). God uses our gifts to accomplish God's purposes and plans accordingly.

As manifestations of God, the concept of the Trinity provides us an example of collaboration. As we work with others, we can keep in mind the unified example of the Trinity, setting aside destructive competitiveness and defeatist comparisons and instead seeking unity in our goals and efforts.

Creator, Redeemer, and Sustainer, thank you for endowing us with gifts so that we can do your work in the world. Help us to be faithful in exercising our gifts for the glory of God. Amen.

SATURDAY, MAY 23 ~ *Read 1 Corinthians 12:7-13*

Like I once did, many believers tend to think that our spiritual gifts are about us. Yet nothing could be further from the truth. A cursory reading of today's passage should dispel that immediately. Spiritual gifts are about God, about God's glory, and about the fulfillment of God's plans here on earth. God graciously works through us mortals in that fulfillment and does so by the bestowal of gifts that will accomplish such plans.

We also mistakenly think that our gifts are based on our natural abilities and talents. While the Spirit, the distributor of gifts, may choose to work within those characteristics, our gifts are not dependent on our abilities. Consider Moses, who professed inadequacy of speech (Exod. 4:10). Through the Spirit, he was empowered to express himself articulately and unapologetically when necessary. Spiritual gifts, rather, are manifestations of the Spirit. The Spirit alone is the agent through whom we receive and apply our gifts. And those manifestations are varied and employed differently, according to the person and their respective ministry.

Because our spiritual gifts are just that—gifts—and are intended for God's purposes, we're not to use them for selfish gain or fame. Rather, we are to be trustworthy stewards who "fan into flame the gift of God" with "power, love and self-discipline" (2 Tim. 1:6, 7, NIV), but above all with love for God and others (1 Cor. 13:1-3).

When we consider all of this, we see that we are really working in partnership with God. How blessed we are to be given this privilege.

God, the giver of gifts, let us not usurp your honor in exercising our gifts. Keep us always mindful of you, to whom belongs all the glory and the good. Amen.

SUNDAY, MAY 24 ~ *Read John 7:37-39*

PENTECOST

Today's passage takes us to the Feast of Tabernacles, the traditional time when the Jews erected temporary shelters of branches and palm leaves. The idea was to live inside these makeshift structures for one week and contemplate God's goodness during their ancestors' nomadic wanderings. During those 40 years, the Israelites often found themselves thirsty but without a source of water from which to drink. Every time, God always miraculously provided the water they desperately needed.

Jesus, however, proclaimed that "rivers of living water" would flow from the hearts of those who believed in him, and that they would never again experience thirst. This was something new. Water from the heart? Never thirst again? Jesus, who often spoke in metaphors, was not referring to literal water but was alluding to the forthcoming Holy Spirit, who would take up residence in believers' hearts.

Throughout scripture, water is symbolic of salvation and eternal life. As the third person of the Trinity, the Spirit is responsible for convicting hearts regarding sin, righteousness, and judgment (John 16:8). Simultaneously, the Spirit awakens hearts to the truth of the gospel, which leads to "rebirth and renewal" (Titus 3:5). The Spirit works to transform us into "new creations" through sanctification (2 Cor. 5:17). Over our lifetimes, we are enabled to grow in and abundantly exhibit the "fruit" of the Spirit's nature: love, joy, peace, patience, kindness, goodness, faithfulness, gentleness, and self-control (Gal. 5:22-23), which, when experienced by unbelievers, causes them to be drawn to the Light.

Holy Spirit, may you, the "living water" pouring out of me, be a blessing and a witness to others. Amen.

Created on Purpose

MAY 25–31, 2026 • ANDY CALL

SCRIPTURE OVERVIEW: The readings this week from the Hebrew Scriptures focus on creation—the Creation stories from Genesis and a psalm of praise for God's creative work. But Creation doesn't end there. God is still on the move, creating even in times of transition. Paul's farewell to the Corinthian church reminds them to continue to create space for the things that are most important. The risen Christ bids farewell to the disciples, but not before commissioning them to carry on his work, thereby creating the movement we know today as the church.

QUESTIONS AND SUGGESTIONS FOR REFLECTION

- Read Genesis 1:1–2:4. What does the first story of Creation tell you about God, about humanity, and about our relationship with God?
- Read Psalm 8. What songs come to your mind when you reflect on God's creating work?
- Read 2 Corinthians 13:11-13. When have you had to say goodbye to people you loved? What were the most important things in those moments?
- Read Matthew 28:16-20. If you were with the disciples on the mountain in Galilee when they met the risen Christ, what do you think you would feel? How do you respond to the Great Commission to "make disciples of all nations"?

Rev. Andy Call is the lead pastor of Church of the Saviour in Cleveland Heights, OH, and is serving as the Chair of The United Methodist Church's Commission on General Conference for 2028. He loves to read and to be a part of everything his wife and kids are into, including music, soccer, art, and just plain quality time.

MONDAY, MAY 25 ~ *Read Genesis 1:1–2:4a*

When God began to create the heavens and the earth, the earth was complete chaos. God began to move, bringing order to the chaos, life out of nothingness, light out of darkness. Our first glimpse of God in the scriptural record is a creative movement. God's nature is to create. From that creative energy spills forth light and life. Everything that ever was, everything that is, and everything that will be comes from God's presence in the midst of chaos.

Chaos did not end when God's creative Spirit brought order. That is a reality we know all too well. As I write these words, we are mired in another contentious election cycle, another school shooting has just occurred, wars rage around the world, and economic uncertainty abounds. Chaos remains. It makes us anxious. It makes us fearful. And it can make us lose hope. But we also remember that, even when there was nothing else but chaos, God was there. We trust that God is still present, no matter the chaos we may experience.

Perhaps chaos is even a precondition for creativity to emerge. As beings created in God's image, our creative acts are reflections of God in us, and our creative work is often inspired by a lack of order or structure that prompts us to find creative solutions to the challenges we face. In another way, God may be most free to work among us when chaos abounds because, in that space, we release any illusion we have that we are in control. We rely on God, because God can do what we cannot.

Holy God, creator of all that was, is, and ever will be, we need your creative Spirit. Chaos abounds. But you are still with us. As once you hovered over the waters, move among us and through us to bring forth light and life. Amen.

TUESDAY, MAY 26 ~ *Read Genesis 1:31–2:4a*

The first time someone told me that there was not one Creation story in Genesis but two, I was incredulous. How could that be? The Bible is the story of God and God's people. I had always believed that the Bible was "true," that every word in it was just as God intended it to be. If there were two different versions of Creation, how could both be true? But as I read and reread the first two chapters, it was unmistakable. Genesis 2:4 marks the end of one story and the beginning of another. And they are markedly different.

That discovery was part of an important journey for me, one that changed the way I view scripture and God's revelation to us. What if the Bible isn't without error, whatever we understand that to mean? What if it wasn't meant simply to be received, but wrestled with? Could there be more to discover in these texts than I thought?

Discovering the multiple Creation narratives in Genesis 1–2 led me to a period of my faith development when I began to engage more deeply with scripture—the various threads of material in the "law" and "history" books, the uniquely different perspectives of the Gospel writers, the authorship and perspective of the Epistles. I began to rely less on certainty and more on curiosity as I engaged in reading and learning from the Bible.

Letting go of the need to defend the literal meaning of every passage of the Bible frees us to discover the deeper truth of scripture. Scriptural witness does not have to be factual in order to be true. Approaching scripture this way can seem scary, but in the discomfort is the movement of the Holy Spirit.

Revealing God, help us to approach your word with reverence, but also with curiosity. As we explore the mysteries of scripture, impart to us what you want us to discover about you and about ourselves. Amen.

WEDNESDAY, MAY 27 ~ *Read Psalm 8*

I spent the first half of my vocational life in music—initially as a music teacher, but mostly as a music minister. Because I spent so much time immersed in the music of the church, certain passages of scripture always evoke memories of particular songs, from choral music to hymns to modern worship music.

Sometimes that can be distracting. I'll find myself reading the same few verses over and over again because my consciousness has been following the rabbit trail of some melody. But other times, the music makes the words come to life, and I descend to a deeper level of consciousness that tunes my soul to the frequency of the Holy Spirit's song.

Psalm 8 is one of those passages for me. Michael W. Smith's "How Majestic Is Your Name" rings in the opening verse, and I find myself almost dancing to that playful melody. But as I read on, the music that captures my attention next is Tom Fettke's "The Majesty and Glory of Your Name." "When I look at your heavens, the work of your fingers . . . what are humans that you are mindful of them?" I pause my reading and indulge in a momentary musical detour.

As the music floods my memory and my consciousness, I am immersed in sound. Though I may be alone, I can hear the voices of others singing alongside me, and in those few moments the music takes hold. I become aware of God's transcendence. I soon find myself so in awe that I can only respond with a simple "Alleluia."

God of all our senses, thank you for the gift of music and poetry, of the connections through the arts that make our imagination come alive. Help us to find you in creative expressions that join our hearts with yours. Amen.

THURSDAY, MAY 28 ~ *Read Psalm 8:3-9*

God is big. God is powerful. God can do things we cannot. That can bring us comfort, knowing that God is able to do far more than we can imagine. But it can also be intimidating. In the presence of God's majesty and glory, we can feel small, powerless, inadequate.

The psalmist writes, "When I look at your heavens, the work of your fingers, the moon and stars that you have established; what are humans that you are mindful of them, mortals that you care for them?" In comparison to God's grandeur, how significant are we?

"Yet," the psalmist writes in the next line. That word is the fulcrum on which the psalm shifts. The poetry goes on to say that we matter in God's eyes. God has given us great honor and great responsibility. God created all that is, but God doesn't manage all of it alone. We are not passive observers or mere beneficiaries of life. God elevates our status, drawing us close. But God also expects us to watch over everything else: the beasts of the field, the birds of the air, the fish of the sea. To put it another way, every life is our responsibility—not ours to do with as we please, but ours to care for and ensure its survival.

Why would God do that? Doesn't God know how selfish we can be, how distracted we are, how often we fail? Of course God does! *Yet* . . . that word provides tremendous grace, as well as wonder, awe, and gratitude.

In the face of such generosity, what can we do other than sing our praise as we work to fulfill God's purposes for us?

O Lord, how majestic is your name! Why you choose me to carry such honor and responsibility is a mystery. But choose me, you do. Help me to live up to your hope for me today, to care for your creation, and to honor the gift you so generously offer. Amen.

FRIDAY, MAY 29 ~ *Read 2 Corinthians 13:11-13*

As a United Methodist pastor, I have been called to move a few times, leaving one faith community and moving to another. Leaving is hard. After years of walking alongside a congregation—learning their stories, celebrating with them, sharing their grief, serving together to do holy work—there is pain in the parting.

Paul was not part of a denominational system with guaranteed appointment. He did not pledge ordination vows that included obedience to an itinerant system. He was forging new territory, doing what no one else had done before, planting churches and imparting faith to people who had never heard the message of Jesus before. And unlike us, there were no standard expectations for how a church should function. They had to learn it together, creating a model under Paul's guidance that would shape the life of Christ's followers for millennia.

So when Paul needed to say farewell, what was on his mind? In each of my moves, the final weeks in one place have been a flurry of activity—scheduling transition meetings, finishing projects, copiously reviewing my notes to check that I've written down the things I had intended to document all along but had never managed to circle back to doing.

But Paul? His final words in the Corinthian correspondence were not about things left undone, checklists to be followed, or even about his own work, really. His parting words were a reminder of who they were and the way they should carry on their work. *Be at peace. Work together. Show one another love and grace.* These are the lasting reminders that truly matter.

God of peace, sometimes our path leads us to change. In times of transition, give us grace to trust in your abiding presence. Help us hold fast to grace and peace. Amen.

SATURDAY, MAY 30 ~ *Read Matthew 28:16-17*

This is a surprising inclusion into the story. Matthew tells us that, when the disciples encountered the risen Christ in what would be the last time they saw him, doubt was mingled with their worship. Most translations read, "but some doubted." The updated edition of the New Revised Standard Version is less equivocal. It simply reads, "they doubted."

The disciples doubted. Really? Jesus' most trusted companions, who had seen and heard everything he did, standing face-to-face with him now on the mountain in Galilee, still harbored doubts? And why would Matthew include such a potentially embarrassing detail in his telling of the Resurrection?

Each of us, if we're honest, wrestles with doubt in some form. Maybe we don't doubt the existence of God or the teachings of Jesus, but we probably wonder about some of the details. Did it really happen exactly this way? Why are the Gospel accounts so different? Do I have to believe every word of the historic creeds of the church to be a real Christian?

Doubt is not the enemy of faith, but an essential element of faith. Without doubt, we would have no questions. And if we don't ask questions, how do we learn? Faith doesn't grow deeper by eliminating our questions or having all the answers, but by asking better questions. Instead of searching for proof or wondering if things happened exactly the way one or another person described it, we might ask, "What does Resurrection faith mean?" or "Where do I experience Christ in my life now?"

I wonder if Matthew wanted us to know that the disciples doubted so we would know that it is okay for us doubt too. Their doubt didn't stop them from being faithful. Ours won't either.

God of the journey, help me to be honest about my questions and to trust you with my doubts. Remind me that doubt does not contradict my faith but helps it to grow deeper. Amen.

TRINITY SUNDAY

The disciples worshiped, but they doubted. Doubted what? Jesus was standing right before them, talking to them! What was there to doubt? Maybe Matthew doesn't mean that they doubted whether Jesus had risen from the dead. Maybe their doubts were about themselves. Could they really continue Jesus' ministry without him?

Jesus did not share their worry. Instead, he sent them out with a Great Commission—to make disciples of all nations, to teach and baptize in his name. It was a tall order. And he left no plan B.

By extension, we are called to carry on that same work—to make disciples. Or, as may be more grammatically correct to the original Greek of Matthew's Gospel, *to disciple*. To engage in this work, we must understand what it means to be a disciple, and dive in to how we can best disciple others. To do that, we go back to the beginning: Here at the end of the Gospel, we return to the start to read again the story of Jesus and what it means to follow him.

There is still no plan B. We are Jesus' plan. How does that responsibility feel? Do we wonder whether we are up to it? Do we have doubts about our ability? We're in good company. Even Jesus' closest companions, the ones who had apprenticed under him for three years, had their doubts. But he called them anyway. He calls us too. He calls you.

Best of all, we don't do it alone. Jesus promised to be with us always, even to the end of the age. We are never alone!

God, you must have great faith in me to trust me to carry on Jesus' work. Help me have more faith in myself to do what you ask. Thank you for your promise to be with me always. Amen.

Following God

JUNE 1–7, 2026 • LAURA AUBERRY

SCRIPTURE OVERVIEW: The passages this week share a common theme: They all showcase what it means to follow God. In the four readings, we look at how specific people followed God, from a tax collector to Abraham to a bleeding woman. These readings also explore what following God looks like in practice, such as letting go of our plans, widening the invitation to the table, and creating a community that is united in inclusivity. As we read about these different people who answered God's call and the practices of following God, perhaps our own vision of faith can expand, as well, as we recognize that there is no one way to follow God or one image of perfect faith.

QUESTIONS AND SUGGESTIONS FOR REFLECTION

- Read Genesis 12:1-9. When was the last time you entered an "unknown"? What scared you the most about it? Where is God calling you to go now?
- Read Psalm 33:1-12. What do you seek to control in your life? What does control look like as we follow Christ? How does this passage encourage you to let go of your plans?
- Read Romans 4:13-25. What does unity look like in your community? How does this passage invite you to believe in the unbelievable?
- Read Matthew 9:9-13, 18-26. What does it mean to follow God? When has it been hard to follow God? What's given you hope on your journey of faith? What is the difference between mercy and sacrifice?

Rev. Laura Auberry is a provisional elder serving two United Methodist churches in Belmont, NC, as both a lead pastor and youth pastor.

MONDAY, JUNE 1 ~ *Read Matthew 9:9*

This is perhaps the simplest passage of them all, yet in practice it might be the most complex. What does it look like to follow God? Scripture offers us some answers, but we do not always appreciate where these answers lead to, such as the fiery furnace or the lion's den. Matthew certainly did not know what his journey would entail when he left his position of power and comfort and ventured into the unknown. In our journeys of following Christ, we might feel the same; we do not know where God will take us.

There was only one thing required of Matthew to start his journey of following God. It is the same thing that is required of us—faith. However, faith does not always look the same at every point on our journey. When I answered God's call to ministry, I never anticipated that my experience of greatest doubt would occur in seminary. Some days all I could do was get through the day and press on toward the next. Other days I was so full of the assurance of God's presence that I felt like my faith was spilling out of me. We often consider faith and doubt to be opposites—one can't exist alongside the other. If I have doubts, that must detract from my faith. However, the two are instead like the opposing sides of a coin, inherently interconnected with one another. The deeper we explore our faith, the more doubts we uncover. The deeper we confront our doubts, the stronger our faith can become.

When we answer God's call, we are never sure where it might take us. Faith and doubt both play an important part of this journey, and neither looks the same as when we initially answered that call. Following God is never going to be a straight line. So let us embrace all the curves in our road, because through it all we know that God is with us.

God of all, as I seek to follow you, grant me the strength to continue to take that next step and to answer your call. Amen.

TUESDAY, JUNE 2 ~ *Read Genesis 12:1-9*

Stepping into the unknown requires a great deal of faith; just ask Abraham! He is an elderly man with a barren wife, and God is asking him to leave his extended family and all that he has ever known to venture into the unknown.

How many times do we actually step into the unknown? I am of the generation that grew up with smart phones. There is truly not much information that I cannot access. Every place I plan to visit, I search for information about it online before I even step foot there, looking at where to park, menus for restaurants in the area, coffee shops, etc. We have gotten out of the practice of stepping into unknown situations because the unknown is an uncomfortable feeling. The unknown places us at risk. We respond to this feeling by trying to collect all the information available. Yet that is not always possible, as it certainly was not for Abraham.

God calls us into the unknown to take a risk. It might look like volunteering with the youth program at church for the first time, starting a new job, moving to a new area, or joining a new church. In these situations we cannot search the internet for how things will work out, whether we will like the new church or area, or whether we will succeed at the new job or in the youth program. We might be tempted to think that Abraham's faith is the belief that everything will go perfectly. But, as one reads more and more of Abraham's story with God, we realize that is not the case at all. Rather, let us look at Abraham's faith as a reminder that when we enter the unknown, God is with us every step of the way.

Holy God, grant me courage as I seek to enter the unknown. May I feel your presence surrounding me on this journey. Amen.

WEDNESDAY, JUNE 3 ~ *Read Romans 4:13-25*

God not only calls Abraham to enter the unknown, but God also makes a promise that seems impossible to fulfill. Abraham becoming a father seems, in every sense of the word, unbelievable. Sarah is barren, and Abraham does not seem to have much life left in him.

Faith is often an exercise in the unbelievable. We see this throughout scripture, from the people asking for water in the desert, to a man being raised from the dead, to the resurrection of Jesus Christ. And despite what our passage says, scripture also shows us that sometimes our faith in the impossible wavers, doubt creeps in, and we feel the need to take it out of God's hands and into our own. You only have to go a few more chapters into Abraham's story to see that doubt creep in.

But when we follow God, we put our faith in a God of miracles. When Jesus walked among the people, so much of what he did seemed unbelievable and shocking—from turning water to wine to eating with sinners. All that Christ did seemed unbelievable at some point, including his very presence. Yet Christ's life, death, and resurrection teach us that nothing is beyond God, even conquering death.

Through God, the unbelievable becomes believable. Over 200 years ago it seemed impossible that women, people of color, indigenous persons, LGBTQ+ persons, incarcerated and formerly incarcerated persons, disabled individuals, addicts and former addicts, and so many others could be ordained ministers. Yet so many faithfully answered God's call to ministry, even when it seemed unbelievable and impossible. Through their courageous work, they made it possible for so many others to follow in their footsteps.

God of miracles, may I embrace the unbelievable as I seek to follow you, remembering that through you, all things are possible. Amen.

THURSDAY, JUNE 4 ~ *Read Matthew 9:18-26*

Interestingly, neither the bleeding woman nor the religious leader in this passage are described as followers of Christ. In other Gospels, the leader is named Jairus, a Jewish leader, who would have likely been in opposition to Jesus' claim to be God's son. Yet their stories are examples of faith, so much so that Jesus says to the woman, "your faith has made you well." What does faith and following Christ look like for the bleeding woman and the leader?

Both the leader and the unnamed woman are at one of the hardest moments in their lives. The leader has lost his daughter and the woman sees no end to her suffering. Yet they both take a chance and turn to someone that they do not know, someone they have only heard rumors or stories about, and reach out a hand for help—metaphorically and literally. When we think of faith, we often think of big acts of faith, like leaving one's home and professing to follow God. Yet faith is also taking a chance, hoping against hope, trying one more time. Neither the leader nor the bleeding woman had any reason to believe that their suffering would change. Others likely laughed at them for even trying, as the crowd laughed at Jesus. But they did not let that stop them from trying one more time, asking for help, or reaching that hand out to touch Jesus' cloak.

In the story of a leader and a bleeding woman, we are reminded that following Christ can look like getting up and continuing to hope and try—even when everything and everyone seems against you. Such perseverance is a miracle, one that is as important as the physical healing miracles named in the passage.

Healing God, when I am at my lowest, grant me the strength to try again, to put one foot in front of the other, and to turn to you. Amen.

FRIDAY, JUNE 5 ~ *Read Psalm 33:1-12*

As I read this psalm, I kept coming back to verse 10: "The LORD brings the counsel of the nations to nothing; he frustrates the plans of the peoples." This might be the understatement of the century. As humans, we often plan beyond our limits, because we want to control. We forget that our bodies need rest as we rush around trying to fix every problem, attend every event, and fit another hour of work into an overloaded day. Yet our bodies will eventually crash, as God reminds us that we have limits. We cannot do it all. God frustrates our plans to do so.

Following God is remembering that God is God, and we are not. Nowhere is that clearer than in Creation. It was God who spoke us into being, God who formed land and sea, and God who made the heavens and the earth. Not only do these gifts of creation speak to God's love for us, but they also remind us that the weight of the world does not rest on our shoulders. In a society obsessed with perfection, God's creation reminds us that even when we fail—and we will—life goes on. The sun still rises, the birds still sing, creation moves on. Following God looks like trusting in God, the Creator of all, to hold it all.

When we recognize that to follow God is to trust God, praise for God can take on new forms. It can look like singing and dancing, as the beginning verses of Psalm 33 highlight. It can also look like caring for our bodies, which are made in the image of God. We can praise God through rest, for rest acknowledges that what matters is not the next item on our to-do list, but trusting in God.

Creator God, help me to let go of all that I cannot control and embrace care for myself. Amen.

SATURDAY, JUNE 6 ~ *Read Matthew 9:9-13*

In high school, where you sat in the lunchroom determined a lot about what others thought of you, such as whether you were viewed as popular or unpopular. The worst was having no one to sit with in the cafeteria. Many of us desperately wished for an invitation to sit with someone, because it meant that we were accepted, that we were not alone. It seems that not much has changed since Jesus' time, for we see the Pharisees judging Jesus for who he sat with—tax collectors and sinners, social outcasts in their communities who just wanted an invitation to the table.

But why were the Pharisees upset? Were they upset because of who Jesus invited to the table, or because of what they thought that invitation meant for their place at the table? Perhaps the Pharisees thought the invitation to the tax collectors meant that the Pharisees must sacrifice their own seats. Yet as Jesus reminds us, he desires mercy, not sacrifice. Throughout Matthew's Gospel, Jesus issues the invitation to all—Pharisees included—and the Pharisees are the ones who continually refuse to show up on Jesus' terms. Jesus does not wish that anyone sacrifice their seat at the table, but rather invites all to the table. This inclusiveness is the gift of mercy, an invitation which is extended to everyone.

It can be hard to remember that accepting the invitation to Christ's table means that we might not always like who is sitting next to us. But part of following Christ is recognizing that all are welcome at Christ's table and extending that invitation to all, no matter where they sit in the lunchroom. For God loves all of us, as beloved children of God, made in God's image.

God of mercy, as I accept your invitation to the table, may I see others in my life who are also hoping for a seat at your table, and may I extend your invitation to them. Amen.

SUNDAY, JUNE 7 ~ *Read Romans 4:13-17*

Paul seems to be drawing a dividing line in this passage between those of the law and those who have faith. However, rather than drawing a division, Paul seeks to unite. He paints a vision of a community united by their identity as siblings in Christ and children of the God of Abraham. In this vision for community, law does not determine who is "in" and "out." All are included.

When we think of our shared identity, we must remember that this unity should not erase our individual identities. We are all made in the image of God, which is reflected in our diversity. Our community is broken when we refuse to celebrate our diversity, falling to the powers of racism, sexism, ableism, antisemitistm, xenophobia, homophobia, and transphobia, among many others. These powers seek to divide, placing certain people "in" and others "out."

The prevalence of these powers make this vision of an inclusive and united community seem all the more impossible. But we can find hope in Paul's reminder that we worship a God "who gives life to the dead and calls into existence the things that do not exist." Through God all things are possible, even an end to the injustices which pervade so much of our world. As Christians, we believe that this day will come, when all can flourish in God's kingdom here on earth. Following God means working toward this day in whatever ways that we can. And when the work gets too hard, when we lose hope and begin to doubt, we are reminded that we follow a God who makes the unbelievable come true.

God of love, help me to have faith on this journey to follow you, especially when your kingdom feels far away. May I not be alone on this journey, but turn to your presence and my siblings in Christ. Amen.

Wonder, Love, and Praise

JUNE 8–14, 2026 • WILL MCLEANE

SCRIPTURE OVERVIEW: Life with God leads us into the mysterious depths of God's compassionate love. Like Sarah, we can't help but stop and laugh at how absurdly wonderful God is. In the psalm and the epistle, we discover a God intimately familiar with the ordinary details of our everyday lives. God's grace is continually transforming us and sustaining us in all seasons. In the Gospel, we are interrupted by the Lord, who calls us by name and commissions us as partners in the extraordinary work of healing and hope.

QUESTIONS AND SUGGESTIONS FOR REFLECTION

- Read Genesis 18:1-15, 21:1-7. When have you waited for a long time for God? Amidst the pain of delay, who and what helped you keep your life open to God's surprising blessings?
- Read Psalm 116:1-2, 12-19. How might God's attention to your life change how you talk with God?
- Read Romans 5:1-8. What gifts have you received during seasons of trial and tribulation? How might you live as one grounded in the peace of Jesus Christ?
- Read Matthew 9:35–10:8. How might God's compassion lead you to partner with God's mission in your everyday life?

Rev. Will McLeane is a United Methodist pastor serving at West End UMC in Nashville, TN.

MONDAY, JUNE 8 ~ *Read Genesis 18:1-8*

Disappointment has a particular sting. It can shrink our imagination of what is possible in our world today. It can cut us off from the people who give us life.

Abraham and Sarah have lived through a cycle of monthly disappointment for years. At this point in the story, the promises of God seem far-fetched, like a cruel joke they must tell repeatedly whenever someone asks why they find themselves wandering through foreign lands. And yet they remain open.

In the heat of the day, Abraham sits at the front of his tent with his eyes on the horizon. Seeing three strangers, he runs to them and offers a gracious welcome. At the call of hospitality, Sarah scrambles as she puts together a feast made up of whatever is in the kitchen. In their acts of love, they receive a blessed company that will refresh their hopes.

Hospitality is a practice that opens us to the power and possibilities of God. When we make room in our lives for unexpected company, we often discover that we are the ones who receive the greatest blessing. Especially in seasons of disappointment, may we remain open to receiving the people of God, even when they arrive unexpectedly.

Generous God, help me make room in my heart for the people you love. Open my imagination to the power and possibilities of new and renewed friendship. Extend your expansive love and welcome through me today. Amen.

TUESDAY, JUNE 9 ~ *Read Genesis 18:9-15; 21:1-7*

Sarah could not contain her laughter when she heard the strangers outside the tent renew the promise: Though her womb was barren and her husband good as dead, she would give birth to a son. That promise so filled with adventure when God first called Abram and Sarai to leave home now feels like a distant dream. They are in the middle space. For their hope, they have been laughed at by many.

The stranger interrupts Sarah's laughter with a question: "Is anything too wonderful for the LORD?" The question frames our journey as God's people. So often, God calls us to inhabit a middle space. We pray to become instruments of peace in a world hell-bent on violence. We seek justice for our neighbors even when leaders and institutions of power are not listening. We long for forgiveness, though we do not know the first healing step.

Sarah's laughter is the answer to the stranger's question. God is faithful to the promise. A baby boy is born, Issac, whose very name means, "God made me laugh." A beautiful reversal, Sarah laughing alone in heartbreak, transforms into a joyful exclamation: "Everyone who hears about it will laugh with me" (Gen. 20:6).

The people of God are those who discover themselves laughing with Sarah: the delight of Joseph when he sees his brother's shock at his forgiveness; the surprise of Moses as he opens his mouth and does not stutter but preaches a word of deliverance to Pharaoh; the wondrous surrender of Mary, believing that her ordinary, insignificant life will become the womb of the world's rebirth; the burning heart of Paul as he celebrates the laughable absurdity of the gospel (Rom. 5:6-8). Don't be afraid to lean into their laughter if you are stuck in a middle space today.

Wondrous God, help us to trust that you will make a way when there seems to be no way. Amen.

WEDNESDAY, JUNE 10 ~ *Read Psalm 116:1-2, 12-19*

It wasn't until I embraced the sport of fly fishing that I learned how much I struggle to pay attention. Standing in a clear mountain stream in Western North Carolina, I often guess where the fish swim and what they might eat. Most of the time, the fish are just beneath my feet, and the bugs they eat crawling on my vest! Learning how to read the water and pay attention to the cycle of life has taken me years.

The psalmist calls upon the help of God, who is attentive to our lives. It is a wondrous discovery to behold the God who created the heavens and the earth as One who is also intimately familiar with all the intricate details of our ordinary, everyday lives. God mourns with us at the death of a loved one. God embraces the monotony of work and blesses it so that it might become a vocation. God receives our wild, outlandish hopes and invites us into the "immeasurably more" of God's abundance. In Jesus Christ, God prays with and for us (Heb. 7:25).

Paying attention is at the heart of our spiritual journey. By grace, God forms us into people who are attentive to the hurts and hopes of our hearts, the gifts and needs of our neighbors, and the teeming beauty of creation. Recognizing our needs leads us into prayerful dependence. Likewise, recognizing the gifts God shares with us opens us into a life of gratitude. As you journey throughout the day, may you discover every singing bird, every encounter with a stranger, and every nudge of your heart as an invitation to prayer. Living in the wonder, love, and praise of God begins with paying attention to the needs and gifts that are right before us.

Listening God, thank you for receiving us in our beautiful complexity. In your Spirit, open us fully to the wonder of sharing all of ourselves with you and one another. Amen.

THURSDAY, JUNE 11 ~ *Read Romans 5:1-8*

His voice shook when he said, "In the name of Jesus Christ, you are forgiven." It was the first Sunday for our seminary intern to lead our congregation through the confession, pardon, and peace. The moment's miracle affected him beyond measure. He froze in the lectern as God's people began joyfully moving about the sanctuary, sharing signs of reconciliation. When I went to him to shake his hand, his eyes were filled with tears.

Paul recognizes the miraculous wonder of Christ's peace. Christ's peace is lasting because it is not a function of empire. It is not achieved through violence, dominance, and possession. The peace of Christ is the fruit of selfless love in Jesus, laying down his life for his friends so that we might forever experience communion with God, free of guilt, shame, and the fear of death.

Like a path emerging to a new future, the peace of Christ Jesus grants us a new, shared future in beloved community. Jesus, the Good Shepherd, guides us in becoming agents of peace even when it requires us to travel through the darkest valley in the presence of our enemies. The Spirit nudges us toward practices of truth-telling, confession, and forgiveness even when we cannot imagine reconciliation. Together, the church discovers its future by claiming the peace of Christ in the present. May that peace be a poignant reminder of Christ's love for us.

Gracious God, you know the places and relationships where I struggle to experience your peace. Through your Spirit, nudge me in the way of life so that I might become an agent of Christ's peace. Amen.

FRIDAY, JUNE 12 ~ *Read Romans 5:3-5*

In my first year as a pastor, the church I served experienced a crisis that consumed the community. It was an exhausting series of days filled with tears, anger, and regret at the height of the Advent season. I didn't know how I was going to find the energy to fulfill my pastoral responsibilities and make it to Christmas Eve. Yet I'll never forget the wisdom of an older saint in the community who could see my weary spirit and sought to offer their wisdom: "The Christian life is not an up-and-to-the-right journey."

Times of trouble have a way of becoming all-consuming. Not only do they dash our best-laid plans, but if we are not careful, they can prevent us from being nourished by the fruit of the Spirit and the gifts of the Christian community. They can shroud us in a veil of desperation and despair that robs us of the irrefutable joy of the Lord. They can cut us off from the wisdom of the saints and the loving hands and hearts of friends who will readily offer their aid if we only ask for help.

Romans 5:3-5 gives us a vision of the Christian life wherein our most significant challenges become opportunities for experiencing God's sustaining and sanctifying grace. Problems become a source of pride, not embarrassment. Trouble provides a fitness plan for strengthening our endurance. Character is formed by living off daily bread and taking the journey one step at a time. In it all, we become people grounded in living hope and nourished by God's lavish love.

If you find yourself in a place of trouble today, I invite you to open your hands to receive the gifts of God, and use your voice to ask for help.

Sustaining God, please help me in times of trouble. Please guide me to the people and resources that will nourish me in the journey of grace. Form me into the character of Jesus Christ, in whose name I pray. Amen.

SATURDAY, JUNE 13 ~ *Read Matthew 9:35–10:23*

There is power in our names. Our names tell where we came from, the experiences we have endured, and the person we are becoming. Whether a parent speaks a word of affirmation, a coach or colleague offers a word of direction, or a friend shouts across the street, we sense a stirring deep within our souls when someone calls us by name.

Jesus calls his apostles by name, grants them remarkable authority, and sends them into the world as agents of healing and hope. Fully aware of all their unique particularities and ordinary inadequacies, Jesus trusts them with the extraordinary purposes of God. They will often fail and falter in their work. Yet through it all, God, the one who calls, is faithful. Simon, Andrew, James, John, and the rest of the apostles will go to people and places they could never have imagined, all in the name of Jesus.

God calls you by name too. Before you even get out of bed in the morning, God speaks a word of your belovedness. As you begin your day, God's Spirit shares an invitation to receive your ordinary, everyday life as a place of ministry. God has an imagination for the names and stories of people you can uniquely bless. You will fail and falter in the work, yet God will work wonders and miracles of healing in and through you beyond your imagination. And finally, as the day draws to a close, God will gently encourage you to receive God's rest and trust in God's never-failing care. Every day, God's voice calls us into the wonder of life with the Divine.

Speaking God, help us listen to your voice. Open our lives to receive your word of blessing and faithfully respond to your call to go and bless others. In the name of Jesus Christ, we pray. Amen.

SUNDAY, JUNE 14 ~ *Read Matthew 9:35-38*

When you set out on a mission with Jesus, you quickly learn he stays on the move. Mark's Gospel says that Jesus traveled "among all the cities and villages" (CEB), devoting himself to teaching, healing, and seeing. With Jesus' daily agenda, one can't help but wonder how he even made time for meals!

Yet the Lord's pace of ministry is never so urgent that he is numb to the beckoning call of compassion. Jesus stops, sees the crowds' fullness of hurts and hopes, and knows them as "sheep without a shepherd" (CEB). With such great need, he encourages his disciples not to do more but instead to pray that God will call more laborers of love to share in the mission.

Cultivating a compassionate heart requires us to move at the pace of the Lord. When we fill our days with endless tasks and responsibilities, we leave little space for the gentle invitations of the Spirit to love ourselves and our neighbors. When we convince ourselves that we are the only ones able to help others, we quickly experience fatigue and burnout. Running is great for exercise, but love is a slow, steady walk.

In reflecting on your daily life, ask God what task or responsibility you can lay aside to make room for love. Go for a slow walk through your neighborhood and receive every person and situation you notice as an opportunity for prayer. Pray for the names of people you believe Jesus is calling into God's mission of boundless compassion.

Compassionate God, form in me the heart of Jesus. Lead me to live within the boundary lines of your abundant provision. Grant me the courage to move slowly and humbly through my day so that I might be fully present to you, myself, and others. Amen.

Divine Presence

JUNE 15–21, 2026 • PAULA BROUSSARD SMITH

SCRIPTURE OVERVIEW: God's unwavering presence in our lives guides us through trials and triumphs. In Genesis, we witness the struggle between Hagar and Sarah, illustrating how God sees and hears those in distress. Psalm 86 offers a heartfelt plea for mercy, emphasizing the importance of reaching out to God in our times of need. In Romans, Paul encourages us to embrace our new life in Christ and walk in the light of his resurrection. Lastly, the verses from Matthew invite us to recognize the true cost of discipleship, assuring us that our worth is anchored in God's love. Together, these passages remind us of God's companionship through every season of our journey.

QUESTIONS AND SUGGESTIONS FOR REFLECTION

- Read Genesis 21:8-21. In moments when you've felt overlooked or unheard, how might you actively seek God's presence to find solace and strength?
- Read Psalm 86:1-10, 16-17. What intentional practices can you adopt to make calling upon God a vital part of your everyday life, providing you with the guidance and strength you need?
- Read Romans 6:1b-11. What does experiencing the newness of life in Christ mean for you personally, and how can it transform your daily living?
- Read Matthew 10:24-39. In what ways can you embrace the obstacles on your faith journey, fully trusting in God's enduring love and divine purpose?

Rev. Dr. Paula Broussard Smith is the Senior Pastor of Gordon Memorial UMC in Nashville, TN.

MONDAY, JUNE 15 ~ *Read Genesis 21:8-21*

As I sat on a huge boulder at the edge of the ocean at daybreak, the grief felt overwhelming. Having lost both my parents just nine weeks apart, I grappled with the fear of facing a future without their guidance. A sense of abandonment enveloped me, and doubts crept into my heart like shadows on the water. Yet as the sun struggled against the clouds, I felt its warmth piercing through the gloom—a tangible reminder that God was present with me.

In Genesis 21:8-21, I see a parallel in Hagar's plight. Cast aside in the wilderness with her son, she faced despair and loneliness. However, in her darkest moment, Hagar encountered a profound truth: God saw her suffering and responded to her cries. This narrative resonates deeply, echoing my own feelings of being unseen or unheard in times of struggle. Just as Hagar brought her burdens before God, we too are invited to lay down our fears, regrets, and isolation at God's feet.

Reflecting on our hardships can create a pathway to transformation. Despite grief and loss, we can hold onto the assurance that God walks alongside us through our wilderness. God's watchful gaze reminds us that we are never truly alone; God is intricately involved in our healing journey. In moments of doubt, we can find comfort in knowing that God is "El-roi," (Gen. 16:13) the God who sees us. Our cries do not go unheard—God is attentive and ready to provide the support we need.

As we meditate on this passage, let us invite God into our struggles, trusting God will meet us in our pain and guide us toward hope and restoration.

Lord, I thank you for your faithfulness. Help me recognize your presence in my life and trust in your promises. May I find solace in your unwavering love as I navigate my own wilderness. Amen.

TUESDAY, JUNE 16 ~ *Read Genesis 21:8-21*

In Genesis 21:8-21, we confront Hagar's plight. Hagar, cast aside, navigates a wilderness with her son, embodying the struggles faced by those who are oppressed or voiceless. In her darkest moment, she discovers that God sees her suffering and responds to her cries. This truth reminds us that even in our most desperate times, we are never overlooked by God.

Hagar's experience invites us to reflect on the burdens we carry and the systemic injustices that constrain us. How often do we feel unseen in a world that prioritizes the privileged? God calls us to lay down our burdens—fears, frustrations, and desires for justice—acknowledging not just our struggles, but the collective pain of marginalized communities.

Recognizing these struggles opens us to the healing and hope God provides. God walks with us through our wilderness, assuring us that we are always under God's watchful gaze, especially when we stand in solidarity with those who suffer.

Reflecting on Hagar's story, I think of the ongoing work of the World Methodist Council, a body of over eighty Methodist denominations that together comprise eighty-two million members across 132 countries. This group's 2024 Conference, themed "On the Move," focused on migration, pilgrimage, and guiding lights, emphasizing our shared responsibility as God's agents in a world of constant change and movement.

God's concern for individual pain can transform our action against systemic injustices both locally and globally. We are called to listen to marginalized voices and work toward a more just society, embodying the love and compassion of Christ.

Lord, thank you for your faithfulness. Help me recognize your presence in my life and the lives of those who suffer. May I be a voice for the voiceless and trust in your promises as I seek justice for others. Amen.

WEDNESDAY, JUNE 17 ~ *Read Psalm 86:1-10, 16-17*

In life's journey, we encounter mountains of trials and seas of blessings. Psalm 86 reveals a heart reaching out to God, pleading for mercy, guidance, and strength. This psalm emphasizes the power and necessity of calling on God in both trials and triumphs.

From a young age, I felt the profound power of the name Jesus. I witnessed people calling on God, exclaiming, "Thank you, Jesus!" in moments of joy, and crying, "Lord, have mercy!" in times of sorrow. I have experienced songs like "Oh How I Love Jesus," "Blessed Assurance, Jesus is Mine," and "Jesus, You Are the Center of My Joy" transform atmospheres, as individuals reach out to a power greater than themselves.

In my mother's Baptist church, no sermon was complete without proclaiming Jesus' crucifixion, death, and resurrection, culminating in, "On the third day, Jesus rose with all power in his hands!" That name—Jesus—remains our anchor, comfort, and strength. When we call on Jesus, we invite his presence into our struggles and victories alike.

We can prioritize our call to God daily by carving out sacred spaces for prayer, whether at dawn or nightfall. I like to imagine myself walking in God's creation, and I speak to God about my joys, fears, and hopes. Our prayers are not mere words; they are lifelines connecting us to the Almighty. Let us trust in God's boundless love, knowing God hears every cry and sees every tear.

Gracious God, as I come before you, I echo the heartfelt cries of the psalmist, "Incline your ear, O Lord, and answer me." Help me to call upon your name in every circumstance, knowing that you are near to all who seek you. Grant me your strength and guidance, and show me the path of righteousness. In the name of Jesus I pray. Amen.

THURSDAY, JUNE 18 ~ *Read Romans 6:1b-11*

In Romans 6, Paul calls us to reflect on the profound gift of grace that transforms our lives. We are not just forgiven; we are made new, invited to consider ourselves "dead to sin and alive to God." This invitation to new life also carries with it the responsibility to let go of what holds us back.

We must ask ourselves: What burdens, pains, or past failures do we need to lay aside? Perhaps it's guilt from past mistakes, fears that paralyze us, or relationships that drain our spirit. These weights can hinder our ability to fully embrace the freedom and joy that God offers.

Letting go is not merely an act of dismissal; it's a powerful step toward healing, a journey made lighter by the hand of the Almighty. In moments of trials, remember that God's unwavering presence remains a constant source of strength. When we surrender our burdens to God, we create space for God's love and grace to flow freely in our lives. Amidst fear, let God's assurance remind us that we are never alone.

In every blessing, we see God's goodness; in every trial, we experience God's faithfulness. God walks with us, never turning away. We can trust God's timing and purpose, even when the path seems uncertain.

Lord, grant me the courage to release my burdens and the wisdom to recognize what hinders my walk with you. Help me to embrace the freedom of living in your grace. May I always feel your unwavering presence guiding me through both trials and blessings. Amen.

While I was serving in a cross-racial appointment, a congregant once remarked, "I can't tell if you are a Republican or a Democrat." I chuckled and replied, "Can you tell I am a Christian?" This exchange brought to mind the song by Rev. Timothy Wright, "Where Do You Stand?" The lyrics challenge the listener to stand on the Lord's side.

Father Michael K. Marsh, an Episcopal priest, once preached a sermon called "Jesus' Line in the Sand." In it, he highlighted the importance of acknowledging Christ in our daily lives through our words, actions, and the policies we support. Consider the pressing social justice issues we face: racism, poverty, violence, inequity in education, and healthcare access. Each of these challenges demands our attention and action. Do we stand with Jesus or deny him in these moments of choice? Our discipleship extends beyond personal belief; it reflects how we embody Christ's teachings. Standing with Jesus involves engaging with societal injustices and confronting our biases—those lines that may isolate us from those who suffer. We must actively choose love over division.

In recognition of Juneteenth, let us recognize that siding with Jesus places us not in comfort but in a commitment to love and serve others. We are called to be ambassadors of hope, extending God's love to all. Each step in faith opens doors to transformation—both within ourselves and in the world around us. We embrace the challenges of discipleship knowing that we are loved by God.

Gracious God, grant us strength to embrace the challenges of discipleship. In doubt, remind us of your presence. May our lives witness to your grace as we navigate our journey and strengthen us to be beacons of hope for others. In Jesus' name we pray. Amen.

SATURDAY, JUNE 20 ~ *Read Romans 6:1b-11*

Physical therapists observe how a person walks, identifying weaknesses, muscle imbalances, pain, and compensatory strategies. This insight allows them to understand not just the mechanics of movement but also the underlying struggles that often go unnoticed. Similarly, in our spiritual journeys, the way we "walk"—how we live our lives—speaks volumes about our inner state and our relationship with God.

In Romans 6, we are reminded of our identity as resurrected people in Christ. This passage invites us to not only let go of our sin but to boldly step into the purpose God has set before us. The transformative power of grace enables us to embrace the abundant life that comes from our relationship with God.

What does it look like to step into God's purpose? It may mean pursuing a calling we've hesitated to embrace, serving others in challenging ways, or sharing our testimony to inspire those around us. Living boldly requires faith and courage, trusting that God equips us for the journey ahead.

As we reflect on our new identity, we look for those moments when we witness God's unwavering presence. In every step we take, God guides our hearts and empowers us to fulfill God's purpose. Each day presents an opportunity to walk in faith, knowing God's light shines through us in every trial.

Just as physical therapy seeks to restore proper movement, our spiritual journey aligns us with God's design, helping us walk worthy of our calling. In blessings, let our gratitude echo God's love; in trials, may we find strength in God's faithfulness. Each challenge is a reminder that God is always supporting us, encouraging us to walk with purpose.

Holy God, help me step boldly into the purpose you have for my life. May I trust in your guidance and embrace every opportunity to glorify you, knowing you are with me each step of the way. Amen.

SUNDAY, JUNE 21 ~ *Read Matthew 10:24-39*

The joy and excitement of watching a group of children play Hokey Pokey was contagious. Their laughter echoed through the air, and soon I found myself singing and dancing along with them: "You put your whole self in, you put your whole self out, you put your whole self in, and you shake it all about. You do the Hokey Pokey and you turn yourself around. That's what it's all about!" The playful rhythm drew everyone into a celebration of movement and connection.

This game mirrors the themes in Matthew 10:24-39, inviting us to fully engage in our journey of discipleship. Just as children immerse themselves in the fun, we are called to put our whole selves into following Christ. Each turn and shake reminds us to release our fears, making space for God's love and strength.

Discipleship is not another task to add to our ever-growing list. Rather, it is a way of living that shapes what goes on our to-do list in the first place. Our discipleship forms every aspect of our lives. For Matthew's early readers, choosing to follow Jesus sometimes involved placing their faith in Christ over their familial relationships. We may find ourselves making similarly life-altering decisions as we choose to follow Christ today. And the choice to follow Jesus does not ensure earthly success. Yet when trials arise, we can embrace our identity as beloved children, celebrating that our worth is rooted not in our actions but in the immeasurable love God has for us.

So let's put our whole selves in and joyfully take steps of faith. In our journey of discipleship, may we discover a rhythm of life, laughter, and love.

Dedicate a few minutes to meditate on your identity as a beloved child of God. Reflect on your challenges and invite God into those moments. As you pray, shake off your fears and doubts, turning your heart toward God's guidance and strength.

The Righteousness of God

JUNE 22–28, 2026 • TIMOTHY J. JOHNSON

SCRIPTURE OVERVIEW: From Genesis we learn of the righteousness of God and the untraversable chasm between God and humankind. Simultaneously, we learn of God's grace and mercy as God intermittently crosses over into human experience as a guide and keeper for Abraham and his descendants. In the psalm, the faith of the psalmist is tutored by the righteousness of God. In the Gospel reading from Matthew, Jesus himself becomes a bridge of righteousness to and from God. And in the epistle to the Romans we learn of Jehovah's eternal transaction. No longer prisoners of the flesh, we become emancipated to freedom in the righteousness of God.

QUESTIONS AND SUGGESTIONS FOR REFLECTION

- Read Genesis 22:1-14. What does it mean to be righteous? How does this scripture passage give you confidence in your faith in God when you find yourself in hard places of ethical and moral dilemmas?
- Read Psalm 13. What does this psalm teach you about who God is and what prayer can and should be?
- Read Romans 6:12-23. How does "fruit" serve as an appropriate metaphor for being righteous and for living out the Christian life? How do you experience God's gift of eternal life in your everyday life?
- Read Matthew 10:40-42. What are the characteristics of a righteous person? What is the reward of a righteous person?

Rev. Dr. Timothy J. Johnson is an ordained Baptist minister and Emeritus Professor of Social Work at Roberts Wesleyan University. He holds degrees in Bible and African American Studies. He is a member of St. Luke Episcopal Church in Brockport, NY.

MONDAY, JUNE 22 ~ *Read Genesis 22:1-8*

We begin this week of devotions deep down in the depths of despair—of Abraham's and of our own—as we read of the patriarch being called by God to sacrifice his son Isaac. This is made all the more abject and egregious given that God, out of God's supposed bounteous grace, blessed Sarah to give birth to Isaac when she was ninety and Abraham was one hundred years of age. When this unfolding drama is placed alongside God's promises to Abraham and Sarah, that their descendants would number the sands of the sea (see Gen. 20:17), it may well appear that Abraham is called to give up everything—his son Isaac, his hopes, his dreams, and any sense of generational continuity. But we who are seated as historical spectators to this drama are called not to lose hope in this off-putting biblical story. Why? Because we are told God is testing Abraham. God wants to see if Abraham is truly faithful to God or only in this for the glory of a long line of descendants. The good news is that Abraham is our forefather in the faith, a role model of true faithfulness to God. He has the power to prevail within the story and to come out on top if he but follows God's will.

Abraham does exactly as God has instructed him. The summarized ending of this story is found in Romans 4:3, "Abraham believed God, and it was credited to him as righteousness" (NIV). What we learn of God in this story is that our understanding of God's righteousness is three-fold: It is our frame of mind, our obedient action, and God's judicial decision that ascribes to us God's righteousness. Thus we are called to enter into the judicially accorded righteousness of God, made assessable to each child of God by obedient attitudes and actions that please the Almighty. This is the pathway into right relationship with God.

God, we pray that you lead us into righteousness by our thoughts, words, and deeds. We thank you that you accord righteousness to us based on the bounties of your grace. Amen.

TUESDAY, JUNE 23 ~ *Read Genesis 22:9-14*

But what about Isaac? What do we know and learn of him in this scripture? It has been suggested that Isaac was a young man, certainly old enough to extract himself from what seems to be an unfolding atrocity. Surely Isaac recognizes that something is amiss when Abraham fails to bring a lamb for the sacrifice.

Conjectures aside, what becomes foundational, upon which the reader can rest, is that Isaac becomes a co-recipient of God's propitious presence in the story. At the cliff-hanger moment of Isaac's sacrifice, an angel intervenes—staying the hand of death—and a ram is miraculously caught in a nearby bush. Abraham understands that the Almighty has provided a substitutionary sacrifice. Isaac is saved and goes on to become the conduit of God's promise that Abraham's progeny will be as numerous as the grains of sand on the seashore. Thus Isaac and Abraham are privileged to institute a new name for God, "Jehovah Jireh," meaning *God will provide.*

It is this name for God that has been the north star, particularly in my African American heritage. Through enslavement and oppression we have looked to Jehovah's justice issuing out of the righteousness of God. The substitution of a ram for Isaac's life is a harbinger of the worship which will be instituted by Jehovah for Israel. All the focus of this story points to Abraham's willingness to be faithful to God—to the very end. So too are we called to be faithful in everything. Are we grateful to God because we are blessed with prosperity, life, abundance? Or are we grateful to God and, therefore, blessed with life abundant? Our position matters—our gratefulness to God for who God is, not for what God has given to us, is the foundation of our righteousness.

Lord, help us to trust you as the God who provides for us. Help us to trust you to lead us into paths of righteousness. Amen.

WEDNESDAY, JUNE 24 ~ *Read Psalm 13:1-6*

Stone soup, anyone? Perhaps some of us will remember this children's fable. A hungry traveler comes to a village seeking a meal but is denied. He then sets up in the village square a boiling pot of water with a stone in it. With this he entices villagers to contribute ingredients to make a finished soup.

What we have here is a ruse of sorts. It's as if the soup were borrowed on account. The fable begins with a fictive pot of soup and ends with the real thing. The villagers' gullibility and contributions to the boiling pot of water lead to an authentic, ready-to-serve pot of soup.

The psalmist trusts in God's unwavering love, rejoices in God's salvation, and sings of God's bountiful provision. These are indeed the ingredients in our own stone soup, given to us from Jehovah's cupboard of righteousness. God fills us with good things by which the fictive soup of our lives is transformed into a stick-to-your ribs recipe for engaging the challenges of life's joys and sorrows with the righteous endurance of God's grace. Unlike the fable, we don't cajole God out of this love, salvation, and bounty. In the purposes of Christ's finished work of salvation, the Lord relates to us as complete in God. In other words, "soup's on"—from the beginning! This is indeed God's righteousness accrued to our accounts on credit.

Holy God, help us to accept that the work of salvation is yours and not ours. Help us to merely rest in it. Amen.

THURSDAY, JUNE 25 ~ *Read Psalm 13:1-4*

The earlier verses of Psalm 13 are both a prayer of complaint on the part of the psalmist as well as a prayer pleading for deliverance. But the prayer is formed by five questions challenging the Lord's way of dealing with the psalmist.

Some cringe at the very idea of questioning God. But my spirituality and relationship with God needs the ability to question God and hold God accountable. Isn't this what Martha, the sister of Lazarus, was doing when she confronted Jesus after his tardy arrival to her brother's death? "Lord, if you had been here, my brother would not have died" (John 11:21). What? Run for cover! How dare Martha speak to Jesus in this way! But that's the point—we serve a God who is connected to our humanity and communicates with us, not as if we are gods, but as human beings in constant dialogue. Jesus' encounter with Martha opens one of the most beautiful theological windows in scripture: "I am the resurrection and the life. Those who believe in me, even though they die, will live, and everyone who lives and believes in me will never die" (John 11:25-26). These words, a doctrinal keystone of our faith, are Jesus' opportunity to elaborate how his righteous nature is manifested among those whom he came to save.

The psalmist's complaints to God and against God are the pathway to affirmation of the righteousness of God even in the midst of trials and tribulations. This prayer of complaint and sought-after deliverance leads to these ending words of affirmation about the righteousness of God: "But I trusted in your steadfast love; my heart shall rejoice in your salvation. I will sing to the LORD because he has dealt bountifully with me."

Lord, we pray you enable us to rest upon your righteousness which helps us to trust in you. Help us to rejoice in you during all the changing experiences of our lives. Amen.

FRIDAY, JUNE 26 ~ *Read Romans 6:12-19*

I love the hymns of the church. I think what I love most is that the melody is readily identifiable as the top note in the chord structure. Perhaps what makes some of the Paul's writings so complex is that he uses huge doctrinal chord structures that have made him the premier doctrinal composer in the New Testament. But if we tease out the melody notes of today's scripture, here is the simple song of our faith. We have been "brought from death to life," an eternal life which continues after our death. We have been set free from the ruling power of sin and are now "slaves to righteousness" on a pathway to sanctification. These melody notes of the faith fit perfectly with the simplicity of the gospel message found in John 3:16: "For God so loved the world that he gave his only Son, so that everyone who believes in him may not perish but may have eternal life." The message is simple, but so often made complicated by the Christian penchant for adding extraneous requirements to the pathway of grace leading to God.

Having identified salvation's alluring melody in today's scripture, this song of the ages is fully sounded by the discordant harmonics of the Edenic shift from being ruled by grace to being ruled by sin, and the discordant harmonics of being imprisoned to the flesh over the ages of human history. Christ's victory returns us to the realm of God's righteousness. For it was at Calvary God made available glorious freedom in Christ Jesus. And the ending harmonic in this hymn of salvation is that those who name themselves as children of God get to live their lives as if enmeshed by the righteousness of God.

Thank you, Lord, for choosing to enmesh us in your righteousness. Lead us. Teach us how to live out the glorious freedom that is ours as recipients of your righteousness. Amen.

SATURDAY, JUNE 27 ~ *Read Romans 6:20-23*

Even as I cull out theological gems from today's scripture, I will candidly share that the use of the term *enslaved* is off-putting for me and my people. It reminds us of the period over several centuries when African Americans were enslaved. Yet the paradox in this writing is that the term *enslaved* is an effective weight-bearing idea for speaking to the devotional life of the readers of the epistle of Romans. Being enslaved to sin carries with it the idea that one does not and cannot experience the freedom that comes with being emancipated from sin.

What is sin? To Paul, sin is a controlling power, a realm to which we can belong. When God freed us from sin through Christ, God freed us from the realm in which we were controlled by sin and moved us to be controlled by the realm of God's righteousness. Today we more often see sin as violation of the divine standards which human beings are called to practice. While this is not exactly what Paul had in mind, with our twenty-first century understanding of psychology and free will, we have a hard time not equating sin and transgressions. In Paul's understanding, though, being enslaved to God or enslaved to righteousness means that as emancipated children of God, we get to choose how we will live. Will we live lives that are anchored to the divine standards that God has laid down for us? Or will we exercise our freedom in Christ haphazardly, continuing to answer the siren call of sin?

In the church of my childhood, there was a woman who would shout out, "I got the 'can't help its,'" referring to her bent for interrupting worship with a personal witness. Perhaps being enslaved to the righteousness of God is best said this way: I got the "can't help its" when it comes to the things of the Lord.

God, thank you for the gift of life. Empower me to accept your grace and live in your freedom. Amen.

SUNDAY, JUNE 28 ~ *Read Matthew 10:40-42*

At the end of Matthew 10, we find Jesus' instructions to his disciples as he sends them out as emissaries. For their mission they are armed with supernatural powers over unclean spirits and over sickness. They are to take vows of poverty, taking with them no money and receiving no reimbursement for their ministrations. Further the disciples are to travel light, and for their sustenance, they are to depend on the good will of those who will receive them. In the midst of this commissioning of the disciples, Jesus signals that they will encounter difficulties—that they will be like sheep among wolves. In the midst of this ominous warning, the good news is that some will courageously support the disciples. And for these people there will be the reward of the righteous.

From 1936–1938, whenever a lynching occurred in the United States, the National Association for the Advancement of Colored People (NAACP) flew a large flag from its downtown New York office window which read "A man was lynched yesterday." They ceased the practice because the building owner threatened to evict the NAACP from their rented offices. The landlord bowed to the destructive powers of this world instead of courageously supporting calls for social justice that would lead to the fullness of every human life.

Proverbs 2 tells us that if we accept God's words and treasure God's commandments then we will "understand righteousness and justice" (v. 9) and will be saved "from the way of evil" (v. 12). As we seek to follow God, we will encounter opportunities that provide us with a choice. Let us courageously claim the righteousness of Christ that is ours, fully expecting that God will reward our faithfulness.

Lord, give us courage to draw continually from the well of your righteousness that has been provided for us. Amen.

Being Obedient to God

JUNE 29–JULY 5, 2026 • AMY SIGMON

SCRIPTURE OVERVIEW: Our four scripture passages this week connect to the discipleship practice of being obedient to God. In the Hebrew Bible we see Abraham's servant and Rebekah take leaps of faith to become part of a great family lineage. The psalm is one for a royal wedding, suited to questions of family and legacy. In Matthew, Jesus promises us that if we choose a path of trusting and following God, he will take up our earthly burdens so that we might find joy in following him. Paul writes to the Romans of his emotional turmoil in trying to be obedient to God, and the relief of knowing that Jesus is always ready to come to our aid.

QUESTIONS AND SUGGESTIONS FOR REFLECTION

- Read Genesis 24:34-38, 42-49, 58-67. When have you felt God calling you to take a leap in faith? How did it make you feel? Can you look back and see the hand of God at work?
- Read Psalm 45:10-17. What kind of legacy do you want to leave behind?
- Read Romans 7:15-25a. Do you ever feel discouraged with yourself and your faith? How do you lean on Jesus, knowing that his resurrection has saved us from sin and despair?
- Read Matthew 11:16-19, 25-30. Think of one burden that is weighing on you right now. Ask God to take it. Who is a wise person in your life? How can you seek wisdom?

Amy Sigmon is a freelance writer based out of Nashville, TN. She is the author of *The Sanctuary for Lent 2026* (Abingdon Press, 2026).

MONDAY, JUNE 29 ~ *Read Genesis 24:34-38, 42-49, 58-67*

Have you ever taken a trip where you weren't quite sure of the destination? Or started a project and you weren't sure how it was going to end? It is hard to take that first step when you're not sure how or if the ending is written.

Shortly after my husband and I got married, he received a job offer several states away, in a new field, away from any of our family and friends. Before we had married, I realized that we were likely going to have to move for his job sooner rather than later. But considering that we might have to move some time in the vague future compared to actually moving four months after the birth of our first child were quite different things. We knew that God would be in this new place, guiding us with a sure hand. Would we be willing to take the leap?

This passage in Genesis speaks to me about putting all your trust in God. First we have Abraham putting his trust in his servant. This servant remains nameless, but shouldn't be discounted. He plays a key role in creating the lineage of Abraham and Isaac, the lineage that will stretch to Jesus Christ himself. Then we see the trust of Rebekah. Talk about taking a leap into the unknown! We could all look to Rebekah as an example of faith and trust. She leaves her family and community to go to a man that she's never met, to live with in-laws she's never met, because she knows that God is calling her.

Wherever you are called in life, know that God goes before you. You can follow where God leads because your faith and trust in God is never misplaced.

Lord, it can be scary to follow you into new places and spaces. But we open our hearts and hands to you, trusting that you will always be with us. Amen.

TUESDAY, JUNE 30 ~ *Read Psalm 45:10-17*

When my husband and I were planning our wedding, we (okay, I) opted to take out the line "to obey" from our wedding vows. I had this image in my head of being ordered around, and I wasn't going to stand for it. (To be sure, my then-fiancé had never ordered me to do anything before.) Something about it felt icky.

Psalm 45 is titled "Ode for a Royal Wedding," extremely apt to be paired with the scripture in Genesis. A dozen years into marriage, and looking at these texts together with the link between trust and obedience, I see things a little differently. Obedience stems from trust. When you trust your partner with your life, your children, your finances, your home; when the relationship is built on solid ground; when you are open and honest—then obedience doesn't feel quite so challenging. Your wife asks you not to go to your guys' weekend this year because the kids are at a really hard age. Your husband asks you not to do any more Amazon shopping this month because finances are tight. These can sound like really controlling requests, but when they're grounded in mutual love and trust, they aren't menacing or unkind. They stem from a place of mutual respect and collective goals.

Choosing to get married or be committed to another person in a long term relationship requires a leap of faith. The same is true of our relationship with God. The good news is God promises to be ever-faithful to us in this relationship, and we can trust God's promises. When we understand that our relationship with God is built on trust and mutual respect, obeying God becomes a whole new experience of joy.

Lord, our hearts often want to go our own ways. We feel constricted by the idea of obedience. Soften our spirits so that we might see obedience to you for what it is: mutual love and trust. Amen.

WEDNESDAY, JULY 1 ~ *Read Genesis 24:34-38, 42-49, 58-67*

Pastors and church leaders often talk about creating a "culture of call." This translates to having a church community that encourages people to see how God is calling them to live and work in the world. This might mean creating leadership opportunities for young people, allowing them to lead in worship, or putting more trust in lay leaders to take on ministry projects. Ultimately, it leaves room for the Holy Spirit to guide people into fitting roles of ministry, perhaps as ordained pastors, but more often as lay servants doing the work of the church.

When we've laid the foundation of trust with God, it is easier to be obedient to God's calling. Obedience is a key piece of discipleship. It might feel strange to change the mindset of being in charge to humbling ourselves before God, asking how God might use us. But that obedience is what we see here in Genesis, and it's how we can follow God into new paths of ministry.

Just as it can be scary to follow God into a new phase of life, it can also be scary to say yes to God's call. But we see in Genesis that obedience is key to lighting the way forward. It can unlock new and exciting paths for us.

Our church is in need of the next generation of leaders. God gifts each of us with talents for ministry, ordained or lay. How can you channel your gifts from God? How do you live out your faith? Your gifts can be used in the church, at your job outside of the church, at your schools, and in your neighborhoods. Be part of a culture that says yes to God's call everywhere, not just in the sanctuary.

God, light within us a fire to follow your guidance. Show us how we can be leaders as well as followers and obey you when you call. Amen.

THURSDAY, JULY 2 ~ *Read Psalm 45:10-17*

My husband's family is extremely close. Both of his parents' families have been in the same area of North Carolina for many generations. My mother-in-law's father inherited seventy-five acres of land that his mother and grandmother had lived on. He held that land in his name, undeveloped, for decades. Now, ten years after he has passed, all three of his daughters and their families live on that land together. Six houses have been built, with plans for a seventh after a cousin marries this year. Nine small kids are being raised on that land, with more to come.

The family speaks about their grandparents often, saying "look what you started," in a warm and thankful manner. It truly is a legacy. The legacy is in the land, saved for their homes. The legacy is in their faith, church members who give of their time and talents and treasure and show up year after year. The legacy is in their relationships, as they care deeply for one another and walk through all of life's valleys and peaks together.

Psalm 45 speaks to family legacy upon the occasion of a royal wedding. Verses 16-17 promise sons to the king. The Lord promises that their name will be celebrated in all generations, that they will be princes in all the earth. Legacy is often connected to the idea of wealth, but it's truly much deeper. How will people speak about you when you're gone? What relationships with your children, family, or friends do you leave behind? Will those relationships go on to build up the kingdom of God? Will your faith inspire the faith of others?

Holy Spirit, you guide and inspire us. May our communion with you inspire our relationships with those around us, so that we might leave legacies of faith, kindness, and courage. Amen.

FRIDAY, JULY 3 ~ *Read Matthew 11:16-19, 25-27*

The idea of secret wisdom is a strange one. In Matthew 11:16-17, Jesus is saying that the current generation has been corrupted by the Pharisees. He is praising John the Baptist, who did hard ministry work in preparing the way for Jesus' ministry. The people aren't seeing John and Jesus for their true selves as messengers from God. When John fasted, the people said he had a demon. When Jesus eats and drinks with his friends, they call him a glutton and drunkard.

Jesus says that God hides wisdom from the intelligent and gives it to infants, ones who haven't yet been corrupted by the world. Jesus says that he is the receiver of God's wisdom, and it is through him that we can find our way to that knowledge. The message is clear: Follow Jesus. Trust and obey him.

In scripture, wisdom is often personified as a woman, the Wise Woman of the Hebrew scriptures. Verse 19b reads, "Yet wisdom is vindicated by her deeds." Here, the author of the Gospel is connecting the personified wisdom with Jesus. Jesus will be vindicated by his deeds, as we see throughout his ministry, death, and resurrection.

How can we cultivate wisdom? First, we follow Jesus, as he instructs in verses 25-27. Second, we carefully examine what comes of our actions. Are we vindicated by our deeds? Do our actions bear good fruit? Or do they wreak havoc and sow seeds of hate and mistrust? Cultivating wisdom is a lifelong process. We are fallible people, easily swayed by false prophets who promise to fix all of life's problems. At times we ignore God or the prompts of the Holy Spirit. That's why it's so important to build a foundation of trust and obedience to God, who will not lead us astray in our pursuit of wisdom, our pursuit of the holy.

Jesus, you are the wisdom of God brought down to earth. We long to follow your good and holy ways. Help us to be receivers of your wisdom and to share it with others. Amen.

SATURDAY, JULY 4 ~ *Read Matthew 11:25-30*

Each of us carry burdens every day. We walk around holding worry about our family members, our friends, our jobs, our communities, and so much more. We wish to take burdens from our children or aging parents. Yet so many of us don't want to set our burdens upon someone else. We don't want to tell someone that we're struggling with the day-to-day demands of life. It can get so bad that you feel like you're drowning. I can assure you—when you believe that the person next to you has it all together, they don't. They are feeling the same thing. We are living in a time plagued by anxiety, driven by the nonstop cycle of news and gossip that we can't seem to get away from. Where is the *good* news?

In this passage I hear the promise that God can handle anything. No matter how heavy the worry—that worry you don't want to hand off to a friend—God can handle it.

I hear in this passage an invitation from Jesus: Give me your burdens. In turn, I will give you my yoke. And guess what? It's light. It's easy. Interestingly, in using the term "yoke," Jesus was using a rabbinic metaphor for joyous obedience to God's law. When we take on obedience to God, we can drop the heavy burdens of the world.

This doesn't mean we give up the work of bringing God's kingdom, the work of justice for all of God's children. But when we take on Jesus' yoke, we take on the work of loving our neighbors and loving God. God is with us in that work. Jesus promises rest for our weary souls. And that is really good news. That is the gospel that can drive us forward, renewed and ready.

Jesus, we come to you with open hearts, ready to hand off our earthly burdens for the yoke of joyful obedience to you. We pray for the power of the Holy Spirit to renew our souls, so that we may go out into the world ready to bring the good news that people are longing to hear. Amen.

SUNDAY, JULY 5 ~ *Read Romans 7:15-25a*

Being obedient is a tall order. The further we get into discipleship, the more we realize just how much God asks of us. It's everything—our actions, our words, our vocations, our very hearts. And what if we want to make our own decisions, follow a different path? Is it wrong or sinful? These are all the questions that Paul is asking of himself in this letter to the Romans: "I do not understand my own actions." This is such an accurate summation of the human condition. Why do we make bad choices? Does it make us bad people? Paul says that when we do something we don't want to do, it's not really us, but the sin that lives in us.

Paul says he finds a pattern: When he wants to do good, evil lies close at hand. While I'm not sure I believe that evil spirits or the devil lies in wait for us, ready to snatch us off to hell, I do believe that temptations look so good because they are easy choices. Deep in our souls, we delight in the law of God but wrestle with temptation and doubt all the time.

But that's where the good news comes in. What Paul wants to emphasize here is that just when we want to give up on ourselves, Jesus is right there. Jesus rescues us from our basest selves and allows us to reach toward God and become more perfect and sanctified.

It's not about being a "good" person, someone who makes all the "right" decisions. It's about being in relationship with the One who guides us perfectly. Christ and the Holy Spirit are the animating factor, the saving grace because we can't save ourselves.

Jesus, you broke our bonds to sin and suffering and instead delivered us to the family of God. You are always waiting to catch us when we fall, ready to redeem us again and again. We give all our praise and thanksgiving for your love and redemption. Amen.

Your Word Is a Lamp to My Feet

JULY 6–12, 2026 • BRUCE REYES-CHOW

SCRIPTURE OVERVIEW: Psalm 119 will serve for us as a pathway of insight into the intertwined and multiple truths that can be revealed when one text is seen through the lens of another. Through a verse of the psalm each day, we'll explore the failures and successes represented in the other scriptures. In Genesis, Jacob should feed his brother out of care and concern, but he takes advantage of the situation and robs Esau of his birthright. Paul in Romans contrasts the life of the flesh and the life in the Spirit. Without the power of God, we are doomed to repeat our mistakes in the flesh, but the Spirit sets us free. Jesus reminds us in Matthew that the effectiveness of the gospel is not based on our efforts. We sow the seed, but we cannot control whether it takes root.

QUESTIONS AND SUGGESTIONS FOR REFLECTION

- Read Psalm 119:105-112. How do you listen and look for how God may be revealing the path that God yearns for you to follow?
- Read Genesis 25:19-34. How might you resist the pull to take advantage of another's desperation (people you know or people with whom you share no adjacency) for your own benefit?
- Read Romans 8:1-11. In a world constantly competing for your imagination, intelligence, and integrity, when have you embraced and navigated the divine call to faith that has been gifted to you?
- Read Matthew 13:1-9, 18-23. Knowing that none of us thrives or "succeeds" one hundred percent of the time, when has your life and faith felt like each of the seeds in this parable?

Rev. Bruce Reyes-Chow is a minister in the Presbyterian Church (USA) and a full-time author and speaker based in San Jose, CA.

MONDAY, JULY 6 ~ *Read Psalm 119:105-106 and Romans 8:1-11*

In the movies, the rule-breaker is often the protagonist and hero. The swashbuckling adventurer who fights off roving mobs of villains, the lawyer that eschews the norms of the day to fight for justice, or the soft-spoken love interest who rejects cultural norms to find love—we love a good rule-breaker.

While I would love to be identified as such, I am not nearly as brave and rebellious as I want to believe I am. Deep down inside I am a rule-follower. The problem is that too often I am not following the rules that God has revealed but human ones. God yearns for us to live according to such rules as "bless those who curse you," "feed my sheep," and "give everything away," but the world wants to us live by the laws of "what's mine is mine," "pull yourself up by your bootstraps," and "you get what you deserve." These are rules designed by the religion of self-centered individualism and not of the ever-expansive Divine.

In his letter to the Romans, Paul contrasts these two sets of rules, identifying them as living "according to the flesh" or "according to the Spirit." Here Paul presents them as two mindsets, two ways of being that we choose between. By choosing the mindset of Christ—of the Spirit—we choose to live by God's rules of love, hope, peace, and joy. And the Spirit of Christ in us empowers us to do so.

Following God's rules is not meant to be restrictive or oppressive, but quite the opposite. God's rules light our way. When we follow the nuanced, complex, and beautiful rules of God, our understanding and experience of God are granted depth, given texture, and made more whole. As enticing as it is to be a rebel and a rule-breaker, we find true freedom when we live according to the law of God's Spirit.

Pray a breath prayer. As you inhale, pray, "God, you reveal your path." As you exhale, pray, "I will follow with discipline."

TUESDAY, JULY 7 ~ *Read Psalm 119:107 and Matthew 13:1-9*

Sometimes, it is difficult to see hope, let alone to live with hope. The constant rage-baiting and abusive onslaught of violent, destructive, and dehumanizing words and actions that are being unleashed upon our collective existence by politicians, institutions, and hoarders of power are determined to extinguish our hope. We are "severely afflicted," as the psalmist cries.

Our hope, however, does not come from an external source in the world. Our hope is born from Christ who lives in us. When we give up hope, we give up on the new life that is in us as a result of the life, death, and resurrection of the one we call Christ Jesus. Yes, suffering and struggle can put up walls and barriers to seeing the fruit of God's labor around us, but no matter how bad it is in the world and our own souls, that suffering is not entitled to access and diminish our hope.

We must always be on the lookout, especially when hope feels so distant, to notice and name hope around us. The laughter of community gives depth to any movement of people trying to make the world a better place. The act of doing something that brings our souls joy rejects the idea that despair will win the day. The moments of silence and stillness allow our senses to observe and absorb the subtle beauty of creation and quiet the noise around us.

Jesus' parable in Matthew's Gospel reminds us of our hope in God. We don't place our hope in the results of our work. We place our hope in God, who calls us to the work of sowing seeds—work we are to do extravagantly. However we each participate in the ongoing revealing of God's intentions for us and the world, we do so grounded in hope.

Pray a breath prayer. As you inhale, pray, "God, you reveal your path." As you exhale, pray, "I will follow with hope."

WEDNESDAY, JULY 8 ~ *Read Psalm 119:108 and Matthew 13:18-23*

When Jesus explains the parable of the sower, he is clear that the different types of ground represent different receptions of his message. We often look at this parable to consider where and how we spread the word of Christ's kingdom. But we can consider how we receive word of this kingdom through the story, as well.

While serving a church in Northern California, I had the privilege of meeting Fred, a man receiving hospice care at his home. I visited Fred in order to share the love that his church offered, to bring him Communion, and to pray with him.

I had not been serving long at this church, but I already knew that Fred and I stood on different sides of every theological and political spectrum. So when, during our conversation, Fred asked his wife to step out of the room so he could have a few moments with me alone, I was half expecting to receive some criticism about what I had preached on Sunday. I thought he might chastise me about where the church was headed or perhaps offer an aggrieved lament over the ills of this fallen world.

To my surprise, Fred began by thanking me for leading the congregation that he so loved. Then, with tears of hope in his eyes, he took my hands in his and asked me earnestly, "What does God want me to do with the rest of my life?" I was stunned. This man—who had maybe a few weeks or months to live—was still seeking God's leading, even to his final breaths. I sat there in pure awe, the kind of awe that transcends respect or admiration.

We would each like to think we would be as faithful in Fred's situation. Have we cultivated good soil so as to receive the word and allow it to bear such fruit in our lives? If Fred can remain curious and teachable at the end of his days, how dare we not?

Pray a breath prayer. As you inhale, pray, "God, you reveal your path." As you exhale, pray, "I will follow with curiosity."

THURSDAY, JULY 9 ~ *Read Psalm 119:109 and Genesis 25:19-34*

When our kids were young, one of our favorite family activities was going to the animal shelter. We'd walk through the rows of crates for an hour or two, talking with the animals and petting them and playing with them when staff allowed it. Our children, now young adults, have fond memories of those visits.

Do you want to know the real reason we took our kids to the animal shelter? We could not afford to take them to the zoo. For a long time when our children were young, we could barely pay for groceries or other necessities. We lived near plenty of family, so we were never in danger of being unhoused or going hungry. But when we lost our home and moved our family of five into a two-bedroom, one-bathroom apartment, we did it out of necessity, not because we wanted to downsize. We were in poverty, and so often we were driven by fear and scarcity.

Like Esau whose hunger completely overwhelmed him, it is so easy for us to be driven by fear—and it is completely understandable. Whether due to economic mobility, access to healthcare, or immigration status, these days far too many are living on the edge. Simply saying "don't live in fear" when the threats are visceral and visible to many is too reductive and often patronizing.

We must have the courage to find ways to places of abundance and liberation, even as we face situations of scarcity and fear. Far from the terrible saying, "God only gives you what you can handle," as if God is doing this to us, we re-frame and have the courage to know that, in the midst of what we are handling, God is still present. Even when we are on the brink of losing everything that we have or know, if we hold on to the assurance of God's presence we can act out of confidence of that presence, and not out of fear.

Pray a breath prayer. As you inhale, pray, "God, you reveal your path." As you exhale, pray, "I will follow with courage."

FRIDAY, JULY 10 ~ *Read Psalm 119:110 and Genesis 25:19-34*

One of the questions I often ask myself when making decisions is, "At what cost?" I think about this not only in terms of my money but my time, my energy, my integrity, and ultimately, my soul. While this is a good question, it is not all of the question. To ask "At what cost?" allows me to only think about my cost and not the cost for others.

In our world of hyper-individualism and greater and greater social separation, we can fall into the trap of believing that our actions do not impact others, or worse, that we can benefit from the dire and desperate situations of others. Like Jacob did with Esau.

In the grand narrative of Genesis, perhaps this small part of the story seeks to explain why Jacob, the second-born, became the inheritor of the promise. We do not know much about the two brothers, and what we do know paints them more as caricatures rather than multi-dimensional people. What can we safely take from this story? We must not use people's fear against them, for fear has a tendency to force poor decisions. The possibility of poor decisions lessens when those with the privilege of not being afraid have the courage not to take advantage of another's fear. God's words to Rebekah have predicted that Jacob will be the preeminent brother. Jacob then acts to make this prediction a reality. But he does so by using the discomfort of his brother to his own advantage.

So yes, "At what cost to me?" must be a discerning lens for our actions, right alongside, "At what cost to others?" When we do that, we ensure the cost does not load more upon those already bearing so much but has the potential to lighten and lift up others, so we may all experience abundance and possibility.

Pray a breath prayer. As you inhale, pray, "God, you reveal your path." As you exhale, pray, "I will follow with wisdom."

SATURDAY, JULY 11 ~ *Read Psalm 119:111 and Matthew 13:1-2*

I often wonder what it was that brought people to Jesus. In those days everything was communicated by word of mouth, so I can only imagine that what drew people in was the hope and joy that spilled from those who had encountered Jesus already and spoke of the new life that was within reach.

Many moons ago, I was the pastor of a church made up of mostly young adults. Our Session—the church leadership—met about once a month. Being on Session isn't generally the most joyful of experiences; in fact it can often be excruciating, soul-sucking drudgery. But at this church we were committed to doing our work differently, not being driven by the business of the day but by the life-giving joy that comes with communal and collaborative work done together. Rather than meeting around a conference room table or treating it as a business meeting, our Session met in our church "living room," and we each brought the food and beverage of our choice. We understood the purpose of Session to be one of mutual support and connection, a sacred task of leading other people in their spiritual journeys. Sure, we had to make decisions about budgets, building maintenance, and other difficult topics. But our true task was to be an extension of an experience that we were creating as a church, an experience that was life-giving and meaningful.

At one of those meetings, one person came up the stairs, arriving right after getting off work, and plopped down on one of our bright orange couches in the living room with a burrito in hand. She exhaled deeply, then said, "I'm so glad to be at Session." That moment affirmed in my mind that the culture we were creating was one of meaning. Like the crowd drawn to Jesus, even amidst the work we knew there was always the possibility for new life, hope, and yes, even joy.

Pray a breath prayer. As you inhale, pray, "God, you reveal your path." As you exhale, pray, "I will follow with joy."

SUNDAY, JULY 12 ~ *Read Psalm 119:112 and Romans 8:1-11*

Choosing to live a life of faith guided by God's teachings is not a journey for the meek and mild. It takes tremendous discipline, hope, curiosity, courage, wisdom, and joy to purge ourselves of patterns, perspectives, and behaviors that place our wants and needs over the needs and struggles of others and, ultimately, over God's ever-revealing path before us.

Yes, choosing to follow God will be exhausting and overwhelming. It will draw mockery and dismissal. It will create tension, conflict, and discomfort. But choosing to follow God is an act of courage that challenges a worldview driven by hatred, dishonesty, and dehumanization. Choosing to follow God is about living a life of integrity in which we daily work at resisting the seductiveness of wealth, success, and self-preservation.

One lesson from the parable of the sower may be that we are not responsible for the results of our labor. But Paul's message about choosing to live in the Spirit over the flesh is clear on the results: Choosing to follow God is life-giving, both for us and for those around us. When we choose to see and respond to the human dignity of any one person, we are all given a little more hope.

We can also consider the alternative. If we do not continue to choose to follow God together, can you imagine how much worse the world will become? The least we can do in response to and in gratitude for all those kindness giants who have paved the way is to do the same for the generations to come.

Pray a breath prayer. As you inhale, pray, "God, you reveal your path." As you exhale, pray, "I will follow you all my days."

God's Presence Is Everywhere

JULY 13–19, 2026 • CHERYL L. PRICE

SCRIPTURE OVERVIEW: This week's readings guide us to the eighth Sunday after Pentecost. Just as God promised land and descendants to Abraham, God confirms these same promises to Abraham's grandson, Jacob. The psalmist meditates on and takes comfort in the fact that God knows everything and is everywhere, asking God to reveal sins from which the psalmist needs to turn. The Romans passage continues Paul's reflection on the life in the Spirit. Because we are children of God, we cry out with confidence that God will hear and answer. Jesus tells a parable in Matthew concerning the final judgment. He says that the wicked will be taken first, then the righteous will be gathered together.

QUESTIONS AND SUGGESTIONS FOR REFLECTION

- Read Genesis 28:10-19a. Identify a time when you recognized God's plan for you.
- Read Psalm 139:1-12, 23-24. List three moments in the psalm when you connect with God's presence. What is holding you back from inviting God to search your heart?
- Read Romans 8:12-25. Paul emphasizes hope. Explain the significance of hope for believers.
- Read Matthew 13:24-30, 36-43. Why is it challenging to know the truth about someone?

Rev. Cheryl L. Price, PhD, is the publisher of Judson Press, and enjoys teaching, planning events, listening to music, traveling, spending time with family and friends, and meeting new people.

MONDAY, JULY 13 ~ *Read Genesis 28:10-19a*

Our faith walk provides us with awe-inspiring or jaw-dropping experiences of God's presence. I remember one such experience from my own life. I was driving my car in Rochester, New York, on a typical cold, snowy, and windy day. However, the day grew into a mightily and significantly windy day. The wind was so strong that it spun my car around in the street, leaving me completely out of control. My car finally stopped, facing the right direction. There were no other cars on the road. I was unharmed and amazed. I said out loud, "Wow! Thank you, God!" I felt God's presence with me in the chaos, and I was reminded of how God shows up in the most miraculous ways.

Jacob's "God moment" was reflected in a dream as he slept on a rock for a pillow. In his dream, Jacob saw angels going up and down a stairway or a ladder, and he heard God reaffirm the promise God had made to Jacob's father and grandfather. God's presence became a transforming moment for Jacob. God pronounced words of encouragement for Jacob, his family, and future generations. These blessings were not limited to Jacob's family alone, but promised for "all the families of the earth." The dream ends with God promising God's presence.

Although Jacob was often in motion or on the run because of his own bad choices, greed, or selfishness, God was constantly with him. We are reminded that the Lord is with us as well. God was with Jacob from triumph to tragedy; God walks with us too. God is with us even when we have created a mess, even when we do things our way instead of God's way. No matter what, God's presence is assured.

O gracious God, thank you for the promise of your presence. We praise and adore you. Amen.

TUESDAY, JULY 14 ~ *Read Psalm 139:1-12, 23-24*

I once knew a woman who had been fired from her job. She did not know what to do, feeling lost, alone, and unsure. She prayed to God, saying, "Lord, help me." As she turned to read scripture to find support, her mind began to rethink her circumstances: "My help is here," she began to understand. Even in the darkness, she felt embraced by God's presence.

Psalm 139 is a meditation filled with the treasure of David's thoughts and relationship with God. David's deep connection with God is expressed in his understanding of God's intimate knowledge. David's prayer compellingly demonstrates the power of the Lord's knowledge and presence, the extent of which even David cannot comprehend. David marvels at the depth and breadth of the God he serves. David is a mighty leader and military genius, but God's thoughts and movements are beyond his capacity.

David's psalm tells us of God's intimate knowledge of ourselves. How does this intimate knowledge shape your life and those around you? David is comforted and intrigued by God's spirit in all aspects of his life. God is omnipresent whether David finds himself ascending to the heavens, rising in the morning, surrounded by darkness, or faced with death.

We can walk in the spirit of the Lord when we are afraid, call on the name of Jesus when we are unsure, and trust the Lord when our tears are overflowing. The woman who lost her job told me that she soon received a phone call asking if she was interested in applying for a new position. She accepted the invitation to apply. God reassured her that she was not neglected. Delay does not always mean denial. God's light was with her.

Lord, we are thankful you never leave us. Guide us to walk with you. Amen.

WEDNESDAY, JULY 15 ~ *Read Psalm 139:23-24*

It is interesting to note that David begins Psalm 139 with a unique statement. He declares emphatically how God has searched him and knows him. David is clear that the Lord is his life's Author and Creator. He affirms who God is in how he does not argue or question God's knowledge or design for all creation. For David was "fearfully and wonderfully made" by God (v. 14). He believes this so much that he repeats it in verse 23, "Search me O God, and know my heart." David was captivated by the Lord's greatness.

David adds a challenge to the Lord. He asks God to evaluate him and dissect his thoughts. Was David a loyal follower of the Lord or a fake follower? David knew he was a true follower. A cross-examination of our spiritual health, as evidenced by our actions, words, and thoughts, may prove shaky. We can take our own inventory of our spiritual and physical moments with the Lord, as long as we are true and honest with ourselves. When we make the time to reassess our relationship with God and the ways that relationship shapes our lives, we can reaffirm our commitment and be empowered in our faith. We can share our assurance with others.

David's response to God encompassed faith in bold acts and humility. He concludes in verse twenty-four that any wickedness in him must be changed. David wanted God to guide him in what he should do. Wicked or evil behavior is not of God. David understood God's road was the best path to take. At times we prefer to choose the path well-walked. It is easier and less burdensome. David chose the "everlasting path" of God. When faced with which life road to travel, what do you do? Stop, look, and listen to what direction God would have you go. God is always with you.

Dear gracious Lord, direct us in your path. Amen.

THURSDAY, JULY 16 ~ *Read Romans 8:12-17*

Romans 8 is a passage of scripture that captures the beauty of freedom and love in Christ. Paul states there are two ways to choose how one can live their life—chained to disobedience that leads to death, or freed for an obedient life in Jesus. Paul's words are adopted and utilized in Christian discipleship. Will the spirit of the flesh and disobedience serve as our god? Or will liberty in Christ become our captain? Paul emphasizes that followers of Christ should abandon sin and disobedience and live a new life in Christ. Jews and gentiles are all free in God and are the children of God.

In Roman society, a male heir could be adopted into a family to maintain the family status and legacy for future generations. The adopted heir received the benefits of a full, natural-born heir. Paul uses this metaphor to indicate the choice we have to choose life in Christ. Paul's clarion call to break free from the oppression that sin keeps over persons is rooted in Christ. Sin brings death, but Jesus' resurrection gives life. Why choose a sinful life when God's spirit allows an unmatched benefits package? Being in the spirit of Christ has benefits that sin can never offer. The superlative benefits package of adoption includes life everlasting with Jesus, a God who always listens, and unconditional love.

As children of God, we are already a part of God's family. The love of God in Christ Jesus is complete. Christians must decide how to live in Christ. Allowing our desires of the body, mind, and soul to keep us bound is against the nature of Christ. Let us boldly decide to live for Christ.

Compassionate Creator, we are your children. We worship you as heirs in the household of faith. Amen.

FRIDAY, JULY 17 ~ *Read Romans 8:18-25*

Paul waves the flag of victory when stating that there is no comparison of suffering in this world to the magnificence of what will come. The revelation of the next world with Christ is far greater than any suffering experienced in this world. Yet the suffering is not mild. Paul uses the analogy of labor pains a woman experiences as she gives birth. The sounds and the pain are intense and undeniable. Paul can only imagine what the woman and the baby are experiencing. He interprets suffering as an act of nature that all of creation has experienced.

We cannot escape the suffering, according to Paul. The suffering of Christ indicates that we must also suffer if we are to experience Christ's glory. The two go hand in hand. But our suffering is not in vain; it is not wasted. Paul encourages believers then and today to have hope in our suffering. The presence of God in our lives through Christ is a fulfilled promise. Victory is ours. We simply must endure the suffering before we experience the victory.

Paul encouraged believers to have patience for the change to happen. Patience requires discipline. Waiting is a slow journey we prefer to avoid. It is even more complicated when we feel unhinged or tread lightly in anticipation of what we desire. Changing our attitudes and perspectives helps us to accept our current reality. Keeping hope in the forefront allows us to rethink what we do and how we do it. When we live in hope, we await the joy to come, and that provides us courage and sustenance to survive the present suffering.

God of hope and care, bless us today. May we show others the hope we have in you. Amen.

SATURDAY, JULY 18 ~ *Read Matthew 13:24-30*

The parable of the wheat and the weeds displays the existence of good and evil living together. The kingdom of God here on earth is divided. Good and wickedness do live together.

The landowner is informed of the evil someone has planted in his field. His demeanor appears calm, and he does not have vengeful outbursts. He gives instructions on the best practices to manage the situation. The owner discourages the field hands from uprooting the weeds. He does not want the grain to be mistaken for the weeds or to be killed in the process. We do mix up good for evil and vice versa. The owner's careful thinking allows for a strategic plan to grow into a healthier outcome.

Several messages arise from this parable. One is that people plot and plan ways to sabotage land and people. Whether we accept it or not, terrible things happen to good people or those who are minding their own business. Why? The answer may lie in the fact that people hurt other people, often without clear reason.

Notice how the wheat and the weeds kept growing together. Another lesson for us is that we too must push forward and continue to grow in the wisdom and justice of Jesus. We cannot let the weeds among us distract us from our intended purpose of Christian discipleship. Even amongst any evil that grows alongside us, we can work together for change and to help one another. When we are faced with a challenging situation, we can remind ourselves to be wheat, working to provide support for others to grow in the fullness of God, not as weeds that may choke out and stall any potential progress.

Finally, we can look to the owner of the field to guide our response in stressful times. Is calmness or calamity our response? We can respond to difficulty with peace and patience, trusting God's work in the process.

Jesus, water and nurture us to spread good news. Amen.

SUNDAY, JULY 19 ~ *Read Matthew 13:36-43*

The disciples, like us, did not always understand Jesus. They misunderstood his actions and his words. We find ourselves in similar predicaments. In yesterday's reading, we read the parable of the weeds among the wheat. The disciples did not get it. They ask Jesus what the parable meant. It is better to ask than to trust what you think is the answer.

The disciples didn't understand the metaphor, but this is likely one of Jesus' clearer parables. Children—people—are the heirs of good or evil, depending on what they work for. The devil is the one who sowed the evil seeds, and the angels will reap the harvest. The cast is set, and the players take the stage on cue. The production grows, and the harvest's applause and gifts belong to God. God's kingdom is displayed in grandeur. With the disciples' question, the secrets of the kingdom are revealed. Their question is a gentle reminder to ask Jesus for guidance. Our vision is sometimes cloudy. Sometimes, we must ask for what we need. Jesus directs us to open our eyes and redirect our vision to him. Jesus is ready.

While this parable may be clearly explained, the implications may not be so. We find helpful reminders for our work today amidst this agrarian metaphor. If we think of the field as the world, we are then reminded that it is not our task to separate the good from the evil in the world today. Attempts to do so may cause harm to the work of God's kingdom. Such work belongs to the master—to Christ—not to us. Our task is to grow in God's light, seeking to share God's love and forgiveness without judgment until Christ deems it time to gather us into the reward of the kingdom.

God, focus our attention on our work in the present moment and keep us from being distracted by that which is not ours to do. Amen.

What Then Are We to Say?

JULY 20–26, 2026 • DONNA GIVER-JOHNSTON

SCRIPTURE OVERVIEW: The apostle Paul's question, "What then are we to say about these things?" shapes our theme for this week's scripture lessons as we read of things that are hard to comprehend. In Genesis, we wonder what to say about deception and the giving and taking of women. In the psalm, as we wonder what to say about God's covenantal promises, we are called to respond with thanks and praise. In Matthew, we wonder what to say about Jesus' parables used to explain what the kingdom of heaven is like. In Romans, as we wonder about what to say in the midst of our groanings and grief, Paul reassures us of the power of the Spirit's intercessions and the promise of God's abiding and eternal presence.

QUESTIONS AND SUGGESTIONS FOR REFLECTION

- Read Genesis 29:15-28. When have you deceived someone? When have you been deceived by someone? In the messiness of life, where have you found God?
- Read Psalm 105:1-11, 45b. Recall some of the wonderful works God has done. What does God's covenant mean to you? How do you respond?
- Read Romans 8:26-39. When have you not known what to say—to a person, in a troubling situation, in prayer? What things made you feel separated or close to God?
- Read Matthew 13:31-33, 44-52. Which of Jesus' parables do you relate to? How would you describe the kingdom of heaven in contemporary language?

Rev. Dr. Donna Giver-Johnston is an ordained minister of Word and Sacrament in the Presbyterian Church (USA). After 20 years as a church pastor, she is currently the Director of the Doctor of Ministry program and Professor of Homiletics at Pittsburgh Theological Seminary.

MONDAY, JULY 20 ~ *Read Genesis 29:15-28*

The Bible is often described as the book of family values, with teachings of how we are to treat one another. And yet some stories, like this one in Genesis, stand in stark contrast to what we would consider "family values." It is the story of Laban's deception, Jacob's polygamy, and the use of women as bargaining chips. What then are we to say about these things?

What we can say is that the story of Abraham's family in Genesis is the story of God working even through flawed humans. This story is but one in the often messy saga of God's people. Their lives are marked by broken promises, hurt, and heartbreak. Read through modern lenses, we see this as a story of sexism, written from a male perspective in which women are devalued, without voice or choice.

God's name is not mentioned in this passage but notice that each of the women is named—Leah and Rachel, and their maids Zilpah and Bilhah—and by this, we understand that they are each seen and valued by God. While Rachel is described as graceful, beautiful, and desired by Jacob, Leah is devalued as one whose eyes were weak. And yet following these verses we read "when the LORD saw that Leah was unloved, he opened her womb." She is blessed with four sons, whom she names Reuben, Simeon, Levi, and Judah—names that continually reassure Leah of her value as beloved and remind her to praise the Lord in the midst of struggles and blessings (vv. 31-35).

What we can say about this story is that when we read between the lines and beyond the verses, we find God at work, even in the messiness, even in the mystery, blessing and calling us each by name.

God, in the messy midst of life, help us to believe that we are each of value to you, even beloved. Amen.

TUESDAY, JULY 21 ~ *Read Psalm 105:7-11, 45b*

In contrast to yesterday's Genesis reading in which God's name was not mentioned, Psalm 105 is all about God. In these five verses, notice the word *covenant* appears three times. In the Hebrew Bible, *covenant* means a formal agreement between *YHWH* and the people of Israel. *Covenant* is from the Hebrew word *bĕriyth*, with the root meaning "to cut." A covenant is literally a cutting, which comes from the ancient Near Eastern practice of taking a fattened animal and cutting it in two pieces. The two parties walk between the cut pieces, as a symbol of their commitment, offering themselves to be slain like the animal if they do not keep the covenant.

God made such a covenant with Abraham, promising him descendants as numerous as the stars in the sky (Gen. 15:5). To seal the covenant, God instructed Abraham to gather animals and cut them in two and lay them on the ground. After Abraham had fallen asleep, in a dream or vision, Abraham sees God (as a smoking fire pot and flaming torch) passing through the cut pieces of animals alone (vv. 17-18). This suggests that God established a unilateral covenant with Abraham and his descendants that does not depend on Abraham's righteousness but on God's graciousness.

The psalm confirms this is "an everlasting covenant," which God is mindful of "forever . . . for a thousand generations." This means that without having to engage in the ancient animal cutting ceremony (thankfully!), we are included in this covenant. God's eternal covenant means that there is mercy enough; there is grace enough; there is love enough for all of us. *All of us.* What then are we to say about these things? We join our voices with the psalmist in saying, "Praise the LORD!"

God of covenant, keep us mindful of and grateful for the covenant you make with us, now and always. Amen.

WEDNESDAY, JULY 22 ~ *Read Psalm 105:1-6, 45b*

Because of God's faithful keeping of the covenant with us (Ps. 105:7-11), we are called to respond with thanks and praise. Psalm 105 is a call to worship God. Notice the verbs in the psalm are not passive, but active. They call us to action today.

O give thanks; call on God's name. How do you give thanks? How do you call on God's name? Take a minute and call on God in prayer. Say thanks for a blessing in your life.

Make known God's deeds. When is the last time you shared your love of God with someone? Maybe it's time to try.

Sing to him, sing praises; tell of his wonderful works; rejoice. You don't have to wait until Sunday to sing praises to God. Why not sing your favorite hymn now? "Great Is Thy Faithfulness" (UMH #140) or "Amazing Grace" (UMH #378) are good options.

Seek the Lord. Surely there are days when you need God's strength. Surely there are days when you need God's presence. Maybe this is one of those days. *Seek* is another word for *pray*: "God, I need you, now."

Remember God's wonderful works, miracles, and judgments. In Hebrew, *to remember* (*zakar*) is not just mindful reflection; it is to engage hands and feet, heart and voice in doing whatever the remembrance requires. If you remember a blessing, give thanks with your voice. If you remember someone you have hurt, get up and go to them, reach out your hand and ask for forgiveness.

As we actively respond to God's abundant blessings, we remember who we are and whose we are, "offspring of . . . Abraham, children of Jacob, [God's] chosen ones." And as God's beloved, we are called to worship God each and every day, in word and in deed.

O God, what shall I say about your abundant blessings you so graciously bestow—morning by morning new mercies I see? I thank you, I praise you, I love you. Amen.

In seeking faithful theological interpretation of Romans 8:26-30, it is important to identify what it does not say as much as what it does say. When Paul writes, "the Spirit helps us in our weakness, for we do not know how to pray as we ought," he is not suggesting that we need not pray at all, nor if we only pray harder, our petitions will be answered. Rather, Paul promises that the Spirit makes intercessions for us when in our grief, we cannot pray, or in our greed, we pray only for ourselves. The Spirit, near to our hearts, reflects our deepest shame and tears, hopes and fears to God's own heart.

In writing, "We know that all things work together for good for those who love God," Paul is not saying that if you love God, nothing bad will happen to you, nor if something bad happens, then God's purpose is to test you. Paul is reminding his readers that even amid the world's evil, God is at work transforming it for good. This is difficult to understand when in the midst of a challenging situation: Seeing the good is often more possible on the other side of suffering.

With "those whom he predestined he also called . . . and those whom he justified he also glorified," Paul is not seeking to cause divisions nor to make a plea for personal piety to attain salvation. This letter is addressed "to all God's beloved in Rome" (1:7). The use of plural pronouns (*those, we, us*) in this passage extend the words to all.

What then are we to say about these things? Together, in Christian community, we have a better chance of praying as we ought through the Spirit, seeing God work for good, and being inspired by those who love God and live according to God's purpose.

Spirit of the Living God, fall afresh on us. Hear our groanings and grief, and reassure us all of your promise and power. Amen.

FRIDAY, JULY 24 ~ *Read Romans 8:31-39*

Fear of being alone is one of our deepest fears. Solitary confinement in prison is one of the harshest and most severe punishments. As humans, we crave connection with other people. And as Christians, we desire connection with God. And yet sometimes, things that we have done or left undone separate us from God. When we confess our sins, our relationship with God is restored with the words of assurance, "In Jesus Christ, we are forgiven." Paul reminds God's people then and now, "It is Christ who . . . was raised, who is also at the right hand of God, who also intercedes for us." The incarnation of God's word becoming flesh in Jesus testifies to the promise of God's connection with humanity: *Immanuel* means *God is with us*.

"Who will separate us from the love of Christ?" Paul asks rhetorically. "Will affliction or distress or persecution or famine or nakedness or peril or sword?" While this list is meant to be inclusive, I wonder what other things make us wonder where God is, things that have wounded us deeply in body, mind, or spirit: injury, disease, injustice, oppression, abuse, violence, war, natural disasters, unemployment, slander, trauma, broken relationships, death of loved ones. What things have happened to us or by us that we fear will forever separate us from God?

Paul emphatically says, "No!" "I am convinced that neither death, nor life, nor angels, nor rulers, nor things present, nor things to come . . . nor anything else in all creation will be able to separate us from the love of God in Christ Jesus our Lord." What then are we to say about these things? Nothing is more powerful than God's abiding presence and eternal love. We need not fear, for God is with us, now and always.

God of love, thank you for your promise to be with us and to love us, no matter what. Amen.

SATURDAY, JULY 25 ~ *Read Matthew 13:31-33*

Stories are powerful. They make us feel. They inspire us to believe, take action, or change our behavior. Knowing the power of stories, Jesus used parables to teach. The word *parable* is from the Greek *parabolē*, meaning "to throw alongside to make a comparison." In telling parables, Jesus put an ordinary object alongside an extraordinary concept to illustrate a deeper truth.

In today's verses, Jesus first compares the kingdom of heaven to a mustard seed, taking an ordinary object and placing it alongside the extraordinary concept of the kingdom of God. Although a mustard seed is small and seemingly insignificant, when it is planted it grows into a tree in which birds can nest. Jesus then compares the kingdom of heaven to yeast. Yeast on its own does nothing, but when mixed in with warm water and flour it leavens the loaf, transforming it, so that it can rise and be baked into bread to feed people. What are we to say about these things? Something so meager and obscure can have great transformative power. This is what Jesus wants us to understand about the kingdom of heaven. The presence of God's kingdom may begin humbly: in Jesus' words, in healing the sick, in welcoming children, and in blessing five loaves of bread. But these small acts done with great love will grow and multiply. They have the power to change the world for good—one person at a time.

What is something small that has become significant for your faith? Was it a word of encouragement someone said to you or a meaningful gift someone gave to you? Was it a beautiful picture someone shared with you? These seemingly small things—once seeds or yeast—have been transformed into meaningful symbols. You have seen the kingdom of heaven is at hand. How can you nurture its growth for someone else?

God, thank you for the small things that hold great meaning. Help me see them and share them with others. Amen.

SUNDAY, JULY 26 ~ *Read Matthew 13:44-52*

Parables are stories Jesus told to illuminate his teachings. But just as we struggle to understand their meaning today, Jesus' disciples sometimes needed help too. "Explain to us the parable," they say in verse 36.

Jesus says that the kingdom of heaven is like a treasure hidden in a field, a merchant in search of fine pearls, and a net thrown into the sea. God's kingdom is hidden in plain sight, but often the trappings of this world prevent us from seeing and seeking what matters most. But those who seek God and God's kingdom with all of their heart, soul, mind, and strength will find it and give themselves fully to it, even sacrificing worldly belongings for eternal reward. In these parables, Jesus shows us what this looks like—a man who found the treasure and sold all he had to buy the field, the merchant who found the pearls and sold all he had to buy the pearl of great value. And when the kingdom of heaven fully comes, the angels will separate the good fish from the bad fish.

Although we want to know what we are to say about these parables, I think a better question to ask is: What then are we to *do* about these things? Elsewhere Jesus warns us against gaining the whole world but losing our life (Matt. 16:26), and he calls us to seek first the kingdom of God and all the things that matter most will be given to us (Matt. 6:33). What are the things of the world you engage in even though they do not feed your soul? How can you seek the kingdom of God and the things that matter most? What are some holy treasures and divine pearls you seek, which you would give everything to have and to hold?

Jesus, I wonder what to say about your teachings. Inspire me to act in response, shaping my life in the way you taught. Amen.

Justice, Transformation, and Abundance

JULY 27–AUGUST 2, 2026 • STEPHANE BROOKS

SCRIPTURE OVERVIEW: The readings illustrate a journey of struggle, transformation, and abundance in God's justice. In Genesis, Jacob wrestles with God, symbolizing the struggle for liberation that leaves us changed but empowered. Psalm 17 expresses the cry for justice and trust in God's faithful presence, affirming that God hears and upholds the oppressed. In Romans, Paul's deep anguish over his people reflects solidarity with those suffering and calls us to grieve injustice with hope for liberation. Finally, the verses in Matthew demonstrate God's abundant provision, revealing a kingdom of justice and inclusion. Together these readings invite us to wrestle with oppression, to trust God in the struggle, to grieve for the marginalized, and to work for an inclusive, abundant community.

QUESTIONS AND SUGGESTIONS FOR REFLECTION

- Read Genesis 32:22-31. What personal or communal struggles have shaped you? Reflect on how God might be present in those struggles.
- Read Psalm 17:1-7, 15. Where do you see injustice in your community? Spend time in prayer, trusting in God's justice and guidance.
- Read Romans 9:1-5. How can you grieve alongside the suffering? Consider an act of solidarity with those who are marginalized.
- Read Matthew 14:13-21. Where can you help share God's abundance? Look for a practical way to include someone in need today.

Rev. Stephane Brooks is married to Claudine Glasgow-Brooks and is the father of three girls. Stephane is a lifelong learner, a contemplative by nature with a love to see human beings achieve their full potential in Christ.

MONDAY, JULY 27 ~ *Read Genesis 32:22-24*

The journey toward liberation often begins in solitude. In Genesis 32, Jacob finds himself alone by the Jabbok River. In the stillness of the night, he wrestles with an enigmatic figure. This encounter is more than a physical struggle; it is a spiritual confrontation with his fears, his past mistakes, and the uncertainties of his future.

Jacob's struggle is active and relentless. He refuses to let go until he receives a blessing. By dawn, he is forever changed. He walks away with a new name, Israel, and a new and profound understanding of his identity and purpose. This transformation is a testament to the resilience of those who fight for justice, holding on to hope when the odds seem insurmountable. The story teaches us that struggle, though painful, can be a gateway to growth and renewal.

Consider the story of a refugee mother fleeing violence and poverty with her children. As night falls a mile away from the border, she wrestles with fear and physical exhaustion, unsure of what the future holds. Her perseverance mirrors Jacob's determination. Through her struggle, she discovers unexpected strength and courage, indeed, a reminder of God's presence even in the darkest moments preceding the dawn of a new day in her life.

In our wrestling, we encounter God not as a distant onlooker but as an active participant in our struggles. God meets us in our pain, strengthens us in our persistence, and transforms us through our endurance. Liberation emerges from this sacred encounter, equipping us to face the journey ahead with renewed hope and determination.

God of the night, you meet us in the depths of our struggles, wrestling with us and drawing us closer to you. Give us the courage to persist, the faith to seek your blessing, and the hope that morning will come. May our struggles lead to transformation and liberation. Amen.

TUESDAY, JULY 28 ~ *Read Genesis 32:25-31*

Struggle leaves its mark but leads to transformation. In his wrestling match, Jacob is struck on the hip, leaving him with a physical reminder of his transformative encounter with God. By dawn, he is no longer simply Jacob but Israel, "the one who struggles with God and prevails." Struggles for justice and dignity often leave scars, yet these marks can serve as reminders of resilience, growth, and God's presence in the midst of the fight.

Jacob's limp embodies a profound paradox: The wounds of struggle are evidence of God's transformative work. Through trials, we discover our true identity and calling. The limp symbolizes the cost of liberation but also the assurance of God's blessing and faithfulness. As Jacob walks away from the encounter, his steps may be slower, but his confidence is renewed—he carries marks of struggle and assurance of God's abiding presence.

This truth resonates in the life of Nelson Mandela. Emerging from twenty-seven years in prison in February 1990, Mandela bore both visible and invisible marks of his fight against apartheid, South Africa's brutal system of racial segregation. Yet he emerged transformed, with a vision for justice and reconciliation. Like Jacob's limp, Mandela's scars became a testimony to the power of hope and the transformative nature of struggle. His story reminds us that suffering can lead to profound change.

As we face challenges—systemic injustices or personal fears—we are invited to see our scars as signs of God's work. Transformation is rarely easy and often comes with pain, but it opens the door to liberation and a closer relationship with God. Our scars become symbols of God's faithfulness, reminding us that even in the hardest struggles, God is present.

God of transformation, you meet us in the struggle and leave us changed. Help us to see our wounds not as signs of failure but as reminders of your faithfulness. Grant us courage to embrace the cost of liberation and faith. Amen.

WEDNESDAY, JULY 29 ~ *Read Psalm 17:1-2*

Naming injustice and trusting in God's righteous judgment are of utter importance. The psalmist's cry is the voice of someone who has experienced injustice and is pleading for divine intervention. In itself, the plea is a reminder that such cries are never futile. For the psalmist, it is clear that God hears the laments of the oppressed and calls us to respond to them with both faith and action. Crying out for justice is both a spiritual act and a courageous declaration that, in God's world, injustice will not have the final word.

In the midst of the Great Depression, Dorothy Day, an American activist and co-founder of the Catholic Worker Movement, devoted her life to advocating for the poor and marginalized. She organized peaceful protests, provided direct aid through houses of hospitality, and fought tirelessly for workers' rights. Her faith informed every aspect of her activism as she saw Christ in the faces of the suffering. One of Day's most profound acts of protest was her consistent resistance to systemic injustices such as exploitative labor practices. She was arrested numerous times for her peaceful protests, but she never wavered in her commitment to justice. Her work not only addressed immediate needs but also inspired a broader movement for social and economic equality.

Day's story reminds us that crying out for justice is both an act of hope and a call to action. Like the psalmist, Day trusted that her cries would reach God and that her efforts, however small, would contribute to the building of a more just and compassionate world.

Think about the injustices you witness in your daily life. What small yet significant steps can you take to stand for justice? Know that whether through a single act of courage, supporting marginalized communities, or joining movements for change, your voice can make a difference. Trust that God walks with you, amplifying every one of your cries for justice.

THURSDAY, JULY 30 ~ *Read Romans 9:1-5*

God's faithfulness throughout history reminds us to trust in God's power to bring true freedom to all. Paul reflects on the profound blessings given to the Israelites: covenants, the law, the prophets, and the lineage of Christ. Despite this rich heritage, Paul is anguished by his readers' inability to recognize the salvation God continually offers. For Paul, this legacy is not just a record of the past; it stands as a testament to God's unwavering commitment to liberation and redemption. It calls us to trust in God's presence, especially in times of oppression and hardship.

The story of salvation is a story of liberation. From the Exodus of the Israelites to Jesus' ministry, God's actions have consistently aimed to set the oppressed free. God's promises, like the covenant with Israel, continue to inspire courage and resilience for those striving for equity and freedom.

This message was central to the work of Richard Twiss, a Native American Christian theologian and activist. Twiss dedicated his life to healing and justice for Indigenous communities in the United States. He worked to reconcile Native American and Christian identities, reclaiming the gospel from the painful legacy of colonialism. Twiss emphasized that Jesus' teachings are a source of empowerment and liberation. His life demonstrated that trusting in God's faithfulness is not just about remembering the past but about acting with hope and purpose in the present to create a future of justice and equality.

God's promises remain active and alive, calling us to partner in the work of liberation and healing. Let this faithfulness inspire us to pursue justice with courage and compassion.

God of all nations, you have shown your faithfulness through generations. Help us remember your promises and be inspired by those who walked in faith before us. May we seek to bring justice and healing, knowing that your vision for liberation includes all people. Amen.

FRIDAY, JULY 31 ~ *Read Psalm 17:3-7; 15*

Psalm 17 is a heartfelt prayer for God's protection and justice. The psalmist cries out for deliverance from the wicked and seeks God's loving care. The words of the psalm reflect a deep trust in God's faithful presence and a firm hope in God's ability to right the wrongs of the world. Liberation theology reminds us that God's presence is found wherever we fight for justice and dignity. To seek God's face is to stand with those who are oppressed and join in their struggle for freedom.

The psalmist's vision offers a powerful image of hope. For those living under oppression, seeing God's face represents the fulfillment of justice and liberation. It is a promise that God's love is not distant or abstract but active in transforming the world. This hope calls us to act, trusting that God's justice moves through our hands and hearts to bring real change.

This truth comes alive in the story of Fannie Lou Hamer, a civil rights leader who dedicated her life to the fight for justice. Born to sharecroppers in Mississippi, Hamer endured poverty, discrimination, and brutal violence as she worked tirelessly to secure voting rights for Black Americans. Her faith was the foundation of her activism. In a 1964 speech, she said, "You can pray until you faint, but if you don't get up and try to do something, God is not going to put it in your lap." Hamer's unwavering courage reminds us that seeking God's face means stepping into action and standing with those in need.

Her life reflects the psalmist's plea for God's justice and faithfulness. It shows us that seeing God's face is not just a spiritual promise but an invitation to create a world where dignity and freedom are shared by all.

God of justice, hold us close. Strengthen our faith and guide our steps, that we may see your face in acts of love and justice. Help us bring hope to a world in need of your light. Amen.

SATURDAY, AUGUST 1 ~ *Read Matthew 14:13-20*

The story of the feeding of the five thousand is a profound testament to God's abundance. In this miracle, Jesus overturns the assumptions of scarcity and reveals the justice and generosity at the heart of God's Kingdom. With only five loaves and two fish, Jesus provides more than enough for everyone, reminding us that in God's economy, there is no lack—only provision for all.

At first, the disciples respond with doubt: "We have only five loaves and two fish." Their words reflect a mindset shaped by limitations and fear, common in a world that prioritizes hoarding and exclusion over sharing. But Jesus doesn't send the crowd away hungry. Instead, he invites the disciples to participate in a miracle of abundance. They bring what little they have, and, in Jesus' hands, it becomes enough to feed the multitude with leftovers to spare.

This moment challenges us to examine the systems and attitudes that perpetuate scarcity in our world. Hunger, poverty, and exclusion are not inevitable. They are the result of greed, fear, and the unjust systems that result from both. When we see God as one who requires justice, we understand that God's provision is meant to be shared by all, not controlled by the few. This story calls us to trust in God's abundance as we work to create communities where no one goes hungry or is denied basic needs.

The miracle is more than an act of compassion; it's a glimpse of God's kingdom—a place where everyone is included at the table and generosity overcomes greed and fear. Jesus' actions remind us that liberation is not only spiritual but also involves ensuring physical nourishment for all people.

God of abundance, you reveal your justice through acts of miraculous provision. Help us to trust in your generosity, to share what we have, and to create spaces of welcome for all. May we reflect your kingdom by working for a world where no one is left hungry and all experience your grace. Amen.

SUNDAY, AUGUST 2 ~ *Read Matthew 14:21*

The conclusion of the feeding miracle contains a significant detail: 5,000 men were fed, "besides women and children." In a society where women and children were often seen as secondary or invisible, this phrase reminds us that they were present and nourished. This inclusion reflects the radical nature of God's kingdom—a place where everyone, especially those on the margins, is valued and embraced.

Our understanding of God as one who invites everyone to the table calls us to notice these details and challenge the systems that perpetuate exclusion. Who are the people whose contributions are overlooked, whose voices are silenced? It is still the women and children, but also the poor, immigrants, and those marginalized due to race, ability, or other forms of inequality. At a time when socio-political ideologies are beckoning us to return to past exclusionary practices, the feeding of the multitude invites us to re-imagine community as one where every person has a place at the table and no one is left out of God's abundance.

This miracle is more than a story of provision. It is a call to action for building communities rooted in justice and inclusion. As followers of Christ, we are challenged to actively work against attitudes and systems that exclude others. Whether through advocacy, service, or fostering genuine relationships, we are called to create spaces where everyone is not just included but celebrated.

Take time today to identify individuals or groups in your community who are excluded or overlooked. What practical steps can you take to include and uplift them? Whether it's through listening, offering support, or advocating for change, commit to one action that embodies the kingdom's radical inclusivity.

Of Faith and Fear

AUGUST 3–9, 2026 • DOUG PAYSOUR

SCRIPTURE OVERVIEW: The strange dynamics in the history of Abraham's family continue in Genesis. We meet Joseph who is sold into slavery by his jealous brothers. God will ultimately use this for good, as we read in Psalm 105, but in Joseph's time, there clearly is significant dysfunction. In the Gospel reading, Peter learns a valuable lesson about trust. He initially shows great faith, but he falters when he allows himself to be distracted by the waves. Paul emphasizes in Romans that every person is welcome to call on the name of the Lord and be saved, but it falls to us to offer them the good news. How can they believe if they never hear?

QUESTIONS AND SUGGESTIONS FOR REFLECTION

- Read Genesis 37:1-4, 12-28. In the face of cruelty, how do you continue to believe in God's dream of unity for us all?
- Read Psalm 105:1-6, 16-22, 45b. How has God used a difficult situation in your life to bring a surprisingly positive outcome? How has that enhanced your faith?
- Read Romans 10:5-15. How does your faith compel you to proclaim God's love for all—no exceptions? What does this look like for you?
- Read Matthew 14:22-33. When have you struggled to trust Jesus through life's trials? How has Jesus revealed his presence and companionship anyway?

Rev. Doug Paysour is a recently retired elder in the Virginia Annual Conference of The United Methodist Church, having served forty years in ministry in churches of all types. Writing is his primary ministry tool, including short stories, devotionals, *Virginia Advocate* articles, skits, news releases, and stewardship programs, in addition to all the usual pastoral writings. Doug lives in Blue Ridge, VA, just outside of Roanoke, with his wife, Gail.

MONDAY, AUGUST 3 ~ *Read Genesis 37:1-4, 12-28*

What a dysfunctional family! The dad, Jacob, also known as Israel, chose a favorite son, Joseph, out of all of his many sons and made him the famous long coat of many colors, a royal robe. Joseph stayed at home with dad while the brothers took the flock to Shechem—Joseph was pampered while his brothers worked. The section in between today's reading recounts Joseph's dreams in which he sees his brothers bow down to him. Small wonder that they hated him.

It's not uncommon for siblings to argue, bully, tattle, and vie for their parents' favor. Yet this family's dysfunction rises to the level of a Steinbeck novel as the brothers in the field see Joseph coming to check on them and, with one voice, plot his murder. Reuben, the eldest, suggests that they should not kill him, just toss him into a pit. He plans to rescue young Joseph and take him home to dad, while telling on the murderous brothers. They throw Joseph in the pit, then later pull him out and sell him as a slave to Midianite traders who are fortunately passing by. Just another day in the dysfunctional household of Jacob.

This family shows the staggering depth of dysfunction that occurs when members are made to feel unloved, overlooked, and unimportant. And this isn't just any family—it's the family God has chosen to work through to bless the entire world. What may be more unimaginable is that God still succeeds—not in spite of the dysfunction, but because of the dysfunction, God works through this family. Years later, Joseph will note that the arrival of the Midianite traders was not just luck or fortune but the very hand of God putting him on a path to preserve the household of Israel in a time of famine. God can, indeed, work through any dysfunction or struggles we might bring to our story.

God, thank you for the times you have taken the horrible parts of our lives and brought some greater good. Amen.

TUESDAY, AUGUST 4 ~ *Read Genesis 37:1-4*

These formative stories in Genesis of Abraham, Isaac, and Jacob are not just about some ancient dysfunctional family, but are about the people of God, the Chosen People. This is indicated with the dual nature of the name *Israel*—this is both the name of the people and the other name of Jacob, the father of the twelve brothers, each who represent one of the twelve tribes of Israel. Genesis tells us that Joseph, one of these brothers, was the favorite son, the Chosen One, the son of Jacob's favorite wife, Rachel. These Genesis stories are earthy and gritty and do not photoshop the flaws in their spiritual complexion. Joseph, the Chosen One, does not enjoy this place of privilege among his brothers, however. As we saw yesterday, he suffers for it, being thrown into a pit, sold into slavery, ending up imprisoned in a land far from home, fearing for his life.

Israel, the Chosen People, suffer as well. If you ask a rabbi, the Suffering Servant songs from Isaiah, in which the servant of God suffers on behalf of the world and brings redemption and hope, are said to be about Israel. For us as Christians, we read the passages about the Suffering Servant and we see Jesus, the Chosen One.

Joseph's brothers were jealous of him as the favored son, the Chosen One, but they didn't understand the suffering that came along with his position. Joseph, the people of Israel, and Jesus all suffered for being Chosen, but always with a redemptive purpose in God's mind.

As Christians, we are tempted to seek the place of honor and glory, forgetting that in following Jesus, the Suffering Servant, we are called to pick up a cross and follow his way, which brings salvation and hope.

Gracious God, may our suffering, like Joseph's, be not only endured but bring healing and wholeness. Amen.

WEDNESDAY, AUGUST 5 ~ *Read Psalm 105:1-6, 16-22, 45b*

My family is surprised that I routinely watch a comedian who, although having been raised as one, is not only admittedly not Christian, but avowedly anti-Christian. He caught my ear one time when he talked about one of his reasons for not being a Christian. He said a God who craves our praise, who needs our praise, who demands our praise is a megalomaniac and not worthy of our praise. As I ruminated on that thought, it occurred to me that God doesn't need our praise as much as we need to praise God, to remind ourselves that God is God and we are not, to place ourselves in a humble, proper relationship to God.

In our reading, the psalmist tells of some of the wonderful works of God, recounting Joseph's story from the time that he was sold into slavery, to his false imprisonment, to his eventual elevation to the king's side, sharing God's wisdom. All of this was God's doing, the psalmist says, so go tell, go sing of God's wonderful works.

I have served as an adult volunteer on several youth mission trips over the years. On each trip, we were encouraged to watch for what we call "God-sightings," specific ways that we saw the hand of God at work in the midst of home repairs and spending time with the residents of those homes. Each evening as we gathered at the end of our work day to worship and praise, we would share stories of these "God-sightings" with one another, celebrating God's presence among us. To hear those stories always reawakens in me a sense of wonder at God's work in our everyday. I am inspired to seek for "God-sightings" not just on mission trips but in my everyday life, and to praise God in response.

God of all creation, we praise you for all the ways that you work in our lives, day by day. Open our eyes to your loving grace. Amen.

THURSDAY, AUGUST 6 ~ *Read Romans 10:5-15*

The letters of Paul collected in our New Testament provide something far short of what could be considered Paul's systematic theology. These letters, far from being sweeping theological statements, represent specific advice to specific communities facing specific situations. But even with acknowledging the specific nature of Paul's writings, we still find within these letters foundational truths of faith that have helped Christians understand our identity and beliefs for over two thousand years. In Romans 9–11, Paul wrestles with the issue of not only the Law, but the Chosen People, the Jews. We can learn so much about faith that is relevant to us today in this short passage.

According to Paul, faith is in what God has done in Jesus: "If you confess with your lips that Jesus is Lord and believe in your heart that God raised him from the dead, you will be saved." For Paul, this act of God brings salvation that cannot be found in the Law. Since we cannot keep the Law, it cannot bring life. Faith in Christ brings life. Jesus' resurrection is a sign of God's grace that overcomes the power of sin and death.

Another point Paul makes is that salvation is not about what we have done, but what God has done. Verses 6-7 point this out in a strange and oblique way. Paul applies a new interpretation to Deuteronomy 30:12-13. It is not up to us to bring salvation through the Messiah into the world. God has already done it.

Finally, salvation is not only for the Jew, but also for the Greek (that is, the Gentile, everyone else). This is a primary theme of the theological treatise of Romans 9–11, and indeed the primary message of Paul's work. In Paul's legacy, we can open wide the doors of salvation, proclaiming to every person the love of Christ.

We are grateful, O God, for the gift of life and life abundant through Jesus. Help us to live out our faith. Amen.

FRIDAY, AUGUST 7 ~ *Read Romans 10:5-15*

A line from the musical *Jesus Christ Superstar* has stuck with me. It conveys the idea that Israel in the time of Jesus had no mass communication, implying that some other time and place would have been a far more beneficial time to spread the word about Jesus. The story of the Christian movement, however, showed that God knew what God was doing, as the church exploded through the verbal witness of what started out as 120 believers gathered in an upper room in Jerusalem after Jesus' resurrection. The faith spread like a wildfire as God's Spirit worked through such a small contingent. In the Acts of the Apostles, they are shown fearlessly proclaiming "Christ is Risen," telling of God's wonderful works. Paul focuses not only on the power of the word, but also on the necessity for tellers, proclaimers. That's what fueled the growth of the early Church.

When I came to my most recent appointment at Windsor Hills UMC, they had just completed a training with another Paul, the Rev. Paul Nickerson, who consulted with us for several years about reaching new people. We learned several things from Paul that I preached about over and over again. One of his key messages is that it is up to all of us—not just the person in the pulpit—to proclaim the good news of Jesus.

Paul Nickerson taught us that we needed to be out and about, making connections in the community as a congregation and as individuals. The Apostle Paul wrote, "How beautiful are the feet of those who bring good news!" This is an apt reminder that it is our feet who carry that good news of Christ's love to the world.

O Lord our God, give us a heart to share and words to share with those who do not yet know you. Amen.

SATURDAY, AUGUST 8 ~ *Read Matthew 14:22-33*

At this point in Matthew's Gospel, it is a fearful time in the life of Jesus and the lives of disciples. Jesus had just heard about Herod having John the Baptist beheaded, so he did what he often did—he went out alone to pray. Perhaps he was processing that "his hour" was nearing also. Jesus' way of dealing with the fearful time to come was to pray.

When the crowds followed him, he had compassion on them, healed their sick, and fed thousands of people, demonstrating his power to do God's work even further. He then sent the disciples away in a boat to the other side, so that he could continue to pray up on the mountain, where he spent all night.

Meanwhile, a storm arose and battered the disciples' boat far from land. That's how they spent their night. It seems strange that in Matthew's version of this story, it doesn't say that they were afraid in the storm like in other Gospels. They were, after all, experienced boatmen, so they would have known what to do. They seem to survive the nighttime storm just fine. Instead, it is only the next morning, when they see Jesus walking on the water toward them, that fear strikes them. "It is a ghost," they cry out. They don't recognize Jesus and they fear the unknown.

Jesus puts their minds at ease, making himself known. "Take heart, it is I," he says. *Eigo eimi,* in the Greek, "I am." This is the same thing God said to Moses from the burning bush, when Moses asked God's name. Jesus is identified as the very presence and power of God. God is near, God is here. Do not be afraid.

In fearful times, do as Jesus did—pray. In fearful times, know that Immanuel, God is with us.

O Lord our God, when we fear the unknown, help us to recognize your presence and that with you all things are possible. Amen.

SUNDAY, AUGUST 9 ~ *Read Matthew 14:22-33*

Peter makes a strange request to verify Jesus' presence. Jesus has come to them walking on water, and Peter asks, "If it is you, command me to come to you on the water." When Jesus tells him to come, he does and, at first, he does okay. Then he recognizes his precarious situation. He notices the wind and that he is walking on water and, small wonder, fear sets in and he begins to sink. He cries out for the Lord to save him. After Jesus rescues him, he tells Peter that he has little faith. Frankly, he had a lot more faith than I would have had, attempting to walk on water like Jesus. What an audacious thing, to step out of a solid boat of safety into the unknown danger of water.

In my first appointment, I failed an early test of faith. Our ministerial association proposed that we hold a community Thanksgiving service, Black and White churches together, something audacious in that time and place. Being a naïve young pastor, not realizing that worship was one of only two things pastors are fully in charge of in our polity, I called a council meeting to ask permission to host such a service. One influential member of the church got wind of the meeting and stormed in, saying that it would happen over his dead body. I rescinded the invitation at the behest of the council. Oh, me of little faith.

The pastor of the Black church, Maynard Jones, instead invited us to worship in their church. We did an audacious thing for God, due to Pastor Maynard's faith. Years later, I returned to the church I had served for a homecoming service and was surprised to see the special music provided by Pastor Maynard and his family. God had clearly changed hearts in that church. God worked through my failure and the failures of that church to teach us that we must have courage in our faith to be bold, to step out of the boat into something new.

Lord, our God, give us faith to attempt great things for you and for your kingdom. Amen.

Faith Beyond Boundaries

AUGUST 10–16, 2026 • ASHLEY BOGGAN

SCRIPTURE OVERVIEW: Joseph has risen to a high position in Egypt, and now his brothers come searching for food in a time of famine. He reveals his true identity and reinterprets their evil intentions as being part of God's plan. Sometimes we too are granted perspective to see God's working in difficult times. The psalmist rejoices when God's people are living in unity. Paul declares that his people are not rejected by the merciful God, for God's promises are unchanging. In Matthew, Jesus teaches that God looks on the inside, not the outside. Thus, what you take into your body is less important than what comes from your heart.

QUESTIONS AND SUGGESTIONS FOR REFLECTION

- Read Genesis 45:1-15. When have you struggled to forgive someone? When have you needed forgiveness? How does recognizing your own need for forgiveness help you to be more compassionate toward others?
- Read Psalm 133. What does it mean to "live together in unity"? What actions can you take to live in unity with those around you, even those with whom you disagree?
- Read Romans 11:1-2a, 29-32. How does the idea of God's "irrevocable gifts" affect your understanding of grace and salvation? What gifts and callings from God might you need to rediscover or embrace in this season of your life?
- Read Matthew 15:10-28. How does the Canaanite woman's faith inspire you to persist in seeking God's help, even when it seems delayed or denied?

Dr. Ashley Boggan is the General Secretary of the General Commission on Archives and History of The United Methodist Church and ultimate "Metho-nerd." She is a laywoman in the Greater New Jersey Annual Conference and attends the UMC in Madison.

MONDAY, AUGUST 10 ~ *Read Genesis 45:1-8*

Joseph's perspective on the hardships he endured is rooted in God's providence. He recognizes that, despite his brothers' betrayal, God has a greater plan to use his situation to save many lives. Joseph's story reminds us that God's purposes can be accomplished even in the midst of pain and betrayal.

Richard Allen was a formerly enslaved man who had purchased his freedom and become a Methodist preacher. He, along with many other Black members of the church, faced racism within St. George's Methodist Episcopal Church in Philadelphia. Despite their contributions and participation, they were often forced to sit in segregated areas. One Sunday, Allen and others were forcibly removed from the church while praying in an area reserved for white congregants.

This moment of betrayal could have fostered bitterness and division. However, rather than responding with anger or seeking retribution, Allen demonstrated a spirit of forgiveness and trust in God's plan, much like Joseph. Instead of abandoning his faith, he recognized that God had a greater purpose for him and his community. In 1787 he established the Free African Society, which became the foundation of the first independent Black denomination in the United States, the American Methodist Episcopal Church.

Allen's decision to forgive the wrongs done to him and his congregation allowed him to focus on creating a space where African Americans could worship freely, without oppression. Just as Joseph's forgiveness of his brothers helped preserve life during a famine, Allen's decision to move forward in faith and forgiveness helped to preserve the spiritual and social life of a marginalized community, planting seeds for justice and equality.

Lord, help me to see your hand in my life, even when things are difficult. Teach me to trust in your plans and to forgive those who have hurt me, just as Joseph forgave his brothers. Amen.

TUESDAY, AUGUST 11 ~ *Read Genesis 45:9-15*

The story of Joseph and his brothers culminates in a powerful moment of reconciliation. After years of separation and hurt, they are finally reunited. Joseph, now in a position of power, chooses compassion over revenge. He not only forgives but also provides for his family's future.

After the Civil War, the United States was deeply divided, with lingering wounds between the North and South. Racial tensions, economic disparity, and regional bitterness plagued the country. Bishop Gilbert Haven, a prominent Methodist Episcopal Church leader, believed that true reconciliation and healing would come not just from forgiveness on a personal level, but from social reform and racial justice.

Haven advocated for racial equality and the full inclusion of African Americans in the life of the church and society. Rather than maintain the status quo of segregation, Haven championed the cause of African Americans during Reconstruction, pushing for equal rights and education. He built relationships with African American leaders, advocated for the rights of freed slaves, and worked tirelessly for their social and spiritual welfare. He envisioned a church and a society where former oppressors and the oppressed could worship and live together as equals.

Much like Joseph, Haven used his influence as a bishop to promote healing and reconciliation for the larger community. He understood that reconciliation wasn't just a personal matter but had profound social implications that could transform the nation. Haven's efforts toward social reconciliation embody the call to be instruments of God's grace in a broken world. We too are called to love others deeply and to work toward healing in our relationships.

God of reconciliation, thank you for the gift of restored relationships. Show me how to bring your grace to others in tangible ways. Amen.

When John Wesley, the founder of Methodism, first began his ministry, the Church of England was deeply divided along social and class lines. Many marginalized groups found little acceptance within established churches. Wesley recognized that the gospel message should transcend these divisions and sought to create a movement that emphasized community, fellowship, and shared life in faith.

Wesley's approach was not just to preach to the well-to-do but to reach out to the poor, the sick, and the marginalized, fostering a sense of belonging and unity among people from diverse backgrounds. He established societies where people could gather for prayer, worship, and mutual support, creating a space where unity could thrive despite differences in social status, race, and life experiences. In America, these gatherings became a significant movement bringing together people from various backgrounds to worship and share their faith. Camp meetings often included both Black and White participants, fostering relationships that crossed racial and social barriers.

The imagery in Psalm 133, with its references to oil and dew, echoes the spirit of these early Methodist gatherings. Just as the oil flowing down Aaron's beard symbolizes divine blessing and sanctification, the unity experienced in these meetings allowed God's grace and love to flow freely among participants, nourishing their spirits and empowering them for service.

True unity does not require uniformity but rather a commitment to love and respect one another, recognizing the inherent dignity of every person. By building bridges of understanding and grace, we can create spaces where God's blessings can flow, leading to healing and peace in a divided world.

Loving God, help me to live in unity with others. Teach me to work for peace, understanding, and love in my relationships and my community. Amen.

THURSDAY, AUGUST 13 ~ *Read Romans 11:1-2a, 29-32*

In Romans 11, Paul reassures the early church that God has not rejected the people of Israel, despite their disobedience. The gifts and calling of God, Paul emphasizes, are irrevocable. God does not abandon God's promises. Whether we have been faithful or faltered, God's faithfulness remains constant.

In May 1738, John Wesley was in a state of spiritual crisis. He had been a clergyman in the Church of England for years, yet he struggled with a profound sense of unworthiness and uncertainty about his faith. Despite his dedication to ministry and his pursuit of holiness, he felt distant from God and questioned whether he had truly experienced salvation.

On May 24, 1738, Wesley attended a meeting on Aldersgate Street in London where someone was reading Martin Luther's preface to the Epistle to the Romans. As he listened, Wesley felt his heart "strangely warmed," a moment he described as a profound encounter with God's grace. He realized that God's love and acceptance were not contingent upon his past failures or feelings of inadequacy. Instead, he understood that God's gifts—salvation, grace, and calling—were irrevocable, just as Paul asserts in Romans 11.

This transformative experience led Wesley to embrace the concept of prevenient grace, the idea that God's grace is always at work in our lives, beckoning us toward repentance, healing, and transformation. Wesley's experience highlights that even in times of spiritual lows or when we falter, God's faithfulness remains constant. Wesley's story is a testament to the understanding that we are continually pursued by God's grace, reminding us that we are never beyond reach, no matter how distant we may feel.

God of grace, thank you for your faithfulness, even when I am unfaithful. Help me to trust in your promises. Renew in me a sense of purpose and calling as I follow you. Amen.

God's mercy extends to all, says Paul. This passage highlights the mystery of God's inclusive grace—that mercy is available to all, no matter their past disobedience. This universal mercy challenges us to think about how we, as followers of Christ, extend that same mercy to others.

Sojourner Truth, born Isabella Baumfree in 1797, was an African American abolitionist and women's rights activist. After escaping from slavery, she became a powerful advocate for both racial and gender equality. Throughout her life, Truth faced immense prejudice and discrimination, yet she embraced a faith that emphasized God's universal love and mercy. One of her most famous speeches, "Ain't I a Woman?" exemplifies her belief in God's inclusive grace. In it, she challenged societal norms that excluded Black women from the conversation about rights and dignity. By doing so, she emphasized that God's mercy and love extend to all, regardless of race or gender.

Truth's life and advocacy serve as a powerful testament to the universality of God's love, demonstrating how a faith grounded in grace can inspire action against injustice. Her commitment to extending mercy to others reflects the very essence of Paul's message about God's inclusive grace.

Truth's story challenges us to embody the same mercy that we have received. It calls us to be conduits of God's grace, extending compassion, understanding, and forgiveness to all people, affirming the boundless mercy of God. Truth's legacy serves as a reminder that through our actions, we can reflect the love and grace of God in a world that desperately needs it.

God of mercy, thank you for the grace you have shown me. Help me to be a vessel of your mercy to others, extending forgiveness and compassion just as you have done for me. Amen.

Jesus shifts the focus from external religious practices to the condition of the heart. The Pharisees were concerned about ceremonial cleanliness, but Jesus challenges their view, teaching that true defilement comes from what is inside a person—the thoughts, intentions, and words that flow from the heart. Holiness is not about mere outward appearances or strict adherence to religious rituals but about cultivating a heart aligned with God's will.

Frances Willard, a prominent figure in the Women's Christian Temperance Union in the late 19th century, was deeply influenced by the teachings of John Wesley, particularly his emphasis on inward holiness and the transformative power of God's grace. Willard understood that true holiness goes beyond mere outward appearances and rituals; it involves a deep, authentic connection with God that leads to a transformed heart and life.

Willard recognized that social issues were often rooted in the condition of individuals' hearts. She believed that personal transformation must precede social change. Rather than solely focusing on legislation, she emphasized the importance of changing hearts and attitudes within communities. Willard wrote extensively about the need for a moral revival, believing that individuals could only contribute to societal well-being if they first experienced inner change through God's grace. Her famous quote, "Do everything in moderation," reflected her belief that true holiness is not about rigid rules but about creating a heart and mind aligned with Christ's teachings.

Frances Willard's story exemplifies the understanding that true holiness is about being inwardly transformed so that our actions and attitudes mirror Christ's love, challenging us to prioritize the condition of our hearts in all that we do.

Lord, examine my heart and purify it. Make me mindful of the words and actions that flow from within me, so that I may reflect your love and truth. Amen.

SUNDAY, AUGUST 16 ~ *Read Matthew 15:21-28*

In the second part of this passage, we encounter the Canaanite woman, an outsider to the Jewish faith, who persistently seeks healing for her daughter. At first, Jesus seems to dismiss her, stating that his mission is for the "lost sheep of Israel." However, her persistence and humility reveal a deep faith, and in the end, Jesus commends her for her great faith and grants her request.

Jarena Lee was the first woman to officially preach in the African Methodist Episcopal Church (AME). She was born in 1783 and grew up in a society that marginalized and excluded both women and people of African descent. Despite these barriers, she felt a powerful calling to preach and share her faith. Initially, she faced significant opposition, because of both her race and her gender. Many dismissed her, believing that she did not fit the mold of a preacher. She was persistent in her efforts, seeking opportunities to share her message and testify to God's goodness.

Eventually, Jarena Lee found a way to preach and began traveling extensively, sharing the gospel and bringing hope to countless individuals who had been overlooked by society. Her ministry was marked by a focus on inclusivity and grace, reaching out to those who had been marginalized.

Lee's story exemplifies the belief that faith can emerge from unexpected places and that God's grace knows no boundaries. Just as Jesus commended the Canaanite woman for her great faith, Lee's ministry demonstrated that God was at work among those whom society often dismissed. She became a powerful voice for the voiceless, showing that faith and calling can transcend societal limitations.

Gracious God, thank you for your mercy that reaches beyond boundaries. Help me to have faith like the Canaanite woman, persistently seeking justice and extending your grace. Amen.

Free For Abundant Life

AUGUST 17–23, 2026 • AMY ODEN

SCRIPTURE OVERVIEW: Our passages share a common theme of being free for the full life God desires for us. In Exodus, we see the stark contrast between Pharaoh's death-dealing fear and the fearless women who step forward to bring life. The psalm celebrates the soaring aliveness that comes with the freedom only God can provide. In Romans, Paul describes being free to not conform to the world's values so that we live our everyday life completely transformed. In Matthew, Jesus offers another kind of freedom. He shows Peter who he truly is, free from labels that have defined him up to this point. Instead, Jesus offers Peter a wider freedom than ever before.

QUESTIONS AND SUGGESTIONS FOR REFLECTION

- Read Exodus 1:8–2:10. How do you long to be free from fear in your life? What might be God's invitation for you?
- Read Psalm 124. Where does being overwhelmed hold your life captive? What's it like to trust that God is for us, setting us free?
- Read Romans 12:1-8. What helps you pay attention and listen to your body's wisdom? How might God be speaking to you through your body in everyday life?
- Read Matthew 16:13-20. How does Christ show you who you really are? Who does Jesus free you to become?

Amy Oden is a seminary professor, retreat leader, spiritual director, and grandmother. She is the author of *Right Here, Right Now: The Practice of Christian Mindfulness* (Abingdon Press, 2017).

MONDAY, AUGUST 17 ~ *Read Exodus 1:8-22*

Fear controls Pharaoh in this story. Pharaoh fears that the Hebrews, a large immigrant group, will grow to outnumber Egyptians. He is afraid of his political enemies, afraid the Hebrews will join forces with them against him. He even fears the babies being born and decrees their deaths. Fear is the corrosive power that drives him, leaving only death and destruction.

When my husband was diagnosed with frontotemporal dementia, my heart sank into fear. Would I lose everything? Would he become a stranger to me? Would all our savings be devoured in his care? I feared the unknown, the terrifying abyss of dementia. The fear made me grip each day tightly, afraid of what I might lose next. I tried to prop up our routines, staving off the chaos of dementia.

Eventually, this fear became its own prison, a stranglehold on our lives that prevented me from really seeing Perry for who he was becoming each day. My fear kept me from surrendering our lives into God's keeping or being present to the life, however painful, we were actually living. My fear robbed me of the life right in front of me.

As God invited me to simply surrender to the actual life before me, to let it unfold and to live in it deeply, fear lost its grip. Here, I could behold the grace shot through every hour of every day. Here, in the flow of grief and awe, fear no longer ruled.

Fear stops our ears from hearing God's voice, blinds us to the grace in front of us, and robs us of this present moment. Yet God consistently works to free us.

Make both hands into fists and grip them as tightly as you can. Then release them and feel the wave of relaxed energy that flows through your body. Allow this physical sensation of release to accompany your prayer.

Free me from fear, O God. Show me your path of life. Amen.

TUESDAY, AUGUST 18 ~ *Read Psalm 124*

Many of us have an almost constant sense of anxiety. Our ability to constantly post, text, and mass communicate on issues small and large, local and global, leads to pervasive and powerful anxiety. Psalm 124 reminds us that while the circumstances may be much different, the experience of anxiety is not new. It's very human to be gripped by anxiety and to feel overwhelmed.

We can feel in our bodies the psalm's visceral descriptions of overwhelming floods and attacks, the terror of being trapped and eaten alive. These visuals provide the metaphors for our own lives: flooded by responsibilities, trapped by never-ending demands, eaten up by toxic systems. We feel stuck with no way out, condemned to put one foot in front of the other in a panicky march through the day.

At the heart of this psalm is the good news: God is for us, "on our side," sparing us from the threat of being devoured. God sets us free to flourish along with all of creation, to take flight and soar.

Our anxiety comes, in part, from outsized expectations and unhealthy systems in which we live. Those loud voices can drown out God's gentle voice. It can help when we sense anxiety to pause, breathe deeply, and ask, "Whose voice is this?" Is it God's voice that pressures us to go faster, to be perfect, or to do more? Probably not. Anxiety is not God's dream for us.

Pause now and take three deep breaths in a row. Notice the release in your body as you breathe in and out. Allow your muscles to relax and let go. Feel some measure of peace. Know that this is God's will for your well-being. God is for us, "on our side," the scripture says, setting us free with each breath, again and again.

Remind me to breathe, Holy One. Remind me that you are on my side. Help me to listen for only your voice. Amen.

WEDNESDAY, AUGUST 19 ~ *Read Romans 12:1-2*

When Paul says, "Do not be conformed to this age," I hear a powerful invitation to be free of society's messaging, expectations, and standards. Another translation puts it this way, "Don't become so well-adjusted to your culture that you fit into it without even thinking. Instead, fix your attention on God" (MSG).

For me, "don't fit in without even thinking" has meant un-learning some key values the world holds dear. A subtle yet powerful one is usefulness. Like many of us, I've believed my worth resided in my usefulness. I was driven to measure my productivity at the end of each day. Productivity has been a functional god in my life.

When faced with my husband's dementia, I felt useless, helpless, even worthless. I couldn't fix it, I couldn't make our lives productive. Yet when I could "fix my attention on God" I could relax into the gift of each breath, each day. I could behold our lives within God's abundant life.

To be sure, usefulness is a good thing, as we all contribute to the well-being of our communities. However, when we value people only for their usefulness, we de-form ourselves into mere machines, only good for getting things done. This betrays our birthright as beloved of God.

When I can root myself in God, my fear of uselessness recedes as I allow God to delight in me, whether I'm productive or not. With my self-worth planted here, placing my "everyday, ordinary life . . . before God," I find that I'm "changed from the inside out" (MSG). Rooted here, I'm free to see myself and others through God's eyes, as precious and beloved, no matter what.

Free me to see myself and others through your eyes of love, no matter what. Amen.

Bold and fearless women take center stage at every turn in this story, though most are unnamed. Let's review. The Hebrew women bear so many children that powerful Pharaoh feels threatened. The midwives, Shiphrah and Puah, outwit Pharaoh with their sophisticated strategy to protect newborns. Moses' mother has the foresight and ingenuity to hide him for three months, keep him alive, then make a waterproof basket for him. Moses' sister watches over him in the dangers of the Nile. Pharaoh's daughter takes Moses to raise but first gives him to his Hebrew mother to nurse, an arrangement made by his sister. The women in this story are effective as powerful, free agents of deliverance!

By Egyptian standards, none of these women (except perhaps Pharaoh's daughter) have status, power, or wealth. None of them have religious standing. Yet each of them refused to be captive to fear. Each one steps into her freedom to act, even at great risk, and in doing so, each brings life.

These agents of God can empower us now. We have all known women in our lives, women who had no status or power, no credential or title, yet who acted in bold freedom to bless and change our lives. We may not remember their names; we may have never even known their names. Yet they were agents of grace, God's outpouring into us and into the world. They inspire us, as our biblical role models inspire us, to act in bold ways to bring deliverance to others. Remember them as concretely as you can and name them now, the unsung saints among us.

Name and thank God for those who have been agents of grace in your life. Pray for God's help to be an agent of grace for others.

FRIDAY, AUGUST 21 ~ *Read Matthew 16:13-20*

What is it like when you feel seen? This phrase has come into parlance in recent years to name a subtle yet powerful experience of being recognized for who we really are. Being known not for the category or box others put us in, not for who others assume we are, but being known as our real, true selves.

When we are seen as merely a label—"soccer mom," "rebellious teen," "old guy," "angry boss"—we feel misunderstood, diminished, invisible. When we relegate others to our assumptive categories, we do harm, failing to recognize the image of God in each precious one, the Christ in you meeting the Christ in me.

I wonder if Jesus felt "seen" when he asked Peter, "Who do people say I am?" Maybe Jesus is asking *do you see me for who I really am? Do you see past the boxes of 'teacher,' 'wonder-worker,' 'friend'? Do you see past who your religion has told you to expect?* Just by asking this question, Jesus invites Peter to truly have eyes to see (see Matt. 13:16). Peter can truly see "the Son of the living God" standing before him.

Immediately, Jesus turns the tables and really sees Peter beyond his social and family roles, even beyond his place as a disciple. Jesus names who Peter really is, the rock on which Jesus will build a church, an active ingredient for this new kindom at hand. Jesus proclaims him blessed.

Maybe when we can really see Jesus, we are freed to see ourselves as Jesus does. Jesus shows us who we really are. Like Peter, we see that we too are active ingredients for God's kindom at hand. We are challenged, called into becoming and into new opportunities and life.

Strip away false labels and show me myself as you see me, God. I long to be seen by you. Amen.

As we move further into the twenty-first century, Christians are reclaiming our bodies as part of our faith life. In the twentieth century, much of Christianity focused on the neck-up, as though faith is a set of thoughts to think or religious concepts to hone. Now Christians are re-discovering a more biblical and faithful reality: Life with God is full-bodied, not just neck-up.

Paul calls attention to our physical existence, telling us to "present your bodies." The Message translates this verse brilliantly, "Take your everyday, ordinary life—your sleeping, eating, going-to-work, and walking-around life—and place it before God as an offering." It's here in our bodily life that God is speaking, moving, challenging, and freeing us. God is not waiting until we enter church doors or until we open our Bible to show up. Wherever our bodies are, God is there, especially in the messy, ordinary world of daily life.

How do we then present our bodies as an offering? A good, first step is taking our bodies seriously. God inhabited a human body in Jesus, so surely God is at home here. We can be too. For me, this means paying attention to my body, not as something to fix or improve, but as a place to listen for God. Christian mindfulness practices have helped me focus on my breath and body so I can slow down long enough to let God have the floor. I focus on a few deep breaths and bring my awareness into my body, noticing sensations, attitudes, feelings. Then I invite God to hold it all with me, placing my current moment "before God as an offering." It's been amazing what I discover this way.

What might be possible if we listened for God in our "everyday, ordinary life—[our] sleeping, eating, going-to-work, and walking-around life?" Try listening for God through your body. How might we be "changed from the inside out" (MSG)?

Free me to listen for your voice in me, in this very body today. Amen.

SUNDAY, AUGUST 23 ~ *Read Psalm 124*

If the LORD had not been on our side . . ." (NIV). The psalm names the many catastrophes that could easily have befallen Israel but didn't: being devoured alive, swept away by flood, snared helplessly in a trap. These vivid scenarios remind us how fragile life is. We are to take nothing for granted, for life can be swept away in a moment. Describing the catastrophes that didn't happen brings my current reality into sharp contrast.

This form of prayer, "If not for God, then . . ." helps me see more clearly the amazing, simple gifts of the life before me: this meal, this person, this tree in all its glory. I find renewed gratitude, even astonishment, in this odd exercise of saying what didn't happen:

- If not for God, I could have withered and starved.
- If not for God, I could be alone without a friend.
- If not for God, this tree could be ravaged by fire.

To be sure, this sort of prayer can be dangerous, suggesting that God must not be on the side of those who experience tragedy or devastation. This can be insidious and spiritually toxic, suggesting that God plays favorites, sparing one neighbor's house while plowing a tornado through the house next door. We must take care to be clear: Claiming God's grace in my life does not require denying the presence of that same grace in others' lives. We can acknowledge with humility the ways God is present in our lives and encourage others to look for God's presence in their lives in a multitude of ways, as well.

As we close the week, try writing your own psalm. See what you discover about how you are freed for life. Experiment using the format "If not for God, then . . ."

Holy One, free us to see you in all things, to embrace the full life you set before us. Amen.

God's Ways Are Not Our Ways

AUGUST 24–30, 2026 • SCOTT GUNN

SCRIPTURE OVERVIEW: Each of the four readings this week remind us that God's purposes may pull us in surprising directions. We might have our own plans, but God's providence is bigger than our thinking. In Exodus, we see Moses taken away from the mundane world of shepherding to meet God in a fire. The psalm recounts how God's people, under the leadership of Moses, were able to defeat mighty Pharaoh. In Romans, Paul teaches us to overcome evil with good, even offering deeds of love to our enemies. And in Matthew's Gospel, we read how Jesus' disciples simply can't fathom that he has come to die for them and to show them an abundant life beyond their imagining.

QUESTIONS AND SUGGESTIONS FOR REFLECTION

- Read Exodus 3:1-15. Have you ever turned aside to meet God in a surprising place, or maybe missed a chance to go find God?
- Read Psalm 105:1-6, 23-26, 45b. Have you ever met an unlikely leader? How is God calling you to a surprising new thing?
- Read Romans 12:9-21. How might it change our world if we all learned to heap kindness on our enemies? When have you tried overcoming evil with good?
- Read Matthew 16:21-28. Jesus' disciples are clearly looking for a different kind of Lord than the Savior whom God sent. What are the aspects of Jesus' life, work, and ministry that challenge your idea of who you'd like Jesus to be?

The Rev. Scott Gunn is an Episcopal priest. He serves as executive director of Forward Movement, a discipleship ministry of the Episcopal Church.

MONDAY, AUGUST 24 ~ *Read Exodus 3:1-3*

When the curtain rises on our scene from Exodus, Moses is taking care of his father-in-law's sheep. Looking after a flock was a pretty big job, made all the more complicated by the fact that they weren't even Moses' sheep. If something happened, it could wreak havoc on family relationships.

As he's minding his own business, Moses notices a bush that is burning but not consumed. It might have been tempting to keep on with his pressing work. Moses had places to go, sheep to look after, and things to do. And yet he decides to turn aside to investigate this surprising phenomenon.

The scriptures don't give us any sense that Moses had an inkling that the mysterious flame was, in fact, God. But the scriptures do tell us that Moses changed his plan: He stopped paying attention to what is sure and certain to turn toward a spiritual possibility. This is a good lesson for busy people living in the twenty-first century. God is present with us as we go through life's journey, though we might have to turn aside from what looks like a sure thing and look toward the unknown to see God.

Years ago, I was busy getting work done at the church I was serving. A parishioner kept trying to talk to me while I was working, mostly small talk. I kept working, getting somewhat annoyed that my busyness and important work wasn't more apparent. Finally, perhaps at the Spirit's nudging, I stopped and focused on this child of God. With my full attention, she told me an important story from her life. It was an important day for her, and she'd been looking for a way to tell me.

Had I not "turned aside" from my seemingly important work, I would have missed out on a sacred conversation I still treasure years later.

Everliving God, open our minds and our hearts to look for you, even in surprising places. Give us courage and imagination to turn aside to seek you. Amen.

TUESDAY, AUGUST 25 ~ *Read Exodus 3:4-15*

As Moses meets the true and living God at the burning bush, God speaks to Moses, summoning him to lead his people to freedom. Every single thing about this was unexpected. No one expects a bush that burns yet is not consumed. Moses did not expect a career change from shepherd to leader. Surely few people could have expected God to desire the liberation of the Israelites from Pharaoh's might.

When Moses hears God's plan to free his people, he responds, "Who am I that I should go to Pharaoh, and bring the Israelites out of Egypt?" Moses doesn't feel worthy to serve as the appointed leader. His humility might be one of the reasons he was such an effective leader. But God assures Moses, telling him that he will not do this work on his own. God will be with him always.

Here is an important truth: When God calls us, God also equips us. If we discern that God is actually calling us to do a thing, we can rest at ease. Of course, the trick is often in knowing whether God is really calling us, or if our prompting comes from somewhere else. We won't usually have something dramatic like a burning bush and a booming voice to make clear God's desire. Instead, we strain mightily to hear the still, small voice of God, relying on the support of our community of faith, family, friends, and mentors to help us hear God's call. But we can trust that if God invites us to embark on a new calling or on new work, God is by that very act promising to equip us.

This doesn't mean that answering God's call will be easy—far from it! But God's vision is bigger than ours. When God calls us to do something, we can say yes in confidence that God will be with us.

God, help us hear you when you call us. Amen.

WEDNESDAY, AUGUST 26 ~ *Read Psalm 105:1-6, 23-26, 45b*

This psalm recounts the glorious deeds of God from the past. The first verse calls us to "give thanks to the LORD; call on his name; make known his deeds among the peoples." The purpose of this psalm, though, is not to get us to yearn for the good old days. Quite the opposite!

In ads for stocks, mutual funds, and other investment products, you're likely to run across the phrase, "past performance is not indicative of future results." The authorities require this disclosure so that we don't assume some investment will continue to increase in value just because that's what happened the last few years. In other words, the future is unknown. The past is not a reliable indicator, at least when it comes to finances.

It's not like that with God, who is the same from generation to generation. God's love is perfect. So when we recall God's deeds in the past, we can be assured that God will continue to act in the present and in the future. Maybe church bulletins should have some fine print at the bottom: "Past deeds *are* indicative of future deeds."

Churches seem prone to sentimentalizing the past. Like the Israelites of old, who longed for the old days with leeks and cucumbers—but who forgot the part about being enslaved by Pharaoh—we might fondly remember full Sunday school rooms and overflowing worship services, forgetting about the ways that the church fell short of making true disciples.

God has been constant through our ups and downs. In times of plenty and scarcity, God has abided with us, bestowing on us many blessings. God will continue to bless us. The sweeping narrative of scripture teaches us that even when we forget about God, God never forgets about us. We might need to look for God in surprising places, but God is there.

Eternal God, give us confidence so that we can trust you. Amen.

THURSDAY, AUGUST 27 ~ *Read Romans 12:9-13*

It's easy to talk about love. It's not so easy to practice what we preach. When Jesus told us to love others as he first loved us, this was no saccharine, emotional love. This kind of love is fierce. Jesus wants us to practice love as a discipline.

Paul fleshes this out in his letter to the Romans. Genuine love means that we will care not just for those we like or for those we find easy to love, but for all. To love as Christ loves leads us to welcome strangers with gracious hospitality, expecting nothing in return. To love fully means to reject evil, even when it is inconvenient or costly for us.

To move from sentimental love to the kind of fierce love Paul writes about is not easy. But when it happens, it's beautiful. Churches at their best can be places where we see genuine Christian love practiced.

I once knew of a church in which a member fell behind on their mortgage. In the spirit of "contributing to the needs of the saints," several other members banded together and paid the mortgage so the house was not seized. They repeated this for a few more months until the person got their footing again. No repayment was expected. It was several Christians caring for a fellow Christian in a way that was literally costly. And the community grew stronger.

The Episcopal Church, where I serve, has an old traditional blessing based on Romans. It offers us all a good word. Use it as your prayer for today.

"Go forth into the world in peace. Be of good courage. Hold fast to that which is good. Render to no one evil for evil. Strengthen the fainthearted. Support the weak. Help the afflicted. Honor everyone. And the blessing of God Almighty, the Father, the Son, and the Holy Spirit be with you now and always." Amen.

FRIDAY, AUGUST 28 ~ *Read Romans 12:14-21*

The world around us teaches us to keep score. We are trained to hope that people get what they deserve, no more and no less. We hear lots of talk about justice and even punishment, but not much talk about mercy. And then we get to Paul's letter to the Romans.

"Do not repay anyone evil for evil." It's tempting to hold a grudge when someone hurts us, or maybe even to try to find a way to get back at the other person. But Paul says to live differently.

I once developed a bit of animosity with another person in the church. We had rubbed elbows a few times and didn't particularly get along well. *Enemies* might be too strong of a word, but not by much. And then one day, when I was in need, this person offered kindness of a staggering generosity. They overcame the evil of estrangement with good. Their willingness to think and to act differently changed me. That's the funny thing about Christian love: It really does change the world, one life at a time.

The few times in my life when I managed to let go of anger and to fill my heart with love instead, I've always been grateful. Perhaps we would do well to follow Paul's advice: to "rejoice with those who rejoice; weep with those who weep." I don't have to agree with someone to share their sorrow, nor to share their rejoicing. After all, we humans are all in this together.

Imagine how different our world would be if we moved from concerning ourselves with justice and punishment to seeking grace and mercy. It's counter-cultural, but every time I've seen this unfold, it's been a shining beacon of Christ's light.

Gracious God, help us to love our neighbors and even our enemies as you have loved us first. Amen.

Pretty much every corner of the world screams to us, "Might makes right!" We are told relentlessly to get whatever we can, that more is better. For centuries, humans have understood that strength and power are in, weakness and suffering are out. And into this world came Jesus Christ.

When Jesus says he is on his way to Jerusalem to suffer and die for his disciples and for the whole world, they just can't fathom it. Perhaps it's understandable: The way of Jesus is profoundly counter-cultural.

Peter gets it spectacularly wrong here, and Jesus rebukes him, "Get behind me, Satan!" This, of course, is the same Peter whom Jesus calls to lead the church. Peter gets things wonderfully right in one breath and completely wrong in another. I find this deeply comforting. If Jesus can call Peter into leadership and love him despite his stunning mistakes, surely the same Lord can find a use for me despite my regular mistakes. And that's not all.

Sometimes as I study the scriptures, I struggle with the demands Jesus seems to make on me and on others. And yet Jesus has a purpose—a portion of which is to love and to redeem sinners like you and me.

The cosmic mission of Jesus Christ to redeem the whole of creation involved his suffering, death, resurrection, and ascension. It's not easy to ponder the depth of love that would lead a man to willingly endure pain and death for people who regularly turn away and reject this gift. Yet that is who our God is.

Lord Jesus, you are mighty to save. Thank you for all that you have done for us, for all that you offer us today, and for all you give us forever. Amen.

Jesus asks a lot from us. Well, more to the point, he asks everything. If we want to follow him, we must deny ourselves. We have to be ready to die.

I've heard quite a few preachers who claim to be biblical literalists, yet I've never heard a sermon on the literal need to deny ourselves and to give up our lives. I've read plenty of people claiming to take the Bible literally who do this in a way that heaps judgment or condemnation on others, but not many who talk about the high demands of the gospel on each one of us.

I don't think that Jesus is suggesting that we all need to die to follow him. In fact, he seems pretty eager to encourage people to live life well. But I do believe Jesus is suggesting that we have to look beyond our own selfish worldview to embrace a God's-eye view of the world that seeks the welfare and redemption of others.

When I was a child, I learned a simple acronym at summer camp: J.O.Y. is *Jesus, Others, You*. It's so simple and yet so profound. It's a pretty solid lens through which to see the Christian life. Our first allegiance is to Lord Jesus. Then we seek the well-being of others, loving our neighbors. And finally, we care for ourselves.

When I manage to live this way, it changes me. It's so freeing not to have to worry about protecting my own ego or status. It feels good to lift up others first, and even better to do so in the name of Christ. I usually don't get this right, but when I do, I sometimes get a glimpse of what Jesus meant when he said "For those who want to save their life will lose it, and those who lose their life for my sake will find it."

Jesus, help us give up everything for your sake. Amen.

The Greatest Commandment

AUGUST 31–SEPTEMBER 6, 2026 • MARJORIE SUCHOCKI

SCRIPTURE OVERVIEW: We move forward in the story of Moses to the climax in Egypt, the tenth plague. God tells the Israelites to prepare for the terrible night to come and establishes the feast of Passover. The psalmist praises God for faithfulness and victory, including overthrowing those who would oppress them. Egypt is not mentioned specifically in the psalm, yet the Passover represents just such a situation. In the Gospel, Jesus provides practical teaching on handling disagreements. Our first responsibility is to go to the other party privately and then include others only as necessary. Paul echoes Jesus in summarizing much of the Law in one simple commandment: "Love your neighbor as yourself" (Mark 12:31).

QUESTIONS AND SUGGESTIONS FOR REFLECTION

- Read Exodus 12:1-14. How has the story of Passover shaped your faith?
- Read Psalm 149. How has God called you to seek freedom from oppression for yourself or others through praise and through action?
- Read Romans 13:8-14. What does it mean to consider love a driving force rather than a warm feeling? How does this understanding change the way you act toward yourself and your neighbors?
- Read Matthew 18:15-20. When have you participated in or witnessed true reconciliation? How did you see compassion at work?

Marjorie Hewitt Suchocki is a Professor Emerita at Claremont School of Theology, where she served as professor and also as dean. She is a member of Fellowship United Methodist Church in Trophy Club, TX.

MONDAY, AUGUST 31 ~ *Read Exodus 12:1-14*

This day of remembrance in the Jewish year celebrates not only escape from certain death but strength for a long journey ahead. Nine plagues had already come, each a response to Pharaoh's refusal to let the Hebrews go. The tenth plague arrives—death to every firstborn. To be protected from this plague, the Hebrews are to put some of the blood of a slain lamb on the doorpost of their house, in which case God will pass over that home. In obedience to Moses' instructions, each Jewish household took a lamb, killed it, put some of its blood on doorposts and lintels, and roasted it. Bread for the meal had to be unleavened—there was no time for it to rise. They would eat this feast of lamb, bread, and herbs quickly while dressed for travel—sandals on their feet, packed bags and staff at the ready, with extra unleavened bread rolled and packed for the journey.

In the middle of the night a great cry went up in Egypt: In every family, from the house of Pharaoh to the least of prisoners in their cells, was the wailing sound of mourning. All firstborn sons had died. And finally Pharaoh sends for Moses, begs him to leave Egypt with all the Hebrews and their livestock. Fortified by their meal, the Hebrews did just that: Freed from bondage, they went. (See Exod. 12:31-32.)

Every year since, the Passover has been solemnly and joyfully celebrated in Jewish households. Some centuries after that first Passover, there was a certain celebration in an upper room in Jerusalem, where a beloved teacher and his twelve disciples gathered to celebrate this holy day of the Jewish year—a passover of deliverance from death and strength for the journey ahead.

O Lord, our God, we give thanks for this defining event of the story of Israel. Call us to continually remember your saving acts. Amen.

TUESDAY, SEPTEMBER 1 ~ *Read Exodus 12:1-14*

These verses in the Exodus story almost act as an interlude. They break the narrative of the plagues and shift to instruction around Passover, a practice that will become so central to the life of the freed Hebrew people. Jesus and his disciples, as faithful Jews, follow these instructions centuries later, eating unleavened bread, bitter herbs, and the meat of a lamb that had been slain. All four of the Gospels describe this otherwise ordinary celebration. The disciples had possibly shared Passover with Jesus in previous years. But this particular meal that had been re-enacted for centuries in Jewish homes would become the pattern for a new celebration for centuries to come in our Christian churches, a continued and expanded celebration of God's saving work.

We call Jesus the "Lamb of God" and see in his death the blood that causes the punishment of death to pass over us too. It's not a great plague from which we are delivered—history is replete with successive plagues that decimate people. The plague from which we are rescued is a plague of consuming hatred, of fear, of looking out only for ourselves. Instead, we live in the freedom of love rather than hate, of welcome rather than rejection, of life rather than death, despite the trials that may await us on life's journey. Just as God released the Israelites from the bondage of slavery, God continues to release the bonds that hold us back. We live both in the freedom of resurrections from the "little deaths" afflicting our present life and in the everlasting freedom in the resurrection life that is to come.

Lord, let us keep the feast, not just on Communion Sundays, but in the strength and power of resurrection all our days. Amen.

WEDNESDAY, SEPTEMBER 2 ~ *Read Psalm 149*

This penultimate psalm is a paean of joy leading into the great hallelujah of Psalm 150. Try approaching it by returning to Psalm 145 and reading consecutively as each psalm adds to those preceding it with yet new praise.

Surely Psalm 149 starts with joy. With those ancient Israelites we sing a new song, rejoice in our Maker, exult in our King. We shout for joy, knowing that through our joy we might . . . "execute vengeance"? Inflict "punishment on the peoples"? "Execute on them the judgment decreed"? Wait. How is it that the joyous beginning of this psalm leads us to such destruction?

Scholars tell us this psalm was written following the return of the exiles from Babylon. Jerusalem was being rebuilt, as was the Temple. At last, Jews could again serve God as God's people. God had freed them. The imagery is of battles now won.

Sometimes we are ensnared by things that only divine power can free us from. If we take the retributive words out of the context of physical war and see them instead as praise for how God has released us from spiritual bondage, we may find new meaning. So many things can hold us captive—addicting substances, psychological disasters, grudges and enmities that destroy families and friendships, loss of physical strength as we weaken through illness or aging. But we serve a God who gives us victories over that which would enslave or destroy us. We must deal with such things in the fragility of our finitude, and sometimes the best imagery for the struggle is warfare. God's resurrection power can help us overcome that which would destroy us, no matter how strong the enemy. Such strength can indeed lead us into even the mightiest hallelujah chorus.

"Praise the Lord! Sing to the Lord a new song!" Amen.

THURSDAY, SEPTEMBER 3 ~ *Read Romans 13:8-14*

Paul's letter to the Romans is a personal correspondence to a specific Christian community. He has not yet met these Roman Christians, but, in Christ, he sees them as neighbors whom he is hurrying to meet. He loves them. In his letter, he extols the teaching of Jesus, who summarized the law thusly: "You shall love the Lord your God with all your heart, and with all your soul, and with all your mind. This is the greatest and first commandment And a second is like it: you shall love your neighbor as yourself" (Matt. 22:37-40). Paul echoes this teaching, reminding the Romans of Jesus' words and their connection to Moses' law.

The definition of "neighbor" moves from the intimacy of one's own circles of family and friends to the wider circles of persons within one's community—one's nation, one's alliances—eventually toward the aim expressed by Julian of Norwich: "All shall be well, and all shall be well, and all manner of things shall be well."

How is it possible to care for the well-being of so large a company? It may be easiest to show our love for others in our own communities, where we respond with active love to the needs of others through our churches' ministries, local food banks, transportation services, and support groups. But global organizations such as United Methodist Committee on Relief, Doctors without Borders, Amnesty International, and the United Nations Food Program serve needs that are beyond what we can do locally. May God help us grow in our capacity to care and grant us wisdom and courage to give care to neighbors we have not yet met.

O God, give me eyes to see and hearts to care for those I am called to love. Amen.

FRIDAY, SEPTEMBER 4 ~ *Read Romans 13:8-14*

In Matthew's Gospel, Jesus is approached by a Pharisee, one who has studied the law. This Pharisee wants to know which commandment is the greatest, or most important. Matthew's Gospel says the Pharisee asked this question "to test him" (22:35). The Pharisee wanted one law; Jesus gave him two.

Paul only states the second here in his letter to the Romans, saying the bulk of the commandments (see Exod. 20:1-17) can be summarized in this one. Some of those original commandments did instruct on how people were to act with one another, while others instructed how people were to act toward God. But what if the first commandment Jesus says is most important—to love God—is only fulfilled through the second? If the God we so dearly love is a God who "so loved the world" (John 3:16), then that must affect how we view the world.

Isn't that how it is with us and those we love? Your son or daughter wants you to meet a "friend" who just might be more than a friend—such an introduction should lead you to regard that friend not only with kindness, but with a hope for the friend's goodness and well-being, hope that your child is safe with that friend. Love for your child opens you to love those who are important to your child.

We love a God who "so loved the world," so we must view the world through the lens of God's love. How is it, then, with that world? Is there laughter and joy? We delight in the joy and share in the laughter. Is there suffering and pain? We mourn for the pain and seek ways to help. Loving God is manifested in how we care for that which God loves—and God so loves the world.

God, let me work with you to relieve pain in whatever way is possible—through prayer and the actions that accompany prayer. Amen.

The clear message Jesus gives and Paul reiterates, to love your neighbor as yourself, is apparently not enough. Still we sin against one another, enough that Jesus and Paul must speak out about how we interact with one another. Even in the community of believers called into being through love, that which opposes love—sin—rears its ugly head.

Many orders of worship provide worshipers the opportunity to confess our collective sin. We are sinners learning through grace, and since we are sinners, we do in fact sin. At this point, the words of the Lord's prayer come to mind: "Forgive us our sins, as we forgive those who sin against us." It is interesting that this is the only part of the prayer that puts a condition on what we ask for. We ask God to forgive us the same way we forgive others. If that is truly what we wish, shouldn't we absolutely rush to forgive those who hurt us? Do we not hope for community's swift forgiveness when we sin?

Sometimes it seems God is like a school teacher—knowing us, teaching us, guiding us, helping us. And Jesus, seeing us clearly, gives us guidance about how to deal with sin in our community: honestly, with kindness and openness, increasing love through mediated forgiveness. When someone trespasses against us, we should not respond by telling even more people about what they've done. We face the issue head-on, go to the source. If that doesn't work, we return to the source with witnesses. And if that still doesn't work—we go on our way. For we are all sinners, saved by grace, with hearts yearning to live ever more deeply into the love of God.

Guide us, God, as we live with and sin against one another. Help us to face our problems head-on with love. Amen.

SUNDAY, SEPTEMBER 6 ~ *Read Matthew 18:20*

Our passage from Matthew concerning sin and forgiveness concludes with the promise of Christ's presence among us. The wonder of Christ's presence is that it is not metaphorical, not an "as if" presence. Christ *is* present in our very midst.

Notice that his presence has no conditions. It's not dependent on whether we feel or even acknowledge Christ's presence, because we do not "make" Christ present. It's not the pastor, the prayers, the lectionary, the choir; it's not the confession of faith; it's not the offering. Christ is present because he said he would be. It's as simple and as amazing as that.

And Christ's presence with us is not limited to the worship service. Indeed, Christ is present with us all the time, at any place where two or more are gathered in his name. That means Jesus is with us when we go to dinner with friends, when we go to a concert, or when we celebrate a birthday. Jesus is present with us in every aspect of our life. And, I would argue, Christ is present with us even when we are not gathered with others, as even then Christ seeks to encourage and support us.

Christ is present whether we're aware of it or not, but this doesn't mean we should ignore Christ's presence. We can acknowledge Christ's presence in every ordinary moment. One of the times in our worship service when we might be a bit more aware of Christ's presence is in the passing of the peace. We turn to look at our neighbor, to give our hand and a smile—so ordinary—so "extraordinarily" ordinary. Perhaps when we next participate in an "ordinary" service where two, three, or more gather together in Christ's name, we can seek to acknowledge Christ's presence with us and be empowered in our collaborative work for the kingdom.

Jesus, may I notice your presence with me wherever I go. Amen.

Transformed by God

SEPTEMBER 7–13, 2026 • PAOLA BARRERA

SCRIPTURE OVERVIEW: This week's readings trace how God transforms us. In Exodus, through the rescue mission that moved heaven and earth, God freed the people of Israel from slavery and bestowed on them a new identity. The psalm echoes the supernatural events that took place during that rescue and issues a stunning declaration whereby a people who had no homeland become God's chosen place of dwelling. The passage from Romans illustrates how the change of status before God leads to an internal transformation, which in turn changes how we see others and ourselves. Finally, in Matthew, a parable outlines the root of forgiveness to show the weight of God's transformation and invites us to model God's grace.

QUESTIONS AND SUGGESTIONS FOR REFLECTION

- Read Exodus 14:19-31. What events mark a before and after in your life? How did God show up, and how are you different because of it?
- Read Psalm 114. What story do you tell yourself and others about who you are? How has knowing God changed your story?
- Read Romans 14:1-12. In what ways has God's accepting you changed how you accept others? How has God recalibrated how you measure yourself and others?
- Read Matthew 18:21-35. When have you found it hardest to forgive someone? What has God forgiven you that changed the way you forgive others?

Paola Barrera is a writer and speaker raised between cultures. She is a Canadian through the gift of immigration. Her work looks at how faith and theology inform and shape everyday life. She writes for various outlets, including *She Reads Truth*, *Fathom Magazine*, and *Propel*, and has contributed to an anthology of essays in French on God's faithfulness. Find more of her work at paolabarrera.com.

MONDAY, SEPTEMBER 7 ~ *Read Exodus 14:19-21*

It can be tempting to breeze through the parting of the Red Sea. We might miss the essence behind this fantastically familiar Sunday school story. The treasure lies in the "why" behind the extraordinary show of power. This is a story of belonging that informs whose we are. It is also a profoundly human story.

Feeling alone, cornered at the end of all possibility—that's the plight of Israel in this text. They literally have no place for safety. They are on the run, at the mercy of an army chasing them. With the sea ahead and soldiers approaching from behind, where can they go? How is this going to work?

Despite the millennia that separates us from this story, it elicits emotions on a visceral level for me. While I've never been chased by an army, I have felt hunted by fear and anxiety over circumstances beyond my ability. I have felt swallowed whole. Hardships push against our limits, leaving us needy and broken. We see no path to move through and no protection from what feels like imminent pain.

The pillar of cloud and fire, we are told, is the very manifestation of God. The angel of the Lord moved from the front to the back of them, to guide them and then to guard them. "One did not come near the other all night." Standing between the people and Pharaoh's army, God then caused the sea to divide, making a path of dry ground walled by the waters of the Red Sea, which obeyed the Lord's command through Moses.

While this is a rescue operation of literally biblical proportions, it is also a statement of ownership. These people belong to the Great I AM. That belonging determines God's personal involvement and presence. God guides, shields, and takes them as God's own.

God, teach me to live like I belong to you, the Lord Almighty, my guide and shield. Amen.

TUESDAY, SEPTEMBER 8 ~ *Read Exodus 14:22-31*

Walking through the hall of an intensive care unit, where life is often measured in heartbeats, I can easily identify the guardians, parents, or spouses: When the hands of the clock signal that hours have passed, the same person is still in the room with their loved one. They help the nurse change the patient; they follow up and ask questions when the doctor makes the rounds. When it comes to abiding care, few things are more telling than time and presence.

The passing from nighttime to daybreak frames the scene in Exodus and anchors the story in a specific time and place. This passage marks a moment when heaven and earth meet in a very real way. The hours leading up to the rescue of God's people are harrowing because the people are not spared the danger and stress of their escape; they are led through it.

The pillar of cloud that "lit up the night" and "came between the army of Egypt and the army of Israel" prevented either group from engaging with the other. In tandem, the Lord caused a powerful wind to turn the sea into dry land. Then sometime between 2 and 6 in the morning ("during the morning watch"), God caused the Egyptians to fall into confusion. At daybreak the sea returned to its depth, drowning them.

These specific hours recorded in scripture serve like time stamps that show the process of God's divine intervention. God was with them on the ground, fighting for them for roughly twelve hours. Why? God—being Lord over all things—could have taken less time or more direct means to eliminate the Egyptian army. The way God did it left a record for them (and for us) of the final hours of their slavery and provided a front row seat to see God fighting to claim them as God's own.

Powerful God, help me remember what you've done for me. Amen.

WEDNESDAY, SEPTEMBER 9 ~ *Read Psalm 114*

I am Canadian through the gift of immigration. My husband and I became immigrants in midlife, emigrating from Venezuela to Canada with enough years of lived experience to remember the past and be shaped by it. It was a challenging blessing, to be sure. Until then, both of us had been educated abroad, and the story we told ourselves about worth and value was based on our accomplishments.

But the two-year legal process leading up to departure was paved with obstacles as we tried to navigate Venezuela's broken system and to comply with all the forms, tests, and fees required by the government of Canada. Whatever strengths we thought we had in our favor did not guarantee our approval. By God's grace we finally boarded a plane to a country we now call home. Despite being well-traveled and having lived in different countries, neither one of us had ever set foot in Canada.

Now, more than a decade later, I look back at that two-year obstacle course as well as our past twelve years in Canada, and I find all along the path evidences of God's grace. They remind me how God's actions reveal our true story, a story of fear, need, and hope. It is a very different narrative than our self-sufficient one.

The psalmist recalls the Exodus of Israel from Egypt and sets the scene with nature in an uproar. A series of whys echo the supernatural happenings, raising the question: What is the reason for these formidable events? The answer: God fought to make them God's. This is their story. The verses document the Lord's track record.

To remember God's action in our past helps us live our present in agreement with that record—to be who God says we are, to live as people who are shaped by God's grace.

Lord, help me remember the mountains you've moved to make a path for me where there was none. May your past faithfulness inform my present. Amen.

THURSDAY, SEPTEMBER 10 ~ *Read Psalm 114:2*

There are experiences that mark a transition from what has been to something new. These shifts alter the very fabric of who we are and how we live moving forward. It could be the transition to a new season of life, like becoming a parent for the first time. Or it could be living through the rupture of a present reality that dies and forever changes our heart, like divorce or the death of a loved one. We become different. A new layer is added to our personhood that becomes part of our identity.

Something of the sort happened to God's people when "Judah became God's sanctuary." The verse is a declaration of what took place when they were led out of Egypt and faced the shores of the Red Sea with no way forward. It was a transformative experience. But what did it mean?

The word *sanctuary* means altar, temple, as well as shelter and asylum. God takes an enslaved people who had no homeland and calls them God's temple. The declaration closes with affirmation that Israel is God's dominion. In other words, Israel is God's territory. The people are God's chosen dwelling.

Psalm 114:2 clearly declares what God calls God's. More than a layer added to an identity, this is a whole new category. To be God's means we are no longer our own. That transformation calls the soul to battle with itself when our own way seems best, when we would rather go back to our own Egypt and would choose bondage instead of worship. That transformation changes obstacles into opportunities. It allows us to behold God's power to do what we can't do and grace to receive what we don't deserve but desperately need. We are God's—God's temple, God's very heart.

Holy God, help me to live into the transformation and renewal of my soul that you have already begun. Amen.

FRIDAY, SEPTEMBER 11 ~ *Read Romans 14:1-6*

Production lines have a standard that helps determine when a product is fit to move to the next stage. When it meets the criteria, the item is compliant. If it doesn't meet the requirements, quality control will flag it to correct the issue and ensure the standard is met.

In matters of faith, who's responsible for quality control? What's the standard? Today's passage answers this question by asking a more pointed one: Who are we to judge someone else's faith? The answer is humbling and, believe it or not, freeing.

Paul's phrasing clues us in: We are all servants. He levels the ground with his analogy of the servant who will stand or fall before their own master. We cannot judge another's faith as wanting; it is only the Lord who can "make them stand." This shift places all believers on equal footing, with God exalted above. God is the master of all, the one who alone can judge who stands or falls.

This is a radically different standard from how the world orders things and, if we're honest, how we as Christians tend to categorize and sort out one another. Whether with denominational differences, worship practices, or theological statements, we often use our own standards as a benchmark for others.

But God's standard confuses whatever bar we use and reorders how we relate to one another. And that is such good news! We're set free from judging others *and* from fear of being judged by others' standards. This changes everything. The acceptance we are called to extend to those with a weaker faith is also extended to us. For we too are found wanting unless the Lord makes us stand.

Thank you, Lord, for removing the human-placed standards of value and judging us by your standards alone. Amen.

SATURDAY, SEPTEMBER 12 ~ *Read Romans 14:7-12*

What do we live for? For the bulk of my adulthood, the answer to that question was my reputation and my validation. In practical terms, that amounted to my work and paycheck. I thought these things would show that I was important, a person of worth. All that changed when I became depressed and suicidal. A burnout sobered me from a life of workaholism and worshiping at the altar of success.

It was a mercy that reoriented my heart and turned things to their right size. I found that I needed and had room for a larger-than-my-life God. I didn't have to relentlessly climb a ladder toward something I had all along—value.

The feeling of belonging is a powerful factor that determines much of human behavior. What we do, think, and feel is informed by the places where we belong or seek to fit in; sometimes even more so by the places that keep us out.

Until I understood that I fit in with Christ and that my life belongs to God, I lived only for what the work of my hands could do for me or say about me to others. That reality was dreadful; I had no peace, no freedom inside the hamster wheel of a life I had created. Living in Christ frees me to live for more. It's a status that overrides any of the definitions the world says I need or the ones I think I lack, who I please or fear displeasing. Our worth is set by the One before whom every knee will bow and every tongue confess as King. We are already God's.

Lord, remind me I belong to you and that nothing can change that. Amen.

SUNDAY, SEPTEMBER 13 ~ *Read Matthew 18:21-35*

How awkward it must have been for Peter to get a lengthy answer to his simple question. He asked for a number. In return Jesus gave him a piercing illustration with impossible implications. It is overwhelming to try to consider the vastness of the debt. But the answer to Peter's question is that the number is not the point. We forgive because we have been forgiven.

The root of such transformation is God's work in us. Today's text shows we have agency in how we join that work. The servant did what any of us would have done—he begged. The king in the story, however, did something downright outrageous. He left millions on the table, so to speak, by taking pity on the man and canceling the debt. He could have designed a payment plan or given the servant a rebate so he would pay less. By the world's standards, these options are unusually kind, not to mention ill-advised and financially foolish.

The answer to Peter's question is in the opening words of the parable: "The kingdom of heaven is like . . ." (NIV). The standard is alien to us. Jesus' work on the Cross is foolishness to the world. And it is the beginning of our true and better story. When there's a disconnect between what we receive from God and what we give our own debtors, we are beckoned to reposition our souls in light of our story. We were beggars given a second chance by a foolish king who came to save the world by dying for it and overcoming death.

Lord, show me how to live forgiven every day. Let my life tell the story of who I am. Help me join your transformative work in and around me. Amen.

In the Gap

SEPTEMBER 14–20, 2026 • CAROLINE VOGEL

SCRIPTURE OVERVIEW: Each of the passages for this week has a way of drawing us into curiosity about how God might most palpably show up in the places where we experience a gap between where we are and where we want to be or think we should be. God provides sustenance for the Israelites as they experience the wilderness that exists between their deliverance from slavery and the Promised Land, and the psalmist praises God's glorious deeds. Paul longs to be with Christ but recognizes his separation provides him the opportunity to serve others. In Matthew, Jesus tells a parable that challenges our understanding of equal access to the kingdom. These passages invite us to question our ideas about how we think life should go versus the reality of what is. The gaps in time or space between where we are and where we want to be can become places that remind us to see joy amidst the suffering and difficulties of life.

QUESTIONS AND SUGGESTIONS FOR REFLECTION

- Read Exodus 16:2-15. When have you found yourself in the wilderness? How did God meet you there? Were you always able to notice God's presence?
- Read Psalm 105:1-6, 37-45. When have you fallen away from seeking God and God's strength? What helps restore your seeking?
- Read Philippians 1:21-30. How have you experienced God's joy even in the midst of suffering?
- Read Matthew 20:1-16. When have you struggled with the vastness of God's grace? When have you felt as if God has been more generous with other people? How did you handle it?

Caroline Vogel is a spiritual writer and lover of the Holy Spirit. She is an EMDR therapist specializing in trauma, anxiety, and fear in Knoxville, TN.

MONDAY, SEPTEMBER 14 ~ *Read Exodus 16:2-3*

The whole congregation of the Israelites complained against Moses and Aaron in the wilderness." Their complaining takes a serious tone: "If only we had died by the hand of the Lord in the land of Egypt . . . for you have brought us out into this wilderness to kill this whole assembly with hunger." It likely never occurred to the Israelites that there would be a huge stretch of space between oppression and promise.

Going into the wilderness is never an easy passage. The circumstances that create our wildernesses are rarely ones we would choose. For us today, wilderness experiences are often created by some sort of loss—of a home, job, relationship, health. All of these situations have a way of writing our narrative in ways that we wouldn't have written ourselves. We therefore feel out of control, wondering where God is in the midst of it all and struggling to find solid ground in the upheaval. It's only natural to cry out to those we think are responsible for our predicament and ask pointed questions like *have you brought us out here simply to kill us?*

As difficult as wilderness experiences are, they always provide an invitation to let go of the way we have seen and understood ourselves, others, and God. Some form of death is an inherent part of a true wilderness experience. Loss often leads us into the wilderness; letting go of what we have lost allows us to rely on God to lead us through and out on the other side. We are forced to see ourselves and everything around us differently, to let die what *was* so that something new might emerge. Wilderness is sometimes welcomed and other times forced, but it is always an invitation to something new.

Holy and gracious God, meet me where I am in the wilderness of my life and allow something new to emerge. Amen.

TUESDAY, SEPTEMBER 15 ~ *Read Exodus 16:2-8*

The Lord makes it clear to Moses that the Israelites' prayers of complaint will be answered. God will test the people and see if they will follow the instructions. In our own wilderness experiences, we often cry out to God for help—either for endurance or deliverance. Crying out to God is not only acceptable, it is expected. Our crying out and questioning brings us closer to our loving God and the inner grace with which we have been empowered.

Jesus' baptism was a sacrament marking the outward sign of God's inner grace. Jesus was empowered by his baptism and then led into the wilderness for forty days before beginning his ministry. The wilderness empowered Jesus with an embodied knowledge of the strength of his baptism and depth of God's inner grace, equipping him for the challenges of his future ministry.

Before they left Egypt, the Israelites were given an outward sign of the inner grace God provided. Before fleeing out of bondage and into the wilderness, the Israelites marked their doors with the blood of a sacrificial lamb. God then passed over all those marked homes, and none of the Israelites died. In that clear act of God, the Israelites were empowered with a deep knowledge that they were marked with an inner grace, a grace that would sustain them through the wilderness to come.

Though our vulnerability is tested in the wilderness, God also supplies us with grace before we enter, strengthens us with that grace through the voyage, and uses that grace for our good on the other side.

Gracious God, as I encounter the wilderness of my life, may I embody the strength you offer me to find my way through. Amen.

WEDNESDAY, SEPTEMBER 16 ~ *Read Exodus 16:9-15*

The Israelites have an idea of how things should be going on the other side of slavery. Given their cries for help, they clearly don't think life is going as planned. God ultimately answers their prayerful cries with quail and bread from heaven. The meat seems to go over okay, but when the Israelites discover the fine, flaky substance in the morning, they fail to see it for the answer to their prayers that it is.

Another challenge of wilderness experiences is our ability to see how God is meeting us in undesired circumstances. The Israelites are experiencing a gap between their reality and their expectations, and this is exactly the space where God shows up and provides transformation. These gaps, these places between our expectations of how we think life should be going and the reality of life as it is, are often the grittiest places in our life. And it's my experience that the bigger the gap between expectations and reality, the harder it is for us to hold that space. That space calls for something greater than ourselves.

Gaps can be momentary, like when a conversation isn't going as planned. Gaps can last for long stretches of time, like difficult periods in a marriage, the aftermath of losing a relationship, going through cancer treatments, or arduous times in a job. I've come to think of these gaps as "God-Appointed Places"—*GAP*s. They are the places where our human minds can't make the leap from where we are to where we hope we're going or feel we already should be. GAPs are those wilderness experiences in which we can't fathom how God will provide for us, but often it's in these very moments that God's answers to our prayers appear at our feet—even if in unexpected ways.

Gracious God, as I reflect on my life, help me to see all the ways you have met me in the wilderness stretches of my life. Amen.

THURSDAY, SEPTEMBER 17 ~ *Read Psalm 105:1-6; 37-45*

It never ceases to amaze me how much I forget to search for God and God's strength. The psalmist sings a song of praise for all of God's works, calling the listener to tell the stories of God's deliverance over and over as a way to remember and praise. This psalm is a reminder to us to turn toward God in good times and bad.

The more I study neurobiology, the more compassion I have for all of humanity as to why we so easily fall away from seeking God. The negativity bias of our brains is constantly scanning for threat and danger. What keeps us alive is our ability to manage perceived threats to our existence. Long ago humanity had to keep an eye and ear out for dangerous animals that could pounce and consume us for an instant meal. Over time, our brains have habituated to perceive threat and danger in all kinds of things, people, and situations. Many of us have a sensitive antenna for potential harm. And though these antennas ultimately keep us alive, they also keep our eyes and ears trained for potential threat rather than seeking the face of God.

One of the many reasons I've enjoyed taking up the spiritual practice of meditation is that in the stillness and quiet, my heart comes home to a loving God. I often have to sift through a lot of brain and heart clutter when I first sit down. Eventually, however, the tumbleweed of my inner being settles, and I search for what I am always truly searching for—God.

It is God's steadfast presence within us that makes us strong, capable, and able to move through difficult times. Due to the negativity bias of the brain, we are tasked with being intentional about seeking God's face. It is there that we can find some ease and solace in our mind, body, and heart.

Holy and loving God, bring my focus to you constantly so that I might remember all the marvels you have done and find strength in you. Amen.

FRIDAY, SEPTEMBER 18 ~ *Read Philippians 1:21-30*

As the letter to the Philippians opens, we read of Paul's struggle to know which he wants more: dying so that he can be with Christ or living in the flesh in fruitful labor with Christ's followers. He decides he will "remain and continue with all of you for your progress and joy in faith." This passage is woven with the acknowledgment of the very real suffering that came with being a follower of Christ for Paul. And joy ends up being Paul's motive. He wants the followers of Jesus to experience the progress and joy in faith alongside any suffering they may be experiencing as well. In the mystery of a loving God, we discover non-dualism as a reality. Life is always both/and.

In the throes of this earthly life, we forget that God is trying to make God's joy complete within us. It's so easy to forget that joy is the second gift of the Spirit listed within the nine gifts Paul spells out in Galatians 5:22-23. Joy? Really? Does God really care about our joy?

In the daily chaos of life, it can be easy to lose sight of the reality that God desires our goodness, our joy, our light, our wellbeing. Our brains and bandwidth can be so consumed with suffering that we altogether fail to see the joy before us, within us, and around us. Sometimes we have to slow down in order to notice what else is here. Yes, the suffering and demands of faith are here—and so is the joy of our faith and lives.

Gracious God, help me slow down and notice how you are making your joy complete within me no matter what I'm experiencing. Amen.

SATURDAY, SEPTEMBER 19 ~ *Read Matthew 20:1-16*

Much like the Israelites complaining to Moses and Aaron in the wilderness, the laborers in this Gospel parable are complaining as well. They believe the landowner should be fair in his distribution of money. Those who have been working the longest should be given the most, and the latecomers should receive wages only for the time they have been working, not the whole day. Jesus' insistence to "give to the last the same as I give to you" is a difficult wisdom for humanity to absorb, much less appreciate. The generosity of the landowner doesn't make sense in a transactional world.

We will always see situations in which God is seemingly more generous with someone else. These are difficult to experience, but they offer us the opportunity to get honest about the jealousy we may be feeling and the motives within us. It's much more comfortable to stay angry and nurse our feelings of injustice. When I identify these situations in my life, I eventually take them to God to hash out what feels unfair, unjust, and even somewhat mean in its seeming imbalance.

I eventually hear God's Spirit whisper to me, reminding me that everyone is on a different journey, has different needs, and requires a variety of graces. The Spirit nudges me to turn back the focus to my own life and attune my heart to God's love without distraction or comparison. Theodore Roosevelt is quoted as having said, "Comparison is the thief of joy." Comparison not only steals our joy, it blurs our attachment and attunement to a loving God.

Holy and gracious God, may your Spirit train the eyes of my heart to you and your love. Protect my mind and heart from the thief of joy. Amen.

SUNDAY, SEPTEMBER 20 ~ *Read Matthew 20:1-16*

This reading from Matthew is ultimately about grace and our discomfort with the last being first and the first being last. Our proclivity to hold on to power can make us think that because we arrived before others we should therefore call the shots. But sometimes I wonder about the parts within me that I consider last and the parts within me I consider first. Does the parable have something to say about our interior lives as well as our exterior relationships?

We all have parts of ourselves that we'd really rather not examine, experiences or attributes that we shove to the back of the line of our personality or attention: experiences that leave us feeling dark or haunted, decisions that weren't our best, failures that loom in the background and occasionally hijack our thoughts and feelings. Whether consciously or unconsciously, many of us try to repress these parts so they don't cause havoc on our minds, hearts, and spirits.

We tend to identify the good things about ourselves and keep those at the front of the line—our accomplishments, our finer attributes, the things that come easily to us. We allow these aspects to shine and lead the way. They are what we put first. But this passage invites us to put what's last first and what's first last.

It's my experience that the things I put last often hold the most shame. Items with shame are the very things God is hungry to love, resolve, ease, and transform. Grace is God's antidote for shame. We must offer these parts of our lives to God in order to receive the grace that enables them to be healed.

Holy and gracious God, may I have the courage to put the things I identify as last before you so that your grace can make them first to be healed. Amen.

The Authority of God

SEPTEMBER 21–27, 2026 • DEA JONES

SCRIPTURE OVERVIEW: The passages this week share a theme of conflict among God's faithful people. The passages from Exodus and Psalms remind us of when God provided water from a solid rock at a time when the people were rebelling against their spiritual leaders. Both detail God's dramatic response, reminding the people of God's authority over everything. To the Philippians, Paul stresses the avoidance of conflict, using a hymn recalling the authority of Christ as God's beloved son. Matthew tells about Jesus' conflict with the religious leaders of the Temple. They questioned his authority, but he turned their questions back on them, indicting them for their hypocrisy. In all these passages, we are reminded that God is the ultimate authority who loves us even when we are rebellious.

QUESTIONS AND SUGGESTIONS FOR REFLECTION

- Read Exodus 17:1-7. Where did you see God at work in the outcome of conflict?
- Read Psalm 78:1-4, 12-16. Reflect on your best teachers. How did they convey important lessons about faith to you? How has your perspective changed about those lessons?
- Read Philippians 2:1-13. What are some of the characteristics that make cohesiveness possible? How does your faith inform your practice when working with others?
- Read Matthew 21:23-32. Have you ever questioned the words and/or actions of someone in authority? How does understanding God's ultimate authority help you discern the right and wrong of those situations?

Dea Jones is a teacher and a writer, living in South Carolina with her spoiled rescue Boston terrier named Winston. She blogs at faithfulconversations.wordpress.com.

MONDAY, SEPTEMBER 21 ~ *Read Exodus 17:1-7*

Imagine the scene. The Israelites were frightened, angry, and desperately thirsty. It would be easy to dismiss their wailing as mere complaint, but on closer inspection, it becomes clear that this is more than complaining. The people had forgotten that God was with them and had been with them every step of the way. God provided the people with their every need. God directed their steps with cloud and fire, sent manna and quail to provide just the right amount of food each day. Miracles all. But the need for water is more serious.

The Israelites were angry with God as a result of their fear. When we are fearful, we wonder how God can allow this to happen, leading us to anger. How could God do that to us? How dare God hurt us in such a way! When we are frightened and angry, we tend to lash out, but it is hard when there is nothing physical to direct that anger toward, so we project that anger toward our leaders. We blame them for getting us into the mess in the first place, and demand that they get us out.

Faith in God, the all-knowing authority with a vision beyond our understanding, slips away in the chaos. Moses, the leader, was caught between God, in whom he had complete faith, and a very large angry group who, in their fear, had lost their faith. Frustrated with them, Moses reached out to God for guidance. And then another miracle occurred. God showed Moses how to access water, from a rock no less, gaining back the faith and trust of the people. Moses' faith never wavered, even when those around him were flailing in a spiritual desert. God showed once again, as always, that God's fearful angry people will never be abandoned. God will always provide.

Gracious God, thank you for providing for my every need, even when I lose faith in your ability to do so. Amen.

TUESDAY, SEPTEMBER 22 ~ *Read Psalm 78:1-4*

As a teacher, it is my job to share knowledge with my students and help them understand its importance in their lives, both right now and in the future. I help them learn new ideas they've never seen or heard before and remind them how older ideas and concepts can lead to new learning and deeper understanding.

This instructional psalm was sung or recited to remind the people about all of God's great deeds, the wonders God performed throughout the history of the Israelites. The beginning is a call to pay attention because the psalmist is going to teach. Teachers have to gain and keep the attention of our students!

Notice how the psalmist talks about sharing "dark sayings," or as the NIV says "hidden things, things from of old." That beginning is a great hook. Who wouldn't want the teacher to continue? Then, the psalmist shares the best part, the *why* of the song: We must share the wisdom passed down to us from our ancestors to new generations. They must know and understand the importance of God's great deeds, God's mighty strength, and the wonders God has wrought. Grasping the importance of this ancient knowledge in their lives allows God's people to greet new learning and have a deeper understanding of God's plan—such as in the teachings of Jesus when his time comes—with an open heart and mind. By reciting these stories, the people, just like us now, are reminded of important things they forgot in the midst of everyday living. God is on our side and always with us through every trial. God is ready to perform mighty deeds on our behalf and has big plans for us. What a lesson!

God of wisdom and might, thank you for teachers, both old and young, who remind me, with wise words and loving hands, of your great works and caring presence in my life. Amen.

WEDNESDAY, SEPTEMBER 23 ~ *Read Psalm 78:12-16*

Who is the keeper of your family lore? Every family needs someone who knows the story of how grandpa and grandma met, or how great-great-grandma crossed the plains in a covered wagon, or how great-grandpa emigrated from another country to start a better life. These are the people who learn the stories and share them with the rest of the family so they can be passed down, generation to generation. In my generation of my family, that job is mine.

When I tell the stories of my ancestors, I try to make them engaging, to paint a picture of the time and place these tales occurred so those listening will feel as though they are there, living the experience. I tell these stories over and over, wanting others in my family to understand how the things that occurred back then affect our lives today.

The writer of the psalm wants the listener to understand how God worked miracles to move an entire population from one place to another at a time long ago and very far away. The listener needs to understand how dire the situation was for those ancestors, so the psalmist stresses the sheer magnitude of God's mighty acts. Notice what the psalmist focuses on: God's intervention in Egypt; God's constant presence, day and night, among the people as they journeyed to their Promised Land; and the provision of abundant water in a dry desert. The psalmist doesn't tell the story with just the facts, but with drama and poetic language to help the listener feel the experience on a more visceral level. These are their stories, sung and spoken, shared continually to remind the people, and us too, of God's presence with the Israelites and God's continual presence with us today.

Mighty God, help me tell the stories of my family and of my family of faith in order that others may know of your great love. Amen.

THURSDAY, SEPTEMBER 24 ~ *Read Philippians 2:1-4*

What makes a community? Humans have banded together over millennia for many reasons: to share resources, for protection, for economic opportunity, for family obligation and loyalty. Members of the group usually have something in common such as shared ancestors, goals, or beliefs. Forming a group is a challenge. Staying together is an even greater one. And facing challenges together usually bonds a group of people more closely or separates them further, depending on how the individuals of the group respond to the challenge and to one another.

The followers of Christ in Philippi formed a community in a vibrant city full of diverse people with varying belief systems, all under the umbrella of Roman rule. This letter of encouragement from Paul to a beloved group of people he had lived and worked with gave them a plan of action to stay motivated. Knowing they were a new community of believers, Paul understood what the group needed to sustain itself and continue to thrive. They must be united in their work and form caring relationships with one another. He says if they share Christ-like qualities as God would wish them to, then they should think of others before considering their own desires.

Paul knows the church at Philippi must do as Christ would do and encourages each member of the community to humble him or herself before the others to create lasting bonds built on love. A community with minds and hands focused on continuing the work of Jesus that genuinely and unselfishly cares for its members can overcome obstacles and accomplish great things for the glory of God. Wise words for any church, then and now.

All-giving Jesus, keep me focused on you and unselfish in my relationships with others so as to further your kingdom on earth. Amen.

FRIDAY, SEPTEMBER 25 ~ *Read Philippians 2:5-13*

Experts say the verses of this reading may be an early hymn or poem of the church. Paul may have written the words, but it's possible this poetry was already known to his readers and that Paul uses familiar words to connect his point to the incarnational truth of Jesus.

The words speak of how Jesus emptied himself. Jesus did not pour out what was inside him. He literally poured himself out in order to become completely and utterly human, but not just human. He became human to the greatest degree. He became the perfect person, utterly obedient to God, even when that obedience led to a brutal death. How absolutely humbling for Jesus to step away from his position as Lord of all for our sake. Jesus is God by his very nature, a concept that is difficult for us to grasp. The power behind Christ's sacrifice is beyond our understanding, leaving us to wonder why God would do such a thing.

The answer is love. Paul used the hymn as a reminder that the selflessness of Jesus is something to be emulated. We should try to be like Christ, sacrificing for others out of love for one another. We will not reach the level of "emptying" ourselves that Christ did. But because Jesus has paved the way for our salvation, we can make our way in the world, continuing to strive for that kind of selfless love out of our own love for God. We can rejoice knowing that God loves us so completely and can strive to love others with that same love. Thankfully, God is at work within us, helping us find the will to help one another and do the work of the kingdom.

Gracious Redeemer, guide my will and my way as I strive to emulate your perfect example of selfless love. Amen.

SATURDAY, SEPTEMBER 26 ~ *Read Matthew 21:23-27*

The chief priests and elders were furious and probably a little frightened. This upstart rabble rouser, who wasn't even officially a rabbi, had been making a name for himself all over the place, inspiring the people to question the status quo and rethink what it meant to be faithful to God. He had the nerve to tear up the Temple, turning over the money changing tables and making a mess. Stirring people up was one thing, but messing with a regular source of income was another. Plus, people were talking, and soon the Roman authorities would take notice. As leaders of the community, they had to put a stop to his shenanigans.

They hit him with this burning question: "By whose authority do you do these things?" Asking them a question in response, Jesus traps them in their blatant hypocrisy. They debate among themselves about the best way to answer him. They claim to be the religious authorities, but they are afraid to give their honest opinion. They take the easy way out, responding with the safe noncommittal answer: "We do not know."

Jesus sees right through them. He understands that the leaders of the religious community were more concerned about the threat he posed to their influence. When faced with the full authority of God, they acted like politicians, not leaders of their faith. Jesus' response was to refuse to answer their question. Jesus knew they weren't ready to accept the truth. This story reminds us that Jesus was unafraid to expose the affected superiority of religious leaders, taking them down a peg in the face of the true authority of God.

Lord of All, keep me ever mindful and thankful of your authority over everything. Amen.

SUNDAY, SEPTEMBER 27 ~ *Read Matthew 21:23-32*

In Jesus' parables, it can sometimes be hard to determine which characters we're supposed to identify with. Perhaps in this parable, though, we are called to identify with both sons, recognizing how we can exhibit qualities they each display. Sometimes we deny what we know God wants us to do. We rebel against doing the work, throwing adult versions of tantrums. It's too hard! I want to do this other thing instead! Our selfish desires get in the way of accepting God's authority in our lives. But then, we reconsider. We recognize God's overwhelming love for us, how God always knows what is best in any situation. We change our minds and do what we know God wants us to do.

Other times we are like the second son. We say yes with a smile to the tasks God asks of us, but we make no real effort to accomplish those tasks. Maybe it is to appease our own conscience or to give the appearance of faithful obedience. It's so much easier to just say yes and then forget about it, isn't it? We give lip service to God.

When Jesus asks the Temple authorities which son did the will of the father, they know the answer: The first son is the more faithful. Jesus points out that they are more like the second son, while the sinners they revile are more like the first. When faced with the work of the kingdom, we have choices. Which son will we emulate? Or better yet let us agree like the second son and work like the first.

Gracious God, help me to discern your will and accept your authority in my life. Thank you for loving and forgiving me when I fail to do so. Amen.

The Laws of the Lord

SEPTEMBER 28–OCTOBER 4, 2026 • BRADLEY BUNN

SCRIPTURE OVERVIEW: A common theme this week is the danger of self-absorption. When we are young, we may struggle to understand the importance of rules because we think that our individual freedom is the highest good. God gives the Israelites commandments to guide their relationships with God and others. These laws will help them thrive because God knows what is best for us. The psalmist understands this: The laws of the Lord are good and sweet. Self-absorption might also lead to pride. Paul shows that a true understanding of the gospel means laying aside our selfishness in the knowledge that God will reward us. In a parable about the rejection of the prophets and Jesus, servants seek to seize a vineyard for themselves, unwisely ignoring that the owner will eventually reclaim what is his.

QUESTIONS AND SUGGESTIONS FOR REFLECTION

- Read Exodus 20:1-4, 7-9, 12-20. Recall your earliest experiences with the Ten Commandments. How do they continue to shape your understanding of God's expectations?
- Read Psalm 19. How does the natural world call you to follow God?
- Read Philippians 3:4b-14. Whom do you emulate? What would it mean for you to emulate Christ in life and in death?
- Read Matthew 21:33-46. When have you participated in or witnessed the rejection of one who could be God in disguise? How might things be different if you had recognized that person as a potential cornerstone of your community?

Rev. Bradley Bunn serves as the senior minister at First Congregational Church in Mansfield, OH. He is a Christian educator and visual artist with interests in spiritual direction, arts in ministry, and leadership studies.

MONDAY, SEPTEMBER 28 ~ *Read Exodus 20:1-4*

My parents and grandparents passed on their most treasured values to me: Finish what you start, live a life of integrity, value education, and lean on God and family for strength. In today's reading, we read about a value system that would form and shape the people of God and reinforce a covenantal relationship with the one, true God who not only delivers the people from an oppressive nation but also surpasses any imitation by any other god in the ancient world. It is by God's authority in who God is—one who brings forth salvation through divine speech and divine action—that we can rest in God's assurances that our lives are meant for abundant living.

As a teenager, I was much more inclined to strive for "being cool" than recognizing spiritual abundance. I was the sort of teen who could navigate decently through junior high and high school social cliques of the day. However, I always felt, even then, that something was missing. All I knew was that God was calling me to do "something." In response to this calling, I asked my pastor if I could serve as one of the group leaders of the church's youth ministry team. Later, as a freshman in college, the church employed me as their first paid youth director. I felt connected to a cause, and I was emboldened to pursue it. I soon realized that abundant living had much more to do with serving others than being served.

The Ten Commandments provide a type of scaffolding for our outlook toward God and one another. They also provide a guidepost toward an abundant life that appreciates God's provisions along the way. In turn, we recognize them for what they are—a clarion call to live a life of abundant service to others.

God of abundance, help me discover the riches of serving others. Amen.

TUESDAY, SEPTEMBER 29 ~ *Read Exodus 20:7-9*

When I began full-time congregational ministry, I was very fortunate to have a wonderful mentor who was my boss as well as the church's senior minister. He took me under his wing and taught me much about ministry. We spent numerous lunches discussing how to empower members for the ministries of the church and how to be sensitive to the needs of parents and youth. During one of our lunches, as I was asking him how to handle some issues that were percolating in the Christian education department, he stopped me midway in the conversation and asked, "Brad, how do you spell your name?" I wondered what he was getting at, but I played along: "Well, I spell it B-R-A-D." "Good!" he said, "Because once you realize that your name isn't spelled G-O-D the better off you'll be!" Those words of wisdom have stayed with me since those early days in my ministry, and I often reflect on them.

As we continue to read through the Ten Commandments, we are particularly challenged in our reading today not to confuse our human identity and role with that of God's. For this is yet another way of misusing the name of God—replacing it with ours. And yet God provides us with a corrective, to take pause and rest in order to marvel at God's abundance in our lives.

The universal church's mission in the world is to make disciples of Christ, and that is our underlining motivation to serve others. However, at times we get in our own way. The apostle Paul said it best: "But we have this treasure in clay jars, so that it may be made clear that this extraordinary power belongs to God and does not come from us" (2 Cor. 4:7). Let's let God be God.

Mighty God, I pray that your abundant love and compassion guide me in all your ways. Amen.

WEDNESDAY, SEPTEMBER 30 ~ *Read Exodus 20:12-20*

As we conclude our reading of the Ten Commandments, we notice how Moses reiterates to the people that the law is to keep sin at bay. In other words, he points to how these latter commandments speak to the licentiousness that can plague a culture and a civilization. Conversely, God's law is to provide guardrails for an otherwise sinful world. Thus, what might be perceived as limitations are really a loving parent's guidance for their children, and we honor our parents by heeding their wisdom.

I do believe there's hope for our hurting world, even as we are confronted with a myriad of problems often caused by individual and societal avarice. My grandfather shared with me once that the reason he joined the U.S. Marine Corps as a young man was because he felt that if he could become a marine, he could do anything in life. Well, I share a similar sentiment: I believe if we can serve others with integrity, passion, love, and humility, then there's no telling how God may use our lives in order to further the work and presence of God's kingdom.

Over the years within the ministry, I have seen children, teenagers, and families give of themselves to serve those in need through various mission camps, outreach projects, and everyday congregational life. I have had the privilege to pray with and sponsor youth and adults who have ministered in places all across the globe. I am fortunate to have come across ordinary folks who are doing extraordinary things in ministry who are impassioned with God's calling in their lives and are eager to respond. This is good news, the good news of the gospel alive in the world! This is abundant living!

Gracious God, help me to honor and praise you through obeying your living word and reaching out to others in need. I pray that you mold and shape me into the best version of myself. Amen.

THURSDAY, OCTOBER 1 ~ *Read Psalm 19:1-6*

I grew up in the country along the dirt roads of Pine Mountain Valley, Georgia. I found our home, ensconced by hundreds, if not thousands, of trees (pines and oaks) to be my refuge, a place where I could daydream as I wandered many wooded treks as a teenager and young adult. My memories of that time are so vivid: hearing the crackling of the leaves under my shoes and seeing the mist of my breath in the cold afternoons while mesmerized by the shards of light breaking through the phalanx of tree limbs. It was a magical place for me, and it was during those walks in the woods where I would encounter God's presence surrounding me.

David begins his psalm with adoration and contemplation of God's creation. He uses romantic imagery about the heavens and the skies—referring to the skies as a tent for the sun like "a bridegroom coming out of his chamber, like a champion rejoicing to run his course" (NIV). For David, God's creation is also magical in that it has the ability to reach into our hearts and capture our imaginations, bringing forth experiences of awe, wonder, and inspiration.

When I was younger, I loved to draw and create art. When I became an adult I quit drawing. I had so many other things vying for my attention—family, graduate school, and career. It wasn't until my late forties that I took up art-making again. One of the first things I began to draw were trees. I would get lost in the roots, the limbs, and especially the leaves, but I soon noticed how creating art allowed me to focus on living in the present and experiencing joy. God's creation can frame our life of abundant living—living in the present—if we're open to it.

Creator God, inspire me through your gift of nature. Amen.

FRIDAY, OCTOBER 2 ~ *Read Psalm 19:7-14*

Attending seminary became a transformational experience for me, especially in the way in which I was taught to engage the scriptures. I remember taking notes in my first New Testament class and suddenly realizing how much I did not know about the Bible. I looked over at one of my classmates bewildered: "That's in the Bible?!" He, a more astute student, grinned and shook his head, probably wondering what in the world I was doing at seminary. But after that first semester, I was hooked. I became enamored with how the scripture could be viewed as a living, breathing exposition of how a loving and righteous God continually reaches out to humankind.

David reminds us that the scriptures are to be trusted, which in turn provides sustenance for our souls. Subsequently, he provides a litany of descriptors about how God's ordinances can affect our interior lives in ways that are known only between us and God. Of course, following God's ordinances would direct us toward being in right relationships with others too.

I'd imagine when Jesus was a preteen, while studying and asking questions in the temple (see Luke 2:42-46), it would have looked very similar to today's yeshiva—a Jewish school or seminary where students study the Torah. Students must be well-versed and knowledgeable about the law and its rabbinical interpretations before they can argue its points. Within the interplay of debates, students are continually formed and shaped by differing points of view in which they all will inevitably hold the Torah in high esteem as an enduring bedrock of the faith. In living an abundant life as a believer, I'm more and more convinced that God is asking us to dive deep into the scriptures and mine the treasures there that provide sustenance for our daily lives.

God of us all, I thank you for the sacred scriptures. I pray that my speech and my actions honor you. Amen.

SATURDAY, OCTOBER 3 ~ *Read Philippians 3:4b-14*

I believe choice, as a requirement for spiritual growth, inherently pushes us out of our comfort zones and into deeper discernment with God. In our reading for today, we can sense Paul struggling with this notion of wanting to know Christ more deeply, even to the brink of his longing to imitate Christ's death and resurrection. Paul chooses to move out of the shadow cast by the law and into the light of Christ's eternal hope.

For most of us, it takes time to learn, observe, and find our way among the choices we make that inevitably branch off into other choices. This type of sifting and sorting is how I define holy discernment. And the goal for holy discernment is really a perceptional change. In other words, we discern so we can see ourselves as God sees us. I believe this is what Paul is getting at when he writes, "Not that I have already obtained all of this, or have already arrived at my goal, but I press on to take hold of that for which Christ Jesus took hold of me" (NIV). Thus, we are all searching for our more authentic selves.

I would suggest that we start the journey or the race with the mindset that all of life is sacred and that God can be discerned even throughout life's nooks and crannies. The abundant life is a sacramental one in that the ordinary things of life can be experienced as holy and extraordinary. This point of view challenges us to take pause and reflect on our day-to-day life, especially if we can accept life with an abundance of gratitude. We benefit in our spiritual lives when we open our hearts and minds toward a God-consciousness that advocates for being grateful—acknowledging that life is a gift, and not one's possession.

Holy God, transform my heart and mind into an abundant and grateful posture toward living. Amen.

In today's passage, we read the dire circumstances of the religious elite. And it stems from dynamics of control: "By what authority are you doing these things?" they asked. "And who gave you this authority?" (v. 23b, NIV). As a clergyperson, I often find myself asking that question when an impassioned church member blurts out a new initiative or ministry idea (usually one that I don't agree with), and a consensus of committee members goes along with said initiative or idea. In retrospect, I've found that if I can take a moment and step back—viewing myself and others, especially others, as having inherent value and as children of God—then my ego is put in check; otherwise, my ego cries out: "Do they know who I am?! This church couldn't survive without me!" The religious elite of Jesus' day are so jealous and defensive. They're holding on to the ways things have always been done and interpreted through their own lenses.

Jesus warns that this ego-driven approach will only lead to dastardly deeds. And though we can't imagine the outright murder of another, especially the landowner's son, we can become guilty of a sort of premeditated crime toward others. In our relationships with others we are privy to the things that can upset or hurt them. And when we allow our egos to run amok, we're inclined to say things we know that become emotional and spiritual arrows, daggers, and stones.

Jesus ends the parable with the caveat that those who are invited into the kingdom of God are the people who create fruitful outcomes. Again, when our egos are kept in check, we have the potential to create something new for the kingdom of God. Abundant living focuses on kingdom outcomes, no matter where they originate from.

God of fruitful outcomes, I pray that I support and follow the Spirit's moving among your people. Amen.

Holding Both Beautiful and Brutal

OCTOBER 5–11, 2026 • VICTORIA LOORZ

SCRIPTURE OVERVIEW: As much as we might like to focus on the easy parts of ancient stories, the golden calf and the parable of the wedding guests this week are particularly difficult, full of betrayal, retribution, and violence. Avoiding those parts can cause us to lose sight of the wisdom at the core. The psalm positions the story of the golden calf alongside God's everlasting love, but still acknowledges the peoples' failure and God's wrath that is tempered only through Moses' intervention. This complicated collection of stories is punctuated by Paul's letter to the Philippians, naming the need for a mindset of love and gratitude no matter the situation. As a result, we are invited to hold the uncomfortable alongside the beautiful in these stories and in our lives.

QUESTIONS AND SUGGESTIONS FOR REFLECTION

- Read Exodus 32:1-14. When have you or your faith community gotten it wrong? When have you interceded with God on others' behalf?
- Read Psalm 106:1-6,19-23. How has forgetting that you can be wrong hurt you or your faith community? How has admitting that you were wrong strengthened you or your faith community?
- Read Philippians 4:1-9. What does the reality of rejoicing always in all situations look like in your life?
- Read Matthew 22:1-14. Why is it so important to be wearing the right clothing at the wedding?

Victoria Loorz is the founder & guide of the Center for Wild Spirituality and co-founder of the Wild Church Network. She is the author of *Church of the Wild: How Nature Invites Us into the Sacred* (Broadleaf Books, 2021), *Field Guide to Church of the Wild* (Broadleaf, 2025), and the upcoming *Wild Spirituality* (Broadleaf, 2027).

MONDAY, OCTOBER 5 ~ *Read Exodus 32:1-14*

The story of the golden calf is usually preached as a cautionary tale about the dangers of idolatry and the heroic prayers of Moses. What is often glossed over is the violence of this tale. We don't like to highlight Moses as the level-headed hero who must talk God out of genocidal wrath. Instead we see Moses as an example of one praying an intercessory prayer, and the lectionary reading stops before we get to the part where Moses has the sons of Levi kill three thousand of the Israelites.

Yet wisdom is hidden in the cracks of the disturbing details. The Exodus and wilderness story is often told in times of catastrophic collapse, when everything seems to be changing and nothing seems to be sure—times, that is, like ours. It is a story told to remind us that the Promised Land doesn't just arrive magically. We must work for the promised vision God has inspired in us. This ancient story about a community of people wrestling to shed their old identity as slaves to an oppressive system shows them struggling with the loss of everything they knew as they try to embrace everything that is promised. A people wandering in the literal wilderness are attempting to create a new identity, an identity that takes rest seriously, that loves elders and neighbors as kin, that honors the sacred reality of God.

Experiencing a shift in our worldview can be brutal, often coming unexpectedly and thrusting us into a new reality that requires a new way of being, a new communal identity. New worlds can't be re-shaped with minimal disruption. New identities often require old identities to be completely surrendered and killed off in the wilderness. In these times of great unrest, we can remember God's faithfulness, even if we have to be the ones to remind God of this faithfulness.

God, may we commit ourselves to the fierce surrender of old ways that no longer serve us so we might be free to serve you and one another with tenderness. Amen.

TUESDAY, OCTOBER 6 ~ *Read Exodus 32:1-14*

Most of us don't have an image of a God that would say things like, "Now let me alone so that my wrath may burn hot against them and I may consume them, and of you—*just you* (my addition)—I will make a great nation." Harsh words indeed.

This is one story among a collection of stories about a nation struggling to understand themselves as "chosen ones." The transition to freedom must have been difficult, to say the least, after four hundred years as slaves in Egypt. Four hundred years of adaptation to doing what you're told. Yet God and the people had just made an agreement, and God didn't even have time to record the commandments on stone tablets before the people had broken the agreement. When Moses delayed his return, the people didn't know what to do without a master. They turned to what they did know—the golden gods of their former enslavers. God isn't so understanding. God wants to start over, expressing to Moses a desire to annihilate all the people who have yet to release the mindset of slavery, choosing instead only the one guy who had never been mistreated as a slave.

Yet Moses reminds God of God's faithfulness. Notice Moses never excuses the behavior of the people, but instead appeals to God's mercy. Perhaps this is the kernel of wisdom for us reading this story in a wholly different time and context. Perhaps those of us in the "chosen" privileged class who have not suffered the trauma of poverty, exclusion, and devaluation are called to step up and raise our voices, even against our own versions of God in our nation, and to defend the people who are still learning that freedom means relationship, responsibility, and mercy.

God, may we who are of the chosen privileged class today have the courage to stand up for our people—which is all people—especially those who have been impacted by the effects of trauma and disregard. Amen.

WEDNESDAY, OCTOBER 7 ~ *Read Psalm 106:1-6, 19-23*

What begins as a psalm praising God and requesting the Lord's favor quickly turns specifically to the confession of sins committed by the Israelites. It is not the Israelites in the desert confessing to God, however. This psalm was written generations later during a traumatic time of profound despair, likely after the Babylonian captivity. The writer is expressing the sorrow of the people of Israel as they search to find meaning in the rubble of the life they knew, now totally dismantled. They look back to the beginning, acknowledging that from the very start they had a tendency to get things wrong. The expression of intense grief is natural. Lamenting "if only I had done something different," acknowledging we were part of the problem that created the traumatic situation is going to create some big feelings.

Israel imagined that it was their own refusal to remember God that caused national devastation. The story of the golden calf is an example of how the Israelites tried to rely on their own self-sufficiency as they forgot who was truly the author of their life and freedom. As a result, we can see that the psalmist beginning with praise is not generic; it is a specific attempt to begin correctly this time with praise of the One who brought them out of slavery and into the Promised Land.

I wonder how we might envision our role in the ecological and cultural destruction of our nations. We also have a tragic loss of memory. We've forgotten that all of life on earth is interconnected, that every part of our planet is sacred, and that God as Creator is the starting point of all life. Perhaps we need to create our own psalms and stories of lamentations that acknowledge how we too have forgotten God and lost everything. It may be the only pathway into new life.

God, we pray for the courage to look honestly at our collective failures, to own them, and to see your loving presence in all things once again. Amen.

The parable of the wedding banquet is found in both the Gospels of Matthew and Luke. I've preached on this parable before, and Luke's version allows us to focus on the benevolence of the king inviting all the peasants and homeless folk to fill the wedding hall after the initially invited guests decline. Luke's version skips right over the king's wrathful murder of all his friends, or former friends, and the burning of all their villages. Luke makes no mention of the friend without proper wedding attire who is summarily tied up and thrown out into the darkness, weeping. Matthew's version, however, requires us to address such violence—a difficult task.

It is no wonder that many argue that the Bible has been used to justify more violence than any other book in all of history. It is easy to see how this parable could easily be twisted to perpetuate a kind of exceptionalism that justifies a caste system of "chosen" and "everyone else distinctly *not* chosen." It happens still today: Those with power exclude and oppress those without power who have been "not chosen."

But that misapplication is precisely the point, I think. Power and privilege isn't the deciding factor of chosenness, even though that is how empires work. What matters is how you clothe yourself—clothing not as a facade to fit into the chosen group but as an authentic reflection of who you are inside. Adorning your life with mercy, beauty, respect for others: This is how you claim and live into relationship with the sacred that dwells in and between all things. Anything less and the relationship is broken, killed off, with weeping and gnashing of teeth.

O Beloved, may our hearts be broken in love so that we treat with fierceness the lingering, judgmental, cruel ignorance that holds us back from truly opening up to compassionate relationship with you and all who dwell on earth. Amen.

FRIDAY, OCTOBER 9 ~ *Read Psalm 106:19-23*

My work is focused on restoring sacred relationship with nature as a foundational aspect of our spirituality. I can see evidence throughout scripture that relationship with God in the wilderness is essential. Every major leader in the Bible was first sent into the wilderness at a critical time in their lives. Their relationship with God is what sustained them and brought them through to the other side.

In this psalm's retelling of this week's story from Exodus, the psalmist laments that the Israelites "exchanged the glory of God for the image of an ox that eats grass." They exchanged the life-giving, redemptive relationship with God for a creation of their own making. In attempting to possess a symbol for their religious faith, they gave up access to the eternal power that freed them from slavery, parted the waters, and protected them from sure death. They did so because, as the psalmist says, they forgot.

In the psalmist's retelling of this story, the followers of God are invited to remember their transgressions. Unlike those who "forgot God, their Savior, who had done great things," the psalmist's song remembers. Not only do hearers of the psalm remember Israel's transgressions, they remember God's mercy provided at the bequest of Moses. They remember the bad and the good, the brutal reality of their failure, the depth of God's wrath, the intercession of Moses, and the beautiful redemption of God. Such remembrance allows them to cling to God in the midst of their own wilderness experiences and to rest in the relationship that will carry them through to the other side.

Redeeming God, may we draw ever closer to you in moments of beauty and brutality. When we suffer, let us suffer knowing you stand beside us. When we rejoice, let us rejoice in you. Amen.

SATURDAY, OCTOBER 10 ~ *Read Philippians 4:1-7*

After a week of difficult passages, this passage brings it all together. This foundational exhortation accompanies the other harsh stories this week to finish the message: This is the clothing of the kingdom of God. This is what chosen means. It is easy to say, "Rejoice!" when we skip over the difficult passages. But rejoicing while looking the other way or hiding our grief under a smile of false belonging is not actually joy. Joy is instead possible "in every situation" when we are in honest relationship with the Holy. We must behold joy as gratitude for the whole—the beginnings and the endings, the suffering and the celebrations, the difficult days as well as the easy, the resting alongside the productivity.

It is so easy to say these words on the shallowest level, like reciting a prayer or a pledge that proclaims forgiveness, inclusion, and justice for all when the speaker really only means some. But this surrender to relationship with God—who is present in all situations, in all places, in all beings—is the path of spiritual aliveness. It is a surrender to practicing love in all situations, which sounds easier than it is, as we all know.

Holding both the grief and the joy, and expressing both in love is the work of the spiritual journey. Allowing death when it comes, rather then turning the other way, is the only way to make room for the new. Can we really rejoice in the midst of all situations, grieving what is lost to make room for the new? This is the peace of God that makes way for authentic gentleness evident to all.

Holy God, I choose to be chosen. I choose to put into practice the responsibilities of love that come with it. Today, I choose the mindset of love. Amen.

SUNDAY, OCTOBER 11 ~ *Read Philippians 4:8-9*

And finally, my kindred siblings, finally, let us think on what is beautiful and alive and life-giving. Rather than figuring out how we can defeat the other political party, or drawing a selfish line around what is ours, or attempting to avoid the necessary death before new life comes, let's finally just put our values of love, kindness, and gentleness into practice.

Let's imagine what life could be and then start living that life now, even while forces of oppression push us back into old ways. Let us gather together on the land and ask the trees and the rivers and the wind and all the beings we are in relationship with to join us. Let's grieve together as wildfires and floods and collective unkindness continue to bring destruction. Let us lament with songs and poems and hold one another close as we face whatever life brings us. Let's create churches that open hearts and welcome the outcasts and grow neighborhood gardens to feed one another. Let us be sanctuaries of safety and acceptance and kindness and help one another remember that God is real in all situations.

And when we forget, may we head back out to the wilderness. We are called there by the Holy Spirit to listen to voices of the holy whispering through the wild, reminding us that we belong, that we have responsibilities of love in the whole interconnected web of aliveness.

The Promised Land isn't a place we need to take over from someone else. It is a way of being in our place, a way of being connected in respectful and kind relationship with the Holy Mystery and all that God loves, which is everyone and everything.

Holy Mystery, today I commit to immerse myself in what is true and real and alive and holy. Today I open my heart to embrace all of life as sacred—both the grief and the beauty of life. Amen.

Where Is God?

OCTOBER 12–18, 2026 • LYNDSEY MEDFORD

SCRIPTURE OVERVIEW: As Christians, we know we believe in Immanuel—God with us. We cling to this idea in theory, but in the everyday messiness of life, we sometimes still wonder where God actually is. This week's readings offer various perspectives on God's presence. In Exodus, Moses feels insecure about the calling on his life and asks to see God. The psalmist remembers the story of God's presence with the Israelites in the wilderness. The Gospel reminds us that even when we ponder momentous decisions about weighty topics, our ultimate security is in our belonging to God. And Paul's letter to the Thessalonians gives us an example of experiencing God's love in everyday friendship.

QUESTIONS AND SUGGESTIONS FOR REFLECTION

- Read Exodus 33:12-23. When have you struggled to believe that God is with you? How did you find a sign of God's presence?
- Read Psalm 99. How has God heard your cry? How can you listen with God for the cries of others?
- Read 1 Thessalonians 1:1-10. When does your faith call you to live in a counter-cultural way? How do you show the world how to live?
- Read Matthew 22:15-22. You belong to God. How do you experience God's call on your life?

Lyndsey Medford is a mom, author, and hope seeker. She writes a newsletter called *Creaturely* at lyndseymedford.substack.com.

MONDAY, OCTOBER 12 ~ *Read Luke 17:11-19*

THANKSGIVING DAY (CANADA)

A few days ago I was deeply frustrated over something that had gone wrong while planning our family vacation. The problem was my own mistake, but I still felt outraged that no one could help me fix it. I also knew, of course, that this was the epitome of a "non-problem"—we get to go on vacation! But knowing that couldn't make my anger go away. Honestly, I was angry because I felt helpless. I'd expected things to be a certain way, but they weren't, and there was nothing I could do about it. And—when I really faced the facts—I couldn't quite believe I wasn't entitled to have things go my way.

It's easy to look at the ungrateful people cured of leprosy in this story and judge them for their attitude of entitlement. We think that if we'd experienced such a life-changing moment, we would have done things differently. But if each of those men were confronted about his ingratitude, each would have a familiar-sounding excuse. As chronically ill, disabled people, the healed men likely weren't used to having everything go their way. But perhaps they felt entitled to God's healing power. Or perhaps they were too eager to return to their lives. Perhaps they intended to return and offer thanks but got distracted. Whatever the reason, only one returned to say "thank you." He saw the miracle in front of him and took the time to mark what God had done.

The excuse isn't all that important. We create excuses for our behavior all the time. As I prayed about my situation this week, I felt God asking me to accept the situation as it was and to be humble and realistic about my place in it. I didn't "use" gratitude to "fix" my anger. My prayer of contrition instead opened up space for gratitude to enter.

Thank you, God, for so much is a gift. Amen.

TUESDAY, OCTOBER 13 ~ *Read Exodus 33:12-18*

Moses already knows that God has called him to lead the Israelites to the Promised Land, but he wants the details. In the previous verses, God has said it's time to go, but clearly says that God will not be going with the people (see Exod. 33:3). *Whoa,* Moses and the people respond. Who will go with them? Moses presses God, arguing that Moses has fulfilled what God has asked of him, so it's time for God to reveal a bit more. God finally relents, "My presence will go with you, and I will give you rest." Still, Moses wants confirmation. He wants to see God.

When I read Moses' words in this passage, they sound familiar. How many times have I been in a similar situation? I might know on some level that God has a direction for me, or that God is with me—but how? When? How can I be sure? Moses has brought all his anxiety right into this meeting with God. Some people might see his worry as a sign of faithlessness. But God is patient with Moses' pleading and questioning. In fact, God even confirms, "I am pleased with you." Maybe it's actually a sign of faith that Moses has chosen to be honest with God. As patient as God is, it also seems that God doesn't want Moses to live with the burden of his anxieties forever. "My presence will go with you, and I will give you rest." Rest, in the middle of the wilderness? Rest, overburdened with responsibilities and hanging on to thin wafers of manna for survival?

God's presence doesn't make those very real needs and struggles go away. But God's presence—exemplified by God's patience and kindness in this dialogue with Moses—offers guidance, reassurance, protection, and abiding love. Rest is not about being free of needs, weaknesses, or cares; it is about looking for the place where God is already waiting to meet with us in the midst of them. This is always a place where we can be honest.

God of patience, please direct my attention to places of your presence today. Teach me how to rest there. Amen.

WEDNESDAY, OCTOBER 14 ~ *Read 1 Thessalonians 1:1-10*

Do you have a friend who puts a smile on your face every time you think about them? First Thessalonians is a letter overflowing with Paul's fondness and gratitude for his friends in the Thessalonian church. He has been waiting to hear how they are doing and has just gotten news from Timothy that their faith remains strong. In fact, they've gone from being hearers of the gospel to proclaiming the gospel through their lives! Both Paul and the Thessalonians have endured hardship, but the news of their flourishing brings him happiness.

Paul writes, "We know, brothers and sisters loved by God, that he has chosen you, because our gospel came to you not simply with words but also with power, with the Holy Spirit and with deep conviction" (NIV). Just as God's presence was the sign in Exodus that the Israelites were God's chosen people, now the Holy Spirit accompanies and reassures the Thessalonians. They don't have to produce faith, hope, and love on their own. Life in the Spirit is a life that overflows with these gifts. Even in the midst of suffering, the Holy Spirit's abiding presence fills them with joy. And perhaps especially in the midst of suffering, their friendship also brings joy.

In the love and the witness of the Thessalonians, God encourages Paul and answers his prayers. God is present to each of them in more than one way, both directly in the presence of the Spirit and indirectly through their friendship. Sometimes when I wonder where God is, I forget that God's presence isn't always found in an earth-shaking experience, but that God cares enough to share our everyday lives with us. The Spirit is near in every breath. And God's love and power are reflected in the faces of those who love us and who bring us joy.

Thank God in your own words for a friend who brings you joy. Then send them a note to tell them you're grateful for them!

THURSDAY, OCTOBER 15 ~ *Read Psalm 99*

I live right at the bottom of a mountain. As I go through my days, I regularly come face-to-face with my own smallness, and I'm reminded of the beauty and majesty of God's creation. A painted sunset, a tree, even a moth or a single leaf can do the same.

The psalmist affirms three times in this psalm that God is holy. The language and imagery inspire wonder, awe, and respect—perhaps even fear. As we read, we feel we are craning our necks to look way up at God "enthroned upon the cherubim," "exalted," on a "holy mountain." The word *holy* means *set apart*. We remember that God is untameable, all-powerful, and unknowable. It can be easy to order our lives to revolve around our own schedules and preferences. We might forget that God is holy, far beyond our imagining, far above our human heroes, far older than time. We might forget to look up. This psalm reminds us that we are made to stand in awe.

But this psalm also does something else. The third stanza shifts from emphasizing God's holiness to telling about God's covenant relationship with Israel. When God promised Moses that God's presence would go with Moses and the Israelites (see Exod. 33:12-17), God fulfilled that promise by accompanying them on their journey in a pillar of cloud. God heard their cries and answered them. God may be high above humanity, but God is also present with us. God is the author of justice, but God is also forgiving. The earth shakes before God, but God also hears our prayers.

The next time I emerge from the grocery store and find myself looking up, and up, and up, I'll remember the holiness and glory of God—and I'll give thanks that God also chooses to descend to be with us.

Lord, I praise your great and awesome name! And I rejoice that when I call your name, you answer me. Amen.

Behind the Pharisees' question in this passage is a test of loyalties. Over and over again in this section of Matthew, some religious leaders have been trying to trap Jesus. They believe that his popularity threatens their power as mediators between the Roman Empire and the Jewish people.

To pay taxes is to offer obedience to the Roman Empire. If Jesus says people should not pay taxes, the powers-that-be will be offended. But if he says they should pay, some of his fellow Jews will view it as an endorsement of a foreign occupying power that oppresses them in their own land. Jesus' answer says more than simply "split your money evenly between taxes and tithes." He answers a question with a question: "Whose image is on this coin?" Coins and currency, he implies, belong to the government, and taxes simply return some to their source.

The Pharisees are anxious about their status within the Empire. But Jesus refuses their framing of the question. He has no need to garner greater popularity with the people, nor does he care to curry favor with the Empire's rulers. His mission is to proclaim the kingdom of God, where status doesn't stem from money, and power doesn't come from violence.

As followers of Christ, questions about our political loyalties and our financial decisions are important, but Jesus reminds us they are not the ultimate questions of our lives. Rather, our decisions about who and what to support with our time, attention, and money come in response to our ultimate loyalty. God's power is greater than that of any earthly power, and it is our status as members of the kingdom of God that directs the rest of our lives.

God, when I am anxious about the powers-that-be or my status under earthly systems, teach me to remember my belonging to your kingdom. Amen.

SATURDAY, OCTOBER 17 ~ *Read Matthew 22:15-22*

Jesus has shown us what is Caesar's. But he leaves us to ask ourselves, "What is God's?" The answer is, of course, everything! Everything we have belongs to God, and how we choose to give, save, and invest our time and money demonstrates where our loyalties lie. All of creation is God's; human systems of exchange and government merely borrow a tiny piece. While political leaders' images are stamped on currency, Genesis 1:26 says that God's image is stamped on every human being. Each of us belongs to God. Each of us must ask ourselves how we return ourselves and our lives back to our source.

Jesus' teachings ask us to think about how we allocate our resources and how we deploy power and status. These practical calculations are affected when we understand all of our lives as belonging to God—and all of creation as a gift God shares with humanity. Regardless of who rules the empire, our responsibility is to invest all we have in loving God and loving our neighbors. We invest resources in pursuit of the dignity of all humans made in the image of God; we give fearlessly in the knowledge of our own belonging to God. Whether we choose to spend money with businesses that share our values, to share our own homes and belongings with our communities, or to offer our time in ministry, we can find creative ways to multiply what we've been given. We honor our Creator by using our resources creatively and generously. We have the opportunity to give to God what is God's—everything—with gratitude and joy.

God, your image is present in every person I encounter today. May I experience the freedom of holding loosely all you've given me and share gladly. Amen.

SUNDAY, OCTOBER 18 ~ *Read Exodus 33:18-23*

Today's reading is a continuation of Tuesday's passage, when Moses asks God more than once to send God's presence along with him and the other Israelites. God agrees to go with Moses and the people, but Moses wants proof: Moses wants to see God. "Now show me your glory," he says. In today's passage, we read God's answer—yes. Yet God also explains that Moses cannot see God's face and live: The fullness of God's glory is more than a human being can bear to experience. So God places Moses in a crack in a rock, from which he can peer out and glimpse God's receding back.

Was this anything like what Moses expected? Surely this was an awesome experience—but did Moses also have to let go of his own ideas for what would happen when he encountered God in a new way? It seems that God could have simply said no. But instead, God devised a plan to grant Moses' request as far as possible. There's a tender grace in the image of God finding a safe refuge for Moses and gently placing him there. Perhaps as much as Moses wanted to see God, God also wanted to be seen.

Many of us dream of enjoying the intimacy with God that Moses had, but Moses could not even catch sight of more than the distant back side of God, let alone comprehend any part of God. God is transcendent, glorious, awesome—well beyond our human frame of reference. Sometimes God is with us in ways we can't understand. Usually, God is with us in ways we don't expect. But always, God is graciously finding a way to meet us where we are, even in our smallness. God is gently pressing us into the cleft of a rock in order to share with us just a little more.

God, help me to notice and see you, even when your presence appears in a way I don't expect. Amen.

The Communal Rule of Love

OCTOBER 19–25, 2026 • FELIPE E. ROJAS CORTÉS

SCRIPTURE OVERVIEW: In the passages for this week, we observe different perspectives on how to understand the image of God within the dynamics of communities. Deuteronomy emphasizes a figure of promise for the social development of a nation. The psalmist reminds us of God's care for the people throughout history. The letter to the Thessalonians presents us with the purpose of being part of and building a community. And Matthew's Gospel gives us essential foundations and guidelines that we must uphold in our own contexts and social world. Through these readings we are able to reflect on our roles and functions in the communities to which we belong.

QUESTIONS AND SUGGESTIONS FOR REFLECTION

- Read Deuteronomy 34:1-12. How does God inspire and challenge you to keep going despite the adversities of life?
- Read Psalm 90:1-6, 13-17. How can you become the image of God who is a refuge for the afflicted, the oppressed, and the brokenhearted?
- Read 1 Thessalonians 2:1-8. How can you contribute to God's work in our communities? How do you create spaces for listening, accompaniment, and fraternity?
- Read Matthew 22:34-46. How do you embody love for God and neighbor? What actions are necessary today to generate examples that reflect that love?

Rev. Felipe E. Rojas Cortés is a priest of The Methodist Church of Chile, a sociologist, and theologian. He is the Director of Outreach and Liaison at the University of the Latin American Educational Center, a member of the Committee on Social and International Affairs of the World Methodist Council, and the Ecclesiastical Secretary of The Methodist Church of Chile.

Organizations often implement transitional processes for people in leadership. These processes ensure the preservation of information and stability as one leader leaves and another takes over. Intentional transition plans prove healthy and wholesome because they offer support as new people take charge. The best ones encourage evaluation of the organization during the time of transition, which can provide new leadership a clearer understanding of potential opportunities for improvement and growth.

The biblical text tells us about the death of Moses, who was the man called by God to lead the liberation of the people from slavery in Egypt. Moses represented God's plans, not his own plans. The text indicates that the community evaluated Moses, characterizing him as a great leader. Although he had many occasions to abandon his task, he stuck with it, leaving a legacy. The story shows us that God too prepares for transition—God prepared for the transition of leadership by equipping a person who could continue to lead the people. Moses, believing in God's plan, presented Joshua as his successor, because he understood that the Israelites' story did not end with his death but continued beyond him.

People often avoid changes and transitions. They do not want to share the mission and cannot envision the continuation of projects beyond their own work. The story of Moses is a challenge to us to prepare others to continue with the project of the kingdom of God. It is necessary to continue believing in God's plans as something continuous, and for that we are challenged to share our responsibilities and tasks, leaving an example that inspires those who will carry on after us.

God, help us to work thinking about the present and the future, leaving traces that contribute to the commitment of others in the work of the kingdom. Amen.

TUESDAY, OCTOBER 20 ~ *Read Psalm 90:1-6, 13-17*

For a number of years I have worked in refugee and migration programs, coordinating initiatives for people who are forced to leave their countries of origin because their lives are in danger as a result of humanitarian crises. It is impressive to see persons in these situations carry a belief that their realities and lives can be transformed, maintaining a hope that they will find refuge and welcome in other places.

The psalmist proclaims God as the dwelling place and contrasts the everlasting nature of God with the finitude of human life. Even though individual lives may be short, the psalmist understands the whole of humanity to continually rest in this refuge, God. God not only allows us to find a refuge, but God actually is that refuge and safe place—and always has been and always will be.

Sometimes we forget that we are fragile human beings, that we live beautiful moments and also complex ones. We forget that we are exposed like the grass of the field. However, we can continue to have confidence and hope because our refuge—God—remains constant during times of challenge and invites us to continue trusting in the Lord who protects us. This protection does not exempt us from difficulties, but it empowers us to continue working even in the face of struggle. It blesses our work. We then find joy and purpose as our lives flourish under the watchful grace of God. When we trust, like the psalmist, that God will always be fighting alongside us on this journey, blessing the work of our hands and providing what we need to move forward, we rest in the refuge of God.

God, confirm in us the declaration of the psalmist to continue advancing and walking in life, with the conviction that you are a refuge for us in moments of insecurity and difficulties. Amen.

WEDNESDAY, OCTOBER 21 ~ *Read 1 Thessalonians 2:1-8*

Often we frame the ideals of a society in ways that support the common good: respect, justice, fraternity, tolerance, and inclusion, among many others. But these ideals cannot be only theories; they must be enacted—lived into—by those in the community in order for them to truly support the community as they are intended to do. Today many people speak of justice without enacting it, of the truth while hiding it, of love while being selfish. It seems that the relationship between discourse and concrete action is tense and distant. We do not practice what we preach.

Paul considers the ministry and the project of the Christian community from the perspective of the social commitment it requires. The faith community of Thessalonica must understand that they have been called by God, and not for merely human projects. It is God who entrusts them with the continuation of the ministry of Jesus Christ, and this work will not be for personal boasting or to take advantage of the call for particular ends. They are to be servants contributing to the social community space where they develop as Christians and live the faith. Their faith must be connected with the surroundings where they give testimony.

Today we are also called to observe our surroundings in order to carry out our call to Christian ministry. We do not work alone but in and through communities of faith that transform realities, that are consistent in both speech and action, and that can inspire a commitment to faith in those around us. We renounce any selfish feelings that hinder the Christian social ministry. We are called to collaborate in the construction of the kingdom of God from our highest commitment that proclaims real freedom, truth, and justice for all.

God, help us to commit ourselves to our communities and our surroundings so that we may bear witness to our call to be servants of the most vulnerable and oppressed. Amen.

Constitutions establish the fundamental regulations for living and coexisting in countries and states. The nations of the world have adhered to the International Declaration of Human Rights, which establishes articles to protect the rights and dignity of all people. In this way, anyone can file a complaint regarding violations of the human rights that are intended to be protected by this universal declaration. Likewise, we have laws in our individual countries that cannot contradict this universal charter that extends throughout the world.

The Pharisees ask Jesus which commandment is greatest. Even with the clarification that they ask this question to test him, it is a logical question. Pharisees kept track of and followed hundreds of commandments and prohibitions. The Ten Commandments were the main laws in Jewish tradition, but the Pharisees followed additional regulations to properly fulfill the commandments. In this way, it made sense to ask if there was any commandment more important than the others.

Without hesitation, Jesus answers the question directly, pulling his answer from the Pentateuch. The books of Deuteronomy (see 6:5) and Leviticus (see 19:18) say that there is no greater commandment than to love God and love one's neighbor. These fundamental commandments are the foundation upon which the rest of the law is established.

Today we need to return to the foundation of God's law, which is love. Love must be the foundation of our faith, something that no one can question. Only in this way do we follow in the footsteps of Christ. When we love, another world is made possible. Through both Jesus' teachings and his model of life we know that love is the most important regulation for living.

God, give us a strong heart to love, a heart to fight for a world built upon the foundation of your love. Amen.

FRIDAY, OCTOBER 23 ~ *Read Matthew 22:34-40*

My son Simon asks me deep questions. Once he asked me, "What is bigger than the universe?" I was captivated by the question, considering the possible answers, but I knew I needed to be more clear and concrete for a little five-year-old like him. Sometimes we make issues more complex and create knots and labyrinths from which we cannot escape. Without being a physics or astronomy teacher, I could only answer Simon that God is bigger than the universe because God created it.

We often struggle to answer questions that are disconcerting or complex. Perhaps if I had been asked what the most important commandment is, I would have attempted to write a summary of the law contained in the Pentateuch, being careful to not leave anything out. However, Jesus wisely summarizes the law in a way that provides both head and heart knowledge. The scripture account shows us that we need both answers to questions and guidance that shows us how to live a consistent faith. Loving God and loving one's neighbor is the most logical answer to achieve God's will.

We can, like my son Simon or like the Pharisees, ask what is the most important or the greatest thing. We will find the answer in Jesus' teaching and in Jesus' life. The greatest and most important thing that a person can do to follow in the footsteps of Christ is to love God and their neighbor. Love is where our mission on earth is established and where all ideas of good for humanity must originate. Everything must be born from love.

God, help us to continue loving above all things, recognizing that loving is the most important and greatest thing we can do as Christians. Amen.

Every day we witness chaotic social events in the world around us: wars, famine, social injustice, violence. In the midst of this context, we wonder what can actually bring change to our challenging reality. Many feel disappointed by those who govern us, losing hope for change to come through new leadership. Most people no longer believe that one system or another will get us out of the crises that we experience, or that any ideology can affect sustainable change.

Given this, we can ask the question the Pharisees asked: What is the main thing we must do to achieve the will of God? To answer, we must understand the will of God. God's will is for us to live in goodness and with the values of the kingdom of God as central axes that guide our living.

Jesus tells us that all we must do to make that life a reality is to practice love. Love is an essential source of change and sustenance in life. Even receiving this answer from Jesus, we struggle to believe in the power of love. We do not want to let love govern us because it challenges anti-values such as envious competition or individualism. We have instead chosen other values that we think are more important than love, and we relegate love to a romantic emotion, diminishing its capacity for transformation.

Today Jesus tells us that the most important thing in our lives is not just to know him, but to love him. It is not enough to know that we must do good—we must actively do good through loving God and our neighbor. We must believe in love as the engine capable of changing the entire world, and we must live lives of love toward every other person we encounter. Love must be our hope for today and always.

Lord, help us to continue believing in the love that transforms lives and societies. Help us to love, believing that a new world is possible. Amen.

SUNDAY, OCTOBER 25 ~ *Read Matthew 22:34-46*

During my university studies I read many books. In order to remember what I read, I would identify the central axes of the topics discussed. I did not try to remember every detail of the whole book, but instead I aimed to understand the author's main idea and related the theories to practical examples. In this way, when I was evaluated I could recall the central themes of the books I had read and used those themes to generate answers.

The Pharisees want to know the axis, the summary, of the law. The answer that Jesus gives provides an umbrella under which all the rest of the laws fall. The ten commandments expand upon what it means to love God (do not have other gods, keep the sabbath, do not take the name of God in vain) and to love our neighbor (do not kill, do not steal, do not covet). The greatest commandment shifts our perspective on the law: It is not that we prohibit ourselves from certain actions, but instead our actions are motivated by love that inspires us to follow the law.

This interchange with the Pharisees is followed by Jesus turning the question on them: "What do you think of the Messiah? Whose son is he?" The Pharisees answer, but Jesus stumps them with a response, calling on Psalm 110 to challenge their thinking. This interesting interchange provides the Pharisees and us the opportunity to consider how the reign of Jesus—the Messiah—is different than that of David. Jesus is trying to convey to the Pharisees that the coming reign of the Messiah will not be a return of the Davidic monarchy, but rather an alternative way of living in the world.

That way of living is love. Love is the guiding force of God's kingdom, the kingdom to which Jesus points over and over. The law of love guides the work of those in this kingdom and calls us all to live within its beautiful boundaries.

God, help us to follow the law of love, understanding that in this way we follow your commandments and your law. Amen.

Faithful Living in God's Presence

OCTOBER 26–NOVEMBER 1, 2026 • MOTOE YAMADA FOOR

SCRIPTURE OVERVIEW: This week's scriptures highlight themes of transition, faith, and living lives worthy of God. They portray God's transformative power, guiding people through moments of uncertainty into new beginnings. The imagery of crossing rivers and turning desolate lands into abundance reflects God's steadfast presence and provision. These texts also call for authenticity and humility, urging us to align our actions with our faith and embrace a life of servanthood. Together, they remind us that God's guidance empowers us to face challenges, move forward in faith, and live in ways that reflect the kingdom of God.

QUESTIONS AND SUGGESTIONS FOR REFLECTION

- Read Joshua 3:7-17. When have you needed to take a step of faith before seeing how God would provide? How did God guide you through the transition?
- Read Psalm 107:1-7, 33-37. What personal stories of God's provision inspire your gratitude? How can you share these with others?
- Read 1 Thessalonians 2:9-13. How does living a life worthy of God challenge your daily actions?
- Read Matthew 23:1-12. How does humility shape your leadership or service to others? What steps can you take to align your actions with God's call for authenticity?

Rev. Motoe Yamada Foor is the Executive Director of Stakeholder Relationships at Discipleship Ministries, a certified coach, and an ordained pastor of the California-Nevada Annual Conference of The United Methodist Church. She was born and raised in Japan.

MONDAY, OCTOBER 26 ~ *Read Joshua 3:7-17*

New beginnings often come at unexpected times. Two months from the end of the calendar year, it may feel strange to focus on starting anew. Yet every day in Christ is an opportunity to begin again. The story of Joshua leading the Israelites across the Jordan River is a powerful reminder of God's presence in moments of transition. After years of wandering in the wilderness, the Israelites were finally entering the Promised Land under a new leader, Joshua, after Moses' death.

Crossing the Jordan echoes the parting of the Red Sea, symbolizing that God is the same yesterday, today, and forever. Just as God guided them out of Egypt, God now leads them into new territory, preparing the way and ensuring their safety. This passage invites us to reflect: What are the "rivers" in our lives that we need to cross? Are there plans, dreams, or spiritual goals we've postponed out of fear or uncertainty?

As churches and individuals plan for the coming year, it's also a time to ask ourselves how we want to grow spiritually. Perhaps you've been sensing God's call to step into something new—serving in a ministry, mending a relationship, or deepening your daily prayer life. Trust that just as God went before the Israelites, God will go before you, parting the waters and guiding your steps.

God, thank you for being with us in every transition. As we step into new beginnings, help us trust your guidance and presence, knowing you will provide a safe path. Amen.

TUESDAY, OCTOBER 27 ~ *Read Psalm 107:1-7, 33-37*

One evening, I was driving home after a discouraging day. As I often do in moments like these, I was looking at the moon—a habit passed down to me by my father, who would admire the moon back in Japan. But that night, the moon seemed different. Its bottom was obscured by clouds, casting shadows over its usual glow. As I drove further, the moon disappeared entirely, swallowed by the darkness. Yet I knew it was still there, constant as ever. Then a faint glimmer of light pierced through the dark—a reminder that even when hidden, the light never fades.

This experience mirrors moments in our faith journey. Like the psalmist in Psalm 107, at times we feel lost in the wilderness, yearning for God's guidance. We may find ourselves wandering through life's struggles, unsure of God's presence. In these moments, it's easy to feel distant from God, as though God's light is obscured by clouds of hardship or doubt. Yet just as the moon remained shining even behind the clouds, so too does God remain steadfast, even when hidden from view.

Psalm 107 recounts God's faithfulness to those who wandered in desert places, guiding them to safety. The same God who led God's people through wilderness journeys is present with us today, shaping us, comforting us, and lighting our path—even in the darkest times. We may not always see God clearly, but God's steadfast love endures forever.

God, when we feel lost or burdened by the shadows of life, help us to trust in your steadfast love. Remind us that even when we can't see you clearly, you are always there, guiding us toward your light. Amen.

WEDNESDAY, OCTOBER 28 ~ *Read Psalm 107:1-7, 33-37*

When people return from exile or a traumatic experience, the road back to normalcy can be long and uncertain. Psalm 107 recounts the struggles of those redeemed by God, wandering in desert places before finding a new beginning. This journey resonates deeply with the experiences of Japanese Americans during World War II.

In the wake of fear and prejudice, over 120,000 Japanese Americans, many of them U.S. citizens, were forcibly removed from their homes and sent to incarceration camps. Families were uprooted, allowed to take only two suitcases, leaving behind homes, livelihoods, and even beloved pets. Visiting the Japanese American National Museum in Los Angeles, I saw an artifact that left a deep impression—a pastor's sermon notes from the final Easter Sunday before his congregation was sent to the camps.

His message was one of hope: "Even though we don't know what will happen, one thing we know is that God is with us." These words, written in the face of uncertainty and suffering, remind us of the sustaining power of faith. Like the Israelites returning from exile, this pastor's congregation clung to the belief that God had not abandoned them, even in the darkest of times.

As we face challenges in our own lives, we too can hold on to the hope that God walks with us. Whether we are stepping into the unknown, recovering from loss, or rebuilding from hardship, God's presence is constant. God's promises endure, and God's love brings us to new beginnings, even when the path is uncertain.

God of hope, in moments of exile and uncertainty, help us to trust in your presence. Strengthen our faith and remind us that no matter where we are, you are with us, guiding us toward a new beginning. Amen.

THURSDAY, OCTOBER 29 ~ *Read 1 Thessalonians 2:9-13*

At one of my former churches, a small group of members formed a Spiritual Renewal Team. Their purpose was twofold: to encourage spiritual renewal both in the church and in their own lives. This team wasn't just about programs or events—it was about transformation. Their commitment inspired tangible change. One couple felt called to attend seminary to prepare for ministry. Another member chose to teach math in one of the most challenged neighborhoods, seeing it as a way to live out their faith in service.

Their stories illustrate what happens when we take Paul's words to heart: "Lead a life worthy of God." When we begin to ask, "Is my life reflecting God's calling?" it shifts our perspective. Life becomes less about achieving personal success and more about aligning our actions with God's will. We stop measuring worth by earthly standards and instead seek to reflect God's kingdom in how we serve, grow, and love.

Paul's encouragement to the Thessalonians wasn't about perfection. It was about intention—choosing to live in a way that honors God's call. The members of the Spiritual Renewal Team did not have all the answers, but their willingness to step forward in faith transformed their lives and the life of their church.

What might it look like for you to live a life worthy of God? Perhaps it's stepping into a new opportunity to serve, deepening your prayer life, or simply being present with someone who needs encouragement. As we seek renewal in our own lives, we can trust that God is shaping us to reflect God's glory.

God, help us to live a life that reflects your love and calling. Renew our hearts and guide our steps, so we may bring honor to your kingdom in all we do. Amen.

FRIDAY, OCTOBER 30 ~ *Read Matthew 23:1-12*

When I was part of a young adult group, I joined a church mission project. During the event, I noticed that the pastor always went first in the food line. This disappointed me; it seemed to me as though the pastor expected to be honored above others. At the time, I told myself, "I will never be like that."

Years later, after becoming a pastor, I found myself in a similar position. In some cultures, it's customary for a guest of honor—often the pastor—to eat first as a sign of respect. I realized that what had once frustrated me was now something I was often expected to do.

Reflecting on Jesus' words in Matthew 23, I see the importance of examining our motives. Jesus warns against seeking honor and elevating ourselves. Leadership in God's kingdom isn't about status or recognition; it's about service and humility.

This doesn't mean traditions of honor are inherently wrong. We have to examine our hearts. Are we leading in ways that reflect Jesus' example of humility? Are we seeking to serve? Are we comfortable being served? Sometimes humility calls for us to serve others; sometimes it calls for us to allow ourselves to be served by others.

Jesus challenges all leaders, not just pastors, to avoid the temptation to exalt ourselves. Instead, we are called to humility—lifting others up and pointing to God, not to ourselves. This may look different in different settings. But leadership rooted in service transforms our communities and reflects the heart of Christ.

Lord, help us to lead with humility and grace. Teach us to serve others as you have served us, and guard our hearts against seeking honor for ourselves. May our actions reflect your love and bring glory to your name. Amen.

SATURDAY, OCTOBER 31 ~ *Read Matthew 23:1-12*

October 31 is Halloween in the United States. Children—and sometimes adults—often dress up as someone they admire or aspire to be. They knock on doors, saying, "Trick or treat," often imagining themselves as superheroes, historical figures, or their future selves. Who do you want to be when you grow up—regardless of your age?

I want to be like Jesus!

I grew up in Tokyo, Japan, with my father, who was a Zen Buddhist monk and knew nothing about Christianity. When I came to the United States for school, I had already committed myself to a life of justice. But when I encountered Jesus—the one who humbled himself to serve others—I knew I wanted to follow him. His commitment to justice, his serving of the least, and his love for others resonated deeply with me. Even more, I was drawn to the people around me who lived out their faith by serving others. Their example is part of the reason I am a pastor today.

As Christians, we are called not only to believe in Jesus but to serve as he served. I remember my ordination service when Bishop Warner H. Brown, Jr. washed the feet of each ordinand, just as Jesus did for his disciples at the Last Supper. It was a powerful reminder that true leadership is rooted in humility and service.

Jesus' words remind us that true greatness is found not in being served but in serving others with humility and love. As we seek to become like Jesus, we are called to live that kind of life.

Lord, help us to follow Jesus' example of humility and service. Teach us to love as he loved, to serve as he served, and to continue serving until every member of your body is lifted up in wholeness and peace. Amen.

All Saints Day

As an Asian woman, it is rare to see someone like me portrayed as an example of a child of God. Even as a clergywoman, I am often questioned because of my gender, my ethnicity, and my accented English. In search of support, I joined with a group of other Asian American clergywomen to form the Asian American Pacific Islander Clergywomen Association (AAPIC), a space to share our stories, uplift one another, and remind ourselves that we are God's children.

Rev. Ingrid Wang was one of AAPIC's founders. She embodied the message of 1 John 3:1-3, continually reminding us of our identity as beloved children of God. Ingrid created programs like the Mary Elizabeth Peer Coaching Program to empower young people. Through her liturgical Chinese dance, she showed us how to praise God with our whole being. Although we all come from different backgrounds, Ingrid reminded us we come together in unity to worship God with everything we have.

I'll never forget my last conversation with Ingrid. She was battling cancer, nearing the end of her earthly life. Yet it was she who encouraged me, saying, "Never, never, never give up." Her unwavering hope and faith left a lasting impact on me.

On this All Saints Day, we remember the saints who have gone before us, who taught us the faith, who helped point to God's presence in our lives. Who in your life has shaped your faith? We give thanks, today and every day, for those who have gone before, and we walk in their footsteps to help build up other followers. We never know how our words or actions might impact someone's life, just as Ingrid impacted mine.

Loving God, thank you for the saints who have come before us, teaching us about your love. Help us to encourage others with your love and hope. Amen.

Now What?

NOVEMBER 2–8, 2026 • RUTH L. BOLING

SCRIPTURE OVERVIEW: On a "Now" clock, the word "now" is repeated around the perimeter where numbers would normally be. As the clock hands rotate throughout the day, the time is always "now." Each passage this week emerges from a particular "now" moment in God's story. In Joshua, the Israelites must choose whom they will serve. For the psalmist, the time has come to tell the story of God's faithfulness in the past to encourage us in the present. Paul assuages the Thessalonians' concerns and reminds them to encourage one another. Jesus' parable teaches that his return will be unexpected, so we should always be ready. Like the hands on a "Now" clock, each passage points to the present moment, summoning us to mindful, wholehearted, unwaveringly joyful service to God and neighbor, *now*.

QUESTIONS AND SUGGESTIONS FOR REFLECTION

- Read Joshua 24:1-3a, 14-25. What gets more attention in churches today, belief or service?
- Read Psalm 78:1-7. Try writing a psalm or prayer about God's faithfulness to you despite your failures and shortcomings.
- Read 1 Thessalonians 4:13-18. Paul's description of Christ's return is meant to be encouraging. Do you find it so? Why or why not?
- Read Matthew 25:1-13. Who do you identify with in this story? What challenges you? How would this parable read differently if the gender roles were reversed?

Ruth L. Boling is a Presbyterian Church (USA) pastor, writer, and author of *Season's Greetings: Christmas Letters from Those Who Were There* (Upper Room Books, 2024) and several children's titles including *Come Worship With Me—A Journey Through the Church Year* (Westminster John Knox, 2010). She is a graduate of Yale University (BA), McCormick Theological Seminary (MDiv), and Pittsburgh Theological Seminary (DMin).

MONDAY, NOVEMBER 2 ~ *Read Joshua 24:1-3a, 14-15*

Joshua gathers the Israelites and their leaders in a solemn assembly at a pivotal point in their history. Yahweh has liberated them from slavery, sustained them in the wilderness, shaped them as a covenant people, instilled in them a distinctive social ethic consistent with the very character of Yahweh's own self, and now—at long last—has established them on a choice stretch of land burgeoning with potential for economic prosperity and future flourishing. Yahweh has been uncompromisingly, single-mindedly, wholeheartedly gracious toward Israel up until this point, despite multiple embarrassing episodes of bad behavior on Israel's part.

Now it's time for Israel to graduate, so to speak, and—hopefully—put all its wilderness training to good use in a new setting. Now, life will be easier, with good soil for crops, good land for grazing, and plenty of opportunities for lucrative trade. But will Israel retain its distinctive character and exclusive devotion to Yahweh? Or will ease and prosperity breed complacency?

Decide, now, what your intentions are, Joshua tells the people. *Don't wait and see how things turn out. Choose.* Joshua presses the matter—once, twice, three times. A casual verbal assent will not do. A decision to serve Yahweh entails a commitment to abide by the ethic of Yahweh, which seeks wellbeing for the whole community, especially for the vulnerable.

Ever the leader, Joshua communicates his personal decision up front—"as for me and my household, we will serve the LORD" —but whether the others follow his lead or not will be entirely up to them. The suspense builds. Will the Israelites break up with Yahweh and one another, or will they renew their vows and carry on together?

God, let my choice to serve you lead me, now and always, into community. Amen.

TUESDAY, NOVEMBER 3 ~ *Read Joshua 24:1-3a, 14-25*

Lifted out of context, this passage depicts God as punishingly harsh, demanding and uncompromising. "He is a jealous God," Joshua says. "He will not forgive your transgressions or your sins. If you forsake the LORD and serve foreign gods, then he will turn and do you harm, and consume you, after having done you good." Taken at face value, verses like these may reinforce the unfortunate and overly-simplistic distinction often made between the Old Testament God (stereotypically angry and violent) and the New Testament God (stereotypically loving and merciful). But God does not change from one era to the next. God's mercy is as much front and center in the book of Joshua as it is in the Gospels.

To find it, we must first look where the story itself points, to the backstory told in the intervening verses (3b-13). Joshua reminds the listeners of God's mighty acts of loving kindness that saved Israel from annihilation. The Israelites have experienced God's mercy in the form of a sacred covenant established and fulfilled in their ancestor Abraham and carried all the way to their current moment in the Promised Land.

Next, we must look for God's mercy in the here and now of the story. Israel has not been a loyal covenant partner. The people have complained, lost confidence, and outright rejected God. Now, through Joshua, God offers restitution, a fresh start. In a move not unlike the risen Christ addressing Peter (see John 21:15-19), Joshua asks for a declaration of loyalty. Like Peter, the people must answer for themselves. Once. Twice. Three times.

A covenant renewal ceremony seals the deal. Israel's relationship with God remains secure. Mercy and loyalty intertwine: Loyalty isn't optional.

Holy God, I choose you. I choose you. I choose you. May my loyalty to you intertwine with your abundant mercy to bless the world, here and now. Amen.

WEDNESDAY, NOVEMBER 4 ~ *Read Psalm 78:1-7*

The church's prayer book—the psalter—is for worship and instruction. The author of Psalm 78 introduces the material as "my teaching" and addresses the psalm not to God but to "my people" as a curriculum of sorts for teaching sacred history to children.

Interpreting verses 1-7 adequately requires that we read the whole psalm. In it, Yahweh's saving acts in history are brought into sharp relief alongside an equally long litany of human failings. The covenant people have gotten themselves into a bloody civil war. The Northern Kingdom has imploded.

We might imagine anxious children asking their elders how the God of Moses and Joshua could allow things to go so horribly awry. We might imagine the psalmist lying awake at night agonizing over that very question, and then coming up with Psalm 78 for an answer.

Psalm 78 takes the position that God's people in the Northern Kingdom were responsible for their demise. They had broken faith with God one too many times. God was justifiably angry, but God showed great restraint in reprimanding them: "He remembered that they were but flesh" (v. 39). History has reached a turning point. God's merciful purposes will now be fulfilled through the Southern Kingdom (Judah) with David as its shepherd king (vv. 67-72).

Questions of meaning arise in every generation. How did things get the way they are now? Who is responsible? What is God doing today? What is the church for? Today's youth do not suffer religious fools gladly. The church will gain nothing by hiding its past or present sins. Our children deserve our honesty. Their faith depends on it.

Holy God, open me like a book for others to read your story and come to know your love now. Amen.

THURSDAY, NOVEMBER 5 ~ *Read 1 Thessalonians 4:13-18*

A heartfelt, compassionate letter from Paul to the Thessalonians takes an apocalyptic turn in this passage, looking ahead to the end times. Through Paul's eyes we see bodies, dead and alive, floating upward as Christ floats downward for a forever-family reunion in the clouds. The passage strains the credulity of scientifically-minded readers. It is best understood as an example of the early church working out in real time the implications of its core belief that "Jesus died and rose again."

The early church expected Christ to return. Soon. When some beloved members of the community died before the blessed event, those left behind grew anxious. Had they missed the return of Christ? Would their deceased friends and family be forever separated from God in death? Paul's response spells out for them the significance of Jesus' resurrection: It was not simply a one-and-done demonstration of Christ's divinity. Rather, it signified God's ultimate victory over sin and death which promised eternal salvation for the faithful in every age. Paul dips into the genre of apocalyptic literature for details and images. Paul seems to have known that in matters of the heart, poetry speaks more powerfully than expository prose.

It is futile—although many have tried—to gather up all of the apocalyptic passages in the Bible for decoding and rearranging into a sequential forecast of "the end times." God did not camouflage mission-critical bits of information in mythical language and sprinkle them into the scriptures the way software developers hide Easter eggs in video games. Paul's writing here is closer to the poetry of Isaiah 40 than to the predictions of Nostradamus. Utilizing a genre familiar to his readers (albeit strange to us) he allays their fears in order to refocus their attention on day-to-day faithfulness.

Merciful Jesus, thank you that I need not worry, but need only love and serve you, here, now. Amen.

FRIDAY, NOVEMBER 6 ~ *Read 1 Thessalonians 4:13-18*

Great is the mystery of faith: "Christ has died. Christ is risen. Christ will come again." These or similar words are spoken during the Communion liturgy in many churches. They serve to connect the worshipers' experience at the Lord's Table with the larger three-act narrative of Christ's redeeming work, integrating past (Christ's death), present (Christ's real presence through the sacrament), and future (Christ's return). In what scholars concur to be the New Testament's earliest piece of writing, Paul proclaims this very mystery and brings it to bear on a burning question troubling the Thessalonians to their core.

Acts One and Two of the mystery—"For since we believe that Jesus died and rose again"—do not alone bring comfort. Act Three is vitally important: Jesus will come again. In verses 14-17, Paul describes Act Three in several disjointed ways that are confusing in the original Greek. "Through Jesus, God will bring with him those who have died." Then, "the Lord himself . . . will descend from heaven." And finally, the faithful "who are left will be caught up . . . to meet the Lord in the air." The details and sequence cannot be ironed out, but the clear implication is that the faithful "will be with the Lord forever." This is Paul's long-winded way of saying to the Thessalonians what the heavenly messengers declared at Christ's birth and again at the empty tomb: "Don't be afraid" (Luke 2:10, Matt. 28:5).

God's watchful care that led Israel out of bondage into freedom and prosperity has widened into a much larger rescue operation transcending time, place, and ethnic identity. None need fear oblivion—not now, not ever. "Therefore, encourage one another with these words," concludes our passage. Stay the course.

Holy Jesus, who died, is risen, and will come again, because of you, I will not fear. Not now. Not ever. Amen.

SATURDAY, NOVEMBER 7 ~ *Read Matthew 25:1-13*

If you have trouble appreciating this parable in which everybody behaves badly toward everybody else, you're not alone. The interaction between the two groups of bridesmaids reads like a scene from a first-century production of *Mean Girls*. The bridesmaids labeled "foolish" arrive ill-prepared for their appointed role. They exhibit a kind of clueless entitlement in their expectation that others should bail them out. And at the exact moment they're needed the most, they go shopping.

Those labeled "wise" confound matters. They're the ones to suggest this fool's errand, which is preposterous on several practical levels. What dealer of oil would be open for business at midnight? And who would ever send unaccompanied bridesmaids out, unchaperoned with a wad of cash at such an hour? Did nobody think of doubling up on their lamps? Did no one offer? An undercurrent of misogyny is hard to ignore in this portrayal of bickering women pitted against one another to outmaneuver the competition for a man's attention and favor.

The bridegroom behaves equally poorly. Why is he so late? Think of the other guests—the cooks, servers, and musicians—not to mention the bride! After keeping everyone waiting and guessing into the wee hours, what entitles this groom to punish the women for being a little tardy themselves? Even the stated moral of the parable causes frustration. The admonition to "keep awake" ought to condemn all ten drowsy bridesmaids, but only five have the door slammed in their faces.

What we consider Christian conduct is nowhere on display in this parable. Perhaps that is the point. In a world booby-trapped with opportunities to behave badly, we must beware! Keep awake! Pay attention!

Holy God, keep me aware, awake, and attentive to my behavior now and in every moment. Amen.

SUNDAY, NOVEMBER 8 ~ *Read Matthew 25:1-13*

This parable comes midway through the "Little Apocalypse" in Matthew 24 and 25. Jesus speaks in frightening detail about a future time of tribulation, followed by a day of judgment. Then he tells a series of severe parables intended to elicit exemplary Christ-like conduct from his followers. The spectacularly harsh punishments meted out at the end of these parables belong to the artifice of the apocalyptic genre and should not be read as a preview of things to come.

It is a mark of Jesus' spiritual genius that these parables about the end times—always a luridly fascinating distraction—serve to divert attention away from the end times and to the task of loving God by serving others now. Five different times in five different ways, five parables evoke urgency, demand loyalty, and prioritize immediate actions over words and lofty intentions.

The Parable of the Ten Bridesmaids illustrates what not to do. It spotlights the "foolish" bridesmaids for their bad choices. They arrive with one job—to carry a lit lamp into the wedding banquet—but only half the necessary equipment. When the bridegroom is delayed, they gain extra time to problem-solve for a solution, but they don't use it. They nap. When the bridegroom finally shows up, they act as if they had neither agency, nor intelligence, nor opportunity, nor responsibility regarding this problem of their own making. They expect to be bailed out. "Give us some of your oil," they demand. To such irresponsibility the other bridesmaids, and the parable itself, deliver a resounding, "No!"

We have one job as Christians and that is to love and serve Jesus. For a job description, consult the Sermon on the Mount. We have agency, intelligence, opportunity, and responsibility at our disposal. Not to use them is beyond tragic.

Merciful God, you know where my heart lies based on what I do and what I avoid. Keep me focused and faithful. Now. Amen.

Deliverance and Mercy

NOVEMBER 9–15, 2026 • SHERRI WOOD-POWE

SCRIPTURE OVERVIEW: Like us, the Israelites struggle to be consistently faithful to God. In Judges, the Israelites have again found themselves at the mercy of God and in need of deliverance. The psalm reminds us of the Israelites' pattern of unfaithfulness: They do wrong. They get in trouble. They cry out to the Lord. The Lord has mercy and delivers them. The cycle repeats. Recognizing this pattern in scripture reminds us of God's mercy toward us and our need to seek it. The New Testament readings continue the themes of deliverance and mercy with First Thessalonians commanding us to always be ready—God has delivered us and will return for us; we just don't know when. The Gospel builds on the theme of God's return, calling us to live a life pleasing to God while we wait by utilizing the gifts God has given us.

QUESTIONS AND SUGGESTIONS FOR REFLECTION

- Read Judges 4:1-7. From what do you need to cry out to the Lord for deliverance?
- Read Psalm 123. What in your life is leading you to seek God's mercy?
- Read 1 Thessalonians 5:1-11. What do you need to do to be ready for the return of the Lord?
- Read Matthew 25:14-30. How are you living a life in gratitude to God for all you have been given?

Rev. Sherri Wood-Powe, a life, leadership, and clergy coach, is a pastor in the Baltimore-Washington Conference of The United Methodist Church and an adjunct faculty for the Course of Study program at Wesley Theological Seminary (Washington, DC).

MONDAY, NOVEMBER 9 ~ *Read Judges 4:1-7*

As Christians, we have come to understand that deliverance and mercy go together. We truly need God to deliver us, and that deliverance is not possible unless God is merciful, overlooking our faults and wiping away our sin. The good news is that God is willing to deliver us over and over again. It is not a one-time occurrence.

The Israelites knew better, yet the text informs us that, "The Israelites again did what was evil in the sight of the LORD." Why is it that we know better but can't seem to do better? Often we come before the Lord asking for deliverance from the same challenges. God is merciful and hears our cries.

Our loving God never leaves us alone, even when we experience consequences for our actions—*especially* when we are experiencing consequences for our actions. Although the Lord "sold them into the hand of King Jabin of Canaan," God did not leave them. God was still with them. Once the Israelites realized the error of their ways and cried out to the Lord for help, the prophet Deborah stepped in and implemented the plan that would free the Israelites.

Sometimes we have difficulty acknowledging our wrongdoing. We don't want to admit that we have disobeyed God and strayed from the path of righteousness. We want to do our own thing without repercussions.

We know better, and we must do better. God is with us always, waiting on us not only to acknowledge our wrongdoing but to seek deliverance. All it takes is acknowledging that we need God's mercy. Cry out to the Lord for deliverance. God is merciful and will lead you in the path of righteousness.

Acknowledging your need for deliverance, pour out your heart before the Lord. Confess any limitations and restrictions you may be placing on God. Trust God to lead you on the path you should go.

Have you ever cried out to the Lord for mercy? The text for today is a supplication for mercy. The psalmist seems to be crying out to the Lord. This does not seem to be a casual plea for mercy, but rather a pouring out of the heart seeking the One who hears and delivers. It serves as a reminder that we can call on the Lord in our time of need. We can go before the Lord trusting and believing that our God who has created all will treat us better than any human would.

We have all experienced times in our lives when we have had more than enough. One thing after another has gone wrong, and we've gotten to the end of our proverbial rope. Like the psalmist, we "have had more than enough of contempt." We are desperate for God to be merciful, to step in and turn things around.

We are living in a time when mental illness seems to be on the rise, or perhaps we are simply more willing to acknowledge the level of struggle many of us experience. More and more people are suffering from depression and having difficulty making it through life. Whether we are struggling more or simply more aware of the struggle, these ancient words can still provide us with hope. We can be persistent in seeking the Lord alongside seeking mental healthcare. God is still in the delivering business. God provides us with the resources to help.

The psalmist exclaims, "Our eyes look to the LORD our God, until he has mercy upon us." We can be persistent in seeking the mercy and support we need, trusting that God is with us. God will deliver us. We must hold on to our faith, never wavering, especially when it seems darkest.

Merciful God, instill in me the persistence and perseverance to face the challenges of life. Let me constantly be reminded that you are my source and my strength as I wait for my deliverance. Amen.

WEDNESDAY, NOVEMBER 11 ~ *Read 1 Thessalonians 5:1-3*

Are you ready? Are you ready for the Lord to return? This question reminds me of the spiritual, "I Wanna Be Ready." We do not know the year, month, day, nor hour. We must be ready. We will not receive a warning.

Our text provides two metaphors for Christ's return: "The day of the Lord will come like a thief in the night," and "as labor pains come upon a pregnant woman." They are both excellent examples, though the latter may be more apt. Many times the first labor contractions come on suddenly, interrupting an ordinary moment and signaling that the time is at hand. While the moment is unknown, the coming contractions are not a surprise. The parent usually has had several months to get ready and has made preparations.

This is what Paul says to us: Though we won't know when Christ will return, we do know it will happen and therefore we are called to prepare. Are we ready for the return of Christ? What preparations do we still need to make? In our reading from Judges earlier this week, we were reminded that we often find ourselves committing "evil in the sight of the LORD" (4:1). We sin by commission and omission, in thought, word, and deed. In order to prepare for Christ's return, we must confess, seek deliverance, and ask for mercy. We get ready by crying out to the Lord.

In Judges, the Israelites cried out to the Lord. They repented, turning back to God. We too can repent, turning from our wicked ways to lead a new life in Christ. We may not know when Christ will return, but we can be sure we are not caught by surprise and live in the freedom of God's redeeming love until that day comes.

Lord, I want to be ready when you return. Please hear my cry and have mercy on me. Forgive me my sins. Let me be ready when you return. In Jesus' name. Amen.

THURSDAY, NOVEMBER 12 ~ *Read 1 Thessalonians 5:4-8*

Life can be full of uncertainty. We do not know what the weather will be, but meteorologists use their skills and tools to analyze data forecast or predict or take an educated guess. In some instances they get it right, and in other instances they are not even close. The one thing we can be certain of is that life is full of changes—some we like and others we don't like. Nevertheless, change comes anyway.

The Thessalonians text for today is clear that we do not need to spend time trying to predict Christ's return, something over which we have no control. Instead, we should use our time to prepare for what is to come. We have no excuse for being caught off guard. We can not be sleeping or engaging in worldly distractions when we should be preparing.

Paul's message to those in the Thessalonian church may seem far removed from us today, who live two thousand years after the promise of Christ's return was made and who are still waiting. But Paul's message places the emphasis on what to do while we wait, which is where we still find meaning in his words. We still do not know when Christ will return. We still can live our lives prepared for Christ's return.

God has delivered us from darkness so that we can walk in the light of Christ. As children of the light, we put aside all that is not of Christ. We must remember that light always overcomes darkness. Our faith is our light in dark times. When we "put on the breastplate of faith and love and for a helmet the hope of salvation," we become prepared and live daily in the light of the One who created and called us, the One who loves us beyond measure. With faith and love, we are able to have hope eternal.

Almighty God, we give you thanks for the light of Christ which shines in the world. Help us to hold on to that light when darkness comes and to bring others to the light. Amen.

FRIDAY, NOVEMBER 13 ~ *Read 1 Thessalonians 5:1-11*

The church in Thessalonica had been going through some challenging times. The validity of their faith had been questioned. They were being pressured about the return of Christ. Doubt was being sown. We know how it is to have others' seemingly innocent questions sow doubt. We sometimes even question things that we know to be true.

Paul has already reminded the church to continue living a life pleasing to God. He is encouraging them to keep the faith because the Lord will return. Not knowing when the Lord will return does not diminish the fact that God will return as promised. So what are they to do? At the very end of this passage they are commanded to "encourage one another and build up each other."

We are better together. When we begin to question God's truths, it is good to have a cadre of believers supporting us, helping us to make sense out of our situation and to recall the love that God has for us. This love promises that God will never leave us nor forsake us. Not only is God always with us, we also have the companionship of all believers. We are communal beings. We must encourage and support one another. No one travels this journey alone. Just as some will encourage and support you in your time of need, you must reciprocate these same acts of love for others.

Don't scorn others who find themselves doubting the love of God, the communion of the saints, or the return of Christ. Love them. Direct them to the word of God. Assist them in recalling times in their past when God made a way althought they thought there was no way out. Share and show the love of Christ.

Lord Almighty, we are grateful for your love and for the love of the body of Christ. Help us to share that love with others on this faithful journey. Amen.

SATURDAY, NOVEMBER 14 ~ *Read Matthew 25:14-30*

Last week as we considered the coming of Christ, we read the Parable of the Ten Bridesmaids, a fitting story encouraging the listener to be prepared. This week our Gospel reading presents the story known as the parable of the talents, which, like Paul's letter, focuses our attention on what we do while we wait. Three servants are entrusted with talents while their master is away. Each servant is given a different number of talents. When the master returns, each servant has to give an accounting of how they used their talents. Those given multiple talents doubled their talents. The servant given only one talent hid it in the ground, explaining that he was afraid of the master.

The key themes of the Gospel lesson are trust and risk. We can admit that being a Christian is risky business. According to scripture, "Faith is the assurance of things hoped for, the conviction of things not seen" (Heb. 11:1). Essentially, our faith is based in hope for something (or someone) that we have never seen. Being a Christian is risky business, indeed.

When Christ returns, we will have to give an accounting of all we have been entrusted with. What exactly is it that we are entrusted with? It is the gospel of Jesus, the love of Christ, which we are called to share with the world. We cannot hide this love, endeavoring to keep it safe and secure. True love requires risk, the risk of sharing it. We cannot be afraid to step out in faith and share God's love with the world.

As we wait for the hope of Christ's return, we are challenged to prepare for that return by living fully in the moment, by taking the risk of loving abundantly. We cannot earn the salvation that is to come with Christ's return, but we can do plenty in gratitude for all God has done for us.

Merciful God, let us walk boldly in our faith, sharing your abundant love with everyone we encounter. Amen.

I have always struggled with the end of the parable of the talents: "For to all those who have, more will be given, and they will have an abundance, but from those who have nothing, even what they have will be taken away." It feels harsh—a version of "the rich get richer and the poor get poorer." It seems contradictory to the God I consider to be kind, compassionate, loving, and just.

With the parable being about money, it makes sense that we would try to make the message about money as well. But upon further examination, the message of this story is not that those with more money will be given more money. We identified yesterday what it is that we are entrusted with: the gospel of Jesus, the love of Christ. We have been given hope, peace, joy, and love. We have been given the precious gift of a Savior who died for the remission of our sins. We have been given salvation.

God has delivered us from darkness and has given us the light of Christ to guide our paths. We walk in the light with confidence, knowing that light has overcome the darkness. We believe in that which we have not seen because we know the power of the God we serve. God has delivered us, and God continues to extend mercy to us time and time again.

Each person who hears the message of the gospel has the opportunity to accept Jesus as their Lord and Savior, and those who accept have a daunting responsibility to live a life that displays the love, grace, and mercy of Christ to all. "To those who have, more will be given." We are given the responsibility to share Christ's love, and the more we do, the more love there is to go around.

God, thank you for the gift of your love. Let me share that gift abundantly with every person I meet. Amen.

Judging the Flock

NOVEMBER 16–22, 2026 • SUSAN THOGERSON MAAS

SCRIPTURE OVERVIEW: These passages speak of God's lordship over the church. Three of the passages compare God or Jesus to a shepherd and the people of God to sheep. Both Ezekiel and Matthew tell how God's true sheep will be welcomed into the kingdom. They also warn that the sheep, or sheep and goats, will be judged and separated by God based on how they treat other people, particularly the poor and vulnerable. The psalm shows sheep in a positive light, describing how God's true sheep worship God with joy and thanksgiving. In Ephesians, while Paul does not use the comparison of a shepherd and his sheep, he does describe Jesus as Lord and judge over all, including the church, which receives a rich inheritance through him.

QUESTIONS AND SUGGESTIONS FOR REFLECTION

- Read Ezekiel 34:11-16, 20-24. When have you felt like God has forgotten you? When have you felt God gathering you in from a distant place?
- Read Psalm 100. How are you able to rejoice before God even in hard times? What can you give thanks for today?
- Read Ephesians 1:15-23. What is "the hope to which [God] has called you"? What is the "glorious inheritance" you receive?
- Read Matthew 25:31-46. In what ways are you called to help the weak and vulnerable?

Susan Thogerson Maas is a freelance writer from Gresham, OR. She has written many devotionals for The Upper Room, Pathways, and other publications, as well as two novels for middle grade kids, *Picture Imperfect* and *Abbie's Woods: Defending the Nest.*

MONDAY, NOVEMBER 16 ~ *Read Ezekiel 34:11-16*

My neighbor has a small herd of sheep and goats. When her field is low on grass, she takes them across our little street to another neighbor's much larger field. The animals scatter throughout the field, munching on grass and resting under the leafy trees. Sometimes they spend several days in the pasture across the street. Yet when she goes to bring them home, they trot eagerly across the road, back into their own yard. They know she will fill the barn feeders with good alfalfa hay and the trough with fresh water. They will be well cared for by their shepherd.

In Ezekiel's time, Israel's "shepherds"—kings—had not cared well for their people. Most of the people had been taken into exile in Babylon, scattered through the land. They felt lost and broken, as though God had deserted them. Through Ezekiel, God promised to remember them. God would be their shepherd, their leader, and would return them to the pastures and mountains of home. They would not always be lost.

We also have times when we feel forgotten, as if we've been scattered on "a day of clouds and thick darkness." We may be physically absent from our home or may feel emotionally distant, like we don't really belong. We may be sick or injured and wonder, "Where is God in all this?" This question has no easy answer, at least not one that assuages our fears or removes our struggle. But we do have God's promise to rescue us, bind up our wounds, and heal us, whether in this life or in the next. One day we will be home and all will be well. We will not be lost forever.

Lord, thank you for the promise that you will rescue me. Help me to trust you through the uncertain times. Help me to remember that you will care for me. Amen.

TUESDAY, NOVEMBER 17 ~ *Read Ezekiel 34:16, 20-24*

A friend of mine bought three young goats. They were cute little things and seemed to get along well at first. But as they have grown up, one male has grown bigger and stronger than the other two. He bullies the others. He chases them away so that he can get to the food first—perhaps the reason he is so stocky and strong. And he is quick to push them with his horns if they get in his way.

Some of the leaders and rich people in Ezekiel's time were like my friend's goat. They grew fat and strong, figuratively and probably literally as well, by taking advantage of the poor and vulnerable. While the means likely varied, the rich may have overcharged for essential goods, paid low wages to their workers, or demanded high interest on loans. The rulers allowed this to continue, perhaps adding to it through taxes on the common people and special privileges for the rich, who could help them financially. They neglected their responsibility to care for all of their citizens.

Not much has changed over the centuries. While many rich people donate to charities and use their wealth to help others, some still take advantage of the poor. Some leaders still put their own wealth and career above the needs of those they are supposed to serve. And we often lack the social structures to care for the weakest among us. The good news is that God's economy doesn't work this way. God will care for the poor and suffering ones. We can do our part to bring God's kingdom by honoring and caring for the poor and hurting people around us, by working toward more just systems in our society, and by standing up for those who can't defend themselves.

Lord, open my heart to the hurting people around me. Help me to be a sheep who is fed by you, not one who pushes others away. Amen.

WEDNESDAY, NOVEMBER 18 ~ *Read Psalm 100*

I have a friend who has dealt with a lot in her life. Many years ago an automobile accident left her with a permanent brain injury. In the aftermath of her accident, her marriage fell apart and her husband left her. Her grown children rarely see her, she struggles to do many ordinary tasks, and her finances are quite limited. Yet when I ask her how she is doing, frequently her answer is, "I'm blessed and grateful."

Psalm 100, as a psalm of praise, expresses this kind of joyful outlook. Using the metaphor of God as a shepherd caring for us, the sheep, the psalmist calls those who hear to take comfort knowing God's care surrounds their lives. Our praise of God is the response we can offer to God's steadfast love.

The hardest part of praising God may be acknowledging the care and grace that God gives us. Many of us would like to think we are the masters of our fate, the captains of our ship. We may see the blessings in our life as something we have earned through our own hard work. And often, the more we have, the more we think we deserve because of our hard work. But everything we have comes from God. We did not create the resources that make our clothing and shelter, the food we eat, or even the air we breathe. We cannot make a mountain or a beautiful sunset. When it comes right down to it, we are often as helpless as sheep in a pen. But God loves us and cares for us. God provides what we need to live and more—food, family, beauty, and joy. We have so much to be thankful for. Praise is the only natural response.

Lord, thank you for the many blessings you have given me. Help me to praise you with a grateful heart and serve you with joy. Amen.

THURSDAY, NOVEMBER 19 ~ *Read Ephesians 1:15-17*

The church I am a part of is small enough that most of us know one another's names. When someone is sick, the church prays for them, and someone calls to provide meals or other support. The same thing happens when someone dies or a baby is born. When people at my church ask me how I am doing, they ask in a way that shows they really want to know. They strive to welcome all who walk through the door of the church building with genuineness. And many members take part in community outreach events that provide practical support and relationship-building to our neighbors. I can honestly say that our church is a place filled with love.

In today's passage, the writer to the Ephesians connects faith in Jesus with love for one another. Jesus himself makes this connection in John 13:35: "By this everyone will know that you are my disciples, if you love one another" (NIV). Yet that love is not always apparent in churches today. Many people have left churches because the other members didn't act lovingly toward them and instead chose to gossip, uphold cliques, and not include others. Some who might be searching for a faith community get turned off by a church they see as judgmental and condemning. Such attitudes dishonor God and hurt the people God loves.

The more we get to know Jesus, the more loving we should become. My church shows love because we make a decision to do so and commit to doing it, even when it is hard. Even when we may not feel love for one another, we live "as if"—our words and actions can be loving, whether or not our emotions are. And in most cases, the feelings of love will follow the actions.

Lord, help me to become more like Jesus, to love those in my community and those beyond it. Amen.

FRIDAY, NOVEMBER 20 ~ *Read Ephesians 1:18-23*

In this passage the writer of the epistle shows Jesus as Lord and head of not only the church, but of all that exists and ever will exist. He speaks in awe of God's mighty power in Jesus that is made available to those who believe. God is awesome in power, far above what we can ever understand.

We sometimes have a tendency to make God smaller, to put God in a box that makes sense to us. Perhaps we are even more inclined to do this with Jesus, knowing that he had human experiences like us. Jesus did say his disciples could call him friend, but we sometimes take that to an extreme. We see Jesus as just our good buddy. He likes the things we like; he hates the things (and people) we hate. He forgives our sins, but doesn't forgive those sins of others that we think are especially bad. He even votes the same way we do, so we can confidently claim that the other side is evil. Trying to remake Jesus, the Son of God, in our image may feel comforting and safe, but it denies the reality of who God is, of the divine Christ we worship.

God's ways are not our ways; God's thoughts are not our thoughts. God is so far above our mortal understanding that sometimes all we can do is fall to our knees in awe and wonder, knowing we will never comprehend. God will never fit into any box we invent. God's power and glory fill and rule the universe. But we don't have to understand God to worship and trust. Ephesians also speaks of the glory of the inheritance we have through Christ. God's love for us means we can face life—and death—without fear, because God gives us a hope that also surpasses anything we can possibly imagine.

Lord, thank you for the wonderful inheritance you have given me. Open my eyes to see your majesty and power and to trust what I can never comprehend. Amen.

SATURDAY, NOVEMBER 21 ~ *Read Matthew 25:31-40*

For several years, my husband, Gary, cooked one day a week at a soup kitchen. He worked hard at the job, going in the night before to chop vegetables and prepare meat, then arriving early in the morning so the food, usually soup or a casserole, would have plenty of time to cook. He sought to make the best meal possible for the people who came to eat, even when others who served in the soup kitchen thought he put in too much effort. For many of the guests it was the main (or possibly only) meal of the day, so he strove to make it both filling and delicious. Gary cared about his diners and found joy in fixing them a special meal.

Those on Jesus' right in this parable weren't serving others out of obligation or to check off a box on their religious checklist. They didn't even recognize that they were serving Jesus by serving others. They had internalized God's love so well that it spilled over into their entire lives. They fed the hungry, practiced hospitality, and visited the sick and lonely simply because they loved them.

We are called to a life of service, to love God and love others. But we choose our attitude. As we go about our daily lives, we can see those around us as obstacles or annoyances, making it harder for us to do what we want to do. Or we can see them as reflections of Jesus, people whom God loves. We can serve grudgingly out of obligation, or we can let Jesus' love fill us so full it automatically spills out in service of love to others.

Lord, open my heart to see Jesus in those I meet each day. Help me to serve you and others with joy. Amen.

REIGN OF CHRIST

When my husband worked at the soup kitchen, it was completely staffed by volunteers, both long-term and short-term. Occasionally volunteers would show up to help because they had been ordered by a judge to do a certain number of hours of public service. Some worked hard, but others did the bare minimum, just enough to get their requirement signed off. They were present in body, but not in spirit.

Some people see their faith that way—both in Jesus' time and now. They want the benefits of the faith but aren't interested in actually living it out. This passage is not talking about non-believers. The "goats" address Jesus as Lord. Jesus is speaking about those who think saying they follow Jesus is enough. Some followers of Christ think as long as they believe in Jesus and get baptized, they are home free. Or they think it's enough to go to church on Sunday and read the Bible, without letting what they learn shape their lives Monday through Saturday. They don't actually want to become Jesus' apprentices and dedicate their lives to him.

It is not that we must earn God's salvation. It's the other way around: Because we are saved by grace, our hearts are filled with gratitude and love for God, and that love flows out to our fellow human beings in caring hearts and deeds of kindness. As James says, "faith without deeds is dead" (James 2:26, NIV). A living faith will automatically lead to good works. We care for others not to gain God's favor or earn heavenly bonus points, but because God's Spirit directs our hearts. If we truly love God, we will love others—and that love will be seen in our words and actions when we serve others as if we were serving the Lord.

Lord, fill my heart with your love and let it flow out to those around me. Let me never close my heart to others. Amen.

Tension with God

NOVEMBER 23–29, 2026 • WESLEY KING

SCRIPTURE OVERVIEW: The readings this week explore experiences of tension with God and with others in our communities of faith. The prophet Isaiah feels tension because he cannot see God in his turmoil. The psalmist feels tension as he asks for restoration and revival. Paul feels tension with the early church and the challenges they faced. Finally, we feel tension in the apocalyptic passage that kicks off Advent. Yet tension isn't necessarily a bad thing. Tension is a way that our faith stretches, evolves, and grows. And as each of these readings shows us, God is faithful—in stressful times or not—always.

QUESTIONS AND SUGGESTIONS FOR REFLECTION

- Read Isaiah 64:1-9. Have you wondered where God was during a tumultuous time? Describe the tension you felt during that period.
- Read Psalm 80:1-7; 17-19. Have you ever felt like you were waiting on God? What might God be teaching us in our waiting?
- Read 1 Corinthians 1:3-9. Who are you giving thanks for during this season of Thanksgiving? Have you shared your gratitude with them recently?
- Read Mark 13:24-37. How might the act of preparation be a spiritual practice? What do you hope for this upcoming Advent season?

Rev. Wesley King is an ordained Disciples of Christ minister. He serves as the associate pastor of Vine Street Christian Church (Disciples of Christ) in Nashville, TN.

MONDAY, NOVEMBER 23 ~ *Read Isaiah 64:1-9*

We are nearing the season of Advent, and the lectionary texts give us hints for what is to come. In the passage from Isaiah, the prophet calls out to God to come down to earth. This exact experience Isaiah desires is the event we will soon celebrate in the coming of Christ. But for the prophet, the time of God's arrival on earth is not yet here.

The prophet Isaiah calls out to God, looking for God in the midst of a difficult time. It seems Isaiah thinks God could change everything if only God would act. Why didn't God come down to Isaiah at that moment? I feel a similar pain to that of the writer. My grandmother has recently received the kind of news that no one wants to receive: "It's back and it's aggressive." God could intervene with my grandmother's diagnosis, but God hasn't.

We believe that God's spirit is always with us. Still, we will experience moments when we cannot feel or see evidence of that presence. Terrible things happen, and we know that God is mighty enough to have prevented them, but God didn't. These are the moments that can lead us to experience crises of faith. The prophet says that God's name alone would make the nations tremble; why doesn't God intervene in these seemingly small matters that would make our individual lives that much easier?

We do not have the answer. But not having the answer is not reason enough to turn away or give in to the despair. I believe that God is with me even in the tough times, even when God doesn't do what I think God should do. Perhaps both things can be true: we can trust that God is with us, and God is big enough for our anger and our questions when we can't feel God's presence. The prophet holds these two truths in tension. We know that even in the tough times, we are God's people.

God of the mountain who is also God of the valley, remind us that you are ever present with us and that we are your people. Amen.

TUESDAY, NOVEMBER 24 ~ *Read Psalm 80:1-7*

Several years ago, I found a piece of furniture at Goodwill that seemed to have "good bones." It had an interesting design and a mid-century modern feel. I restored it with my spouse. It was a long process of slow, difficult work, but seeing its original beauty made anew was exciting.

In this text the psalmist is praying for Israel's restoration. We can tell they have faced hardships by the way the psalmist pleads to God, claiming that God has fed them bread made of tears. We all have moments when we feel as though we are waiting for God to move in our lives and in our communities. We know the frustration of waiting on God, and yet we are called to trust that God's timing is perfect. We live with the tension of these two truths. Even so, it doesn't prevent our own human reactions. We want change. We want to be changed. We want restoration.

God, in God's way, is teaching us that waiting is an act of discipleship and spiritual practice. We live in the world of "right now." Typically, anything we want is easily at our fingertips: food, supplies, connection, communication, and entertainment. We live in a culture that doesn't have to wait on hardly anything. Yet God makes us wait. God made the psalmist wait.

Perhaps waiting provides us a lesson to be learned. Perhaps God is showing just how much we depend on God by making us wait. Perhaps waiting is a form of following Christ, as we must sacrifice our desire for immediacy. As we await the season of Advent, this is an opportunity to begin the practice of waiting on God in an intentional way.

God, we await what you have in store for us. God, we await what you will teach us during this season. God, we await your coming. Amen.

WEDNESDAY, NOVEMBER 25 ~ *Read Psalm 80:17-19*

A friend told me that she recalls as a child seeing her grandmother rock back and forth in hard times, speaking and calling on the name of Jesus. A few years later when my friend found herself in a traumatic situation, she resorted to her grandmother's way of coping: rocking back and forth and speaking the name of Jesus.

In this continuation of Psalm 80, we get an illustration of God's hand upon the people. This hand provides strength. It revives the people, encouraging them to stay focused on God and to continue to call on God's name.

When was the last time you felt revived? What have you done to feel revived? Whether it's a deep dive into the word of God, a new prayer practice, connecting with a friend, or spending time in nature, each of us has practices that nourish our soul. What revives your spirit? When was the last time you called on the name of Jesus? Verbally calling on Jesus may feel strange for some of us, but we believe there is power in that name. Whether it is a comfort in times of trouble, like it was for my friend and her grandmother, or a powerful rebuke in the face of injustice, there is power in speaking aloud the name of Jesus.

The psalmist again cries out that God might restore the people and that God's face might shine upon them. Though we are thousands of years removed from this author, the desire rings true today. Our world is divided and under the stress of war, famine, climate change, racial and political unrest, pandemics, bigotry, and hatred. We need God's revival in our world, our communities, and our lives.

Jesus, Jesus, Jesus, the name above all names. We speak your name as truth to power to heal our world. Revive us, O Christ, as only you can. Restore us, Jesus, as only you can. Shine your face upon us and upon our world. Amen.

THURSDAY, NOVEMBER 26 ~ *Read 2 Corinthians 9:6-15*

THANKSGIVING DAY, USA

For context, in the chapter before today's passage Paul is telling the Corinthians that the church in Macedonia has a need they can help with. Paul knows the heart of this body of early Christians. He is not just asking them to give but illustrating how giving is an act of following Jesus. Sacrifice too is an act of following Jesus. Paul quotes the psalmist saying, "He scattered everywhere; he gave to the needy; his righteousness remains forever" (CEB).

As a people who not too long ago went through a global pandemic in which we hoarded goods and supplies for safety and survival, it isn't tough to imagine what the early church might have felt. Perhaps they were scared to give up too much in a land occupied by the Roman Empire. Yet Paul calls on them to give from what they have to help the church in Macedonia. This is a sacrifice, because it means giving up not only goods and supplies but also security. It means giving up a sense of comfort to support the greater good.

On Thanksgiving, when we reflect on how God has blessed us, perhaps part of our gratitude requires us to give back. We give because we have been given much. As you sit around the table with your friends and families, reflect on how much God has given and how you might be able to give back to God and to God's people. Realize too that this giving may be sacrificial. It may not be comfortable. It will, however, be what we are called to do.

Thank you, God, for your abundance of love, charity, mercy, and grace. As we reflect on all that we have been given, remind us that we have much to give. May it be so, and may we make it so with our living. Amen.

FRIDAY, NOVEMBER 27 ~ *Read 1 Corinthians 1:3-6*

This excerpt is from one of my favorite passages of scripture. I once heard this passage referenced in a lecture on "Holy Friendship." As the opening words of Paul's first letter to the church in Corinth, it sets the stage for the message he seeks to share with his fellow followers of the Way.

Paul starts with a greeting of grace and peace to his friends. Indeed, each of Paul's epistles in the New Testament begins with this prayer for grace and peace. For Paul, grace is the force that creates and sustains a life of faith, and peace describes the status of such life. These aren't throwaway words to get through the introduction of his letter; they are the very core of his message.

Paul then goes on to give thanks for those in the Corinthian church. His immediate gratitude calls us to explore the idea of giving thanks for those relationships we've been given. Each of us can likely attest that God has worked through many people in our lives to reveal God's love for us and God's intention that we have life more abundant. We all have such people in our lives, but how often do we give thanks for them? How often do we thank them for their love and support? Paul tells us that we have been blessed with these relationships because of God's love for us through Christ Jesus. God loves us so much that God has blessed us with holy friendships and relationships.

During this season of Thanksgiving, we give thanks for those people God has placed in our lives. We can also be inspired to be the person our friends, spouses, colleagues, and others thank God for. When we focus on the grace and peace offered through Christ, we become God's signs of grace and peace to those we are blessed to call friends.

List those for whom you are grateful. Pray for each person on your list by name.

SATURDAY, NOVEMBER 28 ~ *Read 1 Corinthians 1:7-9*

Notice the recurring theme of tension in the passages for this week. The opening of Paul's letter seems to present a lovely image of a friend greeting friends with grace and peace. Yet when I read verse 9, I immediately feel tension.

Tension isn't necessarily a bad thing. Tension, by definition, is a force applied to something with the intention of stretching it. A stagnant faith—a faith that doesn't grow and evolve, that doesn't allow room for the Spirit to work in our lives—may need some tension to stretch it. Having an unstretched faith usually means we have checked out on God. Think of a rubber band that has become hardened over time. It will break rather than stretch.

When I read verse 9, I think of the times in my life when it has been hard to proclaim that God is faithful. In times of great loss or sorrow, or in times of great pain and heartbreak, it is often hard to proclaim this truth. And yet I believe within my soul that God is faithful.

Through the tension that the prophet Isaiah felt, God was faithful to God's people. Through the tension that the psalmist felt, God restored and revived God's people. Through the tension of the early church, God was faithful to sustain them. And in the forthcoming season of Advent, as we feel the tension of awaiting the Light of the World, God is and will be faithful.

As you feel tension in your spiritual life, lean into it with the profound assurance that God is faithful. God will never leave you or forsake you. Even in those times when it is hard to feel God's presence, know that God is there with you.

God of tension, may we lean into it, and may it make us stronger, wiser, and more authentic versions of who you've created us to be. Remind us that you are faithful always. Amen.

SUNDAY, NOVEMBER 29 ~ *Read Mark 13:24-37*

First Sunday in Advent

We begin with the ending. We begin the season of Advent with a text that allows us to see into the future. We all have read the synopsis on the back of the book to see how the story unfolds, right? This type of apocalyptic writing has always seemed to me an interesting choice for an Advent text. Why would we read this story about Christ's triumphant return during the season before we celebrate Christ's birth? It is an opportunity to practice preparation.

The author tells us the parable of the fig tree as an illustration of how the tree changes as the seasons change and how we can see the signs of the tree preparing for summer. Likewise, the author says that we won't know the day or the hour when Christ shall return. Instead of looking for a sign of Christ's return and waiting until we think we've pinpointed the moment before we begin to prepare, we must think of it differently. We don't know the day nor the hour, so we should adjust all of our living to be reflective of Christ.

This shift in motivation ensures that we are living a life that is reflective of Christ not because we want the reward of heaven but because a Christ-like life here and now is the reward of heaven. In the same manner, we prepare for Christ's coming as an infant by shifting our motivation. We could treat this as yet another holiday season, or we could truly prepare ourselves to receive the Christ child in a way that we've never received him before.

Loving and gracious God, as we prepare for your arrival, may we make room in our hearts, minds, and lives to reflect you. May your hope, peace, joy, and love be made known by our loving and our living. Amen.

Make Way for the Lord

NOVEMBER 30–DECEMBER 6, 2026 • MITCH TODD

SCRIPTURE OVERVIEW: This week's passages brim over with God's promised blessings and the efforts we must undertake to receive them. Isaiah calls us to remove any obstacles between God and ourselves so that we might fully experience God's glory. Psalm 85 echoes this with the assurance of mercy, peace, righteousness, and salvation—a restoration of God's favor. Second Peter shares an expectation of the Lord's return, but according to God's timing rather than our own. Mark echoes Isaiah, as John the Baptist calls us to repentance and preparation. Together, these passages remind us to take up the work of Advent with both anticipation and delight. God's gifts are many. Are we ready for them?

QUESTIONS AND SUGGESTIONS FOR REFLECTION

- Read Isaiah 40:1-11. What obstacles keep you from receiving God into your life? What obstacles keep you from proclaiming God's blessings?
- Read Psalm 85:1-2, 8-13. When and how have you received God's favor? What list of words would you use to describe it?
- Read 2 Peter 3:8-15a. How is God's time different from your time? How can you cultivate a sense of urgency for the kingdom in a world that continues to languish?
- Read Mark 1:1-8. How do the prophets, especially John, prepare you to receive Christ? How are you qualified to be a prophet as well?

Rev. Mitch Todd is a United Methodist pastor serving in Kansas. He is also the publisher of two devotion collections, *Barefoot* and *In Circles*. He publishes weekly devotions online at weeklydevotion.com.

MONDAY, NOVEMBER 30 ~ *Read Isaiah 40:1-11*

The funniest bumper sticker I've ever seen was on the back of a nice-looking sedan. It read, "Asphalt. The smooth ride." Of all the absurd, mundane public declarations a person could make, this driver decided to profess their favorite paving material! It had to be someone from the "asphalt council" if there is such a thing, but if Isaiah had a car, he might just have put that very sticker on the back of it.

This passage begins what is called "Second Isaiah." It was perhaps written by a student of Isaiah many years later, during the time of the Babylonian exile. In jubilation, the writer issues a proclamation of God's deliverance and comfort for the people of Jerusalem. It's coming soon, but not before preparations are made and some serious groundwork has been laid.

And so a massive spiritual road project must begin. The Israelites are to make a highway for the coming of God. This undertaking involves clearing a path through the wilderness of their lives, flattening mountains and filling in valleys. Some scholars understand the road the prophet calls for to be the road (either metaphorical or literal) back home to Jerusalem. The important point, though, is that it is God's way, not the people's. The work would not be easy, but the purpose is clear: God is coming, and we must get ready.

Are you ready? In this season of preparation, what are the obstacles that obstruct God's path for you? How have you unintentionally (or intentionally) thrown up barriers of sin, distraction, or stubbornness that make it harder for you to receive comfort or deliverance? You may have a road project ahead of you as well. It may not always be a smooth ride, and there is certainly more to it than could fit on a bumper sticker, but clearing a path for Christ is worth the effort.

God, help me see clearly the roadblocks that separate me from you, and help me to remove them. Amen.

TUESDAY, DECEMBER 1 ~ *Read Isaiah 40:1-11*

This passage has a lot of vocalizing going on. In these eleven verses, words like "speak," "cry out," or "lift your voice" are mentioned eleven times. This is a call for the prophet to publicly proclaim good news for Jerusalem. That is, after all, a big part of a prophet's job description. I wonder: Is it part of ours?

The role of a prophet is not always an easy one. Prophets deliver God's news, whether it's good or bad. Prophets try to look at the world through God's eyes to discern God's perspective, intention, and direction. Then they speak boldly about what they see. Are you up for that kind of task? It sounds like a lot of work. If given the choice, I think I'd be more comfortable as a shepherd than a prophet. Shepherds tend their flocks, living a faithful and humble life. Prophets are all about making a fuss, going out on a limb.

Both roles are mentioned in this passage. But the role of shepherd is already taken. The coming Lord will be the gentle shepherd, comforting Jerusalem. The prophets, however, are to function as the loud-and-proud advance team, making joyful noise for all to hear. That includes Isaiah, and it may just include you and me as well.

We can't be timid. We've heard the good news and we can't stay silent about it. Prophecy takes work, so feel free to start small. Maybe your proclamation is a carol sung out in the street, or an invitation to someone to join you at church. Or maybe this is the year you're ready to amplify your voice. Speak up when you feel that prompting. Shout it from the rooftops. Share with the confidence of a believer. Christ is coming!

Lord, give me the courage to speak out and the wisdom to know what to say. Amen.

WEDNESDAY, DECEMBER 2 ~ *Read Psalm 85:1-2, 8-13*

In my bible, the heading for this psalm is "Prayer for the Restoration of God's Favor." It's a celebration of the many blessings God will again bestow upon the people.

The more I think about this heading, the more I struggle. Maybe you struggle with it too. If God is restoring favor to Israel, does that mean God had previously taken it away? I'll admit I've felt like that at times in my life. When things go wrong, it can feel like God is punishing me, even when my theology tells me otherwise. And when life is full of joy, I can't help but feel as though God has blessed me with good fortune.

The beginning and end of this psalm ties the bounty of the land to God's favor. The Bible provides many examples of this more conditional favor. When times are good, the people feel that God is happy with them. When times are hard, they feel God must be angry or absent. This pattern of punishment and reward is built into the whole story of Israel.

Our understanding of grace seems to change this pattern. We're still held accountable for our sin, but the emphasis changes. Instead of tying God's favor to the results we experience, a focus on grace challenges us to see God working through both the good and the bad. God's favor is less a reward and more a gift. Even when bad times come, Christ's victory over death shows us that God's favor is eternally present.

Has God changed throughout the ages, or has our understanding of God simply evolved? Regardless of how you answer the question, the coming of Christ is, without a doubt, a testament to the radical blessings of God's unconditional love.

Gracious Lord, in the midst of my ups and downs, help me become aware of your gracious presence, loving me through my whole life. Amen.

THURSDAY, DECEMBER 3 ~ *Read Psalm 85: 1-2, 8-13*

I look at my online shopping cart. A sweater for my mom, fifty percent off. A fancy gadget for my spouse, with a three-year warranty. A dumb little toy that my niece will break in ten minutes. Black Friday, Cyber Monday, and Giving Tuesday are all reminders that this is a season for bestowing gifts on others. I wonder, am I doing it right? I love to watch loved ones open my presents, but I'm not always mindful when I'm picking them out.

Then I look at Psalm 85. In just a few verses, we're showered with gifts: peace, salvation, steadfast love, faithfulness, and righteousness. This is quite the list, gathered up in one big bundle. It is extravagant, even overwhelming. I long to share the depth of my love too. Can I possibly find a gift that expresses the inexpressible?

Like us, God desires to share love in a palpable, tangible way. Our psalmist identifies and celebrates these blessings. God's work is not done. In time God wrapped these gifts, and put them not in a box, but in a baby. This is the Word, becoming flesh, a sign not just for all people, but for each person.

Maybe before I give, I should remember what I have received. God's faithfulness and righteousness are on full display in Christ. Salvation is there, waiting to be opened. The love of God flows through my veins and aches to pour out into those around me. I'll probably never find a sweater or gadget that can fully convey the depths of this, but that's okay. They say the thought is what counts, and so I will turn my thoughts to God's many blessings. Then, filled with celebration and gratitude, I'll pour a little of what's in my heart into the gifts I give others.

God, may every gift I give be a reflection, however small, of what I have received from you. Amen.

FRIDAY, DECEMBER 4 ~ *Read 2 Peter 3:8-15a*

Ah, what a beautiful passage for Advent. Makes you want to put on some Andy Williams, sit down with a nice cup of hot chocolate, and consider the violent end of the world. The other readings this week all speak of something good coming, and honestly, this passage is no different. We just have to be a little patient.

Why all the violent imagery? Surprisingly, the writer of Second Peter is attempting to be encouraging. This passage is more of a pep talk than you might think.

The early New Testament writers understood Jesus to have talked quite a lot about the end of the world. They understood the kingdom of God as a coming reign that would replace this world. The great turmoil would culminate in unexpected peace, and it could happen at any moment. Disciples were told to be dressed and ready for God's ultimate appearance that could come at any moment. Because of this imminent arrival of the kingdom of God, the disciples felt a sense of immediacy to the work. But time passed, and the end didn't come as expected. These early Christians then faced the same dilemma many contemporary Christians face today: What's the urgency? Maybe we don't need to be quite so driven.

The writer reminds us that God stands outside of time. Even as we are reminded to wait, God is already working the kingdom into our world, to widen the welcome of salvation. Today's verses are a reminder that we must maintain our vigilance. We may be in this for the long haul, but we should remain prepared. Changes are coming—are already here—so drink up your cocoa and put your coat on. You'll want to be ready for what comes next.

Lord, as I stumble through the brokenness of this world, fill me with patience and urgency, always prepared to receive you into my life. Amen.

SATURDAY, DECEMBER 5 ~ *Read Mark 1:1-8*

Strange cousin John. The one who needs a haircut and dresses weird and brings locusts to the family potluck. The one who says the wildest things and is always trying to dunk you when you're in the pool. Why would anybody listen to him? Nowadays he would probably be dismissed as just another homeless person with questionable mental health. Why did the people of Jerusalem take him seriously? Surely they would have been just as dubious about such a character as we would be today. Why did this wild man, alone in the wilderness, capture people's attention?

Because he wasn't alone. Not really. He stood in great company with a long line of prophets. He is, in fact, considered the last of the old prophets, a hinge between the Old and New Testaments. His appearance, with his camel hair shirt and leather belt, resembles the great Elijah. Jesus himself makes the comparison. And John quotes the prophet Isaiah about building a highway in the desert to receive God's deliverance. This spiritual lineage provides context and credibility for John, but it is what he offers that had the most appeal. Drawing from the words of the prophet Jeremiah, John announces a new reality, a covenant of the heart. He points the way to a chance at repentance, a new start. A washing away of sins and a blessing from above.

We can accept this new paradigm by embracing the unlikely gift John offers on God's behalf: forgiveness, new birth, and a deeper connection with God and one another. Strange cousin John wasn't that strange, after all. Instead, he was a herald of something wonderful to come.

God of the ages, help me listen to those who have come before, that they might point me toward what is to come. Amen.

SUNDAY, DECEMBER 6 ~ *Read Mark 1:1-8*

Second Sunday of Advent

The Gospel of Mark begins by talking about baptism. There's no birth narrative, no tales of Jesus as a child. Instead, the story takes you to the Jordan river and jumps right in with John. With such a prominent placement, it must be important.

Do you remember your baptism? I was just a baby when I was baptized. Instead of remembering the day itself, I try to remember that I am baptized. It is a condition that never goes away. It doesn't matter if you were sprinkled, splashed, or dunked fifty years ago. Spiritually, your hair is still wet. Living water never dries.

I think about those first few people, drawn to John there at the Jordan. John baptized people in order to make them receptive to the coming Christ, but did they know what they were getting themselves into? What does it mean to pledge to follow Christ before you are aware of his presence? Of course, the same can be said for those of us baptized as infants.

John revealed more about the meaning of baptism than we might think. He spoke of personal repentance and forgiveness and the promise of a new community. He explained the coming of both Christ and the Holy Spirit, offering just a hint of what was in store. Just like us, the people he baptized had the rest of their lives to grow in their understanding of what that meant. This was only the beginning.

As these days of Advent unfold, remember your baptism. It did not just *happen*—it *is* happening. The relationship that God has offered—and that you have accepted—will not run dry. New beginnings are happening, even now. Remember your baptism. New life keeps coming, wave after wave. Or sprinkle.

Holy Spirit, help me to remember my baptism and be faithful. Amen.

The Coming of Christ

DECEMBER 7–13, 2026 • JUAN GUERRERO

SCRIPTURE OVERVIEW: In a sunrise, darkness slowly gives way to light. It is a gradual process. The birds start singing even in the darkness, and with their songs, they seem to announce the rising of the sun. Similarly, the biblical texts for this third Sunday of Advent announce the coming of the Lord. A new day is already dawning. Isaiah tells us the Spirit is already here. God has already sent a messenger because God wants to speak to us. John tells his listeners that he is not the way, but he shows the way: repentance. The psalmist describes the moment when God intervenes in our lives. Then, in that moment, we will be very joyful. God acted in the past and will act again. First Thessalonians reminds us to rejoice always. The sun is not yet visible on the horizon, but its light is already arriving.

QUESTIONS AND SUGGESTIONS FOR REFLECTION

- Read Isaiah 61:1-4, 8-11. God is coming. How do Isaiah's words of praise and justice inspire you to act?
- Read Psalm 126. How do you celebrate the justice that you have seen come to fruition while hoping for future justice? How does your anticipation of the fullness of justice affect your faith?
- Read 1 Thessalonians 5:16-24. How can you return to the basics of faith during Advent?
- Read John 1:6-8, 19-28. How is this Advent season both familiar and new for you? How might simple announcements of Jesus' coming change your experience of the season?

Rev. Juan Guerrero is a missionary and Methodist pastor, currently serving in a rural church in Cali, Colombia in South America.

MONDAY, DECEMBER 7 ~ *Read Psalm 126:1-3*

Some translations place these verses in the past tense, the psalmist looking back to a time when God intervened. *Remember what God has done,* this kind of interpretation says. Others place these verses in the future tense, having the psalmist look forward to God's coming deliverance. *When God intervenes,* the psalmist implies in these translations, *then our lives will change. Then we will be "like those who dream."*

Many times we are only happy when we dream, when we consider certain and secure what is not yet, when we call things that are not as though they were. We rejoice when we move into a house for which we have worked hard, seeing the hope of our new life and circumstances, but over time our enthusiasm wanes, and we dream of something else new. An age-old saying warns us that everything we own actually owns us. The weight of the past and the present can pull us down.

Being able to dream fills us with joy. Dreamers are happy even though they still haven't achieved what they dream of. They are happy because they have faith and rejoice in hope. Seeing the future with hope is a gift from God. Dreaming is an act of faith typical of those who are liberated from pessimism and fear.

When we dream, we focus our attention on what is to come. When God intervenes, then we will be like those who dream. Under God's intervention, we believe that what seems impossible is possible. God makes this change in our hearts. In the end, Psalm 126 tells us that God's intervention will be like when it rains in the mountains and the water descends in streams, renewing the life of the valleys and even reaching the desert areas (v. 4).

Lord, thank you for inspiring us to dream and for helping our dreams come true. Amen.

TUESDAY, DECEMBER 8 ~ *Read Isaiah 61:1-4*

When I read this passage, I always remember a young man who dressed as Jesus and entered our church, walking slowly down the center aisle to the altar. The young man climbed into the pulpit, took an artificially aged scroll, and read Isaiah 61:1-4. At the end of the reading, some previously instructed individuals pushed the young man, who was playing Jesus, out of the church. Afterwards, the congregation discussed the experience. That reenactment of Luke 4:16-30 became sacred and reverent.

Several centuries after Isaiah, Jesus read this passage in the synagogue in Nazareth. Then he said, "Today this scripture has been fulfilled" (Luke 4:21). Jesus proclaimed that he was the fulfillment of the prophet's vision: Jesus came "to bring good news to the oppressed, to bind up the brokenhearted, to proclaim liberty to the captives and release to the prisoners." We who choose to follow Jesus and read these words today join in this line of those who bring deliverance. The Spirit of God is upon the prophet Isaiah. It is upon Jesus. It is upon the church. It is upon us! What will we do?

The Advent season invites us to pack our bags and embark on this journey with Jesus once again. Christ is coming, Christ is here—Jesus is already in the midst of our world. He is knocking at our door. What will we do? How will we welcome him? Will we postpone our response?

As we restart our walk with Jesus, walking from the manger to the Cross, we can commit anew to following in his footsteps. The time has been fulfilled. Each of us is the person to whom the gospel is announced. It is with each one of us that God speaks. We can respond to the call.

Good God, lead me along your paths. Let me proclaim the good news of your deliverance to all who need to hear it. Amen.

WEDNESDAY, DECEMBER 9 ~ *Read 1 Thessalonians 5:16-24*

Fifteen years ago, I was invited to go as a missionary to a distant country. I thought about it, discussed it with my wife, and we agreed. But then, unexpectedly, everything was postponed. It was a wait with some uncertainty. I still expected to travel eventually, but I no longer knew when, nor did I feel so sure of my decision to go at all. However, I continued to prepare myself. Eventually, I traveled and experienced the most wonderful years of my life.

Similarly, we await the fullness of time when we will see the Lord face to face. But this is not a passive wait. Rather, it is a wait with much to be done. We must praise God and allow that praise to flow into and infect our entire being.

We can go through this life with joy and gratitude, yet some cannot or will not find the joy of a life in Christ. In my homeland, there is a saying: "They are going to heaven, yet they go crying; who understands them?" Many complain continuously, despite being Christians. When we complain, we want to be right, to be justified in our frustration over what we lack or to find solace from some discomfort. Sure, there are worthy reasons to complain, true injustices that need to be righted. But we will not find the kind of justification we seek when our complaints are selfish or from a place of greed. The Holy Spirit that dwells within us has made it possible for us to thank God for everything. Whenever I preside over the Lord's Supper, while handing it to each believer, I like to emphasize the phrase: "Live with joy and be thankful."

"The one who calls you is faithful, and he will do this." Are you aware that God's power is working in you to sanctify you and lead you to promised lands? Is your faith a source of joy?

Thank you, Lord, for working in me. Thank you for blessing me every day in ways beyond what I understand and comprehend. Amen.

THURSDAY, DECEMBER 10 ~ *Read Psalm 126:4-6*

God promises that those who sow with tears will reap with joy. God promises that there will be fruit from our labor, so we can start projects for the glory and honor of God.

Agriculture, in general, is a demanding task. But on an emotional level, sowing can be doubly demanding because the harvest is still far off. After sowing, there is much uncertainty: Rain is needed, pests must be controlled, hard work is required, and there are other factors that we cannot always control. Some trees take years to bear fruit.

However, we have faith to sow and start new projects. Many years ago, I started a small congregation that included a mother and her two children, who lived in extreme poverty. I always picked them up to bring them to church. Eventually they emigrated to another country, and I didn't hear from them for a long time. Years later, one of the children contacted me online and told me that he was serving in a church in New York and that he had a large car in which he transported brothers to the temple. He said he did it because he never forgot what I did for them.

We can work to make our lives kinder, turn our church into a healing community, and help others. But best of all, we can trust that our efforts will be rewarded and that we will return singing and bringing a bountiful harvest. Christians do not live in immobile contemplation; rather, we transform the world for the glory of God.

It is said that in a long journey, the first step is the most difficult. We sow with tears. Many projects that become significant in our lives start with small steps. God promises to bless our labor and bring fruit to our efforts.

Oh God, what a joy it gives us to know that you bless our efforts and labors. May we always serve you with joy. Amen.

FRIDAY, DECEMBER 11 ~ *Read Isaiah 61:1-4; 8-11*

Isaiah speaks of a contrast: the oil of joy instead of mourning, glory instead of ashes, restorations instead of ruins and rubble. A "yes" from God rises and contrasts with a "no." Karl Barth said that God's "no" is embedded within a gigantic "yes." This means that despite everything that has happened in our lives, God offers us hope. God's "yes" is greater than God's "no." We experience a "no" to sin but a "yes" to life. We can fight, overcome, advance, and be more than conquerors in Christ Jesus.

God tells us that, despite everything, joy and gladness are possible. The prophet's words remind us that this joy and gladness have been available to us long before Christ's coming, and Jesus' reference of Isaiah 61 as he teaches in the synagogue (Luke 4:16-19) carries that promise to us today. God accepts us as we are and deals with us in order to ultimately sanctify, orient, guide, and bless not only us but all who come after us. It's as if God is saying: *Despite everything, I love the world and I love you too. Despite everything, you are the person I want.*

Verse 10 turns our attention to our right response for such love. We rejoice because God believes in us more than we believe in ourselves. We are precious clay in the hands of the potter. Instead of rubble and ruins, God wants to transform us, and in response we praise God and share the good news. God has had reasons to destroy us but always prefers to restore us. This is the great "yes" of Christmas. God decides to come into our world again and again to rescue us from fear and lies. God does not rejoice in our destruction but in our transformation. God covers us with the clothing of salvation.

Merciful God, thank you for loving us so much despite our sins. Transform us through the joy made available by the coming of Christ. Amen.

John was an incredible person. God sent him to prepare the way for Jesus.

Humanly speaking, it's difficult for someone to be as straightforward, genuine, and faithful to God as John was. John was incorruptible and honest. What you saw was what you got. He ate simply and dressed the same way. He did not love the things that are in the world, and that is why he was not a man easily blackmailed or manipulated.

Being sent from God, the author needs to clarify that John was not the light but came to bear witness to the light. John decreased so that Jesus could increase. John could have taken advantage of his fame, but he did not. He had to clarify that he was not the Christ because many thought he was. But instead of using this misconception to his benefit, John continually pointed to Jesus as the true Christ, placing the focus of his listeners where it needed to be.

People in scripture like John remind us that this world, despite its shadows, can be transformed by the power of God. It is possible for us to be like John today. We announce the arrival of Jesus Christ, not ourselves. We proclaim that the power of God can still transform lives and the world. It is not about our own power but about the power of God. We can place ourselves correctly underneath Jesus' power, understanding that it is not our own glory we proclaim. It is God's.

Our lives can faithfully point others to Christ. If John could, we can. He was just a person, like you and me. We are those whom God strengthens with the power of God's might.

God, with your help, we can offer a testimony of life that is simple and straightforward so that the world may believe. Help us to make our way of life one that speaks to our world, our community, and our family. Amen.

SUNDAY, DECEMBER 13 ~ *Read John 1:19-28*

Third Sunday of Advent

John defined himself as a voice. Not just any voice, but a voice crying out in the wilderness. This saying is still used today to describe the experience of someone speaking while no one listens. In reality, John was heard. But what was extraordinary is that he didn't say what people wanted to hear, and despite that, he was listened to. Perhaps his genuine nature made the difference.

It's natural to want to be popular and align ourselves with mainstream trends, to be fashionable and fit in with the world. We want applause and recognition. But the Christian faith calls us to walk a narrow path, distinguished precisely because few walk it. When everyone claims to be Christian, perhaps no one is truly Christian. Being Christian implies a calling to be different.

Commercial Christmas pushes us toward consumption and overindulgence, but the Christian faith sets us facing the desert where a voice points the way. This time before Christmas can be used for reflection and to straighten our path, even if it feels culturally unusual. For years, I have stressed over the many activities in the days leading up to Christmas, wanting not to miss an opportunity for activity. But I have learned to slow down, focus, and enjoy time spent striving to live what I feel is right rather than what the world demands. I have learned to trust in God's provision. I do what I can; what I cannot, I peacefully leave to the Lord.

I am struck by John's simplicity. He did not compare himself to the important leaders of Israel but defined himself humbly, saying, *I am just a voice*. Being an honest and transparent voice is more than enough.

Help me, Lord, to be that faithful and true voice crying in the desert. Amen.

Promised Hope for the Future

DECEMBER 14–20, 2026 • BETH RITTER-CONN

SCRIPTURE OVERVIEW: The texts for this week emphasize God's faithfulness throughout history, as well as God's abiding presence with God's people. In 2 Samuel, God promises that the line of David will rule forever. Jesus comes from this line. In the first reading from Luke, Mary rejoices after her visit to Elizabeth, for she understands that her child will play a key role in God's redemption. Paul reminds the Romans that his message about Christ did not begin with him. Instead, it is the fulfillment of promises made through the prophets. These passages help us draw connections between the Old and New Testament as we trace God's promise of presence from the covenant God makes with David to the promise of the birth of Jesus, "God-with-us," that God makes to Mary.

QUESTIONS AND SUGGESTIONS FOR REFLECTION

- Read 2 Samuel 7:1-11, 16. How can these examples of God's presence with our ancestors in the faith give you hope even in times of struggle?
- Read Luke 1:26-38. In this season of giving and receiving, how do you remember that God is the giver of all good gifts? How do you return your God-given gifts to God?
- Read Luke 1:47-55. How have you responded to God's faithfulness and steadfast love in your life?
- Read Romans 16:25-27. How do you see God's faithfulness demonstrated across both testaments of scripture? Where do you see our Hebrew Bible passages for this week echoed in our New Testament passages?

Dr. Beth Ritter-Conn is Assistant Professor of Religion and Honors at Belmont University in Nashville, TN, where she lives with her husband, son, and cat. She holds a Ph.D. in Systematic and Philosophical Theology from the Graduate Theological Union in Berkeley, CA, and she is co-editor of *The Women's Christian Theology Reader* (Wiley-Blackwell, 2025).

MONDAY, DECEMBER 14 ~ *Read 2 Samuel 7:1-11, 16*

In today's passage of scripture, God speaks with the prophet Nathan, who in turn gives God's message to King David. Through Nathan, God reminds David of his humble background. He was a shepherd boy, the youngest son of a large family, hardly the most likely choice to become king. In reminding David of his origins, God declares that God is able to build things—nations, families, temples, the world itself—from scratch.

The major promises here are about hope and presence. For generations, the people of God had been traveling, out of place. They finally have a place to land, a patch of earth to call home. The whole time God has been traveling with them, inhabiting the temporary dwelling of the tabernacle. God promises David that his people will have a home, a place to rest, and that God will live with them there too.

Turbulent times are to come in the story of God's people. There will be a splitting of the kingdom, there will be exile, and the people will be scattered in diaspora like seeds in the wind. But God is steadfast, and these promises of presence and hope are not broken, though they may feel unfulfilled for a time.

Although the context will change, the need for reassurance of God's presence echoes throughout the centuries. The people of God live under Babylonian, Assyrian, and Persian rule in the Hebrew scriptures, and they live under Roman rule in the New Testament. But God always comes through for God's people, promising them liberation and salvation at every turn, as we will see when moving through the lectionary texts for this week.

Help us rest in you, God, knowing that you dwell within and among us even in turbulent times, just as you dwelt with your people in the past. Amen.

TUESDAY, DECEMBER 15 ~ *Read Psalm 89:1-4, 19-26*

Yesterday's passage tells us a story about God's faithfulness; today's passage sings about it. What a beautiful example we have here of the necessity of the many literary genres included in the Bible. Second Samuel is a narrative, a theological history, that chronicles the rise of Israel's monarchy between the time of the judges and the time of the exile. Psalm 89 tells that same story but in poetic, lyrical form. The psalm names the covenant that God has made with David and the promise of an enduring legacy. It praises God for the "steadfast love" extended to God's people throughout the generations.

How did you first learn the stories of your faith tradition? I think about the songs from my childhood in Sunday school that taught me things like, "Zacchaeus was a wee little man, a wee little man was he," and, more importantly, "Jesus loves me, this I know." Then, later, it was the hymns that sustained me—"Blessed Assurance," "Great is Thy Faithfulness," and "How Great Thou Art" will always be reassuring and comforting. When we can't quite remember all the details of a story, we can still probably remember the lyrics to a song, or at least hum along to a familiar tune. Music and poetry have a way of speaking to our souls when other forms of literature fall short.

We can think of the Bible's psalms in the same way. These are the songs of faith that fed God's people for generations and continue to do so today. These psalms, these hymns, sustained God's people even as they experienced the alienation and disorientation of exile and diaspora. These songs of faith are the lifeblood of the people of God, and their rhythms remind them of God's promises and presence even when circumstances become bleak.

When words fail, O God, put a song in my heart that reminds me of your faithfulness and presence. Amen.

WEDNESDAY, DECEMBER 16 ~ *Read Psalm 89:1-4, 19-26*

The figure of the "chosen one" or the one who is "anointed" is the subject of this psalm. Here these terms explicitly refer to King David, widely remembered throughout scripture as the ideal king of Israel who ruled during the height of the nation's glory days. The Hebrew word that means *anointed one* is often rendered in English as *messiah*. A messiah is someone chosen by God and appointed for a special divine purpose, and this special appointment would have been marked by a ceremony in which a prophet or other religious leader poured oil on the head of the chosen one. In the Hebrew Bible, the term *messiah* often refers to kings, most commonly King David. After the end of David's and then Solomon's reign, when the kingdom splits apart in the context of exile (when this psalm was likely finalized), the people turn their hopes for a messiah toward the future: Surely God would raise someone up from King David's line to rescue them from the rising and falling empires at whose mercy they have found themselves.

In Christian interpretation, these ancient hopes for a messiah, recorded in the sacred texts we share with the Jewish community, are understood to be fulfilled in the person of Jesus, known as the Christ—from the Greek translation of the Hebrew word *messiah* (*christos*). Later in the week, notice the similarities between the hope and longing you hear in this psalm and the hope and longing in Mary's song in the Gospel of Luke. God's people, whether Jewish or Christian, have always trusted in God to save them. Our understanding of what we need saving from might shift, but the Bible promises that God is faithful and that God's saving presence is with God's people no matter what.

Thank you, God, for your saving love that is steadfast throughout the generations. Amen.

THURSDAY, DECEMBER 17 ~ *Read Luke 1:26-38*

In response to Gabriel, Mary says, "Here am I." This simple phrase calls to mind the many times in the Hebrew scriptures when God calls someone to a special act of faithfulness and obedience.

In Genesis 22, God says, "Abraham!" And Abraham says, "Here I am," just before God asks for the unthinkable: that he sacrifice his son—a son of divine promise and of anxious longing. Before the act can be completed, God's messenger stops the patriarch mid-knife-swing, calling out again, "Abraham! Abraham!" And Abraham says, "Here I am," ever ready to obey.

In Exodus 3, God beckons from the burning bush: "Moses! Moses!" And Moses says, "Here I am," then proceeds to (reluctantly) accept the honor and burden of leading God's people out of bondage.

In 1 Samuel 3, God's call shatters the silence of the night: "Samuel! Samuel!" In a voice gravelly with sleep, the boy Samuel, who will become the prophet Samuel and anoint God's chosen ones, replies, "Here I am"—and, after a few comedically confusing moments, finally realizes it is God calling, not the priest.

In each of these stories, the Hebrew most simply means what our English translations say: "Here I am." But underneath this phrase is boldness—"Look! I'm here!" It signifies readiness to answer the call.

Mary surely knows these stories—they are some of the central pillars of her faith. Perhaps recalling these scenes of God's faithfulness buoys Mary's own faith and gives her the courage to respond in obedience. The God who was faithful to her ancestors will surely not fail her as she takes on the enormous responsibility of bearing God into the world.

God who has been faithful in the past, give us the courage to say yes to your call. Amen.

FRIDAY, DECEMBER 18 ~ *Read Luke 1:46b-55*

This passage is known as the Magnificat, from the Latin translation of the first line, "My soul magnifies the Lord" *(Magnificat anima mea Dominum)*. Mary launches into this song of praise while visiting her cousin Elizabeth, who is also experiencing a miraculous and auspicious pregnancy: She will become the mother of John the Baptist, who will pave the way for Jesus' ministry.

The Magnificat echoes songs by other women in scripture, most notably that of Hannah (see 1 Sam. 2), the mother of the prophet Samuel. Both Hannah and Mary, whose stories are centuries apart in the biblical canon, experience miraculous pregnancies, and both know that their sons will be dedicated to God and used for extraordinary purposes. Both mothers sing of God's reversal of the typical patterns of the world, praising God for elevating the poor and oppressed, humbling the proud and powerful, filling the hungry, and sending the rich away empty-handed. In a prophetic register, they both sing of God's coming salvation and deliverance.

I wonder if Hannah's song was on Mary's mind in this moment as she celebrated with her cousin. Like Hannah, Elizabeth was very old; both women longed and prayed for children long past the point in their lives when it should have been a biological impossibility. And like Hannah's son Samuel, Elizabeth's son John would be a prophet. What a comfort it must be to these two first-century Jewish women, Mary and Elizabeth, to recall the stories of their foremothers in the faith like Hannah, whose prayers God answered and whose faithfulness makes possible the salvation of God's people.

Holy One, when we struggle to remember that nothing is impossible for you, help us recall the times in the past when we have seen your faithfulness. Like Mary, Hannah, and Elizabeth, may we rejoice in your salvation. Amen.

SATURDAY, DECEMBER 19 ~ *Read Luke 1:46b-55*

The Magnificat, with its ebullient praise of a God who humbles the proud and privileged, has occasionally been viewed as so revolutionary that public readings of this song have been banned by governments at various points in the church's history! Mary's song foreshadows Jesus' teaching later in the Gospel of Luke, when he blesses the hungry and poor and declares woe to the rich and well-fed (Luke 6). It makes sense that these messages of divine reversal of human power might make some uncomfortable, while being supremely comforting to others. How did Jesus' relationship with his mother inform his ministry? Was her voice in his mind as he preached that sermon?

We know that Jesus accompanies his parents to the Temple in Jerusalem as a preteen and participates in the communal process of learning about and interpreting scripture (Luke 2:41-51). The text tells us that the people who hear him regard him as unusually wise, curious, and reflective. Jesus knows the scriptures well. Did he first hear the stories of his faith at his mother's knee? As bedtime stories? Is Mary the one who first told him of the unlikely heroes of the Bible like Hagar and Hannah, Shiphrah and Puah, Esther and Ruth? Was it Mary who first introduced him to the central themes of the Torah, like God's special concern for the poor, the widow, the orphan, and the stranger (e.g., Exod. 22:21-22; Deut. 10:17-18; Deut. 24:17-22)?

Regardless of who was primarily in charge of Jesus' early childhood education, the same Spirit who inspires Mary's prophetic song also inspires Jesus' teaching. In continuity with God's actions on behalf of the oppressed in the Hebrew Bible, both speak about God's nearness to and presence with those who have been rejected or overlooked.

You are the God who sees those who are overlooked and cares for those who have been abandoned. Attune our hearts to the people in our lives in deepest need of your special care. Amen.

SUNDAY, DECEMBER 20 ~ *Read Romans 16:25-27*

Fourth Sunday of Advent

In the epistles of the New Testament, the message of God's liberation and salvation extends further and further, as Paul and other early Christian missionaries take the gospel to new places. What began as a story centered on God's special care and love for the Hebrew people now opens up to reveal more of God's enduring, steadfast love for everyone, including (as Paul says here) Gentiles, or non-Jewish people.

Paul emphasizes the continuity between God's actions in the past—told in the scriptures Paul had that we know as the Hebrew Bible—and God's actions in the present and future, what God has now done through Jesus and through the early days of the church. The "mystery" of God's salvation has now been revealed in the person of Jesus, and everyone, regardless of their background, can receive it. Far from proclaiming that Jesus' advent supplants God's previous activity, Paul declares that Jesus fulfills it. Everything that came before was vital to God's plan.

These verses are the closing exhortation of Paul's letter to the church in Rome, a church threatened both from the outside and from within. Some of the members of the Roman church come from Jewish backgrounds while others have Greek or other gentile roots, so disagreements over how best to be faithful are common. In reminding his audience of God's faithfulness to both the Jewish people and to those encountering Christ outside of that history, Paul is encouraging the church toward unity. In response to God's faithfulness, all God asks is for faithfulness in return. All are now a part of the story of God's people.

God, we praise you for Jesus, Immanuel, God-with-us. As we celebrate Christ's coming during Advent, help us recall the ways you have always been present with your people. Amen.

Joy to the World!

DECEMBER 21–27, 2026 • PURITY MALINGA

SCRIPTURE OVERVIEW: The scripture readings this week have a common theme of praises for God. Isaiah praises God for what God has done, especially cleansing and clothing with righteousness. The psalmist calls all creation to praise the Lord. According to Luke, the song of the heavenly host, "Glory to God in the highest," was audible to the shepherds at the birth of the promised child. It continues to be heard whenever the world celebrates Christmas—"the Lord is come!" The long years of waiting come to a joyful song of praise for Simeon and Anna as they behold the baby Jesus in their arms. Writing to the Galatian church, Paul clarifies how God unifies humanity in Christ. In Christ God has redeemed all humanity (Jews and Gentiles) so all who believe are God's children and therefore heirs with Christ.

QUESTIONS AND SUGGESTIONS FOR REFLECTION

- Read Psalm 148. For what are you praising God in your life this year? Write a list and keep it visible throughout your days.
- Read Isaiah 9:2-7. Where in your life do you need a Counselor? How can Christ be that counselor for you?
- Read Galatians 4:4-7. How does or should the knowledge of your oneness with all believers and with Christ influence your everyday life?
- Read Luke 2:22-40. Human life consists of acceptance and rejection. As a follower of Christ how do you deal with rejection in your life?

Bishop Purity Malinga is the former presiding bishop of The Methodist Church of Southern Africa (MCSA) and the first woman be elected in that role. She is a woman of prayer and a mentor to many.

MONDAY, DECEMBER 21 ~ *Read Isaiah 61:10–62:3*

The joy of Christmas for me as a child growing up in the rural village of Ixopo in South Africa started on the 21st of December each year. That was the date on which my father arrived home from the city of Pietermaritzburg where he worked. Without fail, he brought me a new dress—a Christmas dress! My mother would help me fit it, and, with a smile from ear to ear, I would go show my father how good I looked! It was tradition in my village for everyone, especially children, to wear new clothes on Christmas day. So, with my new dress fitted and nicely put away in my mother's wardrobe, I would joyously look forward to Christmas day.

In this song of praise, Isaiah is proclaiming a new day for God's people. Their transgressions of the past that had led them to exile will be forgotten. On this new day there will be rejoicing and praising of God, who will clothe the people with "garments of salvation" and "a robe of his righteousness."

It was as a grown-up believer that I came to understand that the Christmas dresses of my childhood had a spiritual and theological meaning. They symbolized the newness that Christmas brings. In and through the Jesus of Christmas, God offered the world salvation from sin and the ability to be righteous. God clothed us with the ability to be Christlike.

In these few days before Christmas, let us take time to focus our thoughts and actions on becoming more like Christ. Throughout the year we may have experienced things, people, or events that estranged us from God or from one another. Let us ask ourselves what habits, attitudes, and relationships of ours have been stained by sin and need to be renewed for us to be more like Christ?

Loving God, remind me of the spiritual meaning of this season of joy. I pray that my life reflects the newness and the righteousness gifted to me through your son Jesus Christ. Amen.

I think I was eight or nine years old when my grandfather told my cousin and me that on Christmas morning all plants and animals sing, worship, and talk with God. He told us a story of a boy who was asked to look after the farm animals on his family's farm. The boy hated all animals, so he abused them, not giving them food and water or caring for them when his father was not around. One Christmas morning the farm animals sang and worshiped God and then reported the bad treatment they received from the boy. God and the animals agreed on the punishment for the boy. Every Christmas day the boy would be struck by a stomachache so he would not be able to enjoy Christmas food until he stopped abusing animals.

I still remember the two Christmas mornings my cousin and I woke up before sunrise and went to the cattle kraal trying to listen in on the conversation between my grandfather's cattle and God—to no avail. The story however, influenced how we cared for animals and all of creation.

In Psalm 148, the psalmist is praising God and calling all of creation—the heavens and the earth, all nations of the world—to sing and praise the Lord. Psalms like this are appropriate reminders that God's salvation is for all creation, not just humankind. Our praises, joy, and celebration of Christ must extend to how we relate to all created order. Protection, care, and harmonious living with all creation is a gospel imperative for those who believe in Jesus Christ. Care for the environment is becoming more urgent everyday as we experience the world-wide devastating effects of global warming. In the words of St Paul, "The creation waits in eager expectation for the children of God to be revealed" (Rom. 8:19).

Creator God, your love for all that you have made is beyond our imagination. Increase in all your children love and care for all that you have made. Amen.

WEDNESDAY, DECEMBER 23 ~ *Read Galatians 4:4-7*

One morning I was flying from Johannesburg to Cape Town. It is a two hour flight, and I got a window seat, 20A, in the economy class. I had just settled and fastened the seat belt when the flight attendant called my name and asked me to come to the front. Noticing my worried look when I got to her she said, "Relax lady, you are special, your ticket has been upgraded to business class. Your seat is now 4A." It was the first and only time I've traveled business class! I had a big, comfortable seat, more than enough legroom, a special menu, and special treatment. I felt special indeed!

The systems of the world classify, label, and grade people: the "haves" and "have-nots," upper class and lower class, the firsts and the lasts. In the Galatians' context people were divided into male or female, Jew or Gentile, and slaves or free. Paul therefore uses slavery as an illustration to explain what God has done in Jesus Christ. "When time had fully come," God upgraded all humankind, irrespective of their former grade, into the same class—the best class—God's children and heirs.

In this week of Christmas, we praise God for the gift of Jesus. We are all made special, not because of anything we have done, but by the grace of God through Christ. What a gift!

Many experiences in life try to degrade and enslave us. Let us remind one another of our value as God's children. Let us not allow life's situations take away our faith in Jesus Christ. As we continue to offer prayers for ourselves and for others, let us go boldly into God's presence, knowing that God cares about us and will respond.

Loving God, you are worthy to be praised. Through your Holy Spirit, keep reminding me of my worth. When I seek to divide, may the Holy Spirit draw me nearer to you. Amen.

THURSDAY, DECEMBER 24 ~ *Read Isaiah 9:2-7*

CHRISTMAS EVE

It was in the midst of the darkness of sin and disobedience of ancient Israel that God, through the prophet Isaiah, promised to send a child who would be "the light" and who would "enlarge the nation of God and increase their joy."

Today is Christmas Eve, a day of finalizing the preparations for Christmas. All over the world, people are traveling and arriving at family homes to be with loved ones, making last minute shopping trips and wrapping gifts. It is the last day of waiting, and there is excitement in the air. On this day, we Christians gather to rejoice, sing, and praise God as we remember that silent and holy night when the promise of God was fulfilled. We have become part of God's family and God has increased our joy. "For a child has been born for us."

The birth of a child in a family brings joy and celebration. Friends and family members come bringing gifts to the parents to express their good wishes and joy. However, it is different with the birth of Jesus. It is Jesus who gives gifts to those whose hearts are open to him. He gifts light to those in darkness, advice to those facing contradictions of life, peace to those in conflict—and much more according to people's needs. Take time and reflect on what gift you need and expect from Jesus this Christmas.

Gracious Jesus, Light of the World, come into my heart anew. Let me praise and worship you wholeheartedly as I celebrate your self-sacrificing love for me. Amen.

FRIDAY, DECEMBER 25 ~ *Read Luke 2:1-20*

Christmas Day

I assume Mary and Joseph had prepared for the birth of their baby as all parents do. They kind of had an idea of the time it would happen and perhaps thought they would go to Bethlehem and come back home before the birth. God, however, had a time and place. God's Son arrives in a way like no other.

As Luke reports, Jesus' birth is revealed not to the rulers and the powerful of the land but to the lowly shepherds who were watching their flock. From birth, Jesus turned the world upside down! From birth, he identified with those on the periphery of society and brought them to the center. The shepherds find themselves in the front seats of the heavenly concert, listening to the heavenly song of praise. Having gone to see the baby, the shepherds join the heavens in glorifying and praising God.

Christmas day is and must remain not just a holiday but a "holy" day—a sacred day of glorifying God. We rejoice at God's intervention in human history to save the world from itself. We rejoice because God is with us—Immanuel!

The joy of Christmas calls us to spread the good news of Christ as the shepherds did. To the broken world where there are all kinds of pain, suffering, poverty, inequalities, injustices, hatred, violence, and wars, we are called to spread the love and light of Christ. Today, may we be moved by the Savior born to us and touch our families and communities with love. May we be spiritually re-charged today, to share the hope, peace, love, and joy God has given us in Christ! May the newborn King reign in our hearts forever!

Thank you, Jesus, for bringing light and love to the world. Fill my heart with joy and zeal to live a life that shines your light, as long as I live. Help me to rely on you as my Savior and my guide. Amen.

SATURDAY, DECEMBER 26 ~ *Read Titus 2:11-14*

The day after Christmas can be a stark contrast to what has come before. Many people are back at work, and the shops are open for people to return or exchange some of the stuff they had bought or received as gifts. The significance of Christmas and of the gifts exchanged fades very quickly as the world returns to normal.

In this passage Paul provides Titus and us with the theology of Christmas. Christmas is about what God did in the past, what God is doing in the present, and what God will do in the future. The grace of God here is the person Jesus Christ who appeared in the world and made the unconditional love of God visible in himself. Christmas is also about Jesus who is present and at work through the Holy Spirit teaching believers to live upright and godly lives. Finally, Christmas reminds us that the Jesus who has appeared will come again, and so we celebrate in anticipation of the complete redemption and restoration of creation that he will bring.

How wonderful to be reminded that we are not going through life alone! As we face the challenges of life, Jesus through the Holy Spirit is with us, enabling and empowering us to live Christ-filled lives, as he promised his first disciples: "Remain in me and I will remain in you" (John 15:4). As we await in hope for Christ's second coming, let us continue to represent him in the world by living Christlike lives, Christmas day and every day after.

Remain with me, Holy Spirit. Keep whispering "No" to me when the ways of the world seem easier for me to follow. Amen.

SUNDAY, DECEMBER 27 ~ *Read Luke 2:22-40*

It is the second time the baby Jesus is revealed as the Messiah. He was first revealed to the shepherds and now is revealed to two elderly people at the Temple, where he has been brought to be consecrated. Simeon and Anna have both had been frequenting the Temple, waiting and praying for the promised Messiah. Seeing the Messiah had become Simeon's reason for living. Finally, it happened! As he took baby Jesus in his arms, he broke into song: "Sovereign Lord . . . you may now dismiss your servant in peace. For my eyes have seen your salvation" (NIV).

As Simeon continues to sing, the Spirit reveals to him that the salvation the Messiah brings is not just for Israel, it is for "all peoples." He goes on to proclaim the truth of the paradoxical effect of Jesus on humankind. Some will fall because of him while others will rise. There is no neutral ground about Jesus—we either joyfully accept him or reject him. Anna joins in the song and thanks God, but she does more than that. She speaks about the child to others who were looking forward to the coming of the Messiah! The 84-year-old Anna was one of the first to share the good news of Jesus Christ.

Jesus, the Savior, embraces those that society rejects. In a world that undermines and rejects the elderly, we learn in this story that people are never too old for the promises of God to be fulfilled through them and in their lives. From their experiences of long lives with God flows inspired wisdom. May we embrace the Simeons and Annas in our families and communities. God can and does give messages and prophecies for our times through them. Proclaiming God's light and love has no age limit—it just requires closeness to God.

Merciful and all-embracing God, we thank you for the elderly among us. As I grow old, help me never to leave your Temple. May I never tire of sharing your love and light with those who care to listen. Amen.

A New Heaven and a New Earth

DECEMBER 28–31, 2026 • TEX SAMPLE

SCRIPTURE OVERVIEW: The year ends as it began, with celebrations of God's faithfulness. Although Jeremiah lives in a difficult period for the Israelites, God gives him a vision of a time when the Lord will gather together all those who are scattered and restore their fortunes in Zion, the city of God. The psalmist praises God for protecting the Israelites and being faithful to the promises made to their ancestors. In Ephesians, we read of the blessings that God set aside for us even before the world existed, and we are recipients of those blessings because of the work of Christ. We finish the year by revisiting the opening of John's Gospel. The Word was with God and the Word was God, and in Jesus the Word became flesh and lived among us. Glory to God!

QUESTIONS AND SUGGESTIONS FOR REFLECTION

- Read Jeremiah 31:7-14. When have you failed to comfort or be comforted by someone? How have you recognized who might be able to provide true comfort?
- Read Psalm 147:12-20. How have God's gifts helped you to understand who God is and who you are?
- Read Ephesians 1:3-14. How have you experienced the spirit of adoption into God's family? How has this experience shaped your notions of earthly adoption?
- Read John 1:1-18. When has scripture become intensely personal for you? How might you see the face of Jesus in every child?

Tex Sample is the Robert B. and Kathleen Rogers Professor Emeritus of Church and Society at the Saint Paul School of Theology. An ordained elder in The United Methodist Church, he and his wife, Peggy, are active at Platte Woods UMC.

MONDAY, DECEMBER 28 ~ *Read John 1:1-18*

Two things strike me about the opening verses of John's Gospel. First, "the Word became flesh." We can think of God's Word as God's action and as God's disclosure or revelation. Through this act, God became human (flesh), embodied in Jesus. But not only that, God discloses or reveals the Divine Reality in Jesus. This means that God's very character is made manifest in Jesus—we know what God is like when we encounter the teaching, the life, the death, and the resurrection of Christ.

Second, the text says that the Word "lived among us." The Greek word here translated *lived* is *skeenoo*, which can be literally translated as "pitched tent." This, of course, takes us back to the rich notions of the way that God tabernacled with the people of Israel in their liberation from Egypt. Jesus took up residence in the ordinary lives of the people of his time, and Christ continues to "pitch tent" with us through the Holy Spirit.

This means that those of us in rural or urban settings can trust that God lives among us, works in the daily practices of our lives, and takes on the community practices of our worlds.

As a result of this, God's Word offers an alternative way of being in our world. Christ moves in oral and literate and digital cultures, in working class and corporate sectors, and especially among the dispossessed, the dominated, and the exploited to transform and complete this world.

There are no flyover places, there are no hell holes that Christ has not entered. He pitches tent in the locales of this world to live, to teach, to be crucified, and to be raised.

Dear God, grant us the sensibilities to see the work of Christ in the places of our lives and to live unafraid with courage and faithfulness. Amen.

TUESDAY, DECEMBER 29 ~ *Read Ephesians 1:3-14*

My first crisis of faith came at a very young age following the sudden tragic death of a friend. At age seven, C. L. was thrown from a pony that had been a birthday present from his parents. Only the day before we had had a childhood tiff, arguing over how to play pretend with one another, and I had gone home mad.

Growing up I endured a lot of individualistic revivalism in which I was told that if I would believe in Christ, make a decision for him, and live in faith, that I would be saved. While I didn't have the words or the thoughts to confront that prominent view, I just felt it did not address C. L.'s tragic and untimely death.

Years later, I read Ephesians 1:10, where the writer says that in "the fullness of time" God will "gather up all things in him, things in heaven and things on earth." Theologically speaking, Ephesians doesn't explain or describe this coming consummation, but rather makes this extraordinary proclamation about the God who is working throughout the cosmos, a multiverse, as we now understand it, that is much larger than the writer of these verses could have dreamed or we ourselves can imagine.

As a baseball nut, I once heard someone interpret this passage in language I understood—"God bats last," they said. Only later would I hear the life-giving clarification of that saying I so needed: "And it's a walk-off home run." The destiny of the world is not death; in God all things will be gathered up and completed, my friend C. L. included.

O God, grant us such a vision of the completion of this creation that we may live lives that embody your Word. Amen.

WEDNESDAY, DECEMBER 30 ~ *Read Revelation 21:1-6a*

How in the world can we think about a new heaven and a new earth? It is, I believe, beyond all our thought and conceptualization. So we can only think in terms of metaphors, analogies, poetic reach, and a faithful but limited imagination.

When we have a new heaven and a new earth, I can imagine that the bite of a mosquito becomes a fugue; that the touch of a butterfly is a rhapsody; that rattlesnakes and children play together; that trees clap their hands; that mountains break forth in exaltation; that the sun and moon and stars take on a symphonic magnitude; that every finite thing participates in the infinite magnitude of God's grace and mercy, where justice and righteousness and peace know no limits and where the beauty of the divine vision is unbroken on earth and in heaven, where they have become one.

I can imagine the ages of the universe and the history of all its creatures now gathered in the fullness of God. There they are transformed and transubstantiated into that shalom of completion, where the evil and violations of the past have now been suffered by God's crucified love into their essential and intended reconciliation and goodness.

Surely too the human generations in their personal and corporate existence will have been resurrected into immortal bodies, where all will be the progeny of God, the kinship that overrides alienation, estrangement, exploitation, domination, inequity, injustice, self loss, and war. And where, in that heavenly city of Jerusalem, God's dwelling is with us, where weeping, mourning, crying, pain, and death will be no more. In this eternal consummation, all things will be made new from their creation to their final destiny.

O God, may we be faithful participants in the great journey of creation and alive to your leading in the ordinary places of our lives. Amen.

THURSDAY, DECEMBER 31 ~ *Read John 1:1-18*

In John's Gospel, God loves the world, but in that Gospel the world is hardly lovable. It's a place of darkness, bondage, illusion, and death. These characterizations are expressed throughout the Gospel.

Our text for today teaches us that Christ is the true light of the world; otherwise we walk in darkness. Indeed, it is Christ that breaks the captivity, exposes the falsifications, and conquers the mortality of this world. He not only brings light but is the truth that sets us free and counters death with eternal life. So when we hear that Christ is the light of the world, we see him offering freedom, truth, and life, which means we can envision Christ as the light of the world in terms of the eternal life he brings. These opening verses of John contrast those who recognize the Christ and those who choose not to. For those who do, this "Word" creates a new relationship with God, wherein those who acknowledge the Christ are able to know God in a completely new way through the person of Jesus. This Christ offers us light, the light of all people that brings life.

Remember too that the first thing God does in creating the world is to declare, "Let there be light" (Gen. 1:3). In the new heaven and new earth of Revelation, God will be the light of God's servants (21:23).

So God's light is central to the creation and to its completion, and Christ is the light of that world. That illumination not only counters this world's darkness but provides its inexhaustible, eternal radiance in that new heaven and new earth to come.

Dear God, bless us with the light of Christ that we may participate in his glory and live truthful, emancipated, eternal lives. Amen.

The Revised Common Lectionary* for 2026 Year A—Advent / Christmas Year B *(Disciplines Edition)*

January 1–4
SECOND SUNDAY AFTER CHRISTMAS
Jeremiah 31:7-14
Psalm 147:12-20
Ephesians 1:3-14
John 1:1-18

January 1
NEW YEAR'S DAY
Ecclesiastes 3:1-13
Psalm 8
Revelation 21:1-6a
Matthew 25:31-46

January 5–11
BAPTISM OF THE LORD
Isaiah 42:1-9
Psalm 29
Acts 10:34-43
Matthew 3:13-17

January 6
EPIPHANY
Isaiah 60:1-6
Psalm 72:1-7, 10-14
Ephesians 3:1-12
Matthew 2:1-12

January 12–18
Isaiah 49:1-7
Psalm 40:1-11
2 Corinthians 1:1-9
John 1:29-42

January 19–25
Isaiah 9:1-4
Psalm 27:1, 4-9
1 Corinthians 1:10-18
Matthew 4:12-23

January 26–February 1
Micah 6:1-8
Psalm 15
1 Corinthians 1:18-31
Matthew 5:1-12

February 2-8
Isaiah 58:1-12
Psalm 112:1-10
1 Corinthians 2:1-16
Matthew 5:13-20

February 9–15
THE TRANSFIGURATION
Exodus 24:12-18
Psalm 2
2 Peter 1:16-21
Matthew 17:1-9

February 16–22
First Sunday in Lent
Genesis 2:15-17; 3:1-7
Psalm 32
Romans 5:12-19
Matthew 4:1-11

February 18
Ash Wednesday
Joel 2:1-2, 12-17
Psalm 51:1-17
2 Corinthians 5:20b–6:10
Matthew 6:1-6, 16-21

February 23–March 1
Second Sunday in Lent
Genesis 12:1-4a
Psalm 121
Romans 4:1-5, 13-17
John 3:1-17

March 2–8
Third Sunday in Lent
Exodus 17:1-7
Psalm 95
Romans 5:1-11
John 4:5-42

March 9–15
Fourth Sunday in Lent
1 Samuel 16:1-13
Psalm 23
Ephesians 5:8-14
John 9:1-41

March 16–22
Fifth Sunday in Lent
Ezekiel 37:1-14
Psalm 130
Romans 8:6-11
John 11:1-45

March 23–29
Palm/Passion Sunday

Liturgy of the Palms
Psalm 118:1-2, 19-29
Matthew 21:1-11

Liturgy of the Passion
Isaiah 50:4-9a
Psalm 31:9-16
Philippians 2:5-11
Matthew 26:14–27:66

March 30–April 5
Holy Week

Monday, March 30
Isaiah 42:1-9
Psalm 36:5-11
Hebrews 9:11-15
John 12:1-11

Tuesday, March 31
Isaiah 49:1-7
Psalm 71:1-14
1 Corinthians 1:18-31
John 12:20-36

Wednesday, April 1
Isaiah 50:4-9a
Psalm 70
Hebrews 12:1-3
John 13:21-32

Maundy Thursday, April 2
Exodus 12:1-14
Psalm 116:1-2, 12-19
1 Corinthians 11:23-26
John 13:1-17, 31b-35

Good Friday, April 3
Isaiah 52:13–53:12
Psalm 22
Hebrews 10:16-25
John 18:1–19:42

Holy Saturday, April 4
Job 14:1-14
Psalm 31:1-4, 15-16
1 Peter 4:1-8
Matthew 27:57-66

Easter Day, April 5
Acts 10:34-43
Psalm 118:1-2, 14-24
Colossians 3:1-4
John 20:1-18

April 6–12
Acts 2:14a, 22-32
Psalm 16
1 Peter 1:3-9
John 20:19-31

April 13–19
Acts 2:14a, 36-41
Psalm 116:1-4, 12-19
1 Peter 1:17-23
Luke 24:13-35

April 20–26
Acts 2:42-47
Psalm 23
1 Peter 2:19-25
John 10:1-10

April 27–May 3
Acts 7:55-60
Psalm 31:1-5, 15-16
1 Peter 2:2-10
John 14:1-14

May 4–10
Acts 17:22-31
Psalm 66:8-20
1 Peter 3:13-22
John 14:15-21

May 11–17
Acts 1:6-14
Psalm 68:1-10, 32-35
1 Peter 4:12-14; 5:6-11
John 17:1-11

May 14
ASCENSION DAY
(may be used on May 21)
Acts 1:1-11
Psalm 47
Ephesians 1:15-23
Luke 24:44-53

May 18–24
PENTECOST
Acts 2:1-21
Psalm 104:24-34, 35b
1 Corinthians 12:3b-13
John 7:37-39

May 25–31
TRINITY SUNDAY
Genesis 1:1–2:4a
Psalm 8
2 Corinthians 13:11-13
Matthew 28:16-20

June 1–7
Genesis 12:1-9
Psalm 33:1-12
Romans 4:13-25
Matthew 9:9-13, 18-26

June 8–14
Genesis 18:1-15; 21:1-7
Psalm 116:1-2, 12-19
Romans 5:1-8
Matthew 9:35–10:23

June 15–21
Genesis 21:8-21
Psalm 86:1-10, 16-17
Romans 6:1b-11
Matthew 10:24-39

June 22–28
Genesis 22:1-14
Psalm 13
Romans 6:12-23
Matthew 10:40-42

June 29–July 5
Genesis 24:34-38, 42-49, 58-67
Psalm 45:10-17
Romans 7:15-25a
Matthew 11:16-19, 25-30

July 6–12
Genesis 25:19-34
Psalm 119:105-112
Romans 8:1-11
Matthew 13:1-9, 18-23

July 13–19
Genesis 28:10-19a
Psalm 139:1-12, 23-24
Romans 8:12-25
Matthew 13:24-30, 36-43

July 20–26
Genesis 29:15-28
Psalm 105:1-11, 45b
Romans 8:26-39
Matthew 13:31-33, 44-52

July 27–August 2
Genesis 32:22-31
Psalm 17:1-7, 15
Romans 9:1-5
Matthew 14:13-21

August 3–9
Genesis 37:1-4, 12-28
Psalm 105:1-6, 16-22, 45b
Romans 10:5-15
Matthew 14:22-33

August 10–16
Genesis 45:1-15
Psalm 133
Romans 11:1-2a, 29-32
Matthew 15:10-28

August 17–23
Exodus 1:8–2:10
Psalm 124
Romans 12:1-8
Matthew 16:13-20

August 24–30
Exodus 3:1-15
Psalm 105:1-6, 23-26, 45b
Romans 12:9-21
Matthew 16:21-28

August 31–September 6
Exodus 12:1-14
Psalm 149
Romans 13:8-14
Matthew 18:15-20

September 7–13
Exodus 14:19-31
Psalm 114
Romans 14:1-12
Matthew 18:21-35

September 14–20
Exodus 16:2-15
Psalm 105:1-6, 37-45
Philippians 1:21-30
Matthew 20:1-16

September 21–27
Exodus 17:1-7
Psalm 78:1-4, 12-16
Philippians 2:1-13
Matthew 21:23-32

September 28–October 4
Exodus 20:1-4, 7-9, 12-20
Psalm 19
Philippians 3:4b-14
Matthew 21:33-46

October 5–11
Exodus 32:1-14
Psalm 106:1-6, 19-23
Philippians 4:1-9
Matthew 22:1-14

October 12–18
Exodus 33:12-23
Psalm 99
1 Thessalonians 1:1-10
Matthew 22:15-22

October 12
THANKSGIVING DAY, CANADA
Deuteronomy 8:7-18
Psalm 65
2 Corinthians 9:6-15
Luke 17:11-19

October 19–25
Deuteronomy 34:1-12
Psalm 90:1-6, 13-17
1 Thessalonians 2:1-8
Matthew 22:34-46

October 26–November 1
Joshua 3:7-17
Psalm 107:1-7, 33-37
1 Thessalonians 2:9-13
Matthew 23:1-12

November 1
ALL SAINTS DAY
(may be used on November 5)
Revelation 7:9-17
Psalm 34:1-10, 22
1 John 3:1-3
Matthew 5:1-12

November 2–8
Joshua 24:1-3a, 14-25
Psalm 78:1-7
1 Thessalonians 4:13-18
Matthew 25:1-13

November 9–15
Judges 4:1-7
Psalm 123
1 Thessalonians 5:1-11
Matthew 25:14-30

November 16–22
Ezekiel 34:11-16, 20-24
Psalm 100
Ephesians 1:15-23
Matthew 25:31-46

November 23–29
First Sunday of Advent
Isaiah 64:1-9
Psalm 80:1-7, 17-19
1 Corinthians 1:3-9
Mark 13:24-37

November 26
Thanksgiving Day, USA
Deuteronomy 8:7-18
Psalm 65
2 Corinthians 9:6-15
Luke 17:11-19

November 30–December 6
Second Sunday of Advent
Isaiah 40:1-11
Psalm 85:1-2, 8-13
2 Peter 3:8-15a
Mark 1:1-8

December 7–13
Third Sunday of Advent
Isaiah 61:1-4, 8-11
Psalm 126
1 Thessalonians 5:16-24
John 1:6-8, 19-28

December 14–20
Fourth Sunday of Advent
2 Samuel 7:1-11, 16
Luke 1:46b-55
Romans 16:25-27
Luke 1:26-38

December 21–27
First Sunday after Christmas
Isaiah 61:10–62:3
Psalm 148
Galatians 4:4-7
Luke 2:22-40

December 24
Christmas Eve
Isaiah 9:2-7
Psalm 96
Titus 2:11-14
Luke 2:1-14

December 25
Christmas Day
Isaiah 52:7-10
Psalm 98
Hebrews 1:1-12
John 1:1-14

December 21–27
First Sunday after Christmas
Jeremiah 31:77-14
Psalm 147:12-20
Ephesians 1:3-14
John 1:1-18

December 28-31
Second Sunday after Christmas
Jeremiah 31:7-14
Psalm 147:12-20
Ephesians 1:3-14
John 1:1-18

A Guide to Daily Prayer

These prayers imply worship time with a group; feel free to adapt the plural pronouns for personal use.

Morning Prayer

O Lord, in the morning you hear my voice;
  in the morning I plead my case to you and watch.
—Psalm 5:3

Gathering and Silence

Call to Praise and Prayer

God said, "Let there be light," and there was light.
And God saw that the light was good.

Psalm 63:1-5

God, you are my God; I seek you;
  my soul thirsts for you;
my flesh faints for you,
  as in a dry and weary land
  where there is no water.
So I have looked upon you in the sanctuary,
  beholding your power and glory.
Because your steadfast love is better than life,
  my lips will praise you.
So I will bless you as long as I live;
  I will lift up my hands and call on your name.
My soul is satisfied as with a rich feast,
  and my mouth praises you with joyful lips.

Prayer of Thanksgiving

We praise you with joy, loving God, for your grace is better than life itself. You have sustained us through the darkness: and you bless us with life in this new day. In the shadow of your wings, we sing for joy and bless your holy name. Amen.

Scripture Reading

Silence

Prayers of the People

The Lord's Prayer (ecumenical text)

Our Father in heaven,
    hallowed be your name,
    your kingdom come,
    your will be done,
    on earth as in heaven.
Give us today our daily bread.
Forgive us our sins as we forgive
    those who sin against us.
Save us from the time of trial,
    and deliver us from evil.
For the kingdom, the power, and the glory
    are yours, now and forever. Amen.

Blessing

May the light of your mercy shine brightly on all who walk in your presence today, O Lord.

Midday Prayer

I will bless the Lord at all times;
[God's] praise shall continually be in my mouth.
—Psalm 34:1

Gathering and Silence

Call to Praise and Prayer

O Lord, my Savior, teach me your ways.
My hope is in you all day long.

Prayer of Thanksgiving

God of mercy, we acknowledge this midday pause of refreshment as one of your many generous gifts. Look kindly upon our work this day; may it be made perfect in your time. May our purpose and prayers be pleasing to you. This we ask through Christ our Lord. Amen.

Scripture Reading

Silence

Prayers of the People

The Lord's Prayer (ecumenical text)

Our Father in heaven,
hallowed be your name,
your kingdom come,
your will be done,
on earth as in heaven.
Give us today our daily bread.

Forgive us our sins as we forgive
those who sin against us.
Save us from the time of trial,
and deliver us from evil.
For the kingdom, the power, and the glory
are yours, now and forever. Amen.

Blessing

Strong is the love embracing us,
faithful the Lord from morning to night.

Evening Prayer

For God alone my soul waits in silence;
from [God] comes my salvation.
—Psalm 62:1

Gathering and Silence

Call to Praise and Prayer

From the rising of the sun to its setting,
let the name of the Lord be praised.

Psalm 134

Come, bless the Lord, all you servants of the Lord,
who stand by night in the house of the Lord!
Lift up your hands to the holy place,
and bless the Lord.
May the Lord, maker of heaven and earth,
bless you from Zion.

Prayer of Thanksgiving

Sovereign God, you have been our help during the day and you promise to be with us at night. Receive this prayer as a sign of our trust in you. Save us from all evil, keep us from all harm, and guide us in your way. We belong to you, Lord. Protect us by the power of your name. In Jesus Christ we pray. Amen.

Scripture Reading

Silence

Prayers of the People

The Lord's Prayer (ecumenical text)

Our Father in heaven,
hallowed be your name,
your kingdom come,
your will be done,
on earth as in heaven.
Give us today our daily bread.
Forgive us our sins as we forgive
those who sin against us.
Save us from the time of trial,
and deliver us from evil.
For the kingdom, the power, and the glory
are yours, now and forever. Amen.

Blessing

May your unfailing love rest upon us, O Lord,
even as we hope in you.

This *Guide to Daily Prayer* was compiled from scripture and other resources by Rueben P. Job and then adapted by the Pathways Center for Spiritual Leadership while under the direction of Marjorie J. Thompson.